THE B M W

TROPICAL BEACH HANDBOOK

To my parents, Chris and Joan Hanna
and for my nephew and niece, Hugh and Hayley.

NICK HANNA

THE BMW

ROPICAL BEACH

HANDBOOK

FOURTH ESTATE

LONDON

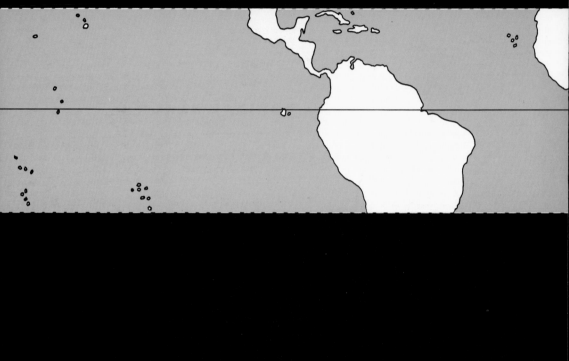

First published in Great
Britain in 1989 by
Fourth Estate Ltd
Classic House
113 Westbourne Grove
London W2 4UP

British Library
Cataloguing in
Publication Data
 Hanna, Nick
  The BMW Tropical
  Beach Handbook.
  1. Tropical regions.
  Beaches. Visitors'
  guides
  I. Title
  910′.0913

  ISBN 0-947795-13-8

Book design by
Kyte and Company
Maps by *Terence Crump*
Typeset in Bembo and
Helvetica by *York House
Typographic Ltd, London*
Printed and bound by
*Sirven Grafic, Barcelona
D. L. B. 18.600-1989*
Origination by *York House
Graphics, London*
Cover photo taken on
Biyadhoo, Maldives.

Publisher's note: Whilst every effort has been made to ensure that the information in this book was correct at the time of going to press, the publishers and author accept no responsibility or liability for any errors, omissions, or alterations, or for any consequences ensuing upon the use of any information contained herein. We plan to keep this guide as up-to-date as possible. Please write to us if there is anything you feel should be included in future editions.

ACKNOWLEDGEMENTS

RESEARCHERS
PAULA LEAVER · BECKY HALLSMITH

I am indebted to Bob Defee of STA Travel for supplying a Round-the-World ticket and to Mike Busuttili of Spirotechnique (UK) for providing snorkelling and diving equipment. Thanks also to Mandy Williams-Ellis, Alain Dupoux, Cheryl Deitsch, Jackie and Colleen, Serena Saffery, Simon and Jackie, James Young, Amanda Levick, Susan Penhall, Megan and Kelvin, Tim Browne, Ruth and Peter, Sonja Wong and Leslie Gosling for their help and comments, and to Mark Kasprowicz for windsurfing advice. Special thanks to the World Conservation Monitoring Centre in Cambridge.

I would like to thank the following hotels, tourist boards, airlines and dive operations for their assistance in compiling this guide:
Australia: Australian Airlines, Heron Island, Hamilton Island, Daydream Island, Hinchinbrook Island, Fitzroy Island, Lizard Island, Air Queensland, Quicksilver Diving and Coral Sea Diving Services. Barbados: Barbados Board of Tourism, Cobbler's Cove, the Coral Reef Club. Cayman Islands: Cayman Airways, Cayman Islands Department of Tourism, Virgin Diver's World. Cook Islands: Cook Islands Tourist Board, Air Rarotonga. Egypt: Egyptian Tourist Board, Sinai Hotels & Diving Clubs. Fiji: The Fijian, the Hyatt Regency, Denis Beckman's Seasports, Dive Taveuni, Qamea Beach Club, Mataqi Resort, Na Koro Resort, Mana Divers and Mana Island Resort, Aquatrek Ocean Sports, Club Naitasi, Beqa Divers. Hawaii: Central Pacific Divers (Maui). Indonesia: Andre Pribadi (Dive Indonesia), Sao Wisata Resort. Jamaica: Sundivers, Blue Whale Divers, Janet Lee, Boscobel BeachClub. Kenya: Wasini Island & Kisite Dhow Tours, Ocean Sports Hotel (Watamu). Malaysia: Pan Pacific Pangkor, Hyatt Kuantan. Maldives: Taj Resorts (Biyadoo), Toni de Laroque (Maldive Travel), Bandos Island Resort, Vadhoo Diving Paradise. Philippines: Philippines Airlines, Anilao Seasports Centre, Badian Island Resort, Reef Rangers (Puerta Galera), Club Pacific, Costabella Tropical Beach Hotel, Tambuli Beach Resort, Argao Beach Club, Bohol Beach Club, Wally's Diving (Boracay). Seychelles: Seychelles Tourist Board, Air Seychelles, Praslin Beach Hotel, Bird Island Lodge, Frégate Island, the Seychelles Underwater Centre. St Lucia: St Lucia Tourist Board, Cariblue Hotel, Anse Chastanet Hotel. Tahiti: Ibis Hotels, Eric Jullian (Rangiroa). Turks and Caicos: Third Turtle Inn.

7

THE BMW TOURING.

THE BMW 3 SERIES RANGE IS AVAILABLE WITH A FUEL INJECTED 1·8 LITRE, 2·0 LITRE OR 2·5 LITRE ENGINE. ALL CURRENT MODELS (EXCEPT THE M SERIES) CAN TAKE UNLEADED FUEL WITH NO MODIFICATION REQUIRED.

HE SAILED ALL THE WAY DOWN HERE.

THE ULTIMATE DRIVING MACHINE

CONTENTS

INTRODUCTION	12
THE INDIAN OCEAN	
KENYA	16
Watamu	21
Shela, Lamu	23
Diani	26
Tiwi	29
Kisite Marine Park	30
SEYCHELLES	31
Mahé:	
Beau Vallon	39
Praslin	41
La Digue	43
Bird Island	45
Frégate	46
THE MALDIVES	48
A–Z of 55 islands	55
SRI LANKA	64
Bentota	70
Ahungalla	71
Hikkaduwa	71
Unawatuna	74
Koggala	76
Dikwella	76
Tangalle	77
INDIA	78
Goa:	
Aguada, Calangute, Baga	82
Colva	83
Anjuna	85
Vagator and Small Vagator	86
Harambol	86
Kovalam	87

Nai Harn	103
Diving	104
Koh Phi Phi	106
Krabi	107
Koh Samui:	
Chaweng	108
Lamai	109
North Coast	110
Choeng Mon	111
Koh Phangan:	
Mae Haat	112
Haat Rin	113
PHILIPPINES	114
Boracay	119
Cebu: West Coast	122
Panglao:	
Bohol Beach Club	123
Alona Beach	124
MALAYSIA	125
Pangkor Pan Pacific	128
Rantau Abang	129
Telok Chempedak	129
Tioman Island	130
INDONESIA	133
Bali:	
Sanur	137
Nusa Dua	138
Kuta	139
Candi Dasa	140
Lombok:	
Senggigi	142
Gili Air, Gili Meno,	
Gili Trawangan	142
Flores:	
Sao Wisata	144

SOUTH EAST ASIA

THAILAND	90
Koh Samet	96
Phuket:	
Patong	98
Surin	98
Karon	99
Kata	100
Kata Noi	102
Relax Bay Meridien	103

THE PACIFIC

QUEENSLAND, AUSTRALIA	146
Lady Elliot Island	153
Heron Island	154
Great Keppel Island	156
Hinchinbrook Island	158
Dunk Island	159
Fitzroy Island	160
Lizard Island	162
Cape Tribulation	164

The Great Barrier Reef 166
FIJI 169
  Viti Levu:
    The Fijian Resort 175
    Hideaway Resort 176
  Nananu-I-Ra 176
  The Mamanuthas:
    Beachcomber and
      Treasure Islands 177
    Mana Island 178
    Malololailai 179
  Namena Island 180
  Taveuni 181
  Qamea Beach Club 182
  Mataqi Island 183
COOK ISLANDS 184
  Rarotonga:
    Muri Beach 186
    The Rarotongan 188
  Aitutaki 190
TAHITI (French Polynesia) 192
  Moorea:
    North-West Coast 199
    Temae Beach 200
  Bora Bora:
    South Coast 201
  Rangiroa 205
HAWAII 208
  Oahu:
    Waikiki 216
    Hanuama Bay 218
    Sandy Beach and Makapu'u 218
    North Shore 219
    Diving 220
  Maui:
    Kaanapali Beach 220
    Diving 222
    Snorkelling 222
    Windsurfing 223

THE CARIBBEAN
JAMAICA 226
  Negril 231
  Silver Sands 235
  Jamaica Jamaica 235
  Frenchman's Cove 236

San San Beach and the
  Blue Lagoon 237
ST LUCIA 238
  Reduit Beach 242
  Anse Chastanet 243
BARBADOS 246
  West Coast 250
  Benston Beach 254
  Silver Sands 255
  South East Coast 257
  Surfing 258
  Diving and Snorkelling 260
  The Atlantis 261
COZUMEL, MEXICO 262
  Pier Beach 267
  El Presidente 268
  Chankanaab 269
  Playa Maya and Playa Francisco 269
  Diving 270
  San Miguel 272

THE RED SEA
EGYPT 274
  Na'ama Bay 280
  Dahab 285

APPENDICES
Suntanning 288
Snorkelling 290
Learning to dive 295
Travelling and diving 297
Travelling and windsurfing 298
Bodysurfing 300
Beach and sea safety 302
Potential Marine hazards 304
Marine tourism and coral reefs 309
Dolphins 310
Marine environmental
  organizations 312
Beach and marine books 313
  Mail order addresses 315
Diving magazines 316

INDEX 317

INTRODUCTION

The BMW **Tropical Beach** HANDBOOK *is a selective guide to tropical beaches and islands in nineteen countries. The tropics have never been as affordable or as accessible as they are now, with a huge growth in charter flights and long-haul holidays bringing exotic destinations within reach of even modest travel budgets. Whether you're interested in exploring underwater, skimming the waves on a windsurfer, or just lazing around under a palm tree, this guide is intended to help you make the most of your trip to the tropics.*

The guide covers a total of 206 tropical beaches and islands, of which 109 are given fully-detailed entries. However you intend to travel, it will tell you where the best beaches are and which beaches (and beach hotels) to avoid. It covers over 400 places to stay, from bamboo beach huts costing US$2 a night to deluxe beach resorts costing US$200 a night or more, and there are 194 recommendations for beach accommodation.

The BMW Tropical Beach Handbook *is a passport to underwater adventure for anyone with a mask, a snorkel and a ticket to the tropics. You can snorkel anywhere in the world but the clearest and warmest seas are in the tropics and, with just a few exceptions, it's only within 23° north and south of the equator that you can snorkel amidst the rich, complex world of a coral reef. Snorkelling is easily learned in a few minutes.*

Scuba diving is an exciting sport which is also at its best in the tropics. The guide covers many of the world's major diving areas along with details on over 100 dive schools. Although it requires formal training, scuba diving is open to people of all ages and abilities.

The ratings for the snorkelling and diving under each entry are based on standards of equipment and service, variety of dive sites, the quality of the marine life, ease of access and value for money. For watersports, the ratings are based on the range of different activities available and the quality of rental equipment.

The overall 'palm tree' rating for each entry is arrived at by adding all the separate ratings together and dividing the total by the number of relevant entries for that beach. Other factors, such as water cleanliness, swimming conditions and the range and quality of accommodation are also taken into account. The rating scale ranges from one to five, with exceptional beaches or islands meriting a 5+.

Two destinations are included here solely because of their diving potential. These are Egypt and the island of Cozumel, Mexico. Neither is particularly recommended for beaches.

The guide is designed to be used by people travelling on multi-country itineraries using fare constructions such as Circle Asia, Circle Pacific or Round-The-World (RTW) tickets. It was researched on an RTW ticket and anyone thinking of setting off on an RTW journey will find that it covers most beach destinations on major RTW trunk routes across Asia and the North and South Pacific within the tropical belt.

13

I haven't attempted to deal with the complexities of airline tickets and I assume that the reader who intends to travel independently is capable of organising their journey to (or across) the tropics themselves, in conjunction with their travel agent.

I haven't included every single hotel on every beach – to do so would require a massive compendium – but you can be sure that all those listed are on a good beach, unless otherwise stated. No island or beach is given a rating unless either myself or a researcher has stayed there. Although individual room rates are given for most hotels, many will work out cheaper as part of an all-inclusive holiday. Where feasible, we've given an overseas reservations number: some of these are international reservation services for hotels, some are tour operators offering complete packages including flights, and others are specialized diving holiday companies. Note that the hotel price categories given in the 'General Information' sections vary from country to country. As this is intended only as a quick reference, prices have been given only in US$. Many hotels at the top end of the market , especially in the Caribbean, only ever quote prices in US$ and I have therefore not converted them to local currencies.

Given the time it takes to research and publish travel guides as well as the unpredictability of exchange rates and volatile inflation rates, it's impossible to ensure total accuracy for room rates or other quoted prices.

Undoubtedly there are plenty of islands and beaches we've missed out, but I hope that the guide will inspire you to explore for yourself: there are thousands more tropical islands and beaches out there waiting to be discovered. There are many more countries which I would have liked to have included – among them, numerous Caribbean destinations – but we had to call a halt somewhere.

KEY:

R.	Recommended accommodation
A:	Hotel address
MSF:	Mask, snorkel, fins
LS:	Low season
HS:	High season
a/c:	air-conditioned
o/w:	one-way
rtn:	return

14

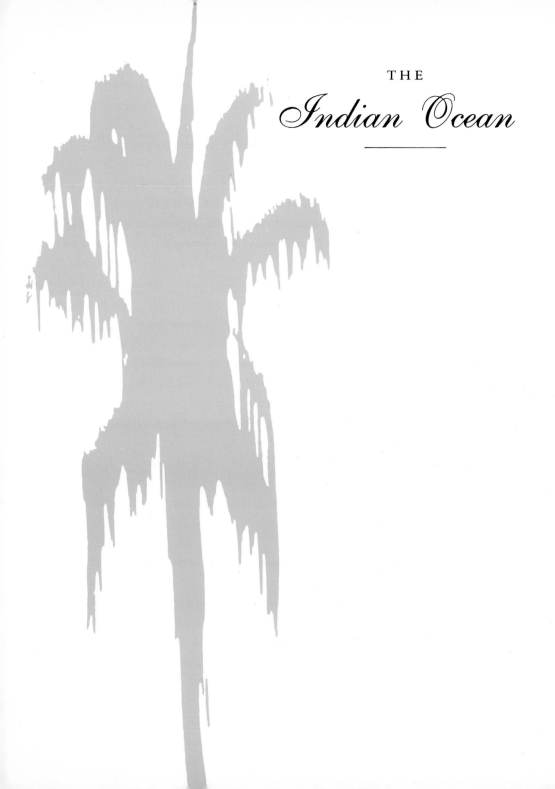

Kenya

F or most people Kenya means 'safari' but for après-safari there are
numerous beaches to choose between with over fifty beach hotels as
well as campsites and scores of self-catering beach bungalows scattered
along the Indian Ocean coast.

The hub of Kenya's coast is Mombasa, a characterful seaport with a
long history and its fair share of equatorial sleaze. From Mombasa, the
coast stretches 55 miles/90 km southwards down to the border with
Tanzania and 280 miles/450 km northwards to the Somali border.

Travel agents seem to be under the illusion that Mombasa is a 'beach
town' but although Mombasa is on an island it doesn't have any beaches –
it's basically an industrial port. When the brochures say 'Mombasa beach'

Giant manta, Kenya

they are generally referring to the coast north of Mombasa, where there
are a dozen or more long-established beach hotels strung out along 13
miles/20 km of shoreline up to Kikambala. The best of this bunch is the
Nyali Beach Hotel but all of the beaches along here suffer to some extent
from pollution from nearby chemical and textile plants, and the cement

16

industry. This has also affected the reefs, and the diving and snorkelling are no good.

Malindi, just over 63 miles/100 km from Mombasa, is Kenya's oldest beach resort and it's seen better days. During the *Kaskazi* (the north/ north-east monsoon) from November to April Malindi beaches are covered in seaweed. Worse still, sea and sand are tinged a dirty mud-red colour by topsoil run-off from the Sabaki River, a problem which has become much more serious in recent years. This annual silting also means that there's no point in coming to Malindi for diving or snorkelling from mid-January to mid-April. If you do come here, choose a beach south of town; the beach to the north is an enormous, sun-baked sand-flat, great for sand-yachting but otherwise quite featureless and unattractive.

Moray eel, Kenya

The best beach on the north coast (if not in Kenya) is **Watamu*****+, to the south of Malindi. There are just four low-key hotels here and the diving and snorkelling are good. An added bonus is that the Gedi ruins, one of Kenya's most important and intriguing coastal archaeological sites, are just nearby.

For a taste of something out of the ordinary, and if time permits, a trip up to the Lamu archipelago near the Somali border is recommended. Lamu is of significant historical and cultural interest and has one enormous beach, **Shela***, a short distance out of town. Options here include staying in a good hotel on the beach or local guest houses in town and it's also possible to go for the day from Mombasa or Malindi.

On the south coast the main resort area is **Diani*****, with neighbouring Galu beach just beginning to be developed. For overlanders the best beach to head for on the south coast is **Tiwi******, where there are several cheap guest houses and a campsite directly on the beach. Sand Island, nearby, is another good choice.

Almost the entire length of the Kenya coast is protected by reef and the lagoons behind the reef on nearly all the beaches are invariably too shallow for swimming or windsurfing at low tide.

Snorkelling (or 'goggling' as it is quaintly known here) is extremely popular.

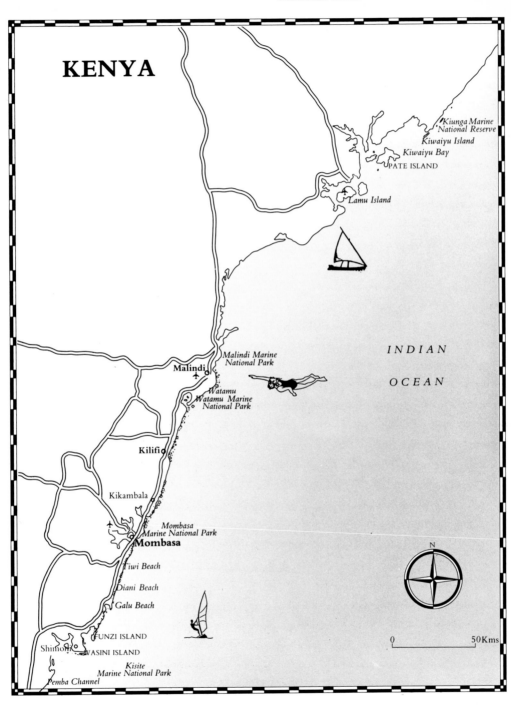

KENYA

Kiunga Marine National Reserve

Kiwaiyu Island

Kiwaiyu Bay

PATE ISLAND

Lamu Island

INDIAN

OCEAN

Malindi Marine National Park

Malindi

Watamu
Watamu Marine National Park

Kilifi

Kikambala

Mombasa Marine National Park

Mombasa

Tiwi Beach

Diani Beach

Galu Beach

FUNZI ISLAND

Shimoni

WASINI ISLAND

Kisite Marine National Park

Pemba Channel

N

0   50Kms

Along with the recent boom in beach hotels there has also been considerable investment in dive clubs to take advantage of Kenya's reefs and warm tropical waters.

Over the years there have been so many negative reports about diving in Kenya that it comes as a pleasant surprise to find that there is anything left underwater at all, but the snorkelling and diving here is surprisingly good and with the commitment now being shown by a few dedicated wardens and rangers (as well as commercial dive guides) to protect the reefs as much as possible, the future for sport diving in Kenya looks healthy. Additionally, there can't be many countries in the world which can offer a combination of a safari holiday and a diving holiday in one go.

There are three major marine parks or protected zones. The best known is the Malindi/Watamu Marine National Park, which is easily reached by boat from either of those beach areas for snorkelling or diving. The season for Malindi is from July to December/January, at Watamu from mid-October to mid-April. The next most popular area is the **Kisite Marine Park** (page 30) and snorkelling and diving here can be arranged from Diani.

The third protected area is the Kiunga Marine National Reserve, 10 miles/16 km south of the Somali border. This is the only park that I haven't visited but scientific reports from the area indicate that reefs are in excellent condition. The reefs cover an area of around 10 square miles/25 square km and you can reach this area by dhow from Lamu (a combined snorkelling/camping trip takes three days) or by booking a holiday at the remote Kiwaiyu Lodge, a safari camp with diving facilities. This exclusive resort costs from around Ksh 5,000 (US$290) per day for a double, fully inclusive. There are scheduled flights from Nairobi, Mombasa and Lamu.

In 1988 they also established the Mombasa Marine National Park, but it will be years before this area recovers.

At whatever level you can afford to travel, costs are extremely reasonable: for the independent traveller, Kenya is still one of the easiest and most rewarding countries in Africa to explore. Nudity is illegal, toplessness is tolerated on the main tourist beaches.

GENERAL INFORMATION

Time
GMT+3 hours

IDD code
254+area code+number

Currency
Kenya shilling (Ksh)
UK£1=Ksh30
US$1=Ksh17

Hotels
Double with B&B
Deluxe: US$88+
Expensive: US$50-90
Moderate: US$20-50
Budget: under US$20

PUBLICATIONS
A Guide to Common Reef Fishes of the Western Indian Ocean
K Bock with photos by J Mackinnon and I Took (Macmillan, London 1985). 122pp. Available from the Bahari Book Centre in Mombasa.
The Rough Guide to Kenya
Richard Trillo (Harrap Columbus, London 1988). 375pp, £6.95. Well-written and informative, available locally.

WEATHER
Kenya has two rainy seasons. The 'short' rains normally fall in late October, November and December, the 'long' rains in late April, May and June. The driest season is December to March. Coastal areas are warm all year round, averaging 78-86°F/28-31°C.

HEALTH
Cholera and hepatitis inoculations advisable, yellow fever compulsory if coming from an infected area. Precautions against malaria are essential.

VISAS
Valid passports required. No visas necessary for citizens of Commonwealth countries (except Australia, Nigeria and Sri Lanka and British citizens of Indian, Pakistani or Bangladeshi origin) or passport holders from Germany, Denmark, Eire, Finland, the Netherlands, Norway, Sweden, Spain and Turkey. All other nationalities, including US citizens, require a visa. Ninety-day visitor pass issued on arrival, renewable either in Mombasa or Nairobi.

TOURIST BOARD
Head office: Nairobi, tel: (02) 331030; London, tel: (01) 355 3144; New York, tel: (212) 486 1300; Los Angeles, tel: (213) 274 6634; Frankfurt, tel: (069) 28 25 52; Paris, tel: (01) 42 60 66 88.

WATAMU

Sometimes known as Turtle Bay, Watamu is 15 miles/24 km south of Malindi – a better choice during the winter when Malindi is covered in seaweed. There are just four hotels on this mile-long beach. You can only swim in the sea at high tide but all four hotels have swimming pools.

Watamu is well-known as a fishing resort and a fleet of deep-sea boats anchor in the bay. A clutch of less high-powered craft are on hand to ferry divers out to the drop-off just a short distance off-shore or to take snorkellers to shallower sections of reef in the Watamu National Marine Park. Diving here is good value and the snorkelling is okay too. You don't have to look any further for a combined beach/diving holiday in Kenya.

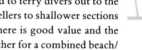

SNORKELLING★★★★

The main area for snorkelling in the Watamu Marine Park is half-a-mile south of the hotel area, usually reached

by boat. The shallow reefs here extend for several hundred yards north and south of the buoyed area: the profile is of plate, leaf and boulder corals starting just beyond the sea grasses in 7-10ft/2-3m of water and dropping to a maximum of 17-20ft/5-6m. The predominant species which will approach to feed include sergeant majors (of course), parrotfish having a change from their normal diet of coral polyps, brassy chubbs, several varieties of small wrasse (including bird wrasse, recognized by their elongated snouts and blue colouring), and orange-striped triggerfish – although the latter are

21

Whaleshark, Kenya

more wary and keep well below the mob of sergeant majors. Shoals of batfish and sweetlips inhabit the reef, as do unicorn fish, Emperor and Koran angelfish, Moorish idols, butterflyfish, snappers, morays and bluespotted stingrays. Boats go anytime, 100 Ksh/US$6 per person (min five).

WATERSPORTS***

The trades average 11-21 knots, 4-5 Beaufort, all year round, reaching a peak at the end of May (May itself is usually rained out) and in June and July. Board hire averages Ksh 120-180/US$7-11/hr, with beginner's, improver and funboard courses available.

DIVING***

There are two dive shops on the beach, both offering essentially the same service with their own individual emphasis: Tom Toendury is the same ever-jesting owner of Tom's Whaleshark Divers at the Turtle Bay Hotel, where no dive is without its share of Tom's jokes or bar stories. Lorenz and Maja Riedl operate Scubadiving Kenya, next to the Blue Bay Village at the north end of the beach − a dive with Lorenz won't be easily forgotten either, since he tends to babble away incessantly underwater, keeping up a running commentary on the creatures he is always pleased to be able to show people.

Both dive shops share 10 buoyed sites on the outer reef, where it drops from 30-50ft/9-15m to 100-130ft/30-40m. The gradual reef slope can't be described as dramatic or spectacular (due to tidal swell, there are very few large coral formations) but it is home to a rewarding variety of marine life. The Big Three Caves, near Mida creek, is famous for its 300kg groupers: trips here are organized monthly by Whale-

shark Divers and fortnightly by Scuba-diving Kenya. None of the sites at Watamu are more than 20 minutes away by boat (except the Big Three Caves) and between the two dive shops there are departures at 8 a.m., 9 a.m. and 10 a.m. so you can breakfast when it suits you and wander down afterwards: easy diving, short boat rides.

Neither dive shop supplies wetsuits as standard; they can be hired, but you're better off bringing your own if you prefer one. BCs aren't standard.

The diving season at Watamu is from September/October to April (although September and the second half of April can be dodgy). From May to August there is no diving here (this is the season for Malindi). Visibility is best in October and November, when I'm told it can reach 150 ft/45 m plus. For the rest of the season the minimum − maximum range is 30-100ft/10-30m. Plankton are present from December through to January/February, with the chance of seeing whale sharks and mantas. Both dive shops offer night dives, intro courses and certifications. The price of a one-tank dive is similar (Ksh400/US$24 including Marine Park ticket) at either.

• *Whaleshark Divers:* **A** PO Box 457, Watamu, tel: Watamu 8 or 80.
• *Scubadiving Kenya:* **A** PO Box 160, Watamu, tel: Watamu 100; also at the Driftwood Hotel, Malindi, tel: 20155.

ACCOMMODATION

• *Turtle Bay Beach Hotel*: Expensive/moderate. The largest hotel on the beach, standard resort facilities (pool, tennis, disco). Single/double fullboard Ksh 900/1,200 (US$53/70). **A** PO Box 457, Watamu, tel: Watamu 3 or 80. Reservations: Nairobi, tel: (02) 21143.

• *Hemingway's*: Expensive/moderate. English-run. Single/double full-board from Ksh 900/1,400 (US$53/82) to Ksh 1,100/1,700 (US$65/100). The old *Seafarer's*, recently completely rebuilt. Rooms in the new wing cost from Ksh 995 (US$58) per person, twin share, half-board. Closed May-June. **A** PO Box 182, Watamu, tel: Watamu 6 or 52. Reservations: Mombasa, tel: (011) 312817; Nairobi, tel: (02) 25255; UK, tel: (01) 730 3585.

• *Ocean Sports*: Expensive/moderate **R**. Casual, friendly, English-run. Convivial sea-front bar, great restaurant. Early morning tea and afternoon tea (with scones) automatically served on your verandah. Simple, cool, spacious rooms. Single/double half-board from Ksh 600/1,000 (US$35/59). Good value, hard to fault. **A** PO Box 100, Watamu, tel: Watamu 8.

• *Blue Bay Village*: Expensive/moderate. Italian. Single/double full board from Ksh 850/1,200 (US$50/70). **A** PO Box 162, Watamu, tel: Watamu 128,129.

ACCESS
Twenty minutes to Malindi airport, six flights daily on Kenya Airways to Nairobi (flight time 90 minutes). Watamu is 65 miles/104 km from Mombasa, about two hours by taxi (Ksh 1,000/US$60).

LAMU and SHELA

This centuries-old seaport is the 'in' destination of the Kenya coast, an intriguing blend of Arabic and African cultures which will reward you with a change of pace from Kenya's game parks and beaches. There are no cars in Lamu's narrow medieval alleyways, just endlessly milling people and donkeys. An overlander's Mecca for a decade or more, Lamu has been dubbed 'the Katmandu of Africa' (I presume the comparison refers to the assault on your nostrils from the open drains running down the streets), and, for insights into the lifestyles and architecture of this ancient town, a visit to the Lamu Museum is a must.

Lamu's only beach, Shela, is a short distance south of town. At the beginning of Shela is Peponi's, a modest hotel whose name has become almost as famous as that of Lamu itself. The hotel has become so famous, complains the manager, that people come here expecting a deluxe resort and are taken aback when they find out it's really very simple and casual indeed. He wishes that journalists would stop name-dropping about their guests, he said. I'm obliged to mention that at this exact moment ex-Rolling Stone Charlie Watts (looking safari-worn) stepped off the boat from the airport.

If you're staying in town Peponi's is an obligatory stop on the way to or from the beach (it's the only place in Lamu where you're guaranteed to find a cold beer at any time of day or night). From town it's easily reached in 30-40 minutes by foot or in 20 minutes by dhow.

Over seven miles long, Shela beach curves endlessly southwards below acres of sand dunes. Keep your belongings in sight when swimming, thefts are common. Women should stay in sight of other people because of harassment and several rapes. There is no shade at all on the beach, and no refreshments, so bring what you need. Body-surfing is possible on spring tides.

With the introduction of frequent air charter services it's quite feasible to visit Lamu and Shela for the day from Malindi or Mombasa.

SNORKELLING*
Dhows can be hired for snorkelling trips to the Kiniyika rocks, south of Lamu. This small outcrop in the middle of nowhere is surrounded by rock gullies and patch reef in maximum depths of 20-25ft/6-8m, colonized by occasional large rock cod or humphead wrasse. Trips to Kiniyika are only possible when the wind is predominantly from the north (December to March/April). Unless you request a motorized dhow, the journey out on a sail-only dhow can take up to four hours, which is not worth doing unless you want to sail all day just for the sake of it (the reefs at Watamu, for instance, are more extensive, more densely populated with fish and easier to reach). Dhows to Kiniyika cost Ksh 100/US$8 per person. Dhow safaris from Lamu also go to nearby islands such as Pate, Siyu and Faza as well as up to the Kiunga Marine National Reserve near Kiwaiyu Island.

Dhow to the Beach, Lamu

BARS AND RESTAURANTS
In Lamu there are as many cheap restaurants as there are guest houses, serving everything from yoghurt and granola to samosas, fruit juices and fresh (and cheap) seafood. Restaurants finish serving in the evenings by around 8 p.m., and everything is closed by 9.30 p.m. Lamu being predominantly Muslim, alcohol is not widely available: the only 'official' bar in town is at Petley's Hotel, which is very gloomy and depressing and often anyway 'runs out' of beer early in the evening, thereafter only serving warm Guinness.

ACCOMMODATION
Shela
● *Peponi Hotel*: Expensive **R**. Sea-facing rooms with verandahs, fans only, no a/c. The restaurant has a good reputation and there is also a lunchtime grill with a reasonably priced menu (oysters, BBQ fish, smoked sailfish, grilled lobster and so on). Sailboards free. Deep-sea fishing, dhow excursions, water ski-ing. Small dive operation, no diving between April and October. Hotel closed May and June. Single/double full-board Ksh 2,200/3,100 (US$125/180). Advance bookings essential. **A** Peponi Hotel, Lamu, tel: (0121) 3029, 3154. Reserva-

tions: UK, tel: (01) 730 3585.

● Guest houses in Shela include the *Samahani* and the *Shela Rest House*, rooms from Ksh 10-300 (US$6-18).

Lamu

● There are over 20 guest houses in Lamu itself, so you should have no trouble finding a suitable room and

400 (US$24), shared rooms from Ksh 125 (US$7.50). If you can't remember (or pronounce) Mlangi Langi, ask for Bushbaby's.

● *Hal-Udy*: Moderate **R**. Hidden away, hard to find, above average. Doubles from Ksh 250 (US$15). Ask at New Mahru's Hotel, near the seafront.

guides approach the minute you step off the boat or out of the airport. There are often water shortages here.

● *Petley's*: Moderate/expensive. Lamu's only hotel, over-priced. Single/double B&B Ksh 700/1,100 (US$41/65). **A** PO Box 4, Lamu, tel: (0121) 3107, 3264.

● *Casuarina Rest House*: Budget **R**. On the seafront, doubles from Ksh 200-300 (US$12-18). **A** PO Box 10, Lamu.

● *Mlangi Langi House*: Moderate/budget **R**. Rooms on the top floor are the best value in Lamu. Doubles from Ksh

● On the seafront you'll find the *New Shamuty*, the *Full Moon Guest House* and *Kisiwana Lodge*, all costing from single/double Ksh 40-200 (US$3-17). Behind the waterfront the best choice is the *Lamu Guest House* **R**, self-contained rooms from Ksh 250 (US$15).

ACCESS

Kenya Airways flies to Lamu direct from Nairobi (one-and-a-half hours); Equator Airlines flies from Nairobi, Mombasa and Malindi, and Skyways and Copper Sky-

Snorkelling at Kisite

25

bird fly from Mombasa and Malindi. One-way fares cost around Ksh 2,000 (US$118) from Nairobi, Ksh 800-1,200 (US$47-70) from Mombasa and Ksh 600-700 (US$35-41) from Malindi. Buses run daily to Mombasa and Malindi.

DIANI

The main beach on the south coast, Diani boasts numerous luxury beach hotels as well as well-equipped and professionally-run diving and windsurfing centres. The beach is tidal and you can't always swim, but all the major hotels have swimming pools.

Camels hoofing it along the shoreline, handsome Samburu or Masai warriors making a buck or two posing for snaps, salesmen flogging wood carvings outside every hotel, tourists tramping up and down – this is a big, busy beach. Hotels are listed starting in the south, and although this is the most crowded area it also has the most attractive hotels. North of the old Tradewinds Hotel the beach is not at its best and most of the hotels up here (with the exception of the Diani Reef) are on the seaweed-strewn and rocky patches. The Leisure Lodge and the Leopard Beach Hotel seem to be the worst affected.

If you want to escape the crowds head for Galu, 3 miles/4 km further south.

SNORKELLING
Resource depletion (fishing, spearfishing, tourist damage, collecting for shells and aquarium fish) on the shallower sections of the reef here have rendered it mostly barren. The best snorkelling on the south coast is at Kisite (page 30).

WATERSPORTS****
The strongest winds are during May, June, July and August (17-27 knots, 5-6 Beaufort, seven days out of ten). September to December and February, March and April are the turn-around months between monsoons when it's calmer (4-16 knots/2-4 Beaufort). In January and February winds can sometimes reach 7-21 knots/3-5 Beaufort, but from September to March it's unusual to have high winds. Windsurfing is only possible at high tide, seagrasses are a problem at other times of day as the lagoon is very shallow. Both monsoons have side-shore winds. There are numerous schools and a wide range of equipment is available. Board hire costs between Ksh 150-250/US$9-15/hr, instruction available in most languages. Hobies can be hired but there is no water ski-ing or parasailing due to the hazardous conditions inside the reef.

DIVING**
Divers are not quite so badly off as snorkellers at Diani, since below 50 ft/15m or so there is more life. The two most-frequented local sites are Tiwi (max depth 60-75 ft/8-23 m) and Kinondo (50-100 ft/15-30 m): Kinondo is perhaps the best of these, with a gradual reef slope starting at 50 ft/15 m, not spectacular for corals but with shoals of snapper and barracuda hovering at close quarters. Visibility here is never more than 30-50 ft/9-15 m, although I'm told it does reach

80 ft/25 m on rare occasions. The best time here for visibility is in the change-over between the monsoons (i.e. September to December and February, March and April) with peak visibility during October, February and March. Dive shops are closed during the rainy season, from April to September. One-tank dives cost Ksh 400-500 (US$24-32); resort courses Ksh 2,500-3,500 (US$150-205); open water certifications from Ksh 5,000-6,000 (US$294-350).

• *Diani Diving*: At Nomad's. Swiss and English PADI instructors; certification courses start Tuesdays; full day two-tank trips to Kisite from Ksh 1,600 (US$94). **A** PO Box 353, Ukunda, tel: (01261) 2074.

• *Diving the Crab*: Italian-run, at the Africana Sea Lodge and Jadini Beach Hotel. PADI five-star centre, top-quality Mares equipment (including Octopus regs as standard). Twice-daily dives, intro courses, PADI open-water and advanced courses.

ACCOMMODATION

All rates quoted are high season (November to February) but in the Christmas peak period many hotels charge up to 30 per cent extra. Low season prices, about 30 per cent less. All prices are inclusive of taxes.

Diani

• *Robinson Club Baobab*: Expensive. German resort, pool, tennis. Single/double full-board Ksh 1,250/2,500 (US$74/147). **A** PO Box 84792, Mombasa, tel: (01261) 2026.

• *Lagoon Reef*: Expensive/moderate. New resort, 120 rooms, VIP block **R** of 24 rooms directly over the beach. Unusual pool, tennis. Single/double half-board Ksh 825/1,250 (US$49/74). **A** PO Box 82352, Mombasa, tel:

(01261) 2627, 2213.

• *Ocean Village/Club*. Expensive. Club Vacenze. Swimming pool, tennis. Villas from Ksh 1,420 (US$84) self-catering. **A** PO Box 88, Ukunda, tel: (01261) 2188, 2003.

• *Safari Beach Hotel*: Expensive. Sister to the Jadini Beach and Africana. Sizeable rooms but no sea views. Pool, squash, tennis. Single/double half-board Ksh 1,450/2,300 (US$83/135). **A** PO Box 90690, Mombasa, tel: (01261) 2726/2311. Reservations: UK, tel: (01) 730 3585.

• *Nomad Beach Hotel*: Expensive **R**. 17 'bandas' (huts made from traditional materials) facing the beach, set amongst palm trees and baobabs. All have verandahs and none are more than a few paces from the sea. No fans, no hot water, no pool, but highly recommended for atmosphere. Great beach bar. Single/double B&B Ksh 920/1,400 (US$54/82). **A** PO Box 1, Ukunda, Mombasa, tel: (01261) 2155.

• *Jadini Beach Hotel*: Expensive. Standard modern beach hotel. Single/double half-board Ksh 1,300/2,000 (US$76/118). **A** PO Box 84616, tel: (01261) 2021. Reservations: UK, tel: (01) 730 3585.

• *Africana Sea Lodge*: Expensive. Twin-room rondavels, single/double half-board from Ksh 1,200/1,900 (US$70/112). **A** PO Box 84616, tel: (01261) 2021. Reservations: UK, tel: (01) 730 3585.

• *Two Fishes Hotel*: Expensive. Old, worn-out hotel. Small pool. Single/double full-board Ksh 1,400/1,900 (US$82/112). **A** PO Box 23, Ukunda, tel: (01261) 2101.

• *Diani Sea Lodge*: Expensive. Large rooms, simple but tasteful. Popular with German tourists. Single/double full-board from Ksh 1,200/1,600 (US$70/

27

Diani

28

Nomads, Diani

94). **A** PO Box 37, Ukunda, tel: (01261) 2060.

- *Tradewinds*: Expensive. Run-down and shabby despite its fame and name. Single/double full-board from Ksh 1,200/1,600 (US$70/94). **A** PO Box Ukunda, tel: (01261) 2016. Reservations: UK, tel (01) 730 3585.
- *Vindigo Cottages*: Budget **R**. Eight self-catering cottages hidden away at the north end of the beach. Good value, although not on the best part of the beach. From Ksh 100-140 (US$6-8) per person. Try and book the Tree House or one of the seafront cottages. English-run. **A** PO Box 77, Ukunda, tel: (01261) 2192.
- *Diani Reef*: Deluxe **R**. 150 well-furnished rooms, all with sea views. Cool white and blue Arabic-style public rooms. Single/double from half-board Ksh 2,400/3,500 (US$140/205). **A** PO Box 35, Ukunda, tel: (01261) 2175. Reservations: UK, tel: (01) 730 3585.

Galu

- *Neptune Village*: Moderate/expensive. The only hotel on this beach, opened 1988. Pool, tennis. Single/double B&B Ksh 950/1,330 (US$56/78). **A** PO Box 83125, Mombasa, tel:

(01261) 2350.

- *Galu Beach Cottages*: Moderate **R**. Cottages (sleeping four) from Ksh 1,000-1,700 (US$59/100). **A** PO Box 80857, Mombasa, tel: (01261) 2133.
- *Nomad Beach Cottages*: Moderate **R**. Spacious, modern self-catering apartments (sleep six) from Ksh 1,600 (US$94). Small pool. **A** PO Box 1, Ukunda, Mombasa, tel: (01261) 2155.

• There are several self-catering places between here and Diani (*Le Paradis, Diani Beach Chalets, Sea View* and *White Rose*) but the beach here is grim. *Diani Beach Cottages*, also down here, are not on the beach.

ACCESS
Diani is 17 miles/27 km from Mombasa. Buses from the Likoni ferry take about an hour.

TIWI

Popular with overland travellers resting up after crossing Africa, Tiwi is just 40 minutes from Mombasa. There are no watersports or diving facilities – no souvenir shops or tourists either. Super beach – you could quite happily slump down here for several weeks without wanting to move.

ACCOMMODATION

• *Tiwi Villas*: Budget. On the headland at the north end of the beach, small pool. Self-contained cottages from Ksh 300 (US$18). **A** PO Box 86775, Mombasa, tel: Tiwi 3Y10.

• *Tiwi Beach Bungalows*: Budget. Self-contained bungalows from Ksh 300 (US$18) for two, Ksh 400 (US$24) for four. **A** PO Box 96008, Likoni, Mombasa, tel: Tiwi 2Y7.

• *Twiga Lodge*: Budget. Popular and sociable, cheap restaurant. Rooms from B&B Ksh 200/350 (US$12/20), cottages from Ksh 360 (US$21) for four. Camping. **A** PO Box 96005, Likoni, Mombasa, tel: Tiwi 2Y2.

• *Minilets*: Budget **R**. Charming tented units with separate cooking areas under thatched roofs from single/double Ksh 125/240 (US$7/14), bungalows on the beach for one to six people from Ksh 410-550 (US$24-32). **A** PO Box 96242, Likoni, Mombasa.

• *Sand Island Beach Cottages*: Budget **R**. Just north of Tiwi beach (from Mombasa take the turning to Tiwi, and then look for signs), on their own beach. Colonial atmosphere, self-contained cottages from Ksh 240 (US$14) for two, Ksh 440 (US$25) for four. **A** PO Box 96006, Likoni, Mombasa.

ACCESS
Tiwi is 14 miles/22 km south of Mombasa, 35-40 minutes by bus from the Likoni ferry. The beach is 2 miles/3 km from the main road: there used to be numerous robberies on this track to the beach, so it might be better to wait for a lift.

Tiwi

Kisite Marine Park

Just near the Tanzanian border, the Kisite-Mpunguti Marine National Park (normally just called Kisite) is the second-most remote reserve in Kenya. The jump-off point for Kisite is Shimoni (34 miles/55 km south of Diani) and from here you can take a day trip in a traditional dhow.

The most popular excursion to Kisite combines snorkelling with a gourmet lunch on the island of Wasini afterwards. This trip is run by a young English couple, Stephen Mullens and Sally Cox, who operate three traditional Arab trading dhows, diesel-powered and converted for passengers.

Stephen Mullens describes Kisite as 'the last unransacked marine park in Kenya' and although some sections near the border have been damaged in the past by dynamite fishing and considerable quantities of shells have been removed over the years, the coral cover and diversity here is high. Dhow crews are vigilant in ensuring that not even a mollusc is now removed by any of the 80-plus tourists they bring here every day.

After an hour's snorkelling the dhows sail back to Wasini Island, where lunch (whole mangrove crabs steamed in ginger followed by Swahili-style fish, fresh fruits and Arabic coffee) is served in an open-air restaurant.

Other options for getting to Kisite include staying at the upmarket (and often fully-booked) Shimoni Reef Lodge or staying in the village on Wasini Island.

Diving trips to Kisite are operated by Diani Diving and Robinson Baobab at Diani, and Gabriella at the Black Marlin Hotel, Msambweni. I've only snorkelled at Kisite and opinion seems divided as to how worthwhile it is to travel all the way down to Kisite to dive: the visibility and the coral cover both tend to be better than at Diani and the shallow reefs allow for much longer dives, but at these depths you'll see most of what there is by snorkelling.

August through to December is the calmest period with the best visibility.

● *Kisite Dhow Tours* and *Wasini Island Restaurant*: The tour costs Ksh 700 (US$40), not including transport Ksh 250 (US$15) from Diani; snorkelling only costs Ksh 300 (US$18). Dhows can also be privately chartered for diving and snorkelling in other areas of the park. Book at the Jadini Beach Hotel, tel: (01261) 2331; in Mombasa, tel: (011) 311752.

● Trips to Kisite are also operated by *Shimoni Dhows & Goggling Safaris*, tel: (01261) 2213, (011) 471771.

● *The Shimoni Reef Fishing Lodge*: Daily dhow trips. Rooms cost from single/double half-board Ksh 1,300/ 1,600 (US$76/94). Reservations, tel: Mombasa (011) 471771.

● More adventurous travellers can get a boat from the Shimoni jetty to Wasini and rent a room in the home of Sharif in the village. From the village, boats can be hired to go snorkelling (you'll need your own equipment). Buses and *matatus* run to Shimoni from the Likoni (Mombasa) ferry.

Seychelles

Hundreds of miles from anywhere in the middle of the Indian Ocean, the Seychelles have some of the most beautiful beaches in the world as well as some superb diving and snorkelling.

The international airport and the country's capital, Victoria, are on the island of Mahé. The biggest and best-known beach on Mahé is **Beau Vallon★★★**, which has a wide choice of accommodation, plenty of watersports, and well-equipped dive shops. For many visitors Beau Vallon is their first stopping point in the Seychelles, and that's how I suggest you treat it: recover from jet lag, relax for a couple of days and then start planning to head out to the other islands. To make the most of the Seychelles island-hopping is a must, whether you're staying in hotels or guest houses, and inter-island transport is cheap and convenient.

Elsewhere on Mahé the two best beaches are Anse Intendance and Grande Anse. Framed by granite outcrops at either end, with wide, clean sand and good swimming, Anse Intendance is worth the trip across the island for a picnic or a day out. Grande Anse, bigger but not as beautiful as Intendance, is good for body-surfing.

Despite what the travel brochures say about Mahé's '68 golden beaches', most of the rest are rubbish. All those on the east side, from the airport down to the Pointe du Sud, are a write-off, principally because they're much too shallow for swimming. This means you should avoid the Reef Hotel, the InterContinental and Barbarons Beach Hotel as well as all guest houses on this coast if you want to be on a decent beach. The Sheraton is also on an awful (man-made) beach, although they have a regular boat shuttle over to Thérèse Island for watersports.

Just past the Sheraton at Port Glaud, L'Islette is a miniscule splodge of an island just 100 yards off-shore with a pocket-handkerchief-size beach

Petite Anse, La Digue

and a handful of bungalows. Despite being so small, this place is really quite chic and it has a lively bar and restaurant serving excellent French and Creole food. Worth considering, perhaps, for a stay of a few days, although any longer and you might go stir crazy for space.

Praslin★★★★★ is the next major island and it has three main beaches, Anse Volbert, Grande Anse and Anse Lazio. The first two are the only ones you can stay on and Anse Lazio, like most of the better beaches in the Seychelles, can only be visited for the day.

One step west of Praslin, **La Digue**★★★★★+ has several beautiful beaches on its east coast. Along with Anse Intendance (Mahé) and Anse Lazio (Praslin), these beaches will fulfil most of your expectations of the Seychelles. At Anse la Réunion on La Digue's west coast there is one hotel directly on the beach, with a handful of guest houses scattered around elsewhere.

Bird Island★★★★★+ is one of two coral cays (the other is Denis Island, which friends have raved about) right on the edge of the Seychelles Bank. It's got just one small resort with miles of empty beach shared between a handful of guests. This is a real beachcomber's island.

St Anne Marine National Park

33

Frégate★★★★, where the resort is housed in an old plantation, also has good beaches. There are no watersports or diving facilities on either of these islands.

Inter-island ferries and flights are inexpensive; bus services (like most other public services in this Marxist country) are cheap, clean and efficient. You'll need to hire a mini-moke if you want to explore some of the better beaches on Mahé (they cost around SR 300/US$60 per day). Praslin and La Digue are small enough to explore by bicycle.

Day trips to islands such as Curieuse, Cousin and Aride are highly recommended. Praslin is more convenient than Mahé for visiting these islands. Cocos Island, which has always had the reputation of being one of the loveliest shallow dive and snorkelling spots in the Seychelles, was closed during 1987-1988 to allow the reefs a chance to recover from heavy traffic but it has now re-opened (with a ranger permanently established on neighbouring Félicité Island to look after it) and this should also be worth visiting.

If you're booking a hotel there's an advantage to choosing one which is part of the Seychelles Hotel Group, since given sufficient notice and subject to availability, you can swap between any of their eight properties at no extra cost (apart from transport). This means that island-hopping is practical for package tourists even if you haven't booked in advance, although obviously it would be safer to do so. There are five on Mahé (the Beau Vallon Bay Hotel, the Northolme, the Reef Hotel, Vacoa Village and the Auberge Club des Seychelles) and three on Praslin (the Côte d'Or Lodge, the Flying Dutchman and the Praslin Beach Hotel). The best of these – for beaches – are the Beau Vallon Bay and all three on Praslin. The Auberge Club is several miles away from any sand at all; the Northolme has its own secluded cove and the Vacoa Village is within walking distance of Beau Vallon. About the Reef Hotel, the less said the better.

Another advantage of these hotels is the Funcard, which gives guests free non-motorized watersports, snorkelling equipment and tennis, and discounts on paragliding, water ski-ing and water scooters. Free introductory scuba dives are available on Mahé, with discounts on diving prices.

A trickle of independent travellers find their way to the Seychelles, and most seem to enjoy it despite the high cost. Bed and breakfast in guest houses costs between US$35-40 for a double. Backpackers are not discouraged but camping is prohibited. There are around thirty regis-

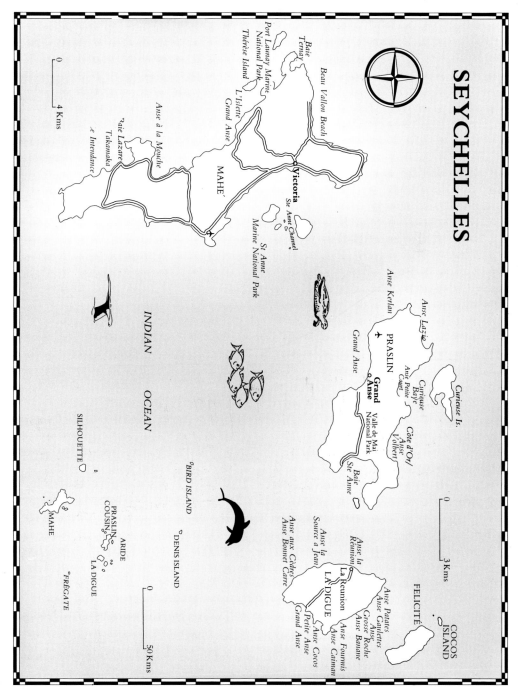

SEYCHELLES

Baie Ternay
Port Launay Marine National Park
Thérèse Island
L'Islette
Grand Anse
Beau Vallon Beach

Anse à la Mouche
'aie Lazare
Takamaka
.e Intendance

MAHÉ

Victoria

Ste Anne Channel

St Anne Marine National Park

0 — 4 Kms

INDIAN OCEAN

SILHOUETTE

MAHE

PRASLIN
COUSIN

ARIDE

°BIRD ISLAND

°DENIS ISLAND

°LA DIGUE

°FRÉGATE

0 — 50 Kms

Anse Kerlan

Anse Lazio

Anse Petite Cour
Curieuse Baye
Côte d'Or/ Anse Volbert

Curieuse Is.

PRASLIN

Grand Anse

Grand Anse

Valle de Mai National Park

Ste Anne

Baie

0 — 3Kms

Anse aux Cèdres
Anse Bonnet Carre
Anse la Source à Jean
Anse la Réunion
La Réunion
LA DIGUE
Petite Anse
Anse Cocos
Grand Anse

Anse Fourmis
Anse Caiman
Grosse Roche
Anse Banane
Anse Patates
Anse Gaulettes
Anse

FELICITÉ

COCOS ISLAND

tered guest houses on the main islands of Mahé, Praslin and La Digue (with the majority on Mahé), and I have listed all those which are close to good beaches.

Diving facilities are available on Mahé, Praslin and La Digue. The topography is similar to the Similans in Thailand, with underwater landscapes of large granitic boulders colonized by brilliantly-coloured patches of soft coral. Spearfishing has been banned here for over a decade and the marine life is both prolific and quite tame. There are no walls or drop-offs: the Seychelles are situated on a granite plateau which covers 12,000 square miles/192,000 sq km of the Indian Ocean but it's never deeper than 200-230ft (60-70m) and most diving is relatively shallow (30-65ft/9-20m).

Denis Island

The Seychelles have very few extensive reefs of the type you might find in the Caribbean or the Red Sea. When snorkelling and diving you'll see a lot of coral rubble but no one seems to know how or why these reefs have died. The usual culprits, such as dynamite fishing or crown of thorns starfish, aren't suspected, and it's thought that long-term temperature changes might be responsible. However, the flourishing marine populations more than compensate for this apparent lack of reefs. *Skin Diver* compares the diving here with Saba and Dominica, which are also volcanic islands with granite drop-offs.

There is good diving around Mahé, with several options for long-range adventure dives for more experienced divers (Silhouette Island and the shark banks, for instance, or the wreck of the *Ennerdale*). Outside of Mahé the top dive areas are considered to be around Frégate, La Digue and Aride. Frégate is apparently sensational, but it is difficult and expensive to reach. Other unexplored areas, such as around Bird Island and, to the south, the Amirantes archipelago and the Aldabras, can only be reached on charter yachts: contact any overseas Seychelles tourist board for a list of charter boats, or the Seychelles Underwater Centre or Marine Divers on Mahé.

Reef fish, Seychelles

Three types of turtle inhabit Seychelles' waters, the hawksbill, green and mock turtles. Green turtles are not yet an endangered species in this part of the Indian Ocean but the hawksbill is much in demand for creating tortoiseshell jewellery, which is sold from market stalls in Victoria. The hawksbill is still on the endangered species list and it's illegal to import tortoiseshell items into most countries. They have had some success in encouraging turtles back into the St Anne Marine National Park, just off Victoria, and there are now 70 or more female hawksbills breeding in the park. It's not unusual to see juveniles feeding around the reefs if you go snorkelling or diving here. 'The number of hawksbills is coming up,' I was told by a conservation official. 'We're trying to kill the market for turtle shell dead and we're almost there.'

The country itself is extremely safe but on the more remote beaches you shouldn't leave your valuables unattended.

In the Seychelles, it is said, everything flowers twice. It's twice as hot, the beaches (some of them) are twice as beautiful – and it's twice the price of everywhere else. Like Tahiti, everyone seems to be hypnotized by the mystique these islands generate – or perhaps it's the advertising – and they don't stop to question the cost. It is, however, an extremely expensive destination.

GENERAL INFORMATION

Time
GMT + 4 hours

IDD code
248 + 5 digit number

Currency
Seychelles rupee (SR)
UK£1 = SR 9.5
US$1 = SR 5.3

Hotels
Bed and breakfast, single/double:
Deluxe: US$150/250
Expensive: US$100/160
Moderate: US$70/120
Budget: under US$30/60

PUBLICATIONS
A Guide to Snorkelling and Diving in Seychelles
Rod Salm (Octavian Books, London, 1977). 60pp. Tri-lingual text (English, French, German). Useful and accurate, unfortunately now out of print: a limited number of copies are available for £5 including UK postage from Nigel Sitwell, tel: (01) 352 5145.
Coral Reef Fish of Seychelles
N Polunin & F Williams (Seychelles Nature Booklet No 8, 1977). 53pp. Available locally.
Hildebrand's Travel Guide – Seychelles

(Karto-Grafik, third edition 1987). 125pp with pull-out map. £4.95.
Life on Coral Reefs in the Seychelles
Dr Peter Vine (Seychelles Nature Booklet No 3). 56pp. Available locally.
The Fishes of the Seychelles
JLB & MM Smith (Institute of Ichthyology, Rhodes University, Grahamstown, 2nd edition 1969). The definitive work, currently unavailable.

WEATHER
The Seychelles have two monsoons: May to October, when the south-east trades blow, is the coolest and driest time of year. From December until March the northwest trades create hotter, wetter conditions. The rainiest months are November, December and January. During the turn-around months between monsoons (October/November and March/April/May) there are periods of complete calm with no cooling sea breezes: whilst this may prove unbearable for people unused to the heat, it's the best time for diving and snorkelling. Hotels are apparently also practically empty in these periods. The mean annual temperature is 80°F/26.7°C. Sea temperatures average 80-85°F/26-30°C.

HEALTH
No vaccination requirements unless coming from an infected area. There are no

major health hazards in the Seychelles.

VISAS
Valid passport and onward or return tick-ets required. Pre-booked accommodation is officially required, but in practice not necessary. A six-week visitor's pass issued on arrival, renewable for up to

three months free of charge.

TOURIST BOARDS
Head Office: Mahé, tel: 22881; London, tel: (01) 439 9699; USA, tel: (831) 864 3013; Tokyo, tel: (03) 2360162; Frank-furt, tel: (069) 292064; Paris, tel: (01) 42 89 85 33; Milan, tel: (02) 49 85 795.

BEAU VALLON

Beau Vallon is Mahé's biggest and most popular beach, with almost any activity close to hand, from paragliding to diving to windsurfing.

SNORKELLING
The best snorkelling near here is in Baie Ternay, for which you need to hire a boat (around SR 100 per person). Other more easily accessible sites include Petit Port, by Frenchman's Cove, and at the Northolme and Sunset Hotels on the road to Glacis.

WATERSPORTS★★★★★
Water ski-ing and beginner's windsurf-ing is best during the calm months from May to October/November. From November to April the north-west mon-soon affects Beau Vallon, with the peak winds during March and April. The bay is wide open and safe, with no danger from rocks or reef except at the extremities.

There are two fully-equipped water-sports centres on the beach renting windsurfers, Hobie cats, sailing dinghies, boogie boards and jetskis. Water ski-ing and para-sailing are also available.

DIVING★★★
Beau Vallon has two full PADI dive centres, both British-managed (Glynis Sanders and Dave Rowat at the Sey-chelles Underwater Centre, Rick How-aston at Marine Divers) and one locally-run (Benny Michel at Le Diable des Mers Diving Club).

Most dive sites are reached by a half-hour boat ride. The best conditions are during the changeover of the mon-soons: October, November and again in March, April and May. December can sometimes be okay but during January (and often December as well) diving from this side of the island is impracti-cal, and divers are ferried to Victoria to dive the other side of the island (princi-pally in the St Anne Marine National Park).

One-tank dives with equipment cost around SR 170-180 (US$35-38) less SR 40 (US$8) for your own equipment; PADI open-water certifications cost around SR 1,800 (US$370), intro courses SR 250-350 (US$50-70).

● *Seychelles Underwater Centre*: At the Coral Strand Hotel. Certifications, underwater photo courses, Nikonos rental, long-range adventure dives, equipment sales. **A** PO Box 384, Vic-toria, Mahé (tel: 47357).

● *Marine Divers*: At the Northolme Hotel. Certifications, underwater videos, Nikonos rentals, long-range adventure dives. French, German,

39

English instruction. **A** PO Box 333, Mahé (tel: 47589).

• *Le Diable des Mers*: At the Baobab Pizzeria. Beau Vallon, Mahé (tel: 47167).

Anse Lazio, Praslin

BARS AND RESTAURANTS

Apart from restaurants in the hotels there are two more reasonably-priced restaurants on the beach, the Beau Vallon Beach Pub and Grill and the Baobab Pizzeria (the latter is great value, terrific pizzas). Evening meals in guest houses cost around SR 40-50 (US$8-10) per person.

ACCOMMODATION

• *Le Fisherman's Cove*: Deluxe **R**. A Meridien hotel. On a headland at the south end of the beach, pool, tennis. Single/double B&B SR 900/1,300 (US$180/260), half-board SR 970/1,500 (US$198/300). **A** PO Box 35, Mahé, tel: 47252. Reservations: UK, tel: (01) 930 6922.

• *Beau Vallon Bay Hotel*: Expensive. Costa del Seychelles at its worst, some would say, although the new management have plans to re-vamp it. Pool. Single/double B&B SR 825/1,000 (US$165/200), half-board SR 900/1,200 (US$180/240). **A** PO Box 550, Mahé, tel: 47141.

• *Coral Strand Hotel*: Expensive. Pool. Single/double B&B SR 725/820 (US$145/165), half-board SR 870/1,100 (US$174/220). **A** PO Box 400, Mahé, tel: 47036.

• *Coco d'Or*: Moderate. Three minutes from the beach, basic. Single/double B&B SR 300/400 (US$61/81), half-board SR 400/520 (US$81/106). **A** PO Box 665, Mahé, tel: 47331.

• *Villa Napoleon*: Budget **R**. Three minutes from the beach, rooms with shared bathrooms from single/double B&B SR175/275 (US$35/55). **A** PO Box 5, Mahé, tel: 47133.

• *Villa Madonna*: Budget. Five minutes from the beach. Rooms with shared bathrooms from single/double B&B SR 180/220 (US$37/45). **A** Beau Vallon, tel: 47403.

• *Beau Vallon Beach Villas*: Budget. Self-catering bungalows with shared bathrooms from single/double B&B SR 125/200 (US$25/40). **A** Beau Vallon, tel: 47442.

• *Beau Vallon Bungalows*: Budget. Single/double B&B SR 175/275 (US$35/55). **A** Beau Vallon, tel: 47382.

• *Panorama Guest House*: Moderate. Doubles B&B SR 320 (US$64). **A** Beau Vallon, tel: 47300.

• *Vacao Village*: Moderate. Half-a-mile north of Beau Vallon beach. 12 a/c self-catering apartments with bathroom and kitchenette from SR 740 (US$148) for four people. **A** PO Box 401, Beau Vallon, tel: 47130.

• *Northolme Hotel*: Deluxe/expensive. One-and-a-half miles north of Beau Vallon beach, with its own small beach (from January to March rough seas sometimes wash this beach away altogether). Single/double B&B SR

800/1,000 (US$160/200), half-board SR 900/1,200 (US$180/240). **A** PO Box 333, Glacis, Mahé, tel: 47222.

• *Sunset Beach Hotel*: Deluxe/expensive **R**. Three-and-a-half miles/5.5 km north of Beau Vallon, above a small beach. Rooms from single/double B&B SR 800/880 (US$160/175), half-

board SR 920/1,200 (US$195/240). **A** PO Box 372, Glacis, Mahé, tel: 47227.

ACCESS
Two miles/3 km from the capital, buses run every half hour; taxi from the airport around SR 60 (US$12).

PRASLIN

Praslin is the second major destination in the Seychelles after Mahé, and also the second largest island, albeit still only seven miles long and five wide (11 by 8 km).

On the east coast there are several low-level hotels (but no guest houses) on a long white sandy beach at Anse Volbert (also known as the Côte d'Or). On the west coast Grand Anse is similarly long and powder-white and likewise has several low-key hotels.

The beaches here look terrific visually but the seabed is extremely shallow on both coasts, which means that although swimming is possible you have to go out a long way before it gets deep. Grand Anse isn't good from October to mid-May because of large quantities of seaweed on the beach.

Anse Lazio is Praslin's third beach, one of those perfect beaches that sells the Seychelles. The seabed here slopes off quickly, so the swimming is better than off the two main beaches. Anse Lazio can be reached by mini-moke, bicycle (40 minutes' bumpy ride from Anse Volbert), or by taking a bus and then walking (one mile/one-and-a-quarter km over a steep hill, about 30 minutes in total from the last bus stop).

An hourly bus goes around the island's one road and bikes, mini-mokes and jeeps can be hired at both main beaches.

41

Anse Volbert, Praslin

WATERSPORTS★★

From January to the beginning of April the north-westerly trades at Anse Volbert mean good conditions for experienced sailors. During June, July and August the southerly winds blow off-shore but since the beach is protected by hills this is a calmer period. Para-sailing and windsurfing are available at the Praslin Beach Hotel. Grand Anse is windiest from June to August; the south-east trades tend to be more constant than the north-westerlies. Windsurfers can be rented at the Indian Ocean Fishing Club and the Maison des Palmes.

SNORKELLING★★

The main snorkelling area from Anse Volbert is around Isle St Pierre, just beyond Isle Chauve Souris, which is reached by boat (SR 35/US$7 per person). Nearly all of the coral is dead but there are plenty of small to medium reef fish. Much of the snorkelling in the Seychelles is like this – good for fish amongst the rocks, but disappointing for coral. Anse Petite Cour, which is next to Anse Volbert, used to have some fine shallow water corals on the right of the bay but these are now dead because the hotel drained a swamp into the bay.

DIVING★★★

The nearest local dive site is Isle St Pierre (five minutes away by boat) a shallow beginners' dive. Experienced divers should request sites around the outlying islands such as Aride, La Digue and Frégate; there is no dedicated dive boat, so divers simply join the regular excursions to these islands. Frégate is said to be the best of these.

I dived Aride, with the first dive on the south-east side and the second on the north-west rocks. Our first dive yielded little apart from small isolated coral heads and a nurse shark, but on the second we came across a profusion of fish behind every rock as well as rays, another large nurse shark, and a family of four large Napoleon wrasse keeping a respectable distance just out of camera range.

Diving is run by Bernard Camille, who can be found at either the Paradise Hotel or the Praslin Beach Hotel on Anse Volbert (or tel: 32148). Intro dives, no certifications. Local dives SR200 (US$40); Aride SR250 (US$50); Frégate SR500 (US$100); all equipment included.

BARS AND RESTAURANTS

Most of the hotels on Praslin have set menus or buffets for around SR 400 (US$25) per person. On Anse Volbert the only restaurant not attached to a hotel is the Laurier, but it's a bit of a rip-off at around SR 120-200 (US$25-40) for two. The best value we found was at the Flying Dutchman on Grand Anse.

ACCOMMODATION

Côte d'Or (Anse Volbert)
● *Hotel L'Archipel*: Expensive **R**. New hotel on its own beach a few minutes from Anse Volbert. Free windsurfing. Single/double B&B SR 700/750 (US$140/150), half-board SR 900/1,050 (US$180/210). **A** Anse Gouvernement, Praslin, tel: 32242/32040.
● *Côte d'Or Lodge*: Moderate. Single/double B&B SR 350/475 (US$71/97), half-board SR 420/605 (US$86/123). **A** Côte d'Or, Praslin, tel: 32200. Reservations: Mahé, tel: 47141.
● *Village du Pêcheur*: Expensive **R**. Whitewash and thatch rooms from single/double B&B SR 575/700 (US$115/140), half-board SR 650/825 (US$130/

165). **A** PO Box 545, Praslin, tel: 32030. Reservations: UK, tel: (01) 930 6922.

• *Praslin Beach Hotel*: Moderate **R**. Comfortable, well-run hotel. Pool, tennis. Single/double B&B from SR 350/475 (US$76/103), half-board SR 420/605 (US$91/132). **A** Côte d'Or, Praslin, tel: 32222. Reservations: Mahé, tel: 47141.

• *Paradise Hotel*: Moderate. Gloomy. Single/double B&B SR 385/520 (US$78/106), half-board SR 450/650 (US$92/133). **A** Côte d'Or, Praslin, tel: 32255.

• *La Réserve*: Expensive. On its own small beach, but the swimming isn't good. Single/double B&B SR 500/640 (US$102/130), half-board SR 620/880 (US$126/180). **A** Anse Petite Cour, Praslin, tel: 32211.

Grande Anse

• *Flying Dutchman Hotel*: Expensive/moderate. Chalets over the road from the beach, restaurant and bar on the beach. Single/double B&B SR 650/825 (US$130/165), half-board SR 745/1,000 (US$150/200). **A** Grande Anse, Praslin, tel: 33337. Reservations: Mahé, tel: 47073.

• *Hotel Maison des Palmes*: Moderate. Swimming pool. Catamaran, dinghies, windsurfers free to guests. Chalets with seaviews from single/double B&B SR 320/420 (US$64/84), half-board SR 390/540 (US$79/110). **A** Amitié, Praslin, tel: 33411.

• *Beach Villa/Plage d'Or*: Budget **R**. Small family-run guest house, rooms from single/double B&B SR 180/260 (US$37/53). **A** Grande Anse, Praslin, tel: 33445.

• *Indian Ocean Fishing Club Hotel*: Moderate/budget. Single/double B&B SR 250/280 (US$51/57), half-board SR 310/380 (US$63/77). **A** Grande Anse, Praslin, tel: 33324.

ACCESS

Air Seychelles has a frequent shuttle between Mahé and Praslin, flight time 15 minutes (SR 150/US$30 o/w, SR 300/US$60 rtn). A ferry operates Mahé to Praslin three times weekly, journey time just over 3 hours (SR 25/US$5 o/w).

LA DIGUE

A favourite with residents and visitors alike, La Digue is a small, unhurried island with several superb beaches. The best of them are Grand Anse, Petite Anse and Anse Cocos on the east coast but there is no accommodation near these beaches, so you have to stay on or near Anse la Réunion, south of the boat jetty on the west coast.

The east coast beaches are 30–40 minutes away by bicycle: the first of these is Grand Anse, day-tripper-ridden for part of the day, empty after mid-afternoon. Climb the path at the north end of Grand Anse and you'll find Petite Anse; Anse Cocos is the next along, and both these dream beaches are likely to be deserted. There is no shade or refreshments over here, so bring sun protection and supplies for the day. Strong currents are present from May to October.

Other beaches on La Digue include Anse Patate, Anse Gaulettes, Anse Grosse Roche and Anse Banane. There are said to be some superb snorkelling spots around La Digue, but when I was here (in January) the sea was too rough for snorkelling.

Bicycles and ox-carts are the main means of transport on La Digue, although a bus service did start up in 1988. There is no airport here – you have to catch a boat.

DIVING

There are several well-known dive sites nearby including Albatross Rocks which Rod Salm (see under 'Publications') refers to as 'the most sensational shallow water fish watching and underwater photography in the Seychelles'. There is a small dive operation based near the La Digue Island Lodge, but they don't have a dive boat and divers can only go out when the schooner is not being used for tourists. The price of diving (SR 280/US$57) is way out of line considering the standard of service and the poor equipment.

Bird Island

ACCOMMODATION

• *La Digue Island Lodge*: Moderate/ expensive. The only hotel on the island, rather gloomy. Swimming pool, hobie cats, windsurfers. Single/double a/c half-board SR 570/815 (US$116/ 166), non a/c half-board SR 359/532 (US$73/108). **A** Anse la Réunion, La Digue, tel: 34237/34233. Dive packages available through Tropical Adventures, USA, tel: (800) 247 3483.

• *Choppy's*: Budget/moderate. Five minutes' walk from the jetty. Single/ double half-board SR 235/340 (US$50/ 75). **A** Choppy's Bungalows, La Digue, tel: 34224.

• *Château St Cloud*: Budget **R**. A ramshackle château with a sociable atmosphere, the best bargain in the Seychelles. Fifteen minutes' walk from the jetty. Basic rooms, half-board single/double SR 135/200 (US$27/40). **A** Château St Cloud, La Digue, tel: 34323.

• *Berenique Guest House*: Budget. Near the Château St Cloud. Single/ double B&B SR 150/200 (US$30/40), half-board SR 225/300 (US$46/61). **A** Berenique Guest House, La Digue, tel: 34229.

ACCESS

Thirty-forty minutes by schooner from Praslin (four departures daily), three hours by boat from Mahé.

Bird Island

BIRD ISLAND

Bird Island is one of two coral cays (the other is Denis) situated on the edge of the Seychelles Bank, with one privately-owned resort on the edge of the beach. The island is aptly named: as well as the birds which nest here all year round (amongst them white-tailed tropic birds, sheerwaters and fairy terns) over two million sooty terns arrive to breed from April to November, with a density of as many as five pairs per square metre of land. This is one of the most accessible sooty tern colonies in the world, if that sort of thing turns you on.

The island has two resident and ancient giant tortoises, Esmeralda and Raphael, who spend most of their time lumbering from the shade of one palm tree to the next in search of a tastier bit of grass – very relaxing to observe.

45

Apart from watching the tortoises, sunbathing, and eating there's very little to do here. There are no watersports and no diving. The lack of diving is a shame, since Bird is only one mile away from the drop-off of the Seychelles Bank into the Indian Ocean proper, but the island's owner, Guy de Savy, has no plans to change anything here. He likes it just the way it is, he tells me, with only the migrating sands changing from one year to the next.

The beach directly by the resort shelves relatively quickly and is perfect for swimming. None of the bungalows is more than ten paces away from the beach.

It's unusual to meet more than a handful of other guests in the 60 to 90 minutes it takes to walk around Bird Island.

Hawksbill turtles nest here during October, November and December; green turtles during July, August and September.

SNORKELLING★★

The snorkelling here is meant to be superb but although the fish life seems okay (I came across several eagle rays, a small reef shark and bump-headed parrotfish so big they could almost have been Napoleon wrasse) the coral mostly appeared to be dead rubble. Also, don't plan on being able to just jump in and go snorkelling when you wish, since you really need to hire a boat to get across the inner reef. Visibility is poor in January.

BARS AND RESTAURANTS

Plentiful buffets at both lunch and dinner, with barbeques twice a week. Creole-style fish is supplemented by fresh salads from the island's own farm and a choice of hot desserts – notably eccentric for a desert island! Bar open until 12 p.m. nightly.

ACCOMMODATION

• *Bird Island*: Expensive R. White-washed and thatch bungalows, straightforward but adequate. Cold water showers only. Twin SR 900 (US$184) per night, full-board. A PO Box 404, Victoria, Seychelles, tel: 21525; direct island line: 44449.

ACCESS

Thirty-five- to forty-minute flight on Air Seychelles, one flight daily. Reservations can be made through the Bird Island office on Independence Avenue in Victoria.

FRÉGATE

Frégate is a small island just 35 miles/56 km east of Mahé, a 'back-to-nature' retreat where visitors can enjoy the relaxed atmosphere of an Indian Ocean plantation and several excellent beaches. It can be visited as a day trip from either Mahé, Praslin or La Digue.

The total island population is under 30 people, most of whom work on the plantation itself (daily tours are free). As well as being something of a hothouse for tropical fruit plants (many of which were introduced by pirate settlers in the eighteenth century), Frégate is also home to the rare magpie robin, of which there are only 23 pairs left in the world – all of them here. The island has a free-living population of over 100 giant tortoises, which you will come across resting in the shade or rooting around in the cashew thickets all over the island. Hawksbill turtles nest on the beaches here from October to December.

There are numerous reefs around Frégate to explore with mask and snorkel and four different beaches to choose between every day. Of the four, the largest is the landing beach, conveniently right in front of the old plantation house. The other three are reached by a fairly strenuous and hilly walk – in some cases more of a scramble than a walk – which means that the chances are you'll have them to yourself. The nearest of these is Anse Parc (15 minutes away), a small beach with good swimming and snorkelling. Also a good swimming beach, Anse Victorin is on the opposite side of the island (40 minutes away), a miniature version of Anse Lazio with inviting, clear turquoise water. The other beach on this side is Grande Anse (again about forty minutes' walk from the Plantation House) which is fringed by a long reef – appealing to look at but too shallow for swimming.

Local wind and weather conditions mean that normally only two beaches at any one time are usable – but one of these is always a good snorkelling beach, the other a good swimming beach.

Frégate has some interesting dive sites (such as Lion's Rock) in the surrounding seas but unfortunately there is no dive operation on the island – you have to dive them from Praslin or La Digue.

SNORKELLING★★★★

Frégate is surrounded by reef, much of it apparently dead, but nonetheless rich in fish life. The best snorkelling on the landing beach is at the south end: the sea can be quite rough here on the shallow reef edge, which means you need a boat.

On Grande Anse the long reef has many gullies heavily populated with fish at a depth of 6-10 ft/2-3m outside the wave break: numerous parrot fish and other common reef fish inhabit the area along with occasional barracuda, Napoleon wrasse and turtles. Again, a boat may be necessary to cross the reef. Just off Grande Anse is a small island, Ilot, with live coral cover (mostly hard corals such as staghorn, fire, plate and brain corals) off the north shore.

At Anse Parc the seabed shelves away steeply from the beach making entry much easier: again, plenty of fish. Anse Victorin is similar but, like the west side of Ilot, inaccessible during the north-west trades.

MSF: free, snorkelling boat SR 200/ US$40/hr (max five people).

BARS AND RESTAURANTS

The restaurant serves a Creole buffet lunch and a five-course set meal in the evening with both Creole and international dishes. There is also a plentiful supply of fruit and fresh salads and vegetables, grown on the island.

ACCOMMODATION

• *Frégate*: Expensive/moderate. **R.** Accommodation is limited to 20 people so book well in advance. The resort is a converted plantation and all 10 rooms have their own individual character. Accommodation is on a full-board basis only, from single/double SR 675/880 (US$135/176). **A** PO Box 330, Mahé, tel: 23123. Reservations: UK, tel: (01) 930 6922.

ACCESS

Air Seychelles flies twice daily from Mahé, flight time 15 minutes.

Maldives

Mention the Maldives to most people and their eyes either glaze over with pleasure at the memory or they go green with envy because they haven't yet been there. What is it about these 1,200 specks in the Indian Ocean which makes them so different? Firstly, it's just that – most of them are literally just specks in the Ocean, minute splodges of sand no more than a few feet high and a few hundred yards across. Here is everyone's fantasy of a desert island, most of them coral cays with sparkling, pollution-free beaches sloping off into paintbox-coloured lagoons and seas.

This 'desert island' appeal is further enhanced by the fact that each coral cay has just one resort on it. There are currently fifty-five in operation, with a further nine due to open in 1989/90 (compare this to the Great Barrier Reef, which has just three resorts on coral cays of this type).

When not lying around indulgently under a palm tree waiting for someone to come along and knock down a coconut, most people are in, on or under the dazzling lagoons.

The scope for windsurfing is excellent, with a variety of conditions to suit most abilities. Boards can be hired on most resorts (for around US$10 per hour, US$120 per week) and the close proximity of some of the islands to each other offers opportunities for island-hopping. Many islands offer cat sailing and water ski-ing, and a few even have para-sailing.

The chug-chug of compressors filling scuba tanks from dawn onwards gives the clearest indication of the other main reason, apart from pure escapism, why many people come here – simply, world-class diving.

There are well-equipped, well-run diving centres on most islands and with shallow lagoons the temperature of bath water there can be few places where it's such a pleasure to learn (open-water courses cost around US$250). With exceptional visibility, thriving, intact reef communities and an abundance of pelagics, this is tropical diving at its best.

Snorkellers will find that in very few other countries is the magic of the underwater world as guaranteed as it is here. Large, tame fish abound on every reef: giant Napoleon wrasse, minute rare tropicals, parrotfish in all their different stages, and some of the fattest, laziest fish you ever saw are right there within a few minutes' swim of your room or thatched hut. In the inner lagoons you might find yourself completely surrounded by a circular wall of fish; snorkelling here is like floating in a gigantic tropical fish tank.

However, this is not the destination to choose if you want culture, sightseeing, sophisticated nightlife or gourmet food. Some resorts seem to achieve a rare combination of the worst of Eastern-bloc cooking and English school dinners. Almost everything except fish is imported and

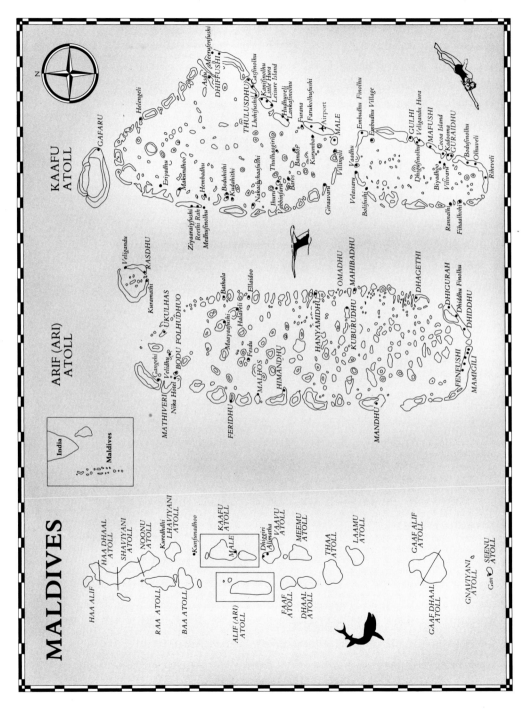

MALDIVES

KAAFU ATOLL

ARIF (ARI) ATOLL

N

GAFARU

Helengeli

Eriyadhu

Makundhoo

Hembadhu

Boduhithi

Kudahithi

Ziyaaraiyfushi
Reethi Rah
Medhufinolhu

Asdu
Meerufenfushi
DHIFFUSHI
THULUSDHU
Lhohifushi
Kanifinolhu
Little Hura
Leisure Island
Hudhuveli
Lankanfinolhu
Furana
Farukolhufushi
Airport
MALE
Villingili

Thulhagiri
Bandos
Baros
Ihuru
Nakachchaafushi
Vabbinfaru
Kurumba

Giraavaru

Velassaru
Bolifushi
Vaadhu

Embudhu Finolhu
Embudhu Village

Dhigufinolhu
Biyadhoo
Vilivaru
Rannalhi
Fihaalhohi

GULHI
Veligandu Hura
MAFUSHI
Cocoa Island
Kadooma
GURAIDHU
Bodufinolhu
Olhuveli
Riheveli

Veligandu
RASDHU
Kuramathi

Gangehi
Velidhu
BODU FOLHUDHUO
UKULHAS
Nika Hotel

MATHIVERIC
Maayafushi
Fesdu
Halaveli
Bathala
Ellaidoo

MALHOS
HIMANDHU
MANDHU

FERIDHU

OMADHU
HANYAMIDHU
MAHIBADHU
KUBURUDHU

DHAGETHI

DHIGURAH
Dhiddhu Finolhu
DHIDDHU

FENFUSHI
MAMIGILI

India

Maldives

HAA ALIF
HAA DHAAL ATOLL
SHAVIYANI ATOLL
NOONU ATOLL
Karedhihi
LHAVIYANI ATOLL
RAA ATOLL
BAA ATOLL
Kunfunadhoo
KAAFU ATOLL
MALE
Dhiggiri
Alimatha
VAAVU ATOLL
MEEMU ATOLL
THAA ATOLL
LAAMU ATOLL
GAAF ALIF ATOLL
GNAVIYANI ATOLL
SEENU ATOLL
Gan
GAAF DHAAL ATOLL
ALIF (ARI) ATOLL
FAAF ATOLL
DHAAL ATOLL

even then it's surprising how infrequently fresh fish appears on the menu at some resorts. However, most people seem to tolerate the lousy food with good humour and some islands are now introducing coffee shops where you can get pizzas and snacks.

Islamic prohibitions on alcohol are strictly observed and all duty-free bottles will be confiscated on arrival at the airport (they will be returned when you leave). Bars in the resorts are open all day and prices aren't outrageous.

Entertainment is fairly restricted and indoor games in the resorts usually means ping-pong, board-games or Maldivian television (the latter is mind-boggling in its dullness). Even in the so-called dry season it rains more often than you might imagine, so take someone with you to play your own indoor games with on rainy afternoons. And while we're on the subject, this isn't a good place for singles unless you're planning on finding an available diving or windsurfing instructor/ress.

Transfers from the airport to your resort are mostly by local boats known as *dhonis*, solid little craft which form the backbone of the transport network between the islands. You'll emerge from the airport to find a fleet of them waiting at the quay just outside the terminal and there can be no better antidote to a cramped and claustrophobic airplane than to stretch out under a shady awning on the deck of a *dhoni*, dangling your swollen feet in the warm sea and watching the flying fish leap across the waves. However, *dhonis* are fairly slow and if your flight is delayed for any reason you might be in for a long and uncomfortable journey on choppy seas at night. *Dhonis* travel at approximately eight to ten mph (13-16 kph) so you can work out how long your transfers will be from the distances given in the A-Z of resorts. Many of the resorts now offer speedboat transfers (at extra cost), which cut transfer times considerably. Helicopter transfers are also now available through the Coral Air Maldive Island Hopper service and there are plans for this to be extended to the nine new resorts in the Alifu atoll, which is expected to cost around US$100 per person return. The islands in Alifu are clustered together more closely than they are in some of the other atolls so this ride promises to be quite spectacular.

The Maldives are currently very popular as a diving destination but it has to be said that this is not wilderness diving. Dive sites are often shared by several resorts and boat traffic can be constant, with shoals of divers almost as common as shoals of fish. As well as this, mismanagement has led to the reefs around some resorts being badly damaged, crown of

Bandos

thorns starfish are a problem in some areas, and some reefs are suffering from extensive bleaching of the corals. Apart from these localized problems, overall the reefs appear to be in excellent shape and most divers won't be disappointed.

Following a considerable number of fatalities in the early 1980s there is now an official depth limit of 130ft/40m on all diving and many resorts have imposed their own limits which are much lower (usually 80-90ft/25-30m). This is deep enough for most sports divers but there are one or two famous and spectacular dive sites which are well below these limits.

Diving in the resorts works out at around US$30-35 for a one-tank boat dive including equipment and between US$150-250 for six days unlimited diving, fully inclusive.

The Maldives are famous for sharks and you'll undoubtedly come across them whilst snorkelling and diving here. If you're snorkelling they'll probably give you a shock the first time you see one but after a few days even the least macho visitor becomes blasé and complains if there aren't any around. They're unlikely to be aggressive and there's no need to worry unduly – just follow normal common sense precautions (see under 'Potential Marine Hazards', p 304). Shark-feeding (page 63) takes place on a regular basis.

The optimum season for diving and snorkelling is from October/ November to May, with the best visibility during February, March and April, when it reaches 100-200 ft (30-60m).

Independent island-hopping is discouraged by the government and difficult (although not impossible) to do, since there are few regular transport links. However, you can go adventure sailing by *dhoni*, sleeping either on deck or camping on beaches along the way, and there are also live-aboard dive cruises. The Air Maldives Travel Bureau, for instance, runs two different cruises, the first of which is an island-hopping trip (aimed at beachcombers and snorkellers) which costs from US$45 per day fully inclusive. The other option is an inner atoll safari, aimed at divers, which costs from US$65 per day fully inclusive (contact: Air Maldives, Marine Drive, Male, Republic of Maldives). Dive cruises on converted *dhonis* are bookable from the UK through Indian Ocean Hideaways (tel: 01-930 6922). It's possible to combine a one-week dive cruise with additional time on the islands.

Toplessness and nudity are illegal; the toplessness rule is rarely disregarded, and then only with a great deal of discretion (with the exception of Club Med). Extras in the resorts are pricey (sunscreens, for instance) but silk-screened T-shirts with tropical fish on them are good value at just a few dollars each. They don't last long, so buy several (Male has the best selection and the lowest prices).

In order to protect the country's Islamic culture from corruption by Westerners, all resorts have been built on previously uninhabited islands but you can visit local communities on day trips.

Information about particular resorts in the Maldives is hard to come by. The only guidebook which exists is Stuart Bevan's *Maldives*, now in its third edition. This is an excellent book to take with you for background information on local customs and the Maldivian people but it doesn't give much information about individual resorts or the diving. Watch out for the forthcoming *Divers' Guide to Fishes of Maldives* from IMMEL (see page 278).

Shark pool, Hudhuveli

53

Because of the difficulties of covering all the resorts in the Maldives in detail, I have compiled an A–Z of resort islands which I hope will give you some pointers when perusing the brochures.

GENERAL INFORMATION

Time
GMT+5 hrs

IDD code
960+4-digit number

Currency
Maldivian Rufiya (Rf)
All transactions in the resorts are in US$
UK£1=11 Rf
US$1= 8 Rf

Hotels
The cost of a double room with all meals varies between US$50-250 a night.

PUBLICATIONS
Common Reef Fishes of the Maldives
Charles Anderson and Ahamed Hafiz (Novelty Printers, Male, 1987). 85 pp, softback. Text in English, French, Japanese, German and Dhivehi (Maldivian). Whilst not up to the standard of fish ID books for other countries, this is a useful little guide. £5.95 including UK postage from Ocean Optics, 4 Greyhound Road, London W6 8NX.
Maldives
Stuart Bevan (Other People Publications, Australia, third edition 1987). 208 pp, softback, £5.50. The only guidebook available, now much improved. Strong on history, language and culture.
The Maldive Mystery
Thor Heyerdahl (Unwin 1988). 323 pp, softback £6.95. Recently re-issued in paperback; essential beach reading.

WEATHER
The peak season is from November to March/April. From May to September showers are more frequent and there are occasional thunderstorms. Water temperatures are a constant 80-86°F/20-30°C year round, and it frequently heats up to 95°F/32°C in the lagoons. The calmest seas and bluest skies are from November through to April/May, with the optimum underwater visibility during February, March and April. The roughest seas and strongest winds are during June and sometimes October or early November. From November to April winds are north-westerly and more gentle. During the transition months between monsoons winds tend to be light and variable. Wave conditions are dependent on storms and Indian Ocean tropical cyclones and will generally be best in high summer and on south-west facing coastlines.

HEALTH
Yellow fever inoculations if coming from an infected area.

VISAS
Valid passports required. 30-day visa issued on arrival, extensions possible.

TOURIST BOARDS
Head Office: Male, Republic of Maldives, tel: 3224/3229. Overseas Representatives: UK, tel: (01) 352 2246, 351 9351; Tokyo, tel: (03) 589 3311.

THE ISLANDS

ALIMATHA AQUATIC RESORT
In the Felidhoo (Vaavu) atoll, close to the Vattaru reefs, which are said to be outstanding. Italian-run resort, Italian food. Free windsurfing. Water ski-ing, dinghy sailing. 64 modern bungalows with fans (a/c available at extra cost). Airport 38 miles/60km.

ASDHU SUN ISLAND
Diving, windsurfing and water ski-ing. 25 rooms. Airport 23 miles/36km.

BANDOS
North Male atoll. Bandos has more facilities than most islands but lacks character. However, they are currently redeveloping the island to give it a more local flavour, with rooms being rebuilt with thatched roofs. Bandos is strong on sailing and windsurfing with a well-equipped watersports centre, Thomaso Sail & Surf, operated by two European cat-sailing pros. They say that the best time here is from November through to March, when winds average 7-21 knots/3-5 Beaufort. Hi-Fly, Merlin and Rainbow boards. Daily and weekly rates, courses, and 'unlimited sail & surf' deals available. Water ski-ing. The snorkelling around Bandos is exceptional with an overwhelming concentration of fish on the outside of the reef. People tend to be put off trying to reach the outside drop-off on this island because of the lack of access channels but there are two boat channels (one by the main jetty and one by the dive shop) which you can snorkel through if you can't get over the reef top. Bandos used to be home to Voightmann's 'shark circus' but Voightmann has since left following at least one if not two diving fatalities (not whilst shark feeding). Bandos is near three other resorts (Furana, Kurumba and Farukolufushi) which share a number of nearby sites and because of considerable traffic over the years the area is now considered over-dived. There is a delightful Sand Bar on the beach, a coffee shop and an a/c restaurant (the latter, however, is anything but delightful). Plans are in hand for a beachside disco and Chinese and Japanese restaurant. 215 rooms, all looking out to sea. 24 VIP suites with mini-bars and other facilities are also planned. Airport 5 miles/8 km.

BAROS
On the periphery of the North Male atoll, popular with the British. Windsurfing, water ski-ing, sailing. The diving school is run by Sub Aqua Reisen of Munich and Baros is said to have a superb house reef (33ft/10m from the beach). 50 bungalows. Airport 10 miles/16 km.

BATHALA
Tiny island in the Ari atoll. Peace and quiet with the emphasis on diving, which is run by Robert Schmidt, the former editor of a West German diving magazine. Bathala is on the edge of the Vadhoo channel and offers drift diving, shark feeding and beach diving; there is a 130ft/40m drop-off within 100ft/30m of the beach. Free windsurfing; occasional strong currents mean that sailors should be experienced. Tennis, volleyball. 36 small, round bungalows with garden shower-rooms. Airport 36 miles/57 km.

55

BI YA DHOO AND VILLI VARU

Bi Ya Dhoo and Villi Varu are neighbouring islands in the Kaafu atoll, both operated by India's Taj Group. You can walk around either of them in 20 minutes. Of the two, Bi Ya Dhoo is the more expensive, and has a better beach, fewer people and more space – 25 acres to Villi Varu's 12. There is a regular boat service between the two islands. Excellent snorkelling: the reefs surrounding both islands are breached by five passages in each case, all signposted, which lead out to the drop-off. Bi Ya Dhoo's house reef has three resident turtles to play tag with – always just too quick to catch a ride from, playfully aware of their underwater superiority. The Nautico Watersports Centre, which operates on both islands, is efficient, well-equipped and looks after both windsurfing and diving. International Windsurfing Association courses available on both islands, conditions suitable for beginners and intermediates. Para-sailing, cat sailing.

Striped sweetlips, Maldives

Thirty or more dive sites are within reach (with an average boat ride of 30-40 minutes), with precipices and overhangs providing plenty of variety. Certified divers can just drop-off over the side of the lagoon (which is 65-100ft/20-30m from the shore), although the deep house reefs (max depth 130ft/40m around the islands) are not as interesting as the off-shore sites. The Taj boasts a hydroponic garden for fresh vegetables and is meant to have one of the highest standards of cuisine in the Maldives but this wasn't reflected in the menus on offer when I stayed here. Tinned Russian salad, spam, cold baked beans and odd mixtures such as cauliflower cheese with curry all appeared in buffets, and fresh, grilled fish was noticeable only by its absence. Lobster was frozen, and expensive.

Bi Ya Dhoo has 96 a/c rooms in a two-storey complex, spacious and simple, all with fresh hot-water showers and fridges. Villi Varu has 42 rooms with fans, 82 with a/c, all with fresh hot-water showers and fridges. Airport 17 miles/27 km.

Villi Varu

BODUFINOLHU TOURIST RESORT

South Male atoll. Very up-market, recently re-vamped. Part of the appeal of this island is that it has two other small deserted islands nearby where you can escape for the day. Dutch-run diving school. Windsurfing, water ski-ing. Attractive over-water bar, disco. 88 rooms with a/c, IDD phones. Airport 24 miles/38 km.

Shark feeding, Lion's Head

BODUHITHI
North Male atoll, full of Italians, very attractive bungalows, nearly always fully booked. Free windsurfing. Water ski-ing and dinghy sailing. 66 bungalows with fans (a/c at extra cost). Airport 18 miles/27 km.

BOLIFUSHI
Windsurfing. 64 beds. Airport 8 miles/12 km.

COCOA ISLAND (Maakunufushi)
Chic, exclusive resort in the South Male atoll, very small island, good beach, expensive. Windsurfing, water ski-ing, para-sailing. Snorkelling, no diving. Eight comfortable, two-tiered bungalows built from natural materials. Good reputation for food and wine. Airport 18 miles/26 km.

DHIGGIRI RESORT
In the Felidhoo (Vaavu) atoll. Free windsurfing. Water ski-ing and dinghy sailing. 30 rooms. Airport 37 miles/60 km.

DHIGUFINOLHU
Recently renovated, up-market, small and exclusive. German clientele. Wind-surfing. 30 bungalows. Airport 12 miles/19 km.

ELLAIDHOO
Italian-run resort. Good diving, including one particularly famous spot known as the Fish Hole. Free windsurfing. Water ski-ing and dinghy sailing. 38 cottages, some located above the water *à la Tahitienne*. Airport 36 miles/57 km.

EMBUDHU FINOLHU
New, very small resort in the South Male atoll. Australian run. No trees or shade. Acres of lagoon, no house reef close by. 'A glorified sand-bank trying to be chic,' according to one brochure. Windsurfing, water ski-ing. 36 beds. Airport 5 miles/8 km.

EMBUDHU VILLAGE
South Male atoll, large island, German clientele. Good diving and house reef. Windsurfing, water ski-ing. 82 rooms. Airport 5 miles/8 km.

ERIYADU VILLAGE RESORT
German clientele. Good beach and a good house reef but some of the surrounding

57

areas appear to be dead. Windsurfing, water ski-ing. 40 rooms. Airport 24 miles/ 36 km.

FARUKOLHUFUSHI

Club Med's island, known as Faru for short, North Male atoll. Attractive beach. Initiation dive and one 'exploratory' dive per day free, second dive at extra cost. Close to Bandos, said to be overdived. Photo lab, underwater slide and video shows and talks on underwater topics. Sailing (6 F Cats) and windsurfing (Fun Cup 11, Speed, Swift, Jibe), yoga, volleyball, aerobics, gymnastics. Limited choice of cuisine by Club Med standards, free wine. Twin-bedded bungalows with shower rooms, fresh water seven hours per day. Airport 2 miles/3 km.

FESDU

Alifu atoll. Good beach with the added bonus of a little deserted island nearby only for Fesdu guests. Very popular. Good house reef, excellent diving. Windsurfing. 45 rooms. Airport 40 miles/64 km.

FIHAALHOLI

Big island with natural jungle in the interior. This island used to have a bad reputation but has recently been rebuilt and is under new management. Most of the staff are ex-Oberoi, which means that standards of service should be high. Subex dive school (English, French, German and Spanish instruction), extensive house reef, good snorkelling. The island has one of the biggest windsurfing schools in the Maldives, with reasonable equipment. Water ski-ing. 130 rooms. Airport 26 miles/40 km.

FURANA

North Male atoll, eastern outer reef. Australian-owned, popular with families and young Aussies. Deep lagoon with yacht anchorage. Top Cat sailing, windsurfing, water ski-ing. Tennis, volleyball. Two or more boat dives daily, intro courses, open-water certifications. Highlights of the diving here include soft corals at nearby Kanduagiri, shark-feeding, diving on the wreck of the *Maldives Victory*, whale sharks off the eastern end of the island and mantas at Manta Point during the monsoon. Restaurant, coffee shop and the only Chinese à la carte restaurant (Mr Lee's) in the Maldives. 88 modern rooms with tiled bathrooms. Airport 2 miles/3 km.

GASFINOLHU

Very, very small island. Windsurfing. 30 rooms. Airport 11 miles/17 km.

GIRAAVARU

Smart resort in the North Male atoll on the Vadhoo channel, recently revamped. Similar to Vadhoo (equally good diving) but with better beaches. Good house reef. Large lagoon for windsurfing and water ski-ing. 50 a/c rooms all with mini-bars, telephones and fresh hot water. Swimming pool. Not much shade and not many palm trees. Airport 7 miles/11 km.

HALAVELI

Italian-run. Water ski-ing, sailing, free windsurfing. Halaveli boasts one of the most beautiful lagoons in the atoll and is also ideally suited for windsurfer trips to nearby Bathala or Maayafushi. Two free dives per day for qualified divers, PADI diving courses. Sand floor dining room specializing in Italian food. 30 white-walled bungalows with thatched roofs. Airport 34 miles/54 km.

HELENGELI
Very much a diver's island, not much else happens here. Windsurfing. 30 bungalows, basic, no a/c. Airport 2 miles/3 km.

HEMBADHU ISLAND
Good beach. Windsurfing, water ski-ing. 30 bungalows. Airport 24 miles/37 km.

HUDHUVELI
One of the smaller Maldivian islands (it's about ten paces from one side to the other). The beaches don't compare to some of the bigger islands and you wouldn't really want to come here on your own – it's extremely quiet. Families with children will find it suitable because of the huge lagoon which children can safely play in; the lagoon likewise makes it ideal for beginners' windsurfing. There are full windsurfing and diving facilities and water ski-ing. A boat leaves twice a day to take snorkellers out to the reef, which is too far to swim to: not the place to come if you want to fall out of bed and go snorkelling every morning. There is a small 'fish farm' with sharks, rays and turtles. Hudhuveli is popular as a stop-over island (packages through Singapore Airlines) if you're just looking for somewhere to unwind for a few days between flights, and it's cheaper than many other islands. There is just one small bar, dining room and coffee shop, all in native style with thatched roofs. 40 rooms, 15 of which are huts, all basic, fans but no a/c. Airport 7 miles/11 km.

IHURU ISLAND
North Male atoll, adorable little island, Australian-managed, one of the best. Swiss-run diving school, high ratio of instructors to students. The reefs here used to be in a terrible state but due to a thoughtful clean-up and a fish-feeding programme the situation has now improved enormously. New growth is starting to emerge, the snorkelling is excellent, and there are now a dozen sting rays in residence: at least half-a-dozen of these will turn up to be fed at dusk every day in shallow water off the island's jetty, an experience which constitutes the highlight of their holiday for many visitors to Ihuru. Water ski-ing, sailing dinghies, free windsurfing. Imaginative food, over-water bar. 28 romantic thatched bungalows with freshwater showers. Airport 10 miles/16 km.

KANDOOMA
South Male atoll, big island with a lake in the middle, but short of beach and has no house reef. Not recommended. Windsurfing, water ski-ing. 98 beds. Airport 19 miles/30 km.

KANIFINOLHU
In the North Male atoll, this island is just 178 metres wide. Water ski-ing, Hobie sailing, para-sailing, free windsurfing. The house reef is 10 minutes away by sailboat, most local dive sites are within half an hour by boat. Eurodivers school. Free tennis (floodlit) and aerobics. Attractive rooms with coral walls and thatched roofs; deluxe rooms have a/c, freshwater showers and mini-bars. Restaurant, lively bar, 24-hour coffee shop, disco. Young clientele. Airport 12 miles/19 km.

KUDAHITHI
North Male atoll. 'Exclusive resort for couples seeking luxury and solitude', they say. Free windsurfing. Diving, water ski-ing, dinghy sailing. For night life you have to get a boat over to Boduhithi, three minutes away by motorized *dhoni*. Six

bungalows, all individually-styled (the Sheikh Room, the Safari Room, etc). All with a/c, fans, hot and cold water, and their own speedboats. Expensive. Airport 18 miles/29 km.

KUDAFOLHUDHOO (Nika Hotel)

Alifu atoll. Up-market Italian-run resort, very small and very smart. Free windsurfing. Two dining rooms, international and Italian food, Italian wine cellar. Bar, coffee shop, nightclub and disco. 16 bungalows each with living room, bedroom, private verandah and bathroom in a garden setting, no a/c. Airport 43 miles/70 km.

KUNFUNADHU

Windsurfing. 25 rooms. Airport 63 miles/100 km.

KURAMATHI

One of the larger islands (two square miles), it actually takes over an hour to walk round! Alifu atoll. *Dhoni* sailing, windsurfing, water ski-ing. Diving operated by Inter Aqua Diving, famous for drift diving and hammerhead sharks, although the latter are by no means guaranteed. Home base of *The Sea Explorer* for dive cruises. Good snorkelling. Recent extensive facelift, including the building of some overwater bungalows. 110 rooms. Popular with Germans. Airport 36 miles/57 km.

KUREDHOO CAMPING RESORT

'Unspoilt diving', word has it: basically a diving resort. Windsurfing. 21 rooms. Airport 80 miles/130 km.

KURUMBA VILLAGE

North Male atoll, bite-sized island only half an hour away from Male, convenient for shopping and sightseeing. Freshwater swimming pool. Water ski-ing, windsurfing. The dive operation, run by EuroDivers of Switzerland, is one of the biggest in the Maldives but the area is considered overdived. The resort recently underwent a million-dollar facelift and now includes a conference centre and deluxe suites all with a/c and full amenities. Only recommended for short stopovers. 70 rooms. Airport 2 miles/3 km.

LANKANFINOLHU

North Male atoll, German clientele, good value. Windsurfing. 51 rooms. Airport 6 miles/8 km.

LEISURE ISLAND

Stuart Bevan (see 'Publications') says: 'The most outstanding feature, one that has amazed and horrified visitors to the island, is that there is no beach or lagoon.' Windsurfing, water ski-ing. 10 bungalows. Airport 10 miles/16 km.

LITTLE HURA

The beach here isn't great and the island has very few palm trees. Not recommended. Windsurfing, water ski-ing. 36 rooms. Airport 10 miles/16 km.

LHOHIFUSHI

North Male atoll. Diving (house reef is just off the jetty), sailing, windsurfing, water ski-ing. 60 duplex-style cabanas. Said to be very bland. Airport 11 miles/17 km.

MAAYAAFUSHI

In the Alifu atoll, recently renovated, good value. Geared towards singles (beach barbeques, discos, plenty of action). Free windsurfing and Hobie sailing. Diving school run by Wolfgang May and Eberhad Lesche, who say: 'Maayaafushi diving is very special – a house reef accessible on the eastern side, a wonderful lagoon stretching for miles to the west, and only 30 minutes from the outer reef at Bathala. All diving in the Ari atoll is unspoilt, as the area has only been open to tourism for a few years. Giant black coral trees, lost forever on Male atoll to make jewellery, stand proudly. Mantas, turtles and millions of fish are so friendly they come to play.' 60 rooms in 4-room units with fans. Airport 38 miles/60 km.

MAKUNDHOO CLUB

Large island on the northern Haa Dhaalu atoll with a reputation for good food, good beaches. Plenty of yachts for charter moored in the lagoon. Diving on an isolated, 25-km long reef with many wrecks. Windsurfing, water ski-ing. 27 rooms. Airport 22 miles/35 km.

MEERUFENFUSHI

North Male atoll, very large island, huge lagoon, terrific for windsurfing and water ski-ing. Because the reef wall is so far away there is no diving or snorkelling from the shore – you have to go by boat (20-30 minutes). This is compensated for by an excellent house reef and uncrowded dive sites. 150 rooms. Mostly German clientele. Due to close in 1991. Airport 5 miles/8 km.

NAKATCHAFUSHI

Appealing small island in the North Male atoll. Huge lagoon for watersports. The long sandspit on the western end of the island is one of the Maldives' most-photographed beaches. Windsurfing, water ski-ing, cat and dinghy sailing. The diving is run by Sub-Aqua Reisen of Munich. 50 round, thatched-roof huts, all a/c. Small disco. Airport 14 miles/22 km.

Scuba lessons in the lagoon,
Biyadhoo

61

CLUB OLHUVELI

On the east side of the South Male atoll, good value. Good for windsurfing but for diving or snorkelling you have to get a boat to the reef. Eurodivers dive school (English and German instruction) with some excellent dive sites in the vicinity, particularly in the Gurudhu Channel. 55 bungalows. Airport 22 miles/35 km.

RANNALHI

Remote resort in the South Male atoll, large island, good beaches. Typically

Maldivian and uncomplicated, fairly wild and natural. Adequate house reef, well-run diving school, but the best local sites are at least one hour away by boat. Windsurfing and sailing. New over-water à la carte restaurant and bar. 50 comfortable, spacious thatched bungalows. Airport 23 miles/36 km.

REETHI RAH (Medhufinolhu)

Swiss-run, better food than many islands. Good for beginner to intermediate windsurfing: the Club Mistral has up-to-date equipment and offers their usual high standard of intruction. The house reef is a fairly long way out (500ft/150m). Eurodivers dive school with attentive, personal service provided by Ueli Weibel and Elaine. Water ski-ing, cat sailing. 50 rooms. Airport 22 miles/35 km.

RIHIVELI

South Male atoll, French-style ambience, popular with honeymoon couples, one of the best Maldivian resorts. Water ski-ing, para-sailing, free catamaran and dinghy sailing and windsurfing. Aerobics. Eurodivers School, PADI courses. No house reef. Bar, open-air dining area, disco once a week. Well-managed, high standard of cuisine. 38 spacious bungalows. Airport 25 miles/40 km.

THULAGIRI

North Male atoll, the Italian version of Club Med. Small sea-water swimming pool. Windsurfing. The house reef has apparently been damaged by crown of thorns starfish. 29 rooms. Airport 7 miles/11 km.

VADHOO

Vadhoo is a 15-minute walk-round island, but whereas other islands are small and charming, Vadhoo is just small. The beach isn't much good and there are no watersports. However, Vadhoo is famous for its diving, thanks to its location on the edge of the Vadhoo Channel. Whereas most islands are part of atolls around sunken craters which go down to maximum depths of around 265ft/81m, Vadhoo and several others are on the edge of a channel over 500 fathoms (1,000m) deep. Within an hour's ride they claim to have 10 of the best dive sites in the Maldives, and at Paradise Point there's drift diving along the channel with a chance of seeing hammerheads. The bar is a bit grim, and accommodation is in modern, ugly two-storey chalets. The diving is run by Japanese instructors. Airport 5 miles/8 km.

VABBINFARU

North Male atoll, recently revamped, young, lively atmosphere, popular with Italians. Free windsurfing, hobie sailing, night fishing. House reef is disappointing (crown of thorns). 30 spacious cottages. Airport 10 miles/16 km.

VELASSARU

South Male atoll. Great beaches and a pretty lagoon, but the rooms are badly in need of a revamp. Diving, large windsurf school (Hifly and Mistral equipment). Close to Male for shopping, good value for money. Airport 6 miles/10 km.

VELIGANDU ISLAND

Remote, long sandspit. Good diving (drift diving, hammerheads). Italian-run. Windsurfing, dinghy sailing. 25 up-market bungalows. Airport 36 miles/58 km.

VILLINGILLI

Large, lively resort. Proximity to Male gives guests plenty of shopping opportunities, but this is another island designated to take the overflow from **Malé**. Near the Vadhoo Channel, top-rated diving, run by Sub-Aqua Reisen of Munich. Coral

pool with sharks and rays. Windsurfing, water ski-ing. A/c restaurant and disco. 125 bungalows, basic. Airport 2 miles/3 km.
VILLI VARU
See under Bi Ya Doo.
ZIYAARAAIYFUSHI
Basic, no natural beach, no house reef. Too many bungalows for such a small island. Great lagoon for windsurfing. 35 rooms. Airport 21 miles/34 km.

Shark Feeding

Sharks are at the top of the marine food chain and most divers enjoy being able to observe the power and grace of their movements under water. Shark feeds are common in the Maldives and take place in at least five specific locations (namely the house reef on Bandos, Lion's Head in the Vadhoo Channel, Banana reef near Furana, Rasfahri near Nakatchafushi and the Fish Hole in the Alifu atoll, the latter being accessible from Bathala, Ellaido and Maayaafushi).

Shark feeding was elevated to an art form on Bandos by German photographer Herwath Voightmann. Voightmann's 'shark circus' took place three times weekly with the maestro feeding them not only by hand but mouth-to-mouth as well, dressed for the part in an underwater Superman costume or an Evil Knievel-style star-spangled wetsuit. Voightmann has since left Bandos. 'The secret of safe shark feeding is simple,' another divemaster explained. 'You just use big fish. We know how big the shark's mouth is, and once you've stuck the fish in there's no room for anything else – like your arm, for instance. You've just got to be careful not to drop the bait.'

However, not everything always goes according to plan, as I found out on a shark feed at Lion's Head. We descended to 60ft/18m and arranged ourselves in a semi-circle on the reef but after waiting for what seemed like an age, nothing happened. Disappointed, the group started to break up, floating off in every direction to have a close look at the reef. At this moment the sharks finally arrived, having been drawn by the smell of blood from several miles downstream. The group was by now totally disorganized and the sharks were passing between and behind the divers, which isn't meant to happen. To make matters worse, one diver had grabbed some fish from the divemaster (without his knowing it) and was also feeding them, so it was impossible to concentrate on where the sharks were at any one time. 'They're wild sharks, not puppy dogs,' commented one angry diver afterwards. 'Voightmann knew what he was doing, and even then he had problems.' An amusing postscript: the divemaster who let this shark feed get so out of control was none other than the infamous 'Richard Harley', a fugitive lawyer who had staged a fake diving accident in the Bahamas after being convicted of taking US$360,000 in bribes in New Jersey. He arrived in the Maldives and took control of several dive centres before Interpol finally caught up with him.

In 1988 *Diver* magazine reported that shark feeding had been banned in the Maldives. This is incorrect, but dive centres are worried that far too many novices are going on shark feeds and much more discretion is now being shown as to who goes on them.

63

Sri Lanka

S ri Lankan beaches conjure up images of the best that the tropics have to offer and a few – but by no means all – fit the picture. As with many countries, the beaches get better the further away you travel from the capital, which in this case means south from Colombo.

Bentota**, 38 miles/61 km south of Colombo, is the first decent beach on this coast. There are several tourist-grade hotels and an enormous lagoon behind the beach for windsurfing and water ski-ing. Next door to Bentota is Beruwala, also a popular tourist beach, but by comparison it is not nearly as good – erosion has seen to that.

Forty-seven miles/75 km south of the capital you'll find **Ahungalla*****+**, a real stunner of a beach and the location of what is unquestionably Sri Lanka's top beach hotel, the Triton.

The country's biggest and busiest beach resort is **Hikkaduwa*****, a well-known rest stop for overland travellers which has recently burgeoned into a tourist-grade resort. Hikkaduwa is also well known for its surfing and snorkelling – although the latter is now poor. A fun beach, but not to everyone's taste.

Just under an hour's drive further south, on the other side of the historic regional capital of Galle, **Unawatuna*****+** is (so far) undeveloped compared to its northern counterparts, with numerous budget guest houses for shoestring beachbums and just one hotel for those who prefer a little more comfort.

Koggala****, which is 5 miles/8 km past Unawatuna, is another superb beach with two enormous tourist hotels on it. Because of the drop-off in tourism all Sri Lankan hotels have reduced their prices dramatically and you can snap up a reasonable room in either of these for US$10 a night. There are no watersports on Koggala – just the surf and

acres of empty sand.

Stilt fishermen, Hikkaduwa

The next main beach is at **Dikwella★**, where there is a smart Italian resort. Finally, in and around **Tangalle★★** there are several secluded coves plus larger, more windswept beaches, all with guest-house accommodation.

Unless mentioned here, all the other south-west coast beaches should be avoided. Mount Lavinia (just outside Colombo) has two beaches divided by the rambling edifice of the old Mount Lavinia Hotel. The beach to the south of the hotel is clean within the 100-yard stretch which is fenced off, but outside of this it is only remarkable for litter and beach-touts. The public beach to the north of the hotel is the nastiest in Sri Lanka with the possible exception of Negombo.

The beach at Negombo has nothing going for it apart from its proximity to the airport, which is only 6 miles/9 km away. The beach is suffering badly from erosion and despite a million-dollar UN pro-gramme to rectify the situation, Negombo is still the pits. If you want to

65

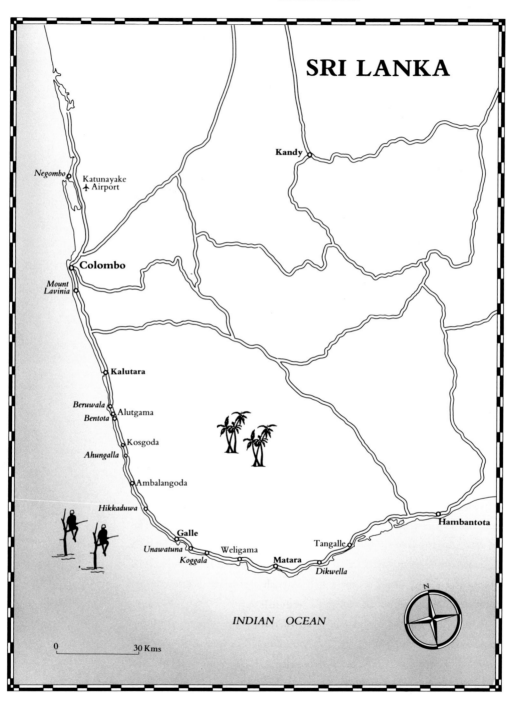

SRI LANKA

Kandy

Negombo   Katunayake
    ✈ Airport

Colombo

*Mount
Lavinia*

Kalutara

Beruwala   Alutgama
Bentota

Kosgoda

Ahungalla

Ambalangoda

Hikkaduwa

Galle

Unawatuna   Weligama   **Hambantota**
Koggala   **Matara**   Tangalle
    Dikwella

INDIAN OCEAN

N

0   30 Kms

stay near the airport before catching a flight out, you're better off booking into the Airport Garden Hotel.

Coastal erosion in the last decade has led to the loss of nearly 165 miles/266 km of beaches on the south-west coast alone. Ironically, it's the tourist industry itself which is mostly to blame: thousands of tons of coral have been removed to build hotels, leaving the beaches unprotected from the ravages of the sea. Over 6,000 men and women are estimated to be involved in the coral mining industry and each of them removes over a ton of coral each year. The result is that on the 220 miles/350 km stretch of coastline between Colombo and Hambantota, three-quarters of it has little or no beach left at all. In addition, nearly 350,000 cubic feet of sand is removed each year for construction, further contributing to the process of deterioration.

Although regulations prohibiting resort construction near the high water mark came into effect in 1983, by then much of the damage had already been done and now each annual monsoon brings with it more erosion, floods and consequent homelessness. Through its new coastal zone management plan the Department of Coast Conservation hopes to try and reverse the trend, but they are battling against heavy odds with limited resources.

Not only are beaches and reefs being lost but fish populations are on the decline in coastal areas, partly due to the loss of their habitat but also because of collection for export for the aquarium trade. The Marine Conservation Society has catalogued 139 species of fish which are exported from Sri Lanka, including 29 species of butterflyfish, 13 species of wrasse, 11 species of triggerfish, 100 species of angelfish and 9 species of surgeonfish. There are no controls governing the trade and at least 29 species of fish which you would normally expect to see on tropical reefs are now rare here. Sadly, 25 per cent of the fish die before they reach their final destination: seven species of butterflyfish exported from Sri Lanka feed exclusively on coral polyps and are therefore virtually impossible to keep alive in captivity.

The degradation of Sri Lanka's reefs means that divers and snorkellers shouldn't expect too much. There is a marine sanctuary at Hikkaduwa but it is consistently abused by both foreigners and locals alike. Diving is incredibly cheap and can cost as little as £5, which is about right for what you get in terms of standards of equipment and diversity of marine life. The off-shore Great and Little Basses reefs in the south-east are considered to be undisturbed and in good condition (practically the only reefs which are) but they can only be visited for a few weeks each year prior to the onset of the south-west monsoon in May and they are limited in extent. It's sometimes possible to get a live-aboard dive charter to go there from Hikkaduwa during April, but don't bank on it.

Sri Lanka offers some good sailing: the wind blows most days at 11-16 knots/4-5 Beaufort with the biggest swells on the south of the island. The right conditions here give waves of 8-12 feet/2.5-4 m with cross-shore winds prevailing.

Some of the best wave sailing spots are on the east coast. In Trincomalee the prevailing winds tend to give off-shores accompanied by a swell of 3-4 feet/1-1.3 m. Uppulevi is immediately north of Trincomalee and the waters here are good for intermediate to expert windsurfers. Further north, Nilaveli boasts one of the most beautiful beaches along this coast and many of the big hotels here hire windsurfing equipment – beware of currents near the lagoon mouth which may be very strong at certain points of the tide. In fact, the whole beach can become hazardous during the course of the day.

A safer place to sail is Kalkudah-Passekudah, two beaches separated from each other by a headland. Passekudah is reef protected, the whole bay being calm, blue and shallow.

For the best surf on the east coast, head for Arugam Bay (just 2.5 km south of the village of Pottuvil), a wide sweeping bay with a low promontory at its southern end where the surf forms. Further on is Crocodile Rock – more surf, but not as good as Arugam Bay.

As with most beaches in developing countries, don't expect those in Sri Lanka to be always neat and clean: most have active fishing communities on them, which adds colour but debris too. Seafood is cheap and plentiful.

Beaches here tend to be more hassle-free than Indian beaches and because of the civil war, prices for accommodation at all levels are going down rather than up; hotel prices are in many cases at 1983 levels. Toplessness upsets local sensibilities, although it is tolerated on the major beaches such as Hikkaduwa.

Because of the civil war we weren't able to cover the east coast in detail and indeed as we went to press the whole country was more or less closed to visitors. However, I have decided not to withdraw this chapter in the forlorn hope that poor, strife-torn Sri Lanka will sort itself out in the near future. In the meantime, check the situation before travelling.

GENERAL INFORMATION

Time
GMT + 5.5 hours

IDD code
94 + area code + number

Currency
Sri Lanka rupee (Rs)
UK£1 = 50 Rs
US$1 = 28 Rs

Hotels
Prices given do not include 10 per cent service.

Bed and breakfast, single/double:
Deluxe: US$35/70
Expensive: US$18/35
Moderate: US$5/13
Budget: US$2

PUBLICATIONS
The Treasure of The Great Reef
Arthur C. Clarke (Ballantine Books, USA 1974). Account of a massive treasure find on the Great Basses Reef.

WEATHER
From the beginning of May to the end of

July the monsoon brings rain to the south and west coasts, although heavy rain and thunderstorms do sometimes occur in the south-west through to December. The north-east monsoon brings rain to the north and east in December and January. The diving season on the south-west coast is from November to March.

HEALTH
Anti-malaria prescription and inoculations against typhoid and polio are advisable. Yellow fever vaccinations are required if coming from an infected area.

VISAS
Nationals of most countries do not need a visa. A 30-day stay is granted on entry and a further 30 days' extension is possible.

TOURIST BOARDS
Head Office: Colombo, tel: (01) 581 801; London, tel: (01) 321 0034; Washington, tel: (202) 483 4025; Tokyo, tel: (03) 585 7433; Frankfurt, tel: (069) 239 221.

BENTOTA

Sri Lanka's top watersports beach, Bentota is also one of the country's oldest resorts. There are three main hotels here as well as several budget guest houses but the beach is so large it never seems crowded – despite the elephants!

The enormous lagoon behind the beach is protected and calm for beginners' windsurfing; the beach itself is more suited to those who are used to open-sea techniques and, when the wind blows strongly, wave sailing. Snorkelling excursions from here go to Beruwela and diving is available at Club Nautique. There are the usual range of tourist bars and restaurants.

WATERSPORTS★★★★★
Water ski-ing (175 Rs/US$6/round), windsurfing (112 Rs/US$4/hr) and water scooters (140 Rs/US$5/15 mins) are available at the *Club Nautique* (based at the *Bentota Beach Hotel* and the *Lihiniya Surf Hotel*), the *Rainbow Boat House* (on the lagoon) and the *Hotel Serendib*. Windsurfing courses are available at all three locations (750-2,000 Rs/US$27-70).

ACCOMMODATION
• *Bentota Beach Hotel:* Deluxe **R**. Tennis, health club, sauna, pool. Family-oriented. Single/double 1,260/1,400 Rs (US$46/50). **A** Bentota, tel: (034) 75176. Reservations: UK, tel: (01) 930 6922.
• *Hotel Serendib*: Expensive: Pool, squash. Single/double 750/1,000 Rs (US$27/35). **A** Bentota, tel: (034) 75248. Reservations: UK, tel: (01) 930 6922.
• *Lihiniya Surf Hotel*: Moderate. Pool, tennis. Single/double 700/800 Rs (US$25/30). **A** Bentota, tel: (034) 75126.
• For budget-priced rooms (200-250 Rs/US$7-9) at the Aluthgama end of the beach try *Susantha Guest House* (near the railway station) and *Nihal's Inn* (on the other side of the main road). By the 63-km marker are several more guest houses: *Sooriya Tourist Inn* and *Club Villa* are the most comfortable and charge around 600 Rs (US$20). *Golden Rock Villa, The Villa, Palm Shade Cabanas, Madame Rosa, Palm Beach* and *Seashells Cabanas* all charge from

single/double 200/300 Rs (US$7/10) including breakfast.

ACCESS
Thirty eight miles/61 km from Colombo.

Trains take around two hours, buses or mini-buses around one-and-a-half hours.

AHUNGALLA

A wild, natural beach – the sort you imagine when dreaming about Sri Lanka, but rarely find. Well, this is it: three miles/five km of sand with nothing in sight except palm trees and surf along its entire length.

Even the biggest hotel here, the two-storey Triton, is low-key. Apart from two small fishing communities and a Buddhist *stupa* (temple) there is nothing else on the beach. Terrific beach for jogging, exploring, or just lazing around in the waves. 'Body-surfing – free of charge' says the hotel brochure – so kind!

The main feature of the Triton is a fabulous 350,000-gallon swimming pool which starts in the lobby and goes right through the hotel all the way out to the beach. This more than makes up for the fact that there are no watersports on this beach. As an alternative to the Triton there is the Lotus Villa, a charming, family-run guest house further down the beach.

Just a few minutes drive north of Ahungalla, at the 73-km mark, a small sign by the side of the road announces the Kosgoda Turtle Farm. For a small fee, visitors to the turtle farm can grab a handful of baby turtles from one of the concrete tanks and take them down to the sea to watch them struggle out of your grip and head off into the surf. Millions of leatherback, hawksbill and green turtles have been released by this small, locally-run operation since it began over eight years ago.

BARS AND RESTAURANTS
The *Triton* has two bars, coffee shop, restaurant and supper club. The *Lotus Villa* has an outside bar/restaurant area.

ACCOMMODATION
• *Triton Hotel*: Deluxe **R** 125 a/c rooms and 6 suites, all with ocean views. Tennis, health club, gym, sauna, massage. Single/double from 1,611/2,013 Rs (US$57/72). **A** Ahungalla, tel: (09)

27228, 27218. Reservations: UK, tel: (01) 930 6922.
• *Lotus Villa*: Deluxe/expensive **R**. Small swimming pool. Half-board single/double 1,000/1,500 Rs (US$35/55). **A** Waturegama, Ahungalla.

ACCESS
Forty-seven miles/75 km from Colombo (around two hours by taxi). Hikkaduwa is 15 miles/23 km away.

HIKKADUWA

Sri Lanka's most famous beach resort, now a huge conglomeration of hundreds of shops, restaurants, hotels and bars strung out along two miles/three km of the main Colombo-Galle road.

There are several different sections to this beach: in the north you'll find dive shops and a whole fleet of glass-bottom boats and outriggers waiting to take you out to the marine sanctuary and reef area. This is the worst part of the beach to stay on, so if you arrive at the railway station keep heading south. Past the Coral Gardens Hotel the beach proper starts, a narrow strip as far as Ranjith's Café (the current 'in' beach bar, popular with surfies). Further south the beach starts to widen out – this is the most scenic part of Hikkaduwa and a good section for body-surfing. This is the village of Narigama and the best part of the beach for meeting people.

Being Sri Lanka's biggest resort, Hikkaduwa attracts a large number of beach vendors and hassles on the beach include the python-round-the-neck wallah, *ganja*-wallahs, boat-wallahs and fruit-wallahs. Needless to say, from a supine position on the sand, mangoes, papayas, coconuts, bananas, pineapples and delicacies such as cooked crab are all instantly available.

Hikkaduwa is no longer as attractive as it used to be but the southern half (Narigama) will fulfil most of your tropical fantasies and the whole area has such a huge selection of hotels and guest houses that it isn't hard to find somewhere suitable to stay. The surf here can be ferocious and there have been several drownings, so take care. Bikes, motorbikes and jeeps can all be rented if you want to explore the rest of the coast.

Hikkaduwa

SNORKELLING★★★

An ancient guidebook to Sri Lanka says of Hikkaduwa: 'Of all the places for skin-diving, and there are many of them around Ceylon's coast, Hikkaduwa is perhaps the best, for this is where the sea sanctuary and coral gardens form the hiding place, the battle ground and the playground for some of the most colourful fish in the world. Here moorish idols and scorpion fish chase blue angels and lion fish, each in their turn a possible meal for the moray eel and the octopus. Go beyond the sanctuary and you can chase the horse mackerel, the marlin yellow fin, barracuda and giant grouper with your spear gun. Or perhaps if you are adventurous enough you may try for the shark. However, they are more easily photographed than speared'(!).

The author's engaging account of the marine hierarchy doesn't obscure the fact that if this is the best that Sri Lanka has to offer I wouldn't suggest coming here on holiday specifically for the snorkelling. Although the area is a well-publicized marine reserve, locals and foreigners alike flout the regulations by spearfishing, hence there are no big fish, the corals have been considerably damaged, and there is a noticeable absence of the small, colourful reef fish of the type caught for

the aquarium trade. However, you should be able to see Sri Lanka's famous blue tangs.

The shallower sections of the reef start right off the beach at the *Coral Gardens Hotel*, and you can easily swim out from here to the deeper sections (or catch a boat), which are on the inside of a large group of off-shore rocks. Due to the number of glass-bottom boats trolling around the area, it's not the most peaceful of reefs to snorkel on either. **MSF:** around 15 Rs/hr.

WATERSPORTS★★
Surf boards (30 Rs/US$1/hr) and windsurfers (100-200 Rs/US$4-7/hr) can be rented on the beach, and windsurfing instruction is available from *Aqua Tours* (in front of the *Coral Reef Hotel)* and *Watersport Diving Paradise* (at the *Coral Sands*). The surfing here isn't as good as at Arugam Bay on the east coast, but this is off-limits during the civil war. Para-sailing (650 Rs/US$23).

DIVING★
There are several wrecks to dive near Hikkaduwa, such as the *Conche*, a 3,000 ton oil tanker which is broken into three sections and lies on the seabed at depths of 40-70 ft/12- 21 m. Partially overgrown with corals, sea rods and feather stars, the wreck is home to morays, grouper and a school of large red snapper. There are at least four other wrecks within easy distance of the beach. The diving season here is from November to April, although sometimes it starts late because of the monsoons or lack of divers.
• *Scuba Safari*: Full PADI courses with theory and training in Colombo and qualifying dives at Hikkaduwa. **A** 25 Barnes Place, Colombo, tel: 94012.
• *Poseidon Divers* (at the north end of

the beach), *Aqua Tours* (in front of the Coral Reef Hotel) or *Watersports Diving Paradise* (at the Coral Sands Hotel) all charge around US$8-15 for one-tank dives including equipment.

Unawatuna

BARS AND RESTAURANTS
There are well over 30 bars and restaurants directly on the beach, with countless others spread out behind it. A great beach for seafood: crab, lobster, barracuda, prawns, calamari, seer fish and tuna all appear on restaurant menus prepared in a dozen different ways and all at bargain prices. At the northern end, *Mama's* is recommended for their fabulous three-course seafood meals. Down in Narigama food is lower priced and mostly basic (grilled fish, chips and salad for around £1/US$2).

ACCOMMODATION
The following is just a small selection of the enormous range of hotels and guest houses available on this beach.
• *The Coral Gardens Hotel*: Deluxe **R**. Hikkaduwa's top hotel. Pool, squash, health club. Single/double 1,300/1,400 Rs (US$46/50). **A** Hikkaduwa, tel: (09)

73

23023.
- *Hotel Lanka Supercorals*: Moderate. On a good part of the beach, pool. **A** Hikkaduwa, tel: (09) 22897.
- *Hotel Reefcomber*: Expensive **R**. Next to the Supercorals, pool. **A** Hikkaduwa, tel: (09) 23374. Reservations: UK, tel: (01) 930 6922.
- *Sunil's Beach Hotel*: Expensive **R**. Good location, pool. **A** Narigama, Hikkaduwa, tel: (09) 22016.
- In the moderate price bracket, rooms get cheaper as you go further south. Down in Narigama there are numerous identical seafront guest houses which consist of two rows of rooms facing each other at right angles to the beach, most with a seafront restaurant. Expect

to pay around 150-250 Rs (US$5-9).
- Rock-bottom budget accommodation can be found on the other side of the road from the beach for around US$2.

ACCESS

Hikkaduwa is just under 60 miles/100 km south of Colombo, 11 miles/17 km north of Galle. Trains from Colombo take around three hours, buses are quicker but more crowded. Although there are frequent mini-buses direct to the airport from the beach (100 Rs/US$4 per person, minimum six) unfortunately no such service is available in reverse, so you have to go via Colombo. A taxi direct from the airport will cost around 1,000 Rs (US$35).

UNAWATUNA

A favourite with many Sri Lanka regulars. Unawatuna isn't as big as Koggalla or Ahungalla but it never seems crowded. The west end of the beach is popular with locals and full at the weekends but during the week the whole beach is more or less yours. If you want a convivial, sociable beach and don't like Hikkaduwa, this is the place to come.

The beach curves round for three-quarters-of-a-mile/one km with just one medium-size hotel, the Unawatuna Beach Resort (the 'UBR'), roughly in the middle and a wide selection of budget guest houses scattered around elsewhere.

Fresh drinking coconuts, pineapples and papayas are all for sale on the beach, so you don't have to move too far for refreshment. Windsurfers can be hired at the Unawatuna Beach Resort.

Unawatuna's name means 'fallen down from the sky' and legend has it that the Hindu monkey god Hanuman carelessly dropped a chunk of the Himalayas here whilst hurrying to treat the wounded Laxman, Prince Rama's brother. The rocks he dropped are at the west end of the beach, a popular sunset-watching spot.

SNORKELLING★★
The best snorkelling is on the shore side of the rocks in the middle of the bay; fishermen will take you over by catamaran for a few rupees. There's also an area of shallow reef opposite the mouth of the creek at the west end of the beach, which is more accessible

but not so extensive as the off-shore reef: apart from a handful of shy fish you might also come across one or more resident turtles. **MSF:** for hire from boys on the beach.

DIVING★
There is a dive operation at the UBR

but it (or rather, 'he') is notoriously in-efficient and equipment is ramshackle. There's no compressor and tanks have to be sent down from Hikkaduwa; this not only means that you have to request one the day before but you're also likely to spend all morning hanging around for the tanks to arrive, and by the time they do the sea is up and the visibility has gone.

The most frequently-used dive area (a few minutes' boat ride outside the bay) is worth a look if you're in the area but don't come here specially. The diving season is November/December to April. One-tank dive US$16, five dives US$70.

BARS AND RESTAURANTS

The beach front at Unawatuna was rad-ically altered by a heavy storm in 1987 which destroyed several popular beachfront restaurants. The only one to be rebuilt right over the beach is the *Sunny Beach Chinese*, which has good food and slow but charming service. The UBR has opened a new *Sun-downer Chinese Restaurant* at the west end of the beach. Depending on the day's catch, devilled fish, sweet and sour fish, and prawn and crab dishes all appear on the menu at prices below US$2, but the service is as appalling as it was in their old restaurant.

At Mensa, over the river at the west end of the beach, a huge rice and curry costs less than US$1 and you can also organise a barbecue here (delicious fish, curry, rice and arrack for US$3 per head). On the road through the village the *South Ceylon (Noble Livelihood) Restaurant* serves healthy meals for under US$2 and cheap wholesome breakfasts.

ACCOMMODATION

● *Unawatuna Beach Resort*: Moderate **R**. Adequate but nothing special. Sin-gle/double from 225/250 Rs (US$8/9), seaview from 300/350 Rs (US$10/12). **A** Unawatuna, Galle, tel: (09) 22147.

● *Sun 'n' Sea*: Moderate **R**. At the east end of beach, on the edge of the sea. Rooms from 200 to 300 Rs (US$7-10). **A** Unawatuna, Galle, tel: (09) 53200.

● Just west of the UBR there is a cluster of standard guest houses: *Rumassala, Sandy Lane, Sunny Beach,* and *Full Moon* all have moderately priced rooms for 150-300 Rs (US$5-10).

● *The Sea View* **R** at the west end of the beach is well maintained and set in a beautiful garden; rooms with attached bath from 250 Rs. Past here *the Strand* has lovely grounds and old colonial fur-niture in the rooms, which cost from 100 to 250 Rs (US$3.50-9), and the owner also runs a small turtle hatchery.

● Budget rooms at the *South Ceylon*, where an English monk holds medi-tation workshops, cost around 50 Rs (US$2).

ACCESS

Unawatuna is two-and-a-half miles/four km south of Galle, a short bus or taxi ride. Trains run to Galle from Col-ombo Fort, journey time around four hours. Buses are quicker (three hours) but more crowded. Unawatuna is just under 25 miles/40 km west of Matara, one hour by bus.

75

KOGGALA

The widest, sandiest, cleanest, longest, most deserted beach in Sri Lanka. There are no watersports or beach bars but the lack of activity is compensated for by acres and acres of uncrowded sand and the unpolluted sea: beautiful clear green rollers tempt you into the water to body-surf.

On Koggala there's just one small fishing village and a tourist complex consisting of the Tisara Beach Hotel, the Koggala Beach Hotel and the Hotel Horizon. The first two hotels have suffered badly from the drop-off in the tourist trade and are almost derelict but if you like the idea of having the hotel almost to yourself you can snap up a room for £5 per night. The Hotel Horizon hasn't suffered so much and is better maintained. Koggala is a terrific beach to visit for the day (from Galle, for instance), but you'd need to rely on your own resources for entertainment if staying here.

Dikwella

ACCOMMODATION
- *Tisara Beach Hotel*: Moderate. 180 rooms (only 30 in use at the time of writing), all sea-facing, from single/double 250 Rs (US$9). **A** Koggala, tel: (09) 2017, 2023.
- *Koggala Beach Hotel*: Moderate. Pool, tennis, 206 rooms (only 130 in use) from single/double 250 Rs (US$9). **A** Koggala, tel: (09) 53260, 53243.
- *Hotel Horizon*: Expensive. Pool. Single/double from 500/600 Rs (US$18/21). **A** Koggala, tel: (09) 53297, 53229.

ACCESS
Eight miles/12 km east of Galle, half an hour by bus or taxi.

DIKWELLA

Stylish Italian resort on a rocky headland between Matara and Tangalle. The beach on the north of the headland isn't that good but the beach to the south, just to one side of the resort, is okay. The resort also has a large salt-water swimming pool. Windsurfers can be hired but conditions are difficult for most of the year because of direct on-shore winds.

DIVING
The diving around here isn't that good but standards of instruction and equipment in the resort are first-rate, so if

you wanted to learn to dive it would be a good place to stay (a PADI open-water course will cost around US$170).

BARS AND RESTAURANTS
The resort has a first-class restaurant (serving mostly Italian food), with views overlooking the sea. An excellent place to stop for lunch if touring the coast. Disco.

ACCOMMODATION
• *Dikwella Village Resort*: Expensive R. Unusual, large bungalows from single/double 700/1,000 Rs (US$28/35). A Dikwella, tel: (041) 2961.

ACCESS
Thirteen miles/20 km east of Matara.

TANGALLE

There are two main beaches areas near Tangalle: to the west of town, a series of small secluded coves are tucked away amongst the palm trees, with several quiet guest houses near the sea. The undertow can be dangerous here, but a couple of these bays are sufficiently hidden away so that you can strip off without attracting attention. To the east of town the main beach goes on for miles, with palm trees receding into the distant horizon. There is heavy surf here, too.

BARS AND RESTAURANTS
All the guest houses have restaurants serving the usual cheap traveller's staples: *Saman's,* on the main beach, is particularly recommended.

ACCOMMODATION
• The only hotel here is the dreadful *Tangalla Bay Hotel*, not recommended. To the west of town on the next headland the *Peacehaven Beach Hotel*, with rooms from 150 Rs (US$5), is a better proposition. Sharing the same two small beaches and hidden away among the coconut-groves are the *Bikini Beach Hotel* and *Palm Beach Cabanas*, with rooms from 250 Rs (US$9). These are amongst the most appealing beach bungalows you'll find in Sri Lanka, with plenty of privacy.
• At the main beach there are a string of cheap guest houses with rooms from 25 Rs (US$1 up). *Saman's* and *Gayana* (the latter is the only one actually on the beach) are recommended.

ACCESS
Tangalle is 120 miles/195 km from Colombo. The coastal railway ends at Matara, from where it's a further 22 miles/35 km by bus or mini-bus.

Triton pool, Ahungalla

India

T ravelling in India is a stimulating, eye-opening experience but canny travellers know that you should always allow yourself time to relax on the beaches of Goa, one of Asia's most famous beach destinations, before going home.

However, a new phenomenon in Goa is the arrival of direct charters from Gatwick and Frankfurt. Numerous beach hotels – including a new Ramada resort – are springing up to meet demand and the number of tourists arriving in Goa is expected to exceed 100,000 during 1989. Ironically, the volume of foreigners now descending on this ex-Portuguese colony (which is culturally and ethnically distinct from the rest of India) is causing more friction and opposition to development than three decades of hippies ever did.

For the moment there are plenty of empty beaches to go round and most, with their picture-postcard swaying palms and golden sands, will fulfil your tropical fantasies. All of the beaches are relatively close together (it takes under two hours by motorbike from the northernmost to the southernmost Goan beach) and bike hire is cheap, so beach-hopping is easy. Watersports facilities are as yet few and far between.

One of the fastest-growing resort areas is around **Aguada, Calangute**, and **Baga★★★★**. Here you'll find a wide range of guest houses and hotels, including the long-established Taj Fort Aguada, Goa's top resort. **Colva★★★** is the biggest of the Goan resorts after Calangute, also currently undergoing a tourist boom. **Anjuna★★★** is one of Goa's more popular travellers' beaches and accommodation is extremely basic (there are no hotels and only a few guest houses).

Just north of Anjuna is the village of Chapora and the neighbouring beaches of **Vagator** and **Small Vagator★★★★**. Like Anjuna, these beaches

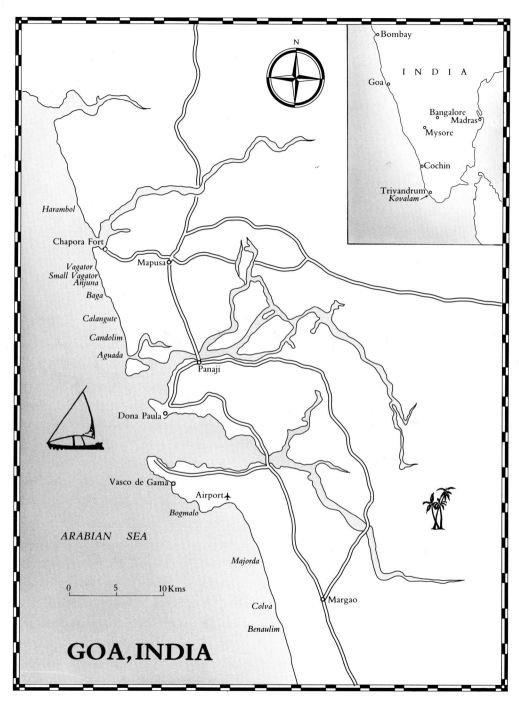

N

Bombay

I N D I A

Goa

Bangalore
Madras
Mysore

Cochin

Trivandrum
Kovalam

Harambol

Chapora Fort
Mapusa

Vagator
Small Vagator
Anjuna

Baga

Calangute

Candolim

Aguada

Panaji

Dona Paula

Vasco de Gama
Airport

Bogmalo

ARABIAN   SEA

0   5   10 Kms

Majorda

Colva

Benaulim

Margao

GOA, INDIA

will appeal to anyone who wants to stay for a long time. **Harambol✱✱✱✱✱**, the northernmost beach, is for people who really want to go for the back-to-nature number.

The only beach in Goa which I don't recommend is Bogmalo beach, near the airport. The Oberoi here is as good as Oberoi hotels always are, but the beach is scrappy.

Kovalam

The capital of Goa state is Panaji, roughly in the middle. For the northern beaches, the nearest town is Mapusa (pronounced 'mapsa') and, for the southern beaches, the jumping-off point is Margao. The railway terminal for trains from Bombay is at Vasco da Gama, which is just south of Panaji, and the airport is nearby at Diabolim.

You can get anything you desire on Goa's beaches, from massages to tropical fruits, without having to lift a finger. The hippy legacy is still much in evidence (despite visa crackdowns which have driven many long-term residents away) and recreational drugs are widely available, although police raids are common. The police are hot on motorbike offences and the normal *baksheesh* for no licence or no helmet or something wrong with the bike (which there will be – this is India!) is around the equivalent of US$4. Toplessness offends local sensibilities and if you insist on stripping off on the more popular beaches, expect to be gawped at by day-trippers who have come here exactly for that purpose. Living costs in Goa are incredibly low (US$10-15 per day is a comfortable budget), and seafood is cheap and plentiful. Except in the tourist hotels a torch is almost essential to find your way around at night, due to frequent power failures or, indeed, lack of electricity altogether.

The monsoon usually lasts from June to September but sometimes it rains well into October. Ferry services from Bombay to Goa normally start up at the beginning of October. High season is November to January, and guest-house rooms can be hard to find at this time. Swimming can be extremely dangerous during the monsoon, with several drownings occurring each year.

Beach massage, Kovalam

The only other notable beach resort on the west coast of India is **Kovalam★★★★**, to the south of Trivandrum in Kerala. Like Goa, Kovalam is rapidly being transformed into a middle-market tourist beach but, unlike Goa, I don't think you would want to travel from overseas just for the beach. However, although Kovalam has none of the natural appeal of some of Goa's more deserted beaches it's a useful stopping point if you're touring south India.

GENERAL INFORMATION

Time
GMT + 5.5 hrs

IDD code
91 + area code + number

Currency
Indian rupees (Rs)
UK£1 = 24 Rs
US$1 = 13 Rs

Hotels
Single/double
Deluxe: US$73/77
Expensive: US$45/60
Moderate: US$8/16
Budget: Under US$8

WEATHER
The south-west monsoon affects both Goa and Kovalam from June through until the

Fort Aguada beach

end of September. October/November to March/April is the best time to visit. Year-round temperatures average 86°F/ 30°C.

HEALTH
Yellow fever inoculation if coming from

an infected area. Cholera, typhoid, gamma globulin and tetanus recommended. Coastal regions are not malarial.

VISAS

All visitors to India now require visas, including Commonwealth subjects. Three-month visas are issued at consulates abroad, and these can be extended for a further three months once in the country.

TOURIST BOARDS

Head Office: Delhi, tel: (011) 332005; Bombay, tel: (022) 291585; London, tel: (01) 437 3677; New York, tel: (212) 586 4901; Los Angeles, tel: (213) 380 8855; Sydney, tel: (02) 232 1600; Tokyo, tel: (03) 571 5062; Frankfurt, tel: (069) 235 423; Paris, tel: (01) 42 65 83 86.

AGUADA, CALANGUTE, BAGA

Although this beach is over 6 miles/10 km long, there are four distinct resort areas. Aguada is the further south and home to Goa's only first class hotel, the Taj Fort Aguada. From its vantage point on the headland the Taj commands magnificent views of the ocean and the whole beach all the way down to Baga. The Taj Holiday Village is a huge complex of villas just below the main hotel and, although it lacks style by comparison, it's a suitable alternative should the main Taj be fully booked.

Nearby Calangute is one of the original Goan hippy beaches, previously the source of many lurid 'sex-drugs-orgy' stories for the Indian press. However, it's now a respectable resort and standards of accommodation are higher than on most Goan beaches (except Aguada) and it's one of the few beaches with a good selection of guest houses. Calangute is convenient for short stays and is also a handy base from which to explore the northern beaches by motorbike, but in terms of beach hassle it's the worst Goan beach.

Baga beach is two miles/three km further north. This ex-fishing village has a distinctive character and is popular with yuppie travellers. You can walk from here to Anjuna in about half an hour. At present Baga is quieter than Calangute but new hotels are springing up all the time between the two beaches and it looks like they will soon merge into one huge resort.

Candolim beach is half-way between the Fort Aguada and Calangute but the beach is awful. There's no point in stopping here unless everywhere else is full and you're desperate for a room.

Sailboards rentals on Calangute and at the Taj complex.

BARS AND RESTAURANTS

Both Taj-run hotels have the standard resort facilities including open-air restaurants, beach bar and so on. In Calangute the range of restaurants matches the number of guest houses, most of them with similar menus typical of Goa (fish, chips and salad, some-times lobster). Elsewhere there are the usual assortment of beach restaurants but worth mentioning are: the *Casa Portuguese* (near Baga, grand colonial-style dining room with food to match); the *Tropicana Bar & Snacks* (in Baga, a cut above the rest in terms of comfort); *Tito's* (between Baga and

Calangute, good food and music, veranda overlooking the sea); and *St Anthony's Bar* (on the seafront in Baga, above-average menu with Goan specialities). Saturday night disco at the *Coco Banana* in Calangute.

ACCOMMODATION

Aguada

● *Fort Aguada Beach Resort*: Deluxe/expensive **R.** Well-appointed rooms, all with sea views, doubles from 650 Rs (US$50) (LS) to 1,400 Rs (US$105) (HS). The sports complex (tennis, squash and badminton) and health club (gym, jacuzzi, sauna, massage) are shared with the next door *Holiday Village*. Non-guests can use these facilities for a small charge. Swimming pool. **A** Sinquerim, Bardez, Goa, tel: (832) 4401. Reservations: Bombay, tel: (022) 2023366; UK, (01) 242 9964; Worldwide: Utell International.

● *Taj Holiday Village*: Doubles from 350 Rs (US$27) (LS) to 1,250 Rs (US$96) (HS). **A** Sinquerim, Bardez, Goa, tel: (832) 4401. Reservations: As above.

Calangute

● There is plenty of choice here but south of the main square there are several guest houses worth mentioning, including the *Concha Beach Resort* **R,** which has a garden and a plant-filled courtyard. Rooms all have mosquito nets, fans and their own bathrooms and cost for 150-350 Rs (US$11-27). The secluded *Calangute Beach Resort* **R** is good value but some way back from the beach. At the *Coco Banana* **R** cottages with bathrooms cost from 150 Rs (US$11).

● Towards town *Varma's Beach Resort* **R** has smart rooms for 150-250 Rs (US$11-20) and has a friendly atmosphere. On the road to Baga (not on the beach) is the *Villa Bonfim* **R,** a large colonial family home with rooms from 150 Rs (US$11). Next door is *Miranda's Beach Resort*, clean and friendly with rooms from 125 Rs (US$10).

Baga

● Rooms are of a similar standard to Calangute, but there is less choice. *The Hotel Riverside* **R** is by the bridge and has large rooms with attached bathrooms from 150 Rs (US$11) or you could try the *Baia de Sol*, also in a good location and with comfortable rooms. There are plenty of small guest houses with rooms costing 40-50 Rs (US$3-4) just back from the seafront in Baga.

ACCESS

Calangute is reached by direct buses from Panaji via Candolim (30-60 minutes) or Mapusa (20-30 minutes). Change at Calangute for Baga.

COLVA

This beach goes on for miles and at present there are three main centres for accommodation, Colva, Benaulim and Majorda. After Calangute this is the biggest of the Goan beach resorts. Colva is at the centre of the beach, popular with Indian holidaymakers. Majorda (to the north) and Benaulim (to the south) are on much quieter sections of the beach.

Beach salesmen wander around offering *lungis* (sarongs) and cheap jewellery, but there aren't many of them and they're not persistent. Beach massages cost 50 Rs (US$4) an hour, and pineapples and other tropical fruit are sold on the beach.

The beach is big enough for it to have isolated sections where you can strip off without offending anyone (go at least a mile north or south of Colva).

BARS AND RESTAURANTS

All the restaurants along here have seafood menus catering to Western tastes. The *Lucky Star* is particularly recommended and the nearby *Sunset Restaurant* is also worth checking out.

ACCOMMODATION

• *Majorda Beach Resort*: Expensive **R**. Set in 20 acres of tropical gardens, two swimming pools, health club, windsurfing. Rooms from 1,000 Rs (US$77). **A** Majorda, Salcete, tel: (832) 20751. Reservations: Bombay, tel: (022) 626269; Delhi, tel: (011) 3010211.

• On the north part of the beach the *Sunset* **R** has clean, basic rooms for 20 Rs (US$1.50). Next door, *Longuinhos Beach Resort* is a Portuguese-style hotel with double rooms from 150 Rs (US$12).

• Most of the up-market hotels in Colva are near the main square (not the most desirable area), amongst them the *Hotel Silver Sanfor*, the *Sukhsagar Beach Resort* and *Williams Resort*, with rooms for 130-260 Rs (US$10-20). Behind the Silver Sands, *Jymis Cottages* and the *Sea View* are less expensive, with rooms for 60-70 Rs (US$5-6).

• To the south you'll find *Camilson's Beach Nests* **R**, where quiet and secluded rooms cost from 45 Rs (US$3.50).

• In Colva village (a fair walk from the beach itself), the *Hotel Tourist Nest* **R** is a large, pleasant Portuguese colonial building with rooms and cottages from

Majorda

40 to 75 Rs (US$3-6).

• Village rooms with families in either Colva or Benaulim are as cheap as you'll find anywhere (from 15 to 25 Rs (US$1-2).

ACCESS

Colva is 4 miles/6 kms from Margao and there are frequent buses via Benaulim. Panaji or Vasco to Margao is about one hour by bus.

ANJUNA

People coming here normally rent rooms in the village or rent whole houses for the winter. Full of weirdos and eccentrics, it's a great beach for people-watching. Unfortunately this is also the attitude taken by the coachloads of Indian tourists who descend on the beach every day, so unless you want to be the subject of someone else's holiday snaps you'll need to go further afield to relax.

During the day you can escape to nearby beaches such as Small Vagator and you can also avoid the day-trippers by going to the south end of Anjuna, which is just a 20-minute walk away.

Most people only come back to Anjuna in the evenings to party, and at night this beach really wakes up. The party season is from mid-November onwards (in December there's one a night) and although venues change all the time they aren't hard to find.

The stylishness of party-goers in Anjuna sometimes makes you wonder if you haven't wandered into a New York disco by mistake – only the ready availability of hallucinogenics gives the game away and reminds you that this is indeed India.

The beach market which takes place at the south end of Anjuna every Wednesday is a typical Goa 'happening'. This is a good place to pick up Rajasthani or Tibetan clothes and jewellery but if you're planning to sell your personal stereo here forget it – supply now exceeds demand and you won't get a good price.

Theft (either from your room or on the beach) is more of a problem on Anjuna than other Goan beaches. This is a good place for motorbike rentals (there are lots to choose from and you're more likely to find one that isn't falling to pieces). Most people stay here for a long time and if you turn up in season you might not be able to get a room for several days.

Anjuna is half an hour from the northern Goan town of Mapusa.

Majorda

BARS AND RESTAURANTS

There isn't much difference between most beach restaurants here except for the *Motel Rose Garden* (above average menu including barbecues, seafood and Chinese food) and the *Sea Rock* (the only place which regularly has lobster). One of the friendliest beach-front restaurants is the family-run *Guru Restaurant*.

ACCOMMODATION

• The three guest houses are the *Poonam Guest House*, the *Palma Sol*, and the *Motel Rose Garden*, where double rooms with showers average 70-100 Rs (US$5-8).

• Rooms in the village cost from 300-500 Rs (US$23-40) per month and are really basic. They don't have bathrooms and you have to wash from the well. Houses near the beach cost from

85

700 Rs (US$54) per month but there aren't many available. If you can't get one on the beach there are others in the village and some people prefer this because it's quieter.

ACCESS
Local buses go from Chapora to Anjuna and then on to Mapusa. From Calangute you can get a motorbike or a motor-rickshaw.

VAGATOR and SMALL VAGATOR

These beaches are within walking distance of Anjuna to the south. Small Vagator is well known amongst Goa regulars, many of whom come here for the day from other beaches. This small, secluded beach has a freshwater creek behind it and a small waterfall at one end. Toplessness is not the problem it is elsewhere and the beach is more sheltered and calmer for swimming than the big Goan beaches. Rumour has it that the best parties happen here too.

On the main beach there's a hotel, the Vagator Beach Resort, but it's a bit of a dump. There is one guest house in Chapora village, next to the beach, but they say that 'every house here is a hotel'. During the day it's a sleepy Indian village but at night the cafés are full of designer hippies.

BARS AND RESTAURANTS
On Small Vagator there are several bamboo-leaf seafront restaurants, all cheap and virtually indistinguishable. In the village the *Noble Nest* restaurant has videos every night.

ACCOMMODATION
• Similar to Anjuna, with rooms in houses or whole houses for 200-400

Rs (US$15-30) per month. *The Noble Nest* is the only guest house and has rooms for 25-60 Rs (US$2-5).

ACCESS
There are regular buses or taxis or motorbike-taxis from Mapusa via Anjuna. Anjuna to Small Vagator is a half-hour walk, Anjuna to Chapora 45-60 minutes.

HARAMBOL

In the far north of Goa, Harambol is a small fishing community on an enormous, empty palm-fringed beach. Apart from herds of cows, this beach is wonderfully deserted but Harambol's secret is hidden away around the corner to the north where, after ten minutes' walk, you'll come across a delightful secluded beach. Behind the beach there's a shallow fresh water lake to swim in and, behind this, paths lead off into a jungle where you can build your own bamboo hut. Harambol is still a great beach to visit for the day even if you're not into the back-to-nature number and indeed guesthouses are now starting to appear here. In the fishing village and along the road up to the main village there are several places to eat.

ACCOMMODATION
• In the jungle behind the lake people

build their own bamboo huts but you can also rent rooms in the village or at the *Ganesh* restaurant or the *Sea Horse*.

ACCESS

Direct (but infrequent) buses from Mapusa take about two hours but its quicker to take a bus from Mapusa to Siolim, catch the ferry across the river, and then get another bus. The same route can be done by motorbike taxi and auto-rickshaw.

KOVALAM

This is the beach to head for if you're travelling around southern India. Kovalam actually consists of several different beaches but they're all close together.

Lighthouse Beach is the busiest and most sociable, with numerous beach cafés and guest houses on it. Just the other side of the promontory to the south there's a small beach which is popular for body-surfing. To the north of Lighthouse are two more beaches, with the government-run Kovalam Ashok Beach Resort on the headland between them.

The ocean swell and undertow at Kovalam is notoriously dangerous and prior to the introduction of lifeguards in 1987 there were frequent drownings here (as many as six to twelve fatalities per year). To onlookers in the beach cafés the Indian lifeguards are the butt of many jokes as they run energetically up and down the beach in their identical yellow shirts blowing whistles at swimmers, but they have been remarkably effective at reducing the annual casualty rate to zero. Needless to say, Kovalam is an excellent beach for body-surfing at the right time of year (December and January are good months).

Tropical fruits (mangoes, coconuts, papayas, pineapples and whatever else is in season) are all instantly to hand and the fruit ladies will bring them to you on the beach. As with many other Asian beaches (like Kuta) where competition for trade is fierce, the way to achieve a peaceful life is to establish early on who you're going to do business with and stick with her.

Beach massages at Kovalam are wonderful and cheap but for women these can prove something of an embarrassment since a woman being massaged is likely to draw large – and I mean large – crowds of Indian day-trippers. As an alternative, ayurvedic massages are available at the Kovalam Beach Resort and the Neelakanta Hotel on Lighthouse Beach.

Finally, watch out for guides who meet the buses and taxis and offer to help carry your bags, since they often steal from them. Thefts from rooms at night (using long, hooked sticks through the windows) is also something to watch out for here.

Kovalam is changing rapidly (new hotels are going up all the time, I haven't listed them all) and it will probably no longer appeal to people looking for beaches off the beaten track.

WATERSPORTS★★

Windsurfer and boogie board rentals from *Casa Nova* on Lighthouse Beach. Sailing, windsurfing and water ski-ing at the *Kovalam Beach Resort*.

BARS AND RESTAURANTS

Most of the local restaurants here are

fairly similar; menus usually include western breakfasts, grilled fish, fish masala, coconut curry (*some do moli*), prawns and spring rolls. Prices are very reasonable. Just back from the beach the charming *Silent Valley* has good food but service is excruciatingly slow. *Restaurant Achutha* on Lighthouse Beach is worth checking out and the *Sea Rock* also has quite a good restaurant. The verandah at the *Rockholm* is a great place to go for tea. At the time of writing there were very few places here with liquor licences (except the *Kovalam Resort* and the *Raja Hotel*) and you had to catch a bus into town to buy alcohol.

ACCOMMODATION
• *Kovalam Ashok Beach Resort*. Expensive. On a headland with great sea views. Swimming pool, tennis. Single/double from 700/800 Rs (US$50/ 57), suites from 1,400 Rs (US$108). **A** Trivandrum 695522, Kerala, tel: (471) 68010.
• *Kovalam Grove and Resort Cottages*. Expensive. Shared facilities with the above. Cottages on the beach cost 650-750 Rs (US$50-58). **A** as above.
• *Rockholm*. Moderate **R**. Hard to get

into in peak season, but worth it if you can. The hotel is just above the small beach past the lighthouse. Rooms from 200 Rs (US$15). **A** Lighthouse Road, Kovalam, Trivandrum 695521.
• *Searock*. Moderate/budget **R**. On the middle beach, rooms cost 50-200 Rs (US$4-15).
• *Raja Hotel*. Moderate. Not on the beach, but from its vantage point up the hill, rooms have terrific sea views. Rooms cost 100-200 Rs (US$8-16).
• Nearly all the budget guest houses are on Lighthouse beach and they normally cost around 100 Rs (US$8) for rooms with private bathrooms. Behind the beach they cost about half that but mosquitoes are a problem and the rooms don't get the sea breezes. *Green Valley Cottages* **R** are well-kept and live up to their name, *Apsara Cottages* **R** have good rooms off a quiet courtyard. It's hard to recommend others because most of them are on annual leases and they change management (and their names) every year. Avoid the *Neela Hotel* and all the small guest houses near the Samudra, since they're all knocking shops.

ACCESS
Kovalam is 8 miles/13 km from Trivandrum, 30 minutes by bus, auto-rickshaw or taxi. Indian Airlines have regular flights to Trivandrum from Bombay and Delhi, and Air India and Air Lanka have flights to Colombo. There are also direct flights to the Maldives. Trains run from Delhi (48 hours), Madras (18 hours), Bangalore (19 hours) and Mangalore (11 hours). With a bit of luck and the right connections it's possible to get from Goa in 36 hours (bus to Mangalore, then train).

South East Asia

Thailand

T hailand's popularity with overseas visitors increases year by year and it's not hard to see why. The combination of Thai culture and nightlife, the ever-hospitable Thai people, superb food and the country's sublime beaches and islands continue to pull in around three million travellers of all descriptions every year. Transport is well organized and there is a range of accommodation to suit everyone, from immaculate hotels which would please the most discerning traveller to simple beach huts for those on a shoestring.

Thailand has dozens of superb beaches but, whatever you do, avoid Pattaya – this notorious resort easily wins the title of the World's Worst Beach. The beach is narrow, dirty and crowded, the sea is polluted and the noise from jetskis, speed-boats and almost every other kind of fuel-driven machine in existence will probably drive you mad. Pattaya is the centre of the country's sex industry and around 8,000 prostitutes make their living in the bars and nightclubs behind the beach. This beach could be damaging to your health in more ways than one.

The nearest good beaches to Bangkok are on the island of **Koh Samet★★★★★**, a few hours' journey to the south-east. Proximity to Bangkok is a big plus point for this little island, making it a natural choice for a short break from the capital. It's not the sort of place you'd come to on holiday (it's too small for that) but if you had a two- or three-day stop-over in Bangkok and couldn't face a long journey to reach the southern beaches, Koh Samet would fit the bill.

Heading off from Bangkok in the opposite direction (south-west) brings you to Hua Hin, Thailand's oldest seaside resort. Both Hua Hin and Cha-am, its neighbour 15 miles/25 km to the north, are currently being promoted as beach resorts. Unfortunately, although the resort hotels here are very comfortable, these mainland beaches just don't compare with those to be found on islands further to the south.

The principal resort island in Thailand is Phuket, 560 miles/900 km south of Bangkok. Phuket has numerous superb beaches and has recently grown into a major international holiday island, drawing around half-a-million people a year. The hub of the island is Phuket town, with roads radiating outwards to all the main beaches.

On the west coast **Patong**** is the most commercial of the Phuket beaches, with a wide range of medium- to top-grade hotels. Patong has been compared to Pattaya but it's not *that* bad (nothing could be). This is a good beach for watersports and diving facilities. To the north of Patong is **Surin Beach****, more secluded than most.

Karon**** is one of the bigger beaches here, a good choice for restaurants and nightlife. New hotels are going up here at a rate of knots but it hasn't yet totally lost its appeal. Next door **Kata Beach****** is one of the most scenic on Phuket and home to Club Med. Karon and Kata are both handy for diving services. **Kata Noi****** is another great beach and, like Karon, you can still stay here on a reasonable budget.

For sheer indulgence the **Relax Bay Meridien******* is hard to beat. This is Phuket's newest and most luxurious hotel. The Phuket Yacht Club on **Nai Harn Beach****** is similarly up-market but given the choice, the Meridien has more atmosphere.

The only resort beach which should really be avoided on Phuket is Rawai, on the east side, which has been totally eroded since its protecting reef was destroyed. The Phuket Island Resort, near Rawai, has no beach left at all, and guests have to take a boat to get to a beach.

Scams to watch out for on all Phuket beaches include vendors selling the same tawdry Gucci copies and fake diamonds found in Bangkok. Those petrol-drive scourges, jetskis and para-sail boats, seem to have been kept to a minimum in Phuket and banned from at least one beach after faulty equipment led to a fatality. Jeeps and motorbikes can be hired almost everywhere, and the roads are good. However, hill roads can be dangerously steep (nearly 80 per cent of Phuket is mountainous – 'Phuket' means 'mountain' in Thai) and accidents often occur – particu-

91

larly on the road over to Patong Beach, which is hair-raising.

Diving (page 104) is flourishing in Phuket, with boats leaving regularly for many off-shore destinations including the fabulous Similan Islands, 50 miles to the north.

Escapists who find Phuket has become too developed for their tastes should head out to **Koh Phi Phi*****+**. Alternatively, back on the mainland you'll find seclusion at budget prices on the beaches near **Krabi*****. If even this is too crowded for your tastes, head off to Lanta Yai, an island 40 miles/65 km south of Krabi.

Koh Samui is a sizeable island off Thailand's east coast which attained cult status in the early 1980s amongst overland travellers. It has now been well and truly discovered by the tourist industry and proper hotels have started to appear amongst the coconut palms, although it isn't yet as smart as jet-set Phuket. However, with the arrival of swanky beach cafés like the Malibu on Chaweng and a glitzy split-level disco on Lamai (more reminiscent of Ibiza than the Orient), Koh Samui is changing fast. In the town of Na Thon European-run sidewalk cafés, complete with parasols and cocktail menus, have sprung up on the seafront. *Die Welt*, *Le Figaro* and the *Herald Tribune* are all available on the news-stands and you can even buy French wine in beach restaurants – all this would have been unthinkable just a few years ago. None the less, Samui is still a lot less 'Mediterraneanized' than Phuket.

Chaweng** and **Lamai*** are Samui's two biggest beaches, both facing east on the opposite side of the island to Na Thon. There are simple beach huts on both beaches, and several more comfortable hotels. On the **North Coast*** are three smaller beaches (Mae Nam, Bo Phut and Big Buddha) which will appeal to those with escapist tendencies, as will **Cheong Mon****. Another beach worth checking out if you're after more privacy is Laem Set, hidden away several kilometres down a track in the south of the island (just follow the signposts). The small hostelry here, the Laem Set Inn, is managed by an Englishman and his Thai wife.

The road which runs around Samui is concrete all the way, great for bike riding but a lot of accidents happen (something to do with Samui's famous herbal cookies, perhaps?). Buffalo fights (quite harmless) are unique to Koh Samui and Thai boxing fights are held regularly.

Diving is in its infancy on Koh Samui and holds the promise of unexplored areas around the adjacent islands, although the underwater visibility on this side of the coast is never as good as it is in the Andaman

Koh Phi Phi

Sea. Dive tours operate to Koh Phangan, Koh Mudsum, Koh Tao and the Ang Thong Marine Park. Koh Samui Divers have offices in Na Thon (one street back from the waterfront), at the Cococabana Club near the Ban Don ferry and at the Malibu Café on Chaweng. Coral Cove, between Lamai and Chaweng, is Samui's best snorkelling spot.

The people that originally raved about Samui have fled to Koh Phangan, the next island on, which is as yet untouched by comparison. For real Crusoe-type beach living you'd be hard pushed to beat **Mae Haat**★★★★★ on the north coast. **Haat Rin**★★★★★+ on Koh Phangan's south-east corner, is much easier to get to from Samui if you're short of time. There are also a few bungalows on the north-east corner of

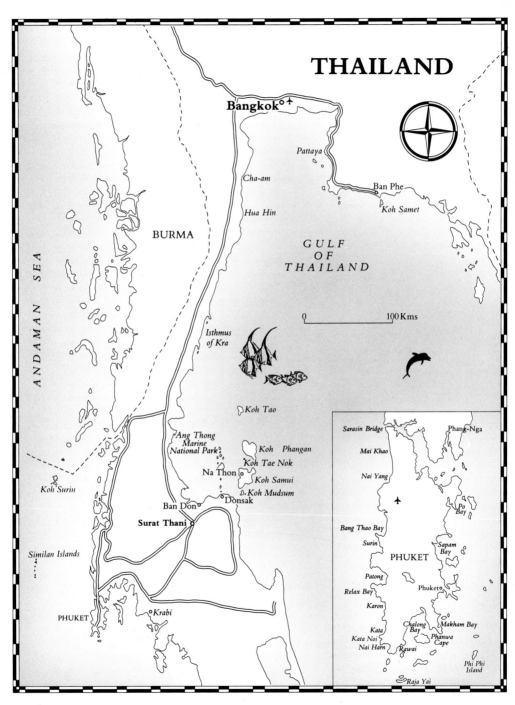

THAILAND

Bangkok

Pattaya

Cha-am

Ban Phe

Hua Hin

Koh Samet

BURMA

GULF
OF
THAILAND

ANDAMAN SEA

0   100 Kms

Isthmus
of Kra

Koh Tao

Ang Thong
Marine
National Park

Koh   Phangan

Koh Tae Nok

Na Thon

Koh Samui

Koh Mudsum

Koh Surin

Ban Don

Donsak

Surat Thani

Similan Islands

PHUKET

Krabi

Sarasin Bridge

Phang-Nga

Mai Khao

Nai Yang

Po
Bay

Bang Thao Bay

Surin

Sapam
Bay

PHUKET

Patong

Relax Bay

Phuket

Karon

Chalong
Bay

Makham Bay

Kata

Phanwa
Cape

Kata Noi

Nai Harn

Rawai

Phi Phi
Island

Raja Yai

Phangan, with the potential for virgin beaches to be discovered up here.

Other nearby islands worth exploring include Koh Tae Nok (just off-shore from Thong Sala on Koh Phangan) and Koh Tao, which is said to be the mirror image of Koh Phi Phi. Both these islands have accommodation and people are just starting to trickle over from Samui or Phangan – go now before the rest of the world does.

GENERAL INFORMATION

Time
GMT + 7 hrs

IDD code
66 + area code + number

Currency
Thai Baht (B)
US$1 = 25B
UK£1 = 40B

Hotels
Rates given do not include tax and service.
Deluxe: US$70-210
Expensive: US$40-70
Moderate: US$20-40
Budget: US$1-20

WEATHER
There are three seasons in Thailand. The hot season lasts from March to April, the rainy season from May to October and the cool season from November to February. The beaches are all in the southern tropical monsoon region with an annual average temperature of 82°F/28°C. Phuket and the west coast have the earliest rain: the monsoon starts here in early May and continues through to October. May sees the annual exodus to Koh Samui, where the rains don't start until July. Although the monsoon on Koh Samui supposedly ends in October heavy rain can sometimes continue through until January. Koh Samet is very dry and has good weather nearly all year round.

HEALTH
No vaccinations required but typhoid, tetanus and cholera are recommended. Malaria precautions necessary for Koh Samet.

VISAS
It's not advisable to arrive without a visa, since you will only be given 15 days. Most people come on a two-month tourist visa, which is extendable.

TOURIST BOARDS
Head Office: Bangkok, tel: (02) 282 1143; London, tel: (01) 499 7679; New York, tel: (212) 432 0433; Los Angeles, tel: (213) 382 2353; Sydney, tel: (02) 277 549; Tokyo, tel: (03) 580 6776; Hong Kong, tel: (05) 868 0732; Singapore, tel: 235 7694; Frankfurt, tel: (069) 295 704; Paris, tel: (01) 54 62 86 56.

Ao Tantawan, Koh Samet

KOH SAMET

Haat Sai Kaew, Ao Hin Klong, Ao Phai, Ao Thap Thim, Ao Nuan, Ao Tantawan, Ao Wong Deuan, Ao Thian, Ao Wai, Ao Kiu, Ao Phrao.

A small triangular island just over 130 miles/200 km south-east of Bangkok, Koh Samet is a perfect retreat from the steamy, humid metropolis.

Along Koh Samet's east coast are 10 wonderful beaches, all with soft white sand. Koh Samet used to be known for the sparkling clarity of its waters, but I regret to say that in 1989 there were reports in the Bangkok press of serious sewage pollution problems. All of the beaches are fairly close together and connected by paths – there are no roads on Koh Samet.

The first beach nearest the village is Haat Sai Kaew (Crystal Sand Beach) but this is the busiest beach and not the best one to stay on. From the next beach – Ao Hin Klong, also known as Mermaid Beach – onwards there is a succession of small beaches such as Ao Phai, Ao Thap Thim (also called Ao Pudsa), Ao Nuan and Ao Tantawan, all of which are popular with people looking for peace and quiet away from the bigger beaches. Ao Wong Deuan is the biggest and busiest beach after Haat Sai Kaew. Beyond here is Ao Thian (Candlelight Beach), Ao Wai, and finally Ao Kiu, which is about as isolated as you'll find on Samet.

Samet's only west-coast beach, Ao Phrao (known also as both Coconut Beach and Paradise Beach) is a half-hour walk over the island. There's no through-traffic, unlike other Samet beaches, and many people consider it the best of the lot.

Until recently there wasn't any electricity or running water on the island, and you had to wash from a bucket dipped in the well: now most bungalows have showers but accommodation here is not such good value as on Samui or Phuket. Prices are also higher at weekends, when the island tends to fill up beyond capacity. Thai students with tents, guitars and bongos descend on the island *en masse* and you might find yourself dossing on the beach due to lack of rooms.

The rains here are from mid-July to September/October and it's a malarial area so anti-malaria tablets are necessary during this period; also, sandflies and mosquitoes can be horrific in the pre-monsoon period.

Although there are patches of reef around Samet, snorkelling here is beginner's stuff; the surrounding sea is poor in corals and fish, and visibility never seems to be very good.

WATERSPORTS★★★★

Windsurfers, Hobie cats and canoes can be rented on the east coast, where conditions are suitable for beginners. Tuition is available from *Choo Kiat Suma*, a member of the Thai National Windsurfing Team (look for him on Ao Phai). Para-gliding and water ski-ing on Haat Sai Kaew at weekends.

BARS AND RESTAURANTS

Most beach restaurants serve a similar menu of seafood, Thai food, snacks, fruit shakes and so on. Restaurant standards here have improved enormously in recent years – you used not to be able to get much more than just rice and fish. Currently the island's flashiest restaurant is at *Vongdeuan Villas*, where the menu includes such mouth-watering delicacies as fresh shrimp salad with mint leaves, fried crabs with curry and baked mussels – expensive but worth it. The restaurant at *Naga Bungalows* is also recommended.

ACCOMMODATION

● Beach huts cost 50-100 B (US$2-4), more comfortable bungalows (with mosquito nets, lights and a shower room) 300-400 B (US$10-15). *Tubtim Bungalows* on Ao Thap Thim are deservedly popular. You can camp on all the beaches.

● As previously mentioned, if you arrive late at night on a weekend it's likely you won't be able to find anywhere and will have to sleep on the beach. This is quite safe. However, a few of the more up-market bungalows can now be reserved in advance from Bangkok; these include the *Vongdeuan Resort* (tel: 250 0423) and *Samet Ville* (tel: 246 3196, 247 1090).

ACCESS

Koh Samet is a 40-minute boat ride from the fishing port of Ban Phe. Buses leave from Bangkok's Ekemai (eastern) bus station all day, and boats make the crossing at irregular intervals or as soon as they are full. All boats go to the village, Na Dang, and some go on to Ao Wong Deuan. You have to walk to all the beaches past here.

Chaweng, Koh Samui

Crown of thorns starfish, Similans

97

PATONG

A huge beach, 2 miles/3 km long with plenty of choice for watersports (wind-surfers, water ski-ing, sailboats, jetskis, and hobie cats) as well as off-shore activities such as yacht charters and dive tours Patong is the most commercial of Phuket's beaches and has more than its fair share of pick-up bars. However scenic the bay itself might be, Patong is a million miles from being 'a Thai village' as several tour operators like to describe it – unless traditional Thai villages are normally lined with banks, supermarkets, nightclubs and discos.

Patong has a wide range of restaurants to suit most budgets and tastes. The most accessible snorkelling is off the pier at the Coral Beach Hotel on the south side of the bay but if you've got the chance, take a snorkel trip to the outlying islands. The hotel itself is on an awful little beach.

WATERSPORTS★★★★
Hobie 14s, 16s, 18s, Laser sailboats, windsurfers, jetskis and water ski-ing.

DIVING★★★
See page 104.

ACCOMMODATION
• *Club Andaman*: Moderate **R**. Standard rooms US$19-25. **A** Patong Beach, tel: (076) 321361. Reservations: Bangkok, tel: (02) 270 1627.
• There are about 40 small to medium-size groups of bungalows on Patong and most are behind the beach road except the following, which are directly on the beach: *Islet Mansions* (tel: (076) 321 404); *Phuket Cabana* **R** (tel: (076) 321 138); *Patong Bay Garden Resort* (tel: (076) 321297); *Patong Beach Bungalows* (tel: (076) 321117) and *Seagull Cottages* (tel: (076) 321238). Expect to pay 600-1,200 B (US$20-55) per night.
• Budget rooms 250-350 B (US$10-13) at *Jeep Bungalows, Aloha, Paradise, Thanee,* and *Coconut Bungalows.*

ACCESS
Ten miles/5 km from town, 20-30 minutes.

SURIN

Secluded Surin is a long way from the bars and social life elsewhere in Phuket – not the place to go if you want to indulge in restaurants or night life, but good for a family holiday. The main hotel here is the Pansea, although I understand there might now be a second.

The Pansea has a Chinese junk which has regular departures for two-, three- and five-day trips to surrounding islands. The wooden junk, which has five comfortable double/twin cabins, is fitted with modern navigational aids and crewed by a European skipper, and a Thai cook and sailor. From Phuket it operates to Raja Yai and Koh Phi Phi; guaranteed departures mean that no minimum of guests is required. It operates from Phuket between November and April, and in Koh Samui from May to October. When they transfer it between the two islands at the beginning and end of each season, you can join it for the nine-day cruise via Singapore (in April it goes from Phuket to Koh Samui, making the return journey in October).

WATERSPORTS★★★
Five windsurfers and one hobie 16, free to guests, free instruction. Sailing dinghies.

DIVING★★★
See page 104.

BARS AND RESTAURANTS
Open-air restaurant overlooking the sea, beach restaurant and bar. There are also several locally-run (and much cheaper) beach restaurants tucked away at the far end of the beach.

ACCOMMODATION
• *The Pansea Phuket*: Deluxe/expensive. Comfortable Thai-style bungalows. Doubles from 875 B (US$35) (LS) to 1,900 B (US$75) (HS). Reopening in November 1989 after renovations. **A** Surin Beach, Phuket, tel: (076) 216137. Reservations: Bangkok, tel: (02) 235 4100. UK, tel: (01) 408 2055.

ACCESS
Twenty minutes from Phuket airport (11 miles/17 km), 30 minutes from the town centre (36 miles/25 km).

KARON

One of Phuket's biggest beaches, most popular at the Kata end (where it tends to be wrongly called Kata beach), much quieter towards the north end.

Karon is rapidly going up-market with the traditional huts being replaced at a rate of knots by luxury bungalows and a huge new hotel (the Phuket Arcadia) has been built right in the middle of the beach, unusually out of scale and out of tune with its surroundings compared to the many low-level properties here. However, there's something to suit every budget on Karon, from cheap beach huts to luxury bungalows. There are several windsurfing rental locations on the beach.

DIVING★★★
See page 104 for full details.

BARS AND RESTAURANTS
The main concentration of bars and restaurants is at the south end of the beach and the choice is enormous. The *Ruam Thepp Inn*, which has terrific seafood at moderate prices, is recommended, as is *Marina Cottages*, which likewise has a crowded, busy restaurant. There are also several video cafés catering for shoestring travellers, amongst them the popular and friendly *Kata Tropicana*. Two bars worth checking out: *On the Rocks* (on the headland, small and sophisticated) and the *Black Rose* (good ambience and late-night music).

ACCOMMODATION
This is a very small selection of what's available.
• *Kampong Karon*: Moderate. Bungalows from 600 B (US$23). **A** PO Box

242, Phuket 83000, tel: (076) 212 901.
- *Karon Villa*: Expensive. Comfortable bungalows from 1,800 B (US$75). Rooms in the new Royal Wing cost from 2,100 B (US$52). Pool, tennis, squash, windsurfing. **A** 36/4 Karon Beach, Phuket 83130, tel: (076) 214 820. Reservations: Bangkok, tel: (02) 251 6228.
- *Marina Cottages*: Moderate **R**. Bungalows from 540 B (US$20). **A** Kata-Karon Beach, Phuket 83000, tel: (076) 212 901.
- *Thavorn Palm Beach Hotel*: Expensive. Well-appointed rooms from 1,700 B (US$68). Pool, fitness centre,

squash, tennis. **A** 128/10 Moo 3, Karon Beach, tel: (076) 214 835. Reservations: Bangkok, tel: (02) 245 0189.
- *Kakata Inn '85*: Moderate. Rooms cost 600-750 B (US$24-28). **A** 62/4 Rasda Road, Phuket 83000, tel: (076) 214 824.
- Budget accommodation costs 100-375 B (US$4-15) at *Golden Sands, Karon Bungalows, My Friend, Karon Seaview, Shangri-La, Kata Tropicana* **R**, *Kata Villa*, and *Kata Guest House*.

ACCESS
Karon is around 30 minutes from Phuket town.

KATA

Kata is as close to perfection as beaches go, a crescent of clean, soft sand with a good selection of beach bars and restaurants with diving facilities and watersports close to hand . . . there's not much lacking on this beach.

Phuket's Club Med is based here, as well as a handful of budget guest houses. The sea is potentially hazardous for swimming during the monsoon (February/March through to October) but this is when windsurfing comes into its own.

WATERSPORTS★★★★
The calmest period is from October to March; April to November has stronger

winds (20-25 knots/seven Beaufort four) and two- to three-metre high waves suitable for shortboards. The

Patong, Phuket

Mae Haat, Koh Phangan

prevailing winds blow off-shore in the mornings, turning in-shore in the afternoons.

• *Club Med*: Tiga Fun Cup II, Speed, Swift, Jibe, plus beginners' boards. Sailing: Lasers, Optimists, catamarans. Lessons in English, French and Japanese. Advanced and funboard lessons available; sailing regattas are held each week. All watersports and lessons free.

DIVING★★★
See page 104.

BARS AND RESTAURANTS
Club Med has its usual gourmet selection of French, Italian, Thai, Chinese and sometimes Japanese buffets, plus a popular annexe restaurant specialising in seafood. A selection of beach restaurants can be found at the opposite end to Club Med.

ACCOMMODATION
• *Club Med:* Expensive **R**. Pool, tennis, squash, yoga. One week fully inclusive from £366 (LS) to £538 (HS), two weeks including flights ex-London from £1,314 (LS) to £1,704 (HS). **A** Kata Beach, Phuket 83000, tel: (076) 214 830.

• Budget rooms at *Island Lodge* **R** or *Chaowkuan* cost from 350 B (US$13) or from 100 B (US$4) at *Boathouse Bungalows* on the hill behind the beach.

ACCESS
Just over the hill from Kata Centre, 30 minutes to town.

KATA NOI

Just around the headland from Kata, Kata Noi is of a similar quality but with less facilities and less going on than at Kata. The main hotel on the beach is the unimaginative Kata Thani but there are also several budget guest houses – and new ones are going up all the time.

DIVING★★★
See page 104.

WATERSPORTS★
Tuition and board rentals (from 100 B/ hr) at the *Kata Thani*.

ACCOMMODATION
• *Kata Thani Hotel*: Expensive. Large resort hotel. The beach bungalows are much better than the rooms, which are grotty. Swimming pool. Bungalows from 1,600 B (US$60) (garden) to 1,900 B (US$76) (beach). **A** 62/4 Rasda Road, Phuket 83000, tel: (076) 214 824.

• Budget accommodation over the road behind the hotel includes the *Kata Noi Beach View*, the *Western Inn* and the *Kata Noi Bay Inn*, with rooms for 150-200 B (US$6-8). Smarter bungalows at the *Kata Noi Beach Club* cost from 400 B (US$15).

ACCESS
Ten-fifteen minutes' walk from Kata.

RELAX BAY MERIDIEN

Superb new hotel designed in contemporary Thai style on its own private beach surrounded by 40 acres of tropical gardens. The hotel has two gigantic swimming pools, one fresh and one salt water, covering a total of 4,800 square metres. Undoubtedly Phuket's top beach hotel.

WATERSPORTS★★
Windsurfers and catamarans with free tuition.

DIVING★★★
NAUI dive shop, free demo dives weekly. See page 104.

BARS AND RESTAURANTS
Seafood restaurant (the *Pakarang*, overlooking the pool), international restaurant, two buffet restaurants, coffee shop, two bars, lounge, and disco-nightclub.

ACCOMMODATION
• *Le Meridien*: Deluxe **R**. Tasteful, well-appointed rooms, all with balconies with sea views. Tennis, squash and a fully-equipped gym. Single/double from 2,300/2,500 B (US$92/100). **A** PO Box 277, Phuket 83000, tel: (076) 321 4803. Reservations: UK, (01) 439 1244; Bangkok, (02) 253 0444.

ACCESS
Two miles/3 km from Patong, shuttle service provided. Thirty minutes from town, 45 minutes from the airport.

NAI HARN

Big, south facing beach in a sheltered bay, dominated by the flashy Phuket Yacht Club which is built into the slope of the hill at the north end of the beach – in truth it's not a yacht club at all, but that's the image they like to project.

In complete contrast, Sunset Bungalows nestles into the opposite hillside, almost the last remaining hang-out for budget travellers after numerous beach bungalows were demolished when the Yacht Club opened. It must be the only beach in the world where you've got the choice of spending either US$100 or US$5 on a room for the night with nothing, literally, in between!

This beach isn't as good for watersports as many in Phuket (although sailboards can be rented at the Yacht Club) and it's also quite isolated: you won't have the same wide choice of seafood restaurants as elsewhere on the island. Diving can be booked through the hotel.

At the T-junction of the road where it arrives at the beach is the Wat Nai Harn (a *wat* is a Thai temple) which has a sauna where the steam is infused with medicinal herbs and plants collected from the surrounding forests (open 10 a.m. to 6 p.m.).

BARS AND RESTAURANTS
Reflecting the same price range as the accommodation, from beach cafés where you can eat for 30 B (US$1) to smart restaurants, all with nautical themes, in the *Yacht Club*.

103

ACCOMMODATION

• *Phuket Yacht Club*: Deluxe **R**. Rooms all have fridges, mini-bars, large private sun terraces and bathrooms with sunken baths/showers. Small pool, tennis. Single/double from 3,400/4,300 B (US$136/172). **A** Nai Harn Beach, Phuket 83130, tel: (076) 214 020-6. Reservations: UK, (01) 995 8211.

• Most of the budget beach huts were demolished in 1987 and only *Coconut* (next to the Yacht Club) and *Sunset* (on the hill) remain. Coconut may no longer be there but a notice on the wall at Sunset promises 'The place is not closing not this year or next year or ever. Problems with authority does not exist.' Huts at Sunset **R** cost 80-200 B (US$3-8).

• Around the headland to the north of the Yacht Club are two moderately-priced resorts hidden away on their own small beaches: at the *Jungle Beach Resort* **R** (tel: (076) 215 969) bungalows cost 500-700 B (US$19-27). *On the Rocks*, just past the hotel, charges 80-150 B (US$3-6).

ACCESS

Thirty minutes from town, 45-50 minutes from the airport.

Koh Samui

PHUKET: Diving and Snorkelling

Phuket is currently one of the busiest dive centres in Asia – even the Crown Prince of Thailand sometimes comes here to go diving. The season is from mid-October to mid-May.

There is a wide choice of dive sites and all over the island blackboards outside dive shops carry lists of times and departure dates: Phuket is a diver's supermarket and prices are extremely competitive.

Most (if not all) of the best diving and snorkelling locations are some way off-shore. There are reefs around the island of Phuket itself but many have been smothered and killed by dredging for tin (which was Phuket's principal industry before tourism) and although you might find some soft corals and macro–photo opportunities, there aren't many fish here. For either diving or snorkelling it's okay for beginners: learn to dive in Phuket's delightfully warm waters and then consider a trip to one of the many quality off-shore locations. Expect to pay about 700-850 B (US$27-33) for a local two-tank dive.

Shark Point and Doc Mai Island (Koh Doc Mai) are two popular sites about one-and-a-half hours away. Shark Point for morays, leopard sharks and sting rays, Koh Doc Mai for its 100-ft/30-m wall. A full day trip with one tank at each site should cost around 700-1,000 B (US$30-40).

Koh Phi Phi is about two hours away and has several good wall dives and a good variety of hard and soft corals as well as white tip sharks. The speciality here, however, is the spectacular underwater limestone caves.

The Raja Islands (Raja Yai and Raja Noi) are further out than Koh Phi Phi but can be dived as a one- or two-day trip (around 1,000-1,200 B (US$40-45 per day). Both the deeper sites and the shallow corals of the Raja Islands are rated by some dive guides as being on a par with the Similans, and mantas and whale sharks are sometimes seen here from January to March.

The Similans are undoubtedly the highlight of Phuket diving. These nine virtually uninhabited islands, 50 miles/80 km north-west of Phuket are rapidly gaining recognition as one of the top diving areas in Asia. Eight of the islands in the group are part of a marine national park. Underwater fissures and canyons between enormous submarine rock structures provide a home for soft pink corals and a rich variety of fish life. Visibility can often be 125 ft/40 m plus and pelagic encounters are common. Those massive coral-crunchers, the crown of thorns starfish, can also be seen trundling their tank-like way across the bottom.

The Similans are around eleven hours from Phuket, so most dive charters leave in the evening and make their way there overnight. With some, you sleep on board the boat, others take you onto the islands to camp. The islands themselves, with their crystal-white beaches and Maldivian-blue waters, are well worth the journey if you've got a non-diving partner in tow.

The Similans

Standards for Similan trips vary widely, so shop around. The most basic trips (on converted Thai fishing boats) cost from 1,200 B (US$45) per day, rising to 2,500 B (US$95) per day for better equipped or European-managed dive boats (such as the *Wanderlust* or the *Andaman Explorer*). For snorkellers or non-diving partners, costs are around 500-1,000 B (US$20-40) per day.

The Similans offer an unbeatable combination of virgin beaches and good snorkelling and diving in crystal-clear water and some dive centres (notably the South East Asia Yacht Charter Co) also now offer a combination of the Similans and diving at Koh Surin, an island near the Thai/Burma border.

• *Fantasea Divers*: Well-established operation with a good reputation. Their 50-ft yacht the *Andaman Explorer* does regular trips to the Similans and Dutch owners Jeroen Deknatel and Maarten Brusselers promise safe, worry-free

diving for everybody from beginners to tank-hungry photographers. Five days from 10,900 to 12,500 B (US$420-480); three-day trips to Koh Phi Phi from US$50/day; PADI open-water certifications. **A** PO Box 74, Phuket 83000, tel: (076) 321 309. Reservations: UK, Twicker's World, tel: (01) 892 7606; The Travel Alternative, tel: (0865) 791636.

• *Ocean Divers*: NAUI courses, Similan trips. **A** Patong Beach Hotel, PO Box 25, Phuket 83000, tel: (076) 321 166.

• *Phuket International Diving Centre*: NAUI courses, Similan trips. **A** Coral Beach Hotel, Phuket 83000, tel: (076) 321 106.

105

Diving in the Similans

● *Santana Diving Centre*: Horst Hinrichs and Dieter Ichler run trips to the Similans, Shark Point, Phi Phi island and the west coast, aboard the *Anjemina*. Open-water certifications, resort courses. **A** PO Box 79, 83000 Phuket, tel: (076) 321 360.

● *South East Asia Yacht Charter & Dive Centre*: Reliable dive centre, PADI courses. Trips to all off-shore sites including the Similans and Koh Surin on board the luxury trimaran *Wanderlust* **A** PO Box 199, Patong Beach, tel: (076) 321 292. Reservations: UK, Virgin Divers World, tel: (0293) 562944.

● *Siam Divers*: Run by American Matthew Hendrick. Off-shore two-tank dives 1,000 B (US$40). **A** Black Rose Café, PO Box 244, Phuket 83000, tel: (076) 212901.

● *Phuket Aquatic Safaris*: Local dives, Phi Phi trips **A** 62/9 Rasda Centre, Rasda Road, Phuket 83000, tel: (076) 216562.

ACCESS TO PHUKET

From Bangkok Thai International flies to Phuket from three to six times daily, flight time 70 minutes (3,900 B/US$155 rtn). Flights also connect Phuket with Penang, Kuala Lumpur, Singapore and Hong Kong.

Air-conditioned and non-a/c buses depart from the Southern Bus Terminal in Bangkok, journey time around 14 hours. From the south a/c buses and local buses run from Haat Yai (seven-eight hrs), Krabi (four hrs), Phang Nga (two-and-a-half hrs) and Surat Thani (six hrs). Private mini-buses are quicker and only slightly more expensive than the a/c buses; in peak season they run from Haat Yai (six hrs), Krabi (two hrs), Surat Thani (four hrs), and Koh Samui (eight hrs).

KOH PHI PHI

Thirty miles/45 km off the east coast of Phuket, the Phi Phi Islands are amongst the most beautiful in Thailand.

Phi Phi Don is the main island in the group, and the only one on which you can stay. Phi Phi Le, a short distance away, is famous for its prehistoric cave paintings, birds' nests, and clear waters for snorkelling in Ma Ya Bay. Phi Phi Le can be visited as either a day or afternoon trip from Phi Phi Don, or as part of the return journey back to Phuket on a tourist boat.

Boats from Phuket or Krabi arrive on Ao Don Sai, Phi Phi Don's main beach. On the isthmus of the island here, with magnificent views of Phi Phi's limestone escarpments, are the Phi Phi Cabanas, the island's main accommodation complex. Windsurfers and sailboats can be rented on this beach.

A second beach, the counterpart to Ao Don Sai, is two minutes away on the other side of the isthmus – both these beaches are fabulous, but if you want more of a Crusoe-type feel to beachlife head off to Haat Yao, which can be reached either by hiring a long-tail boat or by walking around the rocks to the south.

SNORKELLING★★★

Being more isolated from the mainland, both Phi Phi Don and Phi Phi Le have healthier coral cover than Phuket itself.

On Haat Yao there's a reef inside the protection of the rocks at the left-hand end of the beach, just a few minutes' swim out. **MSF**: 70 B/(US$3)/day. You can also hire a boat (around 300 B/ US$12 for six people) for snorkelling trips to Phi Phi Le and Bamboo Island.

DIVING★★
A small dive operation based at the *Phi Phi Andaman Bungalows* on Ao Don Sai takes divers out to Shark Point (1,400 B/US$56) or on local dives (900 B/US$36).

BARS AND RESTAURANTS
The most expensive restaurant – and the only one with any life going on in the evenings – is at the *Phi Phi Cabanas*. There are several cheap restaurants on Haat Yao, some of which are Muslim-run and don't serve alcohol.

ACCOMMODATION
● *Phi Phi Cabanas* **R** are the most expensive and comfortable on the island, and there is even a swimming pool. Reservations through Indian Ocean Hideaways, tel: (01) 930 6922.

● Further down the same beach towards the cliffs, bungalows at the *Tonsai Village* **R** cost from 100 B (US$4); at the opposite end of the beach there is also *Phi Phi Andaman Bungalows*. On Haat Yao there are plenty of beach huts costing 50-100 B (US$2/4).

ACCESS
Boats leave regularly to and from Krabi or Phuket. From Phuket a ticket on a day-trip boat includes mini-bus pick-up from Phuket beaches; since the boat only stops for a couple of hours on Phi Phi Don all you have to do is leave it there and pick it up again going back at 1p.m. on any subsequent day. On the way back the boat stops at Phi Phi Le for snorkelling and swimming. There is also an express boat to and from Phuket.

KRABI

As development begins to overwhelm Phuket and Koh Samui, the quest for undiscovered beaches has led to this area to the west of Krabi town. The scenery here is sensational, with huge eroded limestone cliffs surrounding a series of small sheltered beaches. The water is clear and unpolluted, and the beaches are terrific.

The main beach here is Ao Nang (also called Ao Phra Nang in some guidebooks). This is where the up-market Krabi Resort is located, but it is not the best beach here – the ones to head for are to the south. To reach them you used to have to go via Ao Nang (Ao Nang is the only beach connected to the road) but several of the bungalow developments here now have offices in Krabi, so you can book a room and travel direct to the beach by boat.

The first beach past Ao Nang is known as Pai Plong, as are the bungalows here. Pai Plong is a 20-minute walk from Ao Nang or a short boat ride. Past here are Rae Lae and Phra Nang, both on the bay of Ao Son.

The time to come here is from October to the beginning of May; by late May the sandflies and mosquitoes become intolerable, and indeed many bungalows are closed from May to October. In season, this area is now extremely popular and you might find it crowded. There are apparently also plans in the pipeline for a large resort on Phra Nang, which would be a great shame.

WATERSPORTS★
Windsurfers can be rented at the water-sports centre on Ao Nang.

SNORKELLING
There are shallow reefs around the headlands and snorkelling excursions from here to Koh Dang, Koh Pada and other off-shore sites (from around 150 B/US$6).

BARS AND RESTAURANTS
The usual assortment of budget restaurants; *Gift* and *Pine* have been recommended, particularly for seafood.

ACCOMMODATION
• *Krabi Resort*: Moderate. Smart, comfortable bamboo bungalows from 500 B (US$20) double. Tennis. **A** 53-57 Pattana Road, Krabi, tel: (075) 611 389. Reservations: Bangkok, tel: (02) 251 8094.
• On Ao Nang, budget huts can be found at *Coconut Garden Bungalows*, *Wanna's Andaman*, with slightly better huts at *Ao Nang Villa* (left-hand side of beach) and the *Princess Garden* **R**, both in the 50-250 B (US$2-10) range. *P S Cottage* (rooms from 150 B) has also been recommended.
• *Pai Plong Bungalows* is on its own

Sunrise beach, Haat Rin, Koh Phangan

beach, huts from 70 B (US$3).
• On Rae Lae there's *Pine Bungalows* **R** with huts from 50 B (US$2), *Rae Lae* (40-80 B) and the *Rae Lae Beach Member's Club*, which has superb wooden bungalows owned by a group of friends in Bangkok which rent from around 600 to 1,200 B (US$25-50); tel: Bangkok: 279 3336.
• On Phra Nang there are several groups of huts including *Joy Bungalows* **R**, *Phra Nang Place*, and *Cliff Bungalows*. Huts cost from 50 B (US$2). Behind these, on the mangrove beach over the headland, is *Gift Bungalows* **R**. At the time of writing several more bungalows were under construction between these two beaches.

ACCESS
Ao Nang is 12 miles/18 km from Krabi, 45 minutes by local transport. Long-tail boats from Ao Nang to Pai Plong take five to ten minutes, 15 to Gift and Pine.

Air-conditioned buses run from Bangkok to Krabi daily, and there are direct buses to and from Phuket (four hours), Haat Yai (four hours) and Surat Thani (five hours). In season there are also boats to and from Phuket via Koh Phi Phi.

CHAWENG

Chaweng was one of the original Koh Samui hippy beaches and is now the first with a major hotel – the new deluxe Imperial Samui. Three up-market properties in the middle of the beach (The White House, The Village and The Pansea) likewise cater for affluent tourists. There are, however, still plenty of budget-priced thatched huts along this enormous beach.

The south end of Chaweng is the best part to be on, and beach parties are a regular part of the Chaweng scene. The main part of Chaweng is known as Chaweng Yai and the smaller bay towards Lamai is called Chaweng Noi; Chaweng Noi is less inspiring than the grand sweep of Chaweng Yai, but better for swimming.

WATERSPORTS★★★

Sailboards can be rented at The Pansea, Liberty Bungalows (where they also have funboards), The Village and Chaweng Village (at the extreme northern end). Catamarans are available at the Pansea, water ski-ing at Liberty Bungalows. Cheapest sailboard rentals are at Newstar on Chaweng Noi.

BARS AND RESTAURANTS

Plenty of choice, from real cheapies where meals cost under 40 B/US$2 to swanky beach cafés like the Malibu.

ACCOMMODATION

• *The Imperial Samui*: Deluxe. Terrific

swimming pool, shame about the hotel. Rooms from US$70. **A** Chaweng Beach, Koh Samui, Surat Thani. Reservations: Bangkok, tel: (02) 254 0111.

• *The White House* and *The Village*: Expensive **R**. Both under the same European management, set amidst flourishing gardens right on the beach. Single/double from 1,000/1,200 B (US$40-45), suites from 1,400 B (US$55). **A** PO Box 25, Chaweng Beach, Koh Samui, Surat Thani, tel: (077) 272 222. Reservations: Bangkok, tel: (02) 234 0982; UK, tel: (01) 995 3642.

• *The Pansea*: Expensive. Beach cottages from 875 B (US$35) (LS) to 1,500 B (US$60) (HS). Not as charming as the above two properties. **A** Chaweng Beach, Koh Samui, Surat Thani, tel: (077) 273 410. Reservations: Bangkok, tel: (02) 235 4100. UK, tel: (01) 408 2055.

• Many of the budget places to stay are on Chaweng Noi, with beach huts at *Sunshine* **R**, *Fair House* and *Mellow* costing 50-100 B (US$2/4). On the main beach, bungalows at both *Munchies Bungalows* and *Thai House* are worth the extra cost of 150-250 B (US$6/10).

ACCESS

Thirty minutes from Na Thon.

Snorkelling in the Similans

LAMAI

Smaller than Chaweng but still an enormous beach. As one local pamphlet puts it, 'You go to Lamai. You will see the long beach with the white sand, it's the good looking. Learn Lamai is composed of the big rocks and the small rocks. There are many bungalows for you to choose. It is the best place for you to take sun-bathing and swim because it no have any coral.'

'The good-looking' indeed it is, with most of the bungalows well hidden away in the coconut palms. Lamai hasn't experienced the same transformation as

Chaweng in terms of hotels, but the arrival of the mind-boggling Flamingo disco has transformed that particular part of Lamai into a mini-version of Kuta Beach in the evenings. Like Chaweng, the swimming is better at the south end, elsewhere you might only be able to swim for short periods at high tide. No watersports.

BARS AND RESTAURANTS

Lamai has a wide range of restaurants strung out along the beach, ranging from the expensive Café Roma (pizzas, ice creams and expressos) to budget restaurants like the Fun Club, where you can get a full meal of fish, vegetables and rice for 75 B (US$3) for four people.

ACCOMMODATION

• Plenty of choice with rates from 40 B (US$1.50) and up for a simple beach hut at places like *Lamai Pearl* (at the south end), *Marine*, and *Wish* (half-way along the beach, the cheapest). At the far north end, on the side of the hill, *Bay View* **R** lives up to its name (from 100B/US$4 with fans). *The Weekender* has been a long-time favourite on Lamai, mostly due to the larger-than-life personality of 'Mama', who runs it. Amazingly, they now accept credit cards, which must make it the only place in the world where you can charge a bamboo hut which costs less than US$4 a night to American Express, Visa or Mastercard (not to mention charging up all those unprintable extras which are an integral feature of life on Samui). The Weekender also has more expensive rooms, from 250 B (US$10), as does the *Aloha* at the Café Roma. *Weekender Villas*, towards the north end of the beach, have better than average bungalows in the lower price range.

ACCESS

Thirty minutes from Na Thon.

NORTH COAST

Mae Nam, Bo Phut, Big Buddha.

Three beaches on the north coast of Samui which are becoming increasingly popular, but are still much less crowded than Chaweng and Lamai. Mae Nam is the first you come to heading clockwise around the island from Na Thon, a two-mile/three-km-long beach with just a few bungalows on it. Bo Phut, the next along, has distant views of Big Buddha and is busy with windsurfers out in the water, thanks to some of the cheapest hire charges on the island. The beach at Big Buddha is not as good as the first two.

WATERSPORTS★★

Cobra boards can be hired at *Peace Bungalows* on Bo Phut (60 B/US$2.50/hr), where Kim, who speaks good English, also gives lessons. Water ski-ing at Chaihad's on Bo Phut.

BARS AND RESTAURANTS

On Mae Nam, try the fish curry with coconut at *La Paz*. On Bo Phut there are the usual eateries; restaurant meals on all these beaches are cheaper than those on the other side of the island.

ACCOMMODATION
• Most of the bungalows on Mae Nam are towards the east end of the beach, with prices at *Cleopatra's Palace*, *La Paz*, *Silent* and *Lolitas* ranging between 40 and 150 B (US$2-6). On Bo Phut there's more choice: *Boon Bungalows*, *Smile House* and *Ziggy Stardust* are all up towards the village end of the beach, with the busy and popular *Peace Bungalows* **R** more or less in the middle. At the other end *Sunny Bungalows*, *Charles Bungalows* and the *Bo-Phut Guest House* all have huts for between 60 and 150 B (US$2-6). *World Bungalows* and the smart *Palm Beach* down this end are more pricey. On Big Buddha there are again half-a-dozen groups of bungalows (*Sunset* is recommended) and the more expensive (and tacky) *Nara Lodge*.

ACCESS
All three beaches are easily reached along the coastal road from Na Thon but make sure you get on a Chaweng-bound pick-up truck.

CHOENG MON

Tucked away in the north-east corner of Koh Samui, Choeng Mon is another hideaway beach for people escaping the building boom on Chaweng. A great beach – despite the ugly Imperial Group villas development on the headland – Choeng Mon is sheltered and calm when the sea is rough elsewhere on Koh Samui and has its own small island at the right-hand end of the beach which is is cut off at high tide. All the beach bungalow complexes have small restaurants attached.

ACCOMMODATION
• Budget beach huts cost 30-80 B (US$1-3), more comfortable bungalows (at the *Chat Kaewo Resort*, *P S Villa* and *Cheong Mon Bungalows*) from 80 to 200 B (US$3-7).

ACCESS
Thirty-five minutes from Na Thon by pick-up truck. It's no problem to get out here but more difficult to get back: you might have to book in advance for the return journey.

ACCESS TO KOH SAMUI
There have been rumours of an airport opening on Koh Samui for several years; although it has now been built, it is not yet operational. You still have to catch a boat from either Ban Don (8 miles/12 km from Surat Thani) or Don-sak (a new car ferry terminal 37 miles/ 60 km east of Surat Thani).

To reach Surat Thani from Bangkok you can fly (one flight daily) or take the train or coach. Rapid and express trains leave from Hualamphong station daily and take 12-13 hours (first-class sleeper around 500 B (US$20), second-class sleeper from 314 B (US$12). The most convenient trains leave at 5.30 p.m. and 6.25 p.m. Coaches leave Bangkok's southern bus terminal in the evenings and take 11 hours (seats cost 125-225 B (US$5-9).

From Ban Don the Songserm Express boats leave three times daily and take two hours; some services connect with the ferries to Koh Phangan (total four hours). There's also a night boat to Koh Phangan. From Don-sak the car and passenger ferry runs four times daily, crossing time one-

and-a-half hours. There's also a speedboat service in the afternoon which takes an hour.

Getting to Koh Samui sounds complicated, but in fact through tickets (which combine either buses, trains or flights with ferry tickets and transfers) are the easiest way to do it and these are widely available from Bangkok travel agents.

Direct air-conditioned mini-bus services (ferry tickets included) connect Koh Samui with Phuket (eight hours), Hat Yai (eight hours) and Penang (twelve hours).

MAE HAAT

This is one of my favourite beaches in Thailand, much harder to get to and therefore much less crowded than Haat Rin. In recent years the number of beach huts here has doubled – there are now around thirty – but this still isn't enough to cope with demand and when you first arrive here you will probably find yourself sleeping around a bonfire on the beach. It's perfectly safe but be prepared to wait several days (or nights) before you can rent a hut – the trouble is, no one ever wants to leave this beach!

In front of the main beach there's a shallow lagoon which is as warm as bath water to float around in but at low tide you sometimes can't swim at all. There are two small beach restaurants. The Island View recently doubled in size, which isn't saying much: it still manages to be the world's most uncomfortable beach bar if you're in bare feet, since the floor consists of a painfully sharp layer of dead corals. Snorkelling equipment and a bottle or two of the infamous Mae Khong (Thai whisky) are about all you need to bring with you.

Travelling on Koh Phangan is still an adventure compared to the better-known Thai islands, but this is one of the beaches it's well worth the adventure to get to, right up on the north coast of the island. Most of the beaches below here, on Koh Phangan's west coast running down to Thong Sala, are no good: don't be sidetracked until you get to Mae Haat. Government plans to develop Koh Phangan include the building of a proper road across the island, so this isolated beach might not remain so for much longer.

SNORKELLING★★★
The area around the island in front of the main beach is worth exploring (take a straight line from the Island View over the sand dune in front, snorkel straight towards the rocks on the left of the island and you'll come across a huge expanse of sea anemones.

ACCOMMODATION
• *Island View Cabanas* **R**, 21 huts cost-ing 30-60 B (US$1-2); *Mae Haat Bay Resort* **R**, 12 huts from 30 B (US$1).

ACCESS
Mae Haat is a 20 to 30 minute hike, or a 15-minute motorbike ride, from the northern fishing village of Ban Chaloklum. Travel to Ban Chaloklum is erratic and although Chaloklum to Thong Sala is only 6 miles/9 km it can take up to an hour in a battered pick-up truck with the

present state of the road. Off-road bikes can be hired in Thong Sala, or you can hire a bike-taxi if you miss the regular pick-up truck. There's also a boat which goes three times a day between Chaloklum and Thong Sala (45 minutes).

HAAT RIN

Sunrise and Sunset Beaches

Fabulous beaches with mint-condition sand sloping off into clear, shallow water. The main beach on the east side of the promontory (Sunrise Beach) is the better of the two – the beach on the south-west side (Sunset Beach) is too shallow for swimming because of the off-shore reefs. However, it's only two minutes' walk away from the main beach.

Sunset Beach runs intermittently for several miles along the south-west coast of Koh Phangan, all the way down to Ban Tai: there are several remote bungalows scattered along here if you're looking for somewhere more isolated to stay. There's no road, so you have to walk along the beach.

SNORKELLING★★★

A clearly visible reef curves around the headland from the right-hand side of the main beach with easy entry, plentiful small tropicals and healthy coral growths including gigantic boulder corals. There are also reefs to the left of this beach and directly off-shore on the south-west side.

BARS AND RESTAURANTS

A great beach for seafood: shark, king prawns and barracuda regularly appear in beach restaurants as daily specials. Most of the beach restaurants here are similar (they even use the same printed menus) and great value. On the south side the *Rin Beach Kitchen and Bakery* is more expensive but a culinary treat no matter what you choose from their extensive menu.

ACCOMMODATION

● There are around sixty beach bungalows or huts on each beach so you shouldn't have a problem finding somewhere suitable. On Sunrise they cost 50-90 B (US$2-4), on Sunset 20-50 B (US$1-2). *Sunset Bungalows* on Sunset are recommended.

ACCESS

Direct boats from Bo Phut on Koh Samui leave daily, crossing time 45 minutes. Boats also go from Haat Rin to Thong Sala, the main village on Koh Phangan, which connect with the ferry for Koh Samui and Surat Thani on the mainland, and vice versa.

113

Philippines

U nquestionably the best beach – or beach island – in the Philippines is **Boracay*****+. This enchanting and hard-to-reach island has been a hot tip for years and is already so popular that boatloads of people have had to be turned away because there is simply nowhere to put them all. Once you do get there, however, a month won't seem long enough. People often ask me which is the best beach in the world, and the reply is invariably Boracay.

Elsewhere in the Philippines the picture is remarkably unpromising.

The large, centrally-located island of Cebu has half-a-dozen tourist beach resorts on its east coast, all of which we visited and found to be uniformly third rate. The best of the bunch is the Argao Beach Club, but for anything longer than a weekend break its attractions would wear thin.

On the **West Coast*** of Cebu the beaches are just as bad but there are one or two worthwhile dive sites. Divers have a choice of staying at the up-market Badian Island Hotel or in budget-priced Moalboal a short way up the coast. Astonishingly, Cebu is considered to be one of the Philippines' top beach islands.

The two best beaches in the Cebu region are on the island of Panglao, which is reached via Bohol, to the south-east of Cebu. The **Bohol Beach Club***** and **Alona Beach***** are a pair of aces, one at either end of the budget spectrum. At last, the sort of beaches the brochures promise but rarely deliver.

Philippine Airlines promotes beach resorts through its 'Swingaround Philippine Beaches' packages. They feature sixteen resorts, and we tried eight of these. Out of these sixteen, at least three have no beach (these are the Anilao Seaport Centre, the Puerto Azul Beach Hotel and Country

Club, and the Salawaki Beach Resort). Of the thirteen that remain, five were either on poor beaches or the resorts themselves were dreadful. These are: the Club Pacific Beach Hotel, the Costabella Tropical Beach Hotel, the Tambuli Beach Resort, the Argao Beach Club and the Badian Island Beach Hotel. Of the beaches we stayed on that only leaves Boracay and Bohol, both of which, however, are highly recommended.

Those not covered here are the Isla Resort (Isla Naburot, Iloilo), Nagarao Island Resort (Iloilo), Maya-Maya Reef Club (Batangas), Punta Baluarte (Batangas), El Nido (Palawan) and the Sicogon Beach Resort (Roxas). The latter two are both first-class resorts which have received several independent recommendations, the first for the diving and the second for the beach, and we hope to review them in future editions.

For weekend breaks from the capital of Manila, the nearest beaches within striking distance to the south are at Puerta Galera on the north coast of Mindoro Island. In the vicinity of Puerta Galera's classically-beautiful natural harbour there are five popular beaches with budget-to medium-priced accommodation. The main beach here, Sabang, has been ruined by over-building and is anyway becoming increasingly insalu-brious: this is where Ermita bar girls bring their clients from Manila. If you're broke and need to get out of Manila (there can't be any other reason for coming here) the best beaches to head for in the vicinity of Puerta Galera are La Laguna and Small La Laguna or White Beach and Talipanan (to the west); beach huts cost US$5-10.

For divers, the Philippines is said to have more dive areas to choose from than any other country in the world. Unfortunately although there are 13,000 sq miles/20,000 sq km of reefs surrounding the Philippines, 75 per cent of it is dead. Dynamite fishing and pollution are the main culprits. Dynamite fishing is illegal, but widespread. The penalties are harsh but unenforceable in a country where fishermen earn less than half the subsistence wage. The Philippines earns over £6 million per annum exporting fish for the aquarium trade, but sodium cyanide is used to anaesthetize and collect the fish and this kills the coral polyps it is squirted on or near. Although the use of sodium cyanide is illegal, the law is, again, unenforceable. Sickness amongst Filipino children who have eaten

115

cyanide-poisoned fish is an even more tragic side-effect of this practice. It's estimated that at least 2,000 collectors here currently use this method and many of the fish will die because of the failure of their vital functions before they reach the aquarium.

Coral is also collected illegally for sale abroad, with over 1,000 tons being exported annually.

Another potent factor in marine destruction here is a highly intensive fishing method known as *muruami*. On the *muruami* boats, young boys are used to chase fish off a reef by banging weights on to it, driving whole reef populations into the nets. These huge ships carry as many as 500 crew – around half of them children – and spend 10 months of the year at sea, sweeping clean up to 10 whole reefs a day. *Muruami* has been banned since 1986 but at least 30 boats still operate illegally and as many as 15,000 Filipinos depend on *muruami* for a living.

One marine biologist is quoted as saying that nowhere else in the world have reefs been abused as much as they have in these waters, either directly or indirectly. However, there are signs of change. The Aquino government is committed to the preservation of the country's marine resources and is trying to phase out the use of sodium cyanide with the help of the International Marinelife Alliance and the World Wide Fund for Nature, who are training fishermen to collect ornamental species with hand nets. An artificial reef programme is underway and the country's first national marine park, off Sumilon Island, has proved remarkably successful in helping to increase catches in neighbouring areas. Aquaculture, which relieves pressure on the reefs, now accounts for 10 per cent of fish eaten in the Philippines.

As in many countries, the best sites are at remote locations and experienced divers would be wise to consider a live-aboard to make the most of them. The *Lady of the Sea* runs scheduled trips to the Sulu Sea, North Palawan and the Cuyo Islands (USA, tel: (800) 854 9334, CA, tel: (714) 644 5344); as does the *Tristar* (USA, tel: (415) 434 3400 or 1–800 DIV EXPRT). If you're in Manila and considering a short diving break the nearest reasonable diving to the capital is on the southern coast of Luzon, where there are around a dozen dive resorts. The diving here is not at all bad and some areas – such as Sombrero Island – have surprisingly intact coral cover.

Inter-island travel in the Philippines is not without risks, as the tragic ferry disaster in December 1987 showed. This hit the international headlines because it was the biggest civilian maritime disaster since the war, but the small native pump boats which ply the inter-island routes are equally prone to capsize. Over the last couple of years there have been several incidents of over-loaded boats capsizing and drowning everyone on board. One of these had over two hundred passengers on board. Another, which was on its way to Boracay from Roxas in Mindoro, capsized in rough seas at night with the loss of 14 lives (nine of them European).

Philippines Airlines has a network of frequent, cheap flights and if you arrive on a PAL international flight you qualify for a 30 per cent discount on domestic tickets (you must book and pay for the domestic sectors in advance to qualify).

Boracay

Independent travel in the Philippines requires a considerable amount of time and island-hopping is a slow business.

Evidently there must be countless other beaches in this enormous archipelago but after six weeks' travelling around the Philippines I failed to find more than three (out of 16 we stayed on) which I can honestly recommend.

Boracay

GENERAL INFORMATION

Time
GMT + 8 hours

IDD code
63 + area code + number

Currency
Peso (P)
UK£1 = 35P
US$1 = 20P

Hotels

Deluxe: US$60-90
Expensive: US$25-40
Moderate: US$15-25
Budget: US$3-10

PUBLICATIONS
The Divers Guide to the Philippines
David Smith and Richard Westlake, 128 pp, hardback. US$13.95 from Helix Books (p 315).
The Philippine Diver
Free newspaper distributed in Manila

117

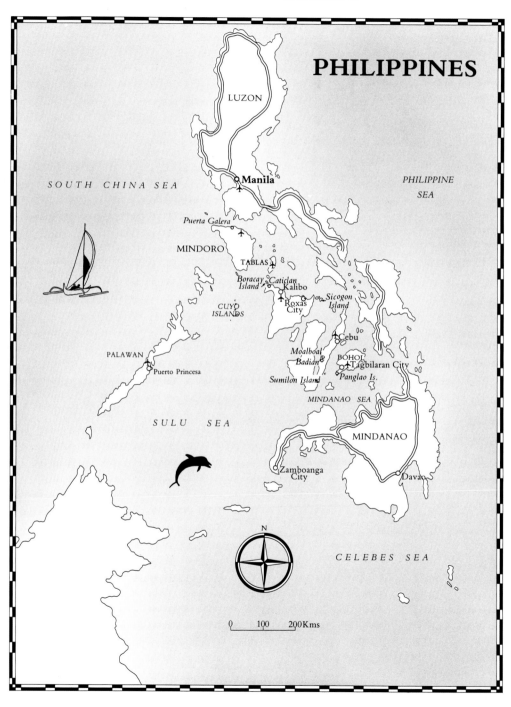

PHILIPPINES

LUZON

SOUTH CHINA SEA

Manila

*PHILIPPINE
SEA*

Puerta Galera

MINDORO

TABLAS

*Boracay
Island* *Caticlan*
Kalibo

CUYO
ISLANDS

*Roxas
City*

*Sicogon
Island*

PALAWAN

Puerto Princesa

Cebu

Moalboal
Badian

BOHOL
Tagbilaran City

Sumilon Island

Panglao Is.

MINDANAO SEA

SULU SEA

MINDANAO

*Zamboanga
City*

Davao

CELEBES SEA

N

0   100   200 Kms

bars, clubs and dive shops.

Philippine Dive Versions

Gretchen Hutchinson, Edgar Ventura and Lynn Funkhouse (1988). 182 pp, softback. US$19.95 from Helix (p 315).

Philippine Shore Fishes of the Western Sulu Sea

Robert E Schroeder. 266 pp. Covers 525 species. US$39.95 from Helix (p 315).

WEATHER

The dry season is from November to May. Annual average temperatures vary between 84-90°F/28-32°C. The water temperature averages 88°F/30°C. The hottest months are March to May, the coolest are November to February. The rainy season is from June to October, with most of the rainfall occurring in August to October. The diving season is January to May.

HEALTH

No vaccinations required unless coming from a yellow fever area. Malaria precautions are necessary and typhoid, cholera and tetanus vaccinations are advisable.

VISAS

Valid passports and onward or return tickets required. A 21-day visa is issued on arrival to most nationals. Extensions are possible but if you want to stay longer than three weeks it's better to get a visa in advance from a Philippines consulate abroad.

TOURIST BOARDS

Head Office: Manila, tel: (02) 599 031; London, tel: (01) 439 3481; New York, tel: (212) 575 7915; Los Angeles, tel: (213) 487 4527; Sydney, tel: (02) 267 2675; Tokyo, tel: (03) 464 3635; Frankfurt, tel: (069) 20893; Paris, tel: (01) 555 3492.

BORACAY

This relatively inaccessible island has become famous so quickly that it is already becoming overcrowded. There's not actually a shortage of space (the island is quite large) but, even with over 500 beach huts spread out around Boracay, rooms are sometimes hard to find. It's really not difficult to see why: Boracay's main beach (prosaically called White Beach) is over two miles/3.5 km of pristine, vanilla-coloured sand sloping off into the pure blue water, strewn with handsome, pastel-painted sailboats and the tanned bodies of jet-setting beachcombers. You can hire the boats – which bear such poetic names as *Wind Song*, *Love Song* and *Wave Song* – for the equivalent of under US$2 an hour and you can even have one made for US$100.

Boracay has hundreds of bamboo bungalows to choose between (most with verandahs and hammocks in which to escape the heat of the day) with prices of US$3-15 a night. Once you've settled into a little bamboo hut you can get the necessities of life – tropical fruits, mosquito coils, drinks, even wholemeal bread from an English bakery – delivered to your verandah.

Music on the beach, a couple of smart restaurants, tasty Filipino food, cheap seafood . . . Boracay's got the lot. There used to be an off-shore floating bar, but it has now been removed for environmental reasons.

Regulars claim that nowhere in Asia is as well set up for the hedonistic beach life as Boracay. If you wanted to conjure up the perfect beach island it couldn't be

119

done better (and if the magic isn't real, the mushrooms certainly are).

When I was here Boracay had no central electricity, no telephone link, no travel agency, no banks, and no proper exchange facilities. The lack of somewhere to book flights or change money is a hassle, but the lack of any other communications can only be considered a virtue. How long it will last, no one knows.

White Beach is where most of the bungalows and restaurants are located. On the other side of the island is Bulabog Beach, wild and empty with hardly a hut in sight, a welcome escape from what seems like non-stop beach life on the other coast. No one comes here except to walk (the seaweed is notoriously fly-infested) or to sail.

Boracay

At Puka Beach, which is a stop-off on round-the-island tours, one used to be able to see people sunbathing amidst small groups of Filipino women sifting and grading the sand all around them: the beach was literally being sorted and bagged up to be used for building in Manila, but thankfully this has now been stopped.

Balingay beach, on the north-east of the island, is extraordinary: this smidgen of a beach, with rocks and sand set in zen-like perfection beneath the cliffs, looks like it was freshly created yesterday. There are a few huts for rent stacked into the hillside above the beach, and one beach bar – very chic, very Boracay.

Cagban, in the south, is a get-away-from-it-all retreat reached by a half-hour forest walk from the south of White Beach: simply follow the signs to Captain Sinbad's. Manoc-Manoc, next to Cagban, is convenient for blasting in the channel between here and Panay (sailboards were advertised as free to guests staying on this beach at the time of writing). Boracay has excellent conditions for wind – surfing as well as some reasonable diving.

Beach Bar, Boracay

SNORKELLING*

The two main snorkelling locations are at the south end of White Beach and on Cagban beach. The north end of White Beach is a waste of time, and the east coast too rough to snorkel. Cagban is the most popular spot, with scattered reef which starts on the other side of the rocks past *Captain Sinbad's,* extending to just over half-way back down the beach. Not brilliant, but worth a look if you're here.

WATERSPORTS★★★★

There are at least two windsurfing centres here with rentals and tuition. Winds reach 34-40 knots/eight Beaufort between December and February, with the peak during January. During the monsoon (June, July, August) there are strong in-shore winds. Mistral, Vinta, Hi-fly, Wylot, Tiga and F2 boards for rent.

DIVING★

The main dive centre is the *Donaire Dive Centre* in the middle of White Beach, good value at around 300P (US$15) per dive.

BARS AND RESTAURANTS

There are plenty of beach bars, with the liveliest at the south end of the beach. *Friday's*, at the north end of the beach, lays claim to the island's most civilized dining. *Chez Deparis*, at the south end, serves above average French food (for the Philippines, that is) but service is excruciating. There are also Italian- and Mexican-style restaurants on the island. Meals tend to be a bit of a hit-and-miss affair on Boracay, with service even more unpredictable: 'Wow, it's arrived and it's still today' is a commonly-heard remark from hungry travellers. Special rate menus (three or four courses for around 40-70 P (US$2-4) help cut costs. Several restaurants have regular seafood buffets with up to seven or eight different seafoods for around 100 P (US$5).

ACCOMMODATION

Friday's: Moderate **R**. At the top end of the beach, English-managed with large, tastefully-appointed double bungalows costing US$32. **A** Lotty Green, PO Box 35, Karibo, Aklan. Reservations: Manila, tel: (02) 521 5440.

• *The Pearl of the Pacific, Sea Paradise Inn* and the *Boracay International Garden Beach Resort* all have moderately-priced and comfortable rooms from 300 P (US$15).

• Budget bungalows on Boracay vary as much as the bamboo they're built from. There are over 500 huts to choose between with varying degrees of privacy, cleanliness and seafront views. Most have verandahs, hammocks and shower-rooms (no hot water). Cups and hot water are provided on tip-toe at dawn so you can make tea and coffee. The majority of huts are set back a few paces from the beach although you can find a few (principally at either end) which open directly on to the beach. Bungalows

normally cost around 50-200 P (US$3-7). Most are on White Beach, although there are others scattered around the island.

Night diving in the Philippines

ACCESS

Boracay doesn't have an Boracay doesn't have an airport (yet) so to fly here you have to go to either Kalibo or Tablas. PAL flies daily from Manila but flights are heavily booked, so if you're coming from overseas it would be worth trying to make reservations well

121

in advance.

From Kalibo a jeepney or bus to Caticlan takes one-and-half to two hours, and from there a boat to Boracay takes 30 minutes. From Tablas airport a jeepney to Santa Fe takes 45 min - utes, and a boat from there to Boracay a further two-and-a-half hours.

There are also daily flights to Catic- lan from Manila, operated by Aerolift (tel: (02) 817 2361). The cost is 2,000 P (US$100) rtn.

Getting to Boracay by island-hop- ping can take a considerable amount of time and energy. The journey from Puerta Galera, for instance, can take up to three days of non-stop travelling.

CEBU: WEST COAST

Moalboal, Badian Island

There is no reason to be on this coast apart from diving, and even then its appeal is limited. The beaches at both Badian and Moalboal are awful. Moalboal lost what was apparently once a super beach during a hurricane in 1984 and mere shreds remain. At Badian, the beach is on a shallow tidal area between the island and the shore, so watersports are restricted to certain times of day, and you can only swim in a small, marked-off area because of sea urchins. However, the hotel (supposedly Cebu's best) has a swimming pool.

The snorkelling along this coast is no good. Most of the shallow reefs are dead.

Moalboal's dusty waterfront houses four dive shops in the space of 400 yards and numerous bars and restaurants as well as cheap huts to stay in. A Hong-Kong- based reader wrote to a British diving magazine complaining that their holiday in Moalboal was ruined by 'vile food, poor accommodation, communal loos, showers that worked spasmodically, an aggressive and threatening proprietor, coral reefs wrecked by typhoons, blasting and overfishing, all in all an expensive total disaster, never to be repeated.' This type of diver would obviously be better off at Badian, but I don't know why they didn't like Pescador (if they went there).

WATERSPORTS*

Winds of 22-33 knots/6-7 Beaufort are found in the Tanon Straight during December, January and February. March, April and May are calm. *Aquarius Watersports* at Sumsid Lodge have Hi-flys and Bic funboards, The *Reef Club* has Mistrals. Hobie cat rentals at the Reef Club. The *Badian Resort* has Mistral equipment.

DIVING**

From Moalboal at least three or four dive boats leave regularly, several times a day, to local sites such as Pes- cador, Sunken Island and the in-shore reef of Tonga Point. At Pescador a coral shelf drops off from 40 ft/12 m down to 200 ft/60 m replete with soft and hard corals, sea fans and a full quota of reef fish. Caves are a feature of the wall: the cave of the lionfish (which is 75 ft/23 m down), is home to at least two dozen lionfish. Sunken Island is said to be as good if not better than Pescador; Tonga Point is mediocre but it can be dived as a shore dive. Night dives between Badian and Pescador are popular.

● At the last count there were four dive shops in Moalboal (*Sa-Avedra Diving,*

Ocean Safari/Nelson's Dive Shop, Aquarius Watersports and the Moalboal Reef Club) with an average Two-tank dive price of 320 P (US$16) including guide, boat and equipment.

• The PADI/VDTL/ADSI dive shop on Badian, run by Bernhard Jackenroll and Andreas Veits, is thorough and well equipped. One-tank dives cost around US$27.

BARS AND RESTAURANTS

At Moalboal eating and drinking is as cheap as the accommodation and the diving. At Badian they specialize in Filipino cuisine plus steaks and lobsters.

ACCOMMODATION

• At Moalboal accommodation is basic, with the price of a standard hut being 50-200 P (US$2.50-10). The exceptions are Oscar Regner's Reef Club R, where rooms cost 350-500P (US$17-25) full board and Sumsid Lodge, where they charge from 300 P (US$15) per person, also full board. An important consideration when choosing a room at Moalboal is noise: music is constant and goes on until late at night.

• Badian Island Beach Hotel: Deluxe. Spacious bungalows designed in semi-Japanese style, single/double from US$65 (LS) to US$90 (HS); dive packages through Philippine Airlines from single/double US$360/500 for three nights including four/eight dives per person. A Badian, Cebu, tel: (032) 61306. Reservations: Manila, tel: (02) 581 835, 506 041; Worldwide: Utell International.

ACCESS

PAL has 10 flights a day from Manila to Cebu City, flight time just over one hour. Moalboal and Badian are two to three hours away by car or bus.

BOHOL BEACH CLUB

Terrific beach, easily worth the extra flight (30 minutes by turbo-prop) on from Cebu – as is its neighbour, Alona Beach. This wild, natural beach is two miles/three km from end to end and there is nothing else on it except the low-key Bohol Beach Club. The fringing reef is around 350 ft/100 m off-shore but local spearfishermen have worked most of the fish and shells off this reef.

WATERSPORTS*

Sailing and windsurfing is dependent on the tide. Hi-fly and Hobie cat rentals and tuition.

DIVING

Bohol is 30 minutes away from Balicasag Island, where the diving is said to be superb with visibility of up to 200 ft/60 m. Local two-tank dives including equipment cost around US$30; off-shore sites such as Balicasag are considerably more expensive (from US$50). Resort dives and certifications available.

BARS AND RESTAURANTS

The hotel has a restaurant and poolside bar with above average food at normal resort prices.

ACCOMMODATION

• Bohol Beach Club: Expensive R. Comfortable, rustically-designed rooms, single/double from US$35/40. Tennis, sauna, jacuzzi, massages.

123

Dive packages through PAL from single/double US$250/300 for three nights and four-eight dives. **A** Panglao Island, Bohol. Reservations: Manila, tel: 522 2301.

ACCESS
PAL flies from Manila to Cebu a mini-mum of six times daily. Twice-daily PAL flights from Mactan (Cebu) to Tagbilaran take a further 30 minutes. Transfer time from the airport to the resort is around 30-40 minutes. There are also twice-daily boats from Cebu to Tagbilaran, crossing time four hours.

ALONA BEACH

On the east coast of Panglao, fabulous beach. 'Welcome to Alona Beach – Have A Nice Swimming' is what the signboard at the junction says, and that's just what you'll get: the clear, warm sea is swimmable along the entire length of the beach. Diving facilities are available through Jacques Trotin at the Bohol Diver's Lodge and although the price is double what it is at Moalboal at least there's a beach here. Jacques says 'many drop-offs, coral gardens and the famous Snake Island are on the programme'. The snorkelling is similar to the Bohol Beach Club and not at all promising. Jacques has one sailboard for rent but otherwise the only beach sport around here is swinging from a rope on a palm tree – very relaxing.

BARS AND RESTAURANTS
There are several cheap beach restaurants. Filipino, Chinese and seafood are all on the menu at the *Bohol's Diver's Lodge*, where crêpes Suzettes are the house speciality and cocktails, wines and pastis are available at the bar and restaurant above the beach.

ACCOMMODATION
● *Bohol Diver's Lodge*: Moderate **R**. Bungalows with private bathrooms from single/double US$15/25. Two nights/three day packages cost from single/double US$75/100 inclusive of meals and transfers from the airport. **A** Jacques Trotin, Bistro de Paris, Tagbilaran City, Bohol, tel: 2663.
● Budget rooms cost 50-100 P (US$2.50-5) at half a dozen locations on the beach.

DIVING
All dive sites are reached by boat. The best months are apparently March, April and May. Two-tank dives US$45 (US$30 each for two people) including tanks, weights, boat and guide.

ACCESS
One hour from Tagbilaran (see above).

Malaysia

T he Malaysian peninsula has very few good beaches compared to its neighbour to the north, Thailand. The biggest and best known beach resort in the country is Batu Ferringhi on the island of Penang, where there are half-a-dozen international-class beach hotels, with more under construction. Penang is a fascinating island and the port of George-town is an intriguing blend of Indian, Malaysian and Chinese cultures and cuisines. Unfortunately, the sea at Batu Ferringhi is so polluted that it poses a considerable health hazard. If you do happen to be staying here, stick to hotel swimming pools until they've cleaned up the sea. With considerable investment going into new and existing hotel properties on Batu Ferringhi (including a new Pan Pacific and a new Regent) something should be done about it soon.

Beach hut, Tioman Island

Further down the coast to the south the island of Pangkor is the complete opposite to Penang, unpolluted and isolated. The best resort here is the smart **Pan Pacific★★**, comfortable but very, very quiet. It's miles from anywhere and there are none of the culinary delights or historical sights which make Penang so interesting, but the beach is superb.

Malaysia's east coast is famous for its turtle-nesting beaches. From May to September each year giant leatherbacks come ashore to lay their eggs along a 20-mile/32-km stretch of beach at **Rantau Abang★★**. Beach huts for turtle-watching are around US$2-10 per person per night. The moderately priced Tanjong Jara Resort is slightly further along down the coast but it has an annexe on the turtle beach. Peak turtle watching season is June, July and August and advance bookings are advisable.

South of Rantau Abang, Malaysia's Club Med is located at Cherating. This old and rather run-down property was one of the original Club

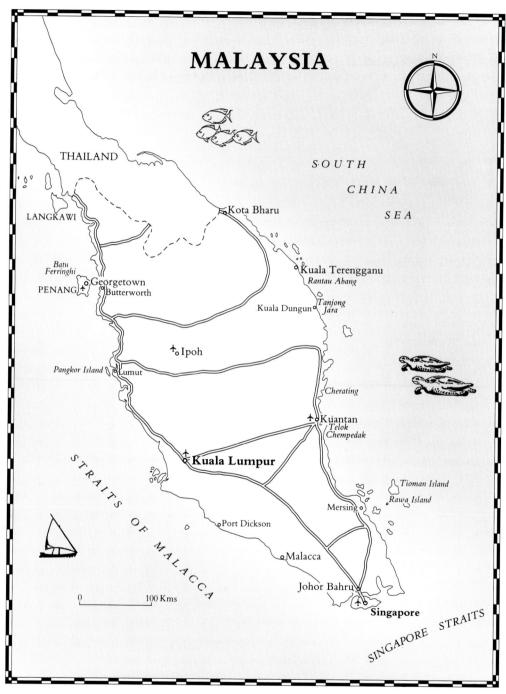

MALAYSIA

N

THAILAND

LANGKAWI

Batu Ferringhi
Georgetown
PENANG Butterworth

Pangkor Island Lumut

S·O·U·T·H

C H I N A

S E A

Kota Bharu

Kuala Terengganu
Rantau Abang

Kuala Dungun *Tanjong Jara*

Ipoh

Cherating

Kuantan
Telok Chempedak

Kuala Lumpur

Tioman Island

Rawa Island

Mersing

Port Dickson

Malacca

Johor Bahru

Singapore

S T R A I T S   O F   M A L A C C A

SINGAPORE STRAITS

0   100 Kms

Meds and although it has two good beaches, the rooms are very cramped. Club Meds to the north (in Phuket) and to the south (in Bali) are livelier with better facilities.

Just outside of the coastal town of Kuantan is **Telok Chempedak**★★, the southernmost beach resort on the east coast. Telok Chempedak is perfect for weekend breaks or short trips from Kuala Lumpur if you were in the capital on business and it's also a good stopping point for independent travellers exploring the coast by bus (there are two guest houses behind the resort hotels).

The jewel in Malaysia's crown is **Tioman Island**★★★★★+, off-shore at Mersing, which has one medium-grade hotel and numerous simple beach huts to stay in. Tioman is an ideal weekend retreat from either Singapore or Kuala Lumpur (there is a small airstrip with flights to both these cities) and for independent travellers it's one of the few islands worth stopping at between Thailand and Bali. Good beaches and reefs for snorkelling can also be found on neighbouring Rawa Island, likewise reached from Mersing.

GENERAL INFORMATION

Time
GMT + 8 hours

IDD code
60 + area code + number

Currency
Malaysian ringgit or dollar (M$)
UK£1 = M$4.50
US$1 = M$2.45

Hotels
Rates do not include tax and service
Single/double
Deluxe: US$45/80
Expensive: US$38/65
Moderate: US$8/32
Budget: US$2.50/8

WEATHER
The rainy season on the west coast is from August through to November, with September, October and November being the wettest months. October/November through to January is the rainy season on the east coast. Humidity is high all year round, with temperatures of 70-90°F/ 21-32°C.

HEALTH
Yellow fever vaccinations required if coming from an infected area.

VISAS
Visas not required for most nationalities. One-month visas are granted on arrival extensions up to three months possible.

127

TOURIST BOARDS
Head Office: Kuala Lumpur, tel: (03) 293 5188; London, tel: (01) 930 7932; Los Angeles, tel: (213) 689 9702; Sydney, tel: (02) 232 3751; Tokyo, (03) 279 3081; Frankfurt, tel: (069) 283 782.

PANGKOR: PAN PACIFIC

First-class resort located on Pulau Pangkor, off Malaysia's west coast. Apart from the stylishly designed hotel itself there is very little else here except the untouched forest canopy (jungle trekking is popular) so anything longer than a weekend break would require a huge stack of paperbacks. Scuba diving is the most recent addition to the hotel's programme, although this side of Malaysia is not renowned for its reefs.

The hotel has a terrific pool and a great beach. In terms of facilities and restaurants the Pan Pacific is far superior to anything Tioman (for instance) has to offer and the beach is clean and unpolluted (unlike Batu Ferringhi). This sounds like an ideal combination and usually the more isolated a hotel is the more I prefer it, but – possibly due to low occupancy rates and the lack of guests when I was here – I found it rather dull. Perhaps it just needs a few beach parties to get it going. Turtles nest on the island from May to July.

Nesting turtle, Rantau Abang

WATERSPORTS★★★
Mistrals, Hobie 14s, Topper dinghies, water ski-ing. Yacht charters.

BARS AND RESTAURANTS
Pool bar, coffee shop, lounge bar, two restaurants, disco open at weekends. High standard of food and service.

ACCOMMODATION
• *Pan Pacific*: Deluxe **R**. Unusual, stylish hotel. Creatively designed rooms all with tv/video, fridges and IDD phones. Single/double from M$170/US$70, suites from M$280/US$115. **A** Teluk Belanga, Pulau Pangkor, 32300 Perak, tel: (05) 951 091. Reservations: Pan Pacific worldwide.

ACCESS
Malaysian Airline System (MAS) flies daily from Kuala Lumpur and Penang to Ipoh, which is just over an hour by road from Lumut on Malaysia's west coast. Pangkor is 25 minutes by boat from Lumut. Coaches take from four to five hours from Kuala Lumpur, four from Penang.

Tioman Island

128

RANTAU ABANG

Giant leatherback turtles come ashore on this coast to nest from May through to September, with the peak during June, July and August. If you want to come and watch the turtles you've got the choice of budget huts on the beach or more comfortable bungalows at the Rantau Abang Visitor Centre. Just down the road is the Tanjong Jara Resort, which is affiliated to the Visitor Centre.

Turtle watching here is very popular and to get one of the more comfortable chalets on the beach you should book in advance. There is also a Turtle Information Centre in Rantau Abang for visitors (never mind educating the visitors, I wish they would inform locals not to ride the turtles). During the season local people will come and fetch visitors and drive them to where the turtles have come ashore in the night if they don't turn up on the beach outside your chalet.

ACCOMMODATION

• *Rantau Abang Visitor Centre*: Moderate. Chalets sleep four people, from M$90 (US$35) per chalet. **A** Thirteenth Mile, off Dungun, 23009 Terengganu, tel: (09) 841 533.

• *Merantau Inn*: Moderate. Chalets sleep four people, M$44- 66 (US$17- 26) per chalet. **A** Kuala Abang, Dungun, 23050 Terengganu, tel: (09) 841 131

• Advance reservations for the above are advisable during the peak turtle-watching season.

• Rock-bottom places on the beach at Rantau Abang include *Sunny's* and *Ismail's*, where huts cost around M$15-

25 (US$6-10) for four people.

• *Tanjong Jara*: Expensive. A quiet backwater with characterful, wood-built rooms in two-storey Kampong-style buildings. The hotel's *Danau* restaurant is promoted as 'a gourmet's dream come true' but the food is terrible. Single/double from M$100/US$41. Diving, windsurfing. **A** Dungun, Terengganu, tel: (09) 841 801. Reservations: Kuala Lumpur, tel: (03) 291 4299.

ACCESS

Two hours from Kuantan airport, accessible by bus from anywhere on the coast.

Tioman Island

TELOK CHEMPEDAK (KUANTAN)

Even though Telok Chempedak is only 3 miles/5 km from the town of Kuantan, monkeys roam the beach and eagles are a common sight riding the thermals above the headlands. Facing the South China Sea, this sizeable beach has safe swimming and is uncrowded despite the presence of two big resort hotels, the Hyatt and the Merlin (with a third hotel planned). There is also a natural, undeveloped beach five minutes away through the jungle.

This is a good beach, good value and cheaper for watersports than Penang (the sea is cleaner too). The Hyatt is probably the best resort on this coast but I think a week or even a long weekend here would be enough – the town of Kuantan is distinctly uninteresting and there isn't much else to do in the surrounding area.

WATERSPORTS★★★★
Mistral and Alpha boards, Hobie cats, Topper dinghies, canoes, water ski-ing.

DIVING
Dive trips to Tenggol Island (further up the coast) can be booked at the Hyatt. I haven't dived this area but the blurb says 'Pulau Tenggol is rated as one of the better dive sites in Malaysia, with prolific hard and soft corals, gorgonians and fish life. Attractions range from flat reefs in protected coves to sharp walls along the island's face with diving depths ranging from 20 ft/6 m to 130 ft/40 m. Underwater visibility can better 100 ft/30 m but averages 60 ft/18 m year round.' The trip involves a one-and-a-half-hour drive and a two-hour boat ride: Pulau Tenggol would be good – that's seven hours' travelling for a day's diving. Two-tank dives cost M$200 (US$82) fully inclusive. Two days' notice required. The diving season here is from April to October.
• Pulau Tenggol can also be dived on a six-day trip from Singapore aboard the 90-ft/27-m *Sea Eagle*. For more information contact: Kwok Tai Tour, Singapore, tel: 273 3333.

BARS AND RESTAURANTS
The Hyatt has an in-pool bar, café restaurant, gourmet restaurant, disco and a seaside bar in a converted refugee boat which brought 162 Vietnamese to Kuantan's shores in 1980. The Merlin has Malaysian, European and Chinese restaurants plus a disco. There are a string of cheap restaurants two minutes' walk from the hotels on the main road, as well as hawker stalls in a food complex on the beach.

ACCOMMODATION
• *Hyatt Kuantan:* Deluxe **R**. Spacious, tasteful rooms with mini-bars, tv/video, 24-hour room service. Swimming pool, tennis, squash, health club, sauna. Regency Club. Rooms from M$160 (US$62). **A** PO Box 250, Kuantan, tel: (09) 525 211. Reservations: UK, (01) 580 8197.
• *Merlin Inn:* Moderate. Tacky but comparatively cheap. Pool, tennis. Rooms from M$100 (US$40). **A** Telok Chempedak, 25050 Kuantan, tel: (09) 522 388. Reservations: UK, tel: (01) 439 2651.
• There are two budget hotels behind the Hyatt: the *Kuantan Hotel*, with large, clean double rooms for M$28 (US$11) is the only one I recommend. The *Asrama Bendahara* is a flea-pit.

ACCESS
The beach is 3 miles/5 km from Kuantan, 20-30 minutes from Kuantan airport. Malaysian Airlines flies from Kuala Lumpur, Singapore and Johor Bahru.

TIOMAN ISLAND

Formerly an important South China Sea trading post, Tioman was first mentioned in *Tales from China and India*, an early Arabic work on which the *Tales of Sinbad* was based. Surrounded by virgin jungle, Tioman's uncrowded beaches are now a magnet for twentieth-century beachcombers.

Tioman has been so isolated from the mainland over the centuries that separate sub-species of squirrels, butterflies, insects and small cats have evolved within the rainforests and as much as a 25 per cent of the plant life here is unique to the island. Huge bats swoop down on the beach at sunset and the island's single primate, the long-tailed macaque, can be seen roaming the forest fringes near the sea.

The island's rich natural history is complemented by an equally absorbing maritime history. Thanks to abundant fresh water supplies and its twin peaks – easily visible to seafarers – it became an important trading post and shelter for traders in the spice trade, an exchange centre for cloves, camphor, wood, incense, rhino horns and ambergris. In the early 1960s Lord Medway discovered quantities of Oriental ceramics on the island which correspond with designs from the kilns of eleventh- and twelfth-century China, and previous finds have been matched with ceramics from Sarawak, Japan and Sri Lanka, which gives some idea of the extent of Tioman's role as a trading post.

The only hotel on the island is the Tioman Island Resort, recently upgraded under new management. The hotel has a beach to itself and a dive shop, watersports centre and swimming pool. On the opposite side of the airstrip and Kampong Tekek (the island's main village) are a series of A-frame huts stretched out along the beach where you can stay for the equivalent of a few dollars a night.

Past ABC Bungalows at the end of this beach there are a series of small beaches with fabulous views over the east side of Tioman and little to disturb your contemplations of the South China Sea except the cacophony of the forest behind.

As well as the places mentioned here there are also huts for rent on Kampong Jara on the east coast but it's not popular, largely because the beach is plagued by sandflies. However, the rainforest trek over the island to Kampong Jara is worth doing: the track starts by the mosque in Kampong Tekek, and traverses the neck of the island. Pausing frequently to watch Tioman's red-faced black squirrels jumping from tree to tree, or to drink from, or swim in, the clean, ice-cold waters of the river Sungei Ayer Besar whose course the track follows, the trip will take about three hours each way (two hours non-stop).

The number of people visiting Tioman has been limited up until now, partly because it's such a long boat ride from Malaysia's east coast but also because the airport can only handle small planes. However, the authorities are looking into the possibilities of finding a site for a bigger airport and there is even talk of a condo development.

SNORKELLING*

Although I've snorkelled here often and friends from Singapore come here just for that purpose, I'm still not convinced that it's any good. There are considerable amounts of dead coral close inshore and, although there are occasional reports of turtles, rays and the odd shark further out, the marine life isn't as prolific as you might expect. Visibility never seems to be very good here, rarely exceeding 30-40 ft/8-12 m.

MSF: M$614 (US$2.50-56)/day. If you're coming by boat several shops in Mersing sell cheap masks and snorkels which would repay their cost in a few days.

DIVING

There is an efficient, well-equipped dive operation at the resort and nearby off-shore sites include Tulai Island, Labas Island, Rengis Island, Tut Island, Sepoy Rock, Magicienne Rock and

Chebeh Island.

• *Dive Asia*: Two-tank boat dive M$95 (US$36) fully inclusive, open-water certification M$450 (US$160). **A** PO Box 4, Mersing, Johor, tel: (09) 445 445.

• You can also dive around Tioman on a three- or four-day trip from Singapore aboard the aluminium cruise boats *Sea Eagle* and *Sea Rover*. The latter leaves Singapore on Thursday nights, returning Sunday noon; the *Sea Eagle* departs Saturday afternoon, returning Tuesday afternoon. Contact: Kwok Tai Tour, tel: 273 3333.

Tioman Island

WATERSPORTS★★★

Windsurfers, Hobie cats, dinghies and canoes at the resort.

BARS AND RESTAURANTS

This is not a gourmet's island: standards of food and service at the Tioman Island Hotel appear to have remained as low as they were under the old management and food at the budget end on Tioman tends to be limited to fish and rice. However, *jahau* (which resembles catfish only in appearance) is a tasty local fish, and fresh tuna and shark are also sometimes on the menu at Nazris or ABC. Alcohol is expensive on Tioman but foreign brand liquors are available in Mersing – stock up before catching the ferry.

ACCOMMODATION

• *Tioman Island Resort*: Moderate. Rather down-market (the recent expansion included the addition of a slot machine arcade) but reasonable value. Malaysian Airlines have very reasonably priced packages for short breaks from KL (US$110-180 including

flights). Swimming pool, tennis. Rooms M$75/230 (US$30/92). **A** PO Box 4, Mersing, Johor, tel: (09) 445 444. Reservations: Kuala Lumpur, tel: (03) 230 5266; Singapore, tel: 737 1259; UK, tel: (01) 287 1566.

• Budget beach huts cost M$5-10 (US$2-4), with the most popular ones at *Nazri's* **R** and ABC (Zul's Place). Nazri also has a block of proper rooms with their own bathrooms and fans (around M$30-40 (US$12-16) for four people) if you don't want to go totally primitive.

ACCESS

Flights to Tioman from Singapore on Tradewinds, tel: 225 4488; from Kuala Lumpur on MAS, tel: (03) 746 3000.

Access by sea to the island has improved with the addition of a small hovercraft and a hydrofoil to complement the normal fishing boats from Mersing, but because of the tides you still might be forced to stay overnight before making the crossing. This is not a very desirable prospect so ask around to see if there is a boat going over on the midnight tide or later (try Giamso Safari on Jalan Abu Baker). This will leave you on the beach at Tioman at around 4-5a.m., which is preferable to wasting a whole day and night in Mersing.

From Mersing the hotel launch takes one-and-a-half hours, regular boats (M$15/US$6) around four hours.

Buses connect Mersing with Kuala Lumpur (six hours) and Johor Bahru for Singapore (two-and-a-half hours). There are also direct air-conditioned buses to and from Singapore.

Indonesia

M ost of the 200,000 people who visit Bali each year spend their holidays on the three main beaches on the south coast of the island. The original tourist resort is **Sanur★★★**, which faces east with wonderful views of Mount Agung, Bali's holy volcano. **Nusa Dua★★★** is a purpose-built tourist enclave on a peninsula to the south of the airport, hard to beat if you want first-class beach hotels with the bonus of Bali on your back doorstep. Sanur is the better of the two for eating out in local restaurants, Nusa Dua has a better beach for swimming and watersports.

The best-known beach in Bali is **Kuta★★★★**, famous for surfing and body-melting Balinese beach massages. Next door Legian beach is similar. Most of the people on Kuta and Legian are either overlanders at the end of their Bangkok-to-Bali travels or young Australians on holiday packages.

If Kuta gets too much to handle (which it sometimes does), alternative choices on the east coast include **Candi Dasa★** and nearby Buitan. Candi Dasa is gaining in popularity rapidly but unfortunately losing

Sanur

133

beach sand just as fast. The beach is small and rather grotty, but a short stay will at least give you some respite from the non-stop action at Kuta.

On the north coast there is a volcanic beach at Lovina, to the west of the town of Singaraja. Like all black sand beaches Lovina is uncomfortably hot and, in this case, dirty too. However, if you're passing through, the large patch reef off-shore (15 minutes by outrigger) is one of Bali's best known snorkelling locations.

That's about it on Bali. The next major island to the east is Lombok, which is becoming increasingly popular as a side trip from Bali itself. In 1988 the first resort hotel was opened on **Senggigi Beach★★★★**, on Lombok's dramatic west coast. There are also several guest houses (*losmen*) for budget travellers. A great beach to escape to, with some reasonable snorkelling and Lombok's only dive operation. At present the only other beach with accommodation on Lombok is Kuta, on the south coast, where there are two basic *losmen*. A complete contrast to its namesake on Bali, this wild and unspoiled beach is best visited on a day trip unless you don't mind roughing it.

Off Lombok's north-west coast are three coral cays, **Gili Air, Gili Meno** and **Gili Trawangan★★★**. These are well known for their surrounding reefs and will appeal to Crusoe-types who want to just tumble out of bed everyday and go snorkelling. You can live out here on around US$3-6 per day.

There are half-a-dozen dive operations on Bali, with most of the dive sites on the east and north coasts. If you want more adventurous diving in virgin territory consider a side trip to the purpose-built dive resort of **Sao Wisata★** on Flores.

The island of Nusa Lembongan near Bali is famous for its surfing but otherwise you can give it a miss. The beach and the sea are full of seaweed and in fact there's so much of the stuff on this island that it forms the basis of the local economy and is exported for cosmetics manufacture.

Bali – and indeed the whole of Indonesia – is currently one of Asia's best travel bargains. For independent travellers a reasonable budget to cover accommodation, meals and transport is around £50 (US$90) per week. Travelling around is easy and anyone who takes the trouble to

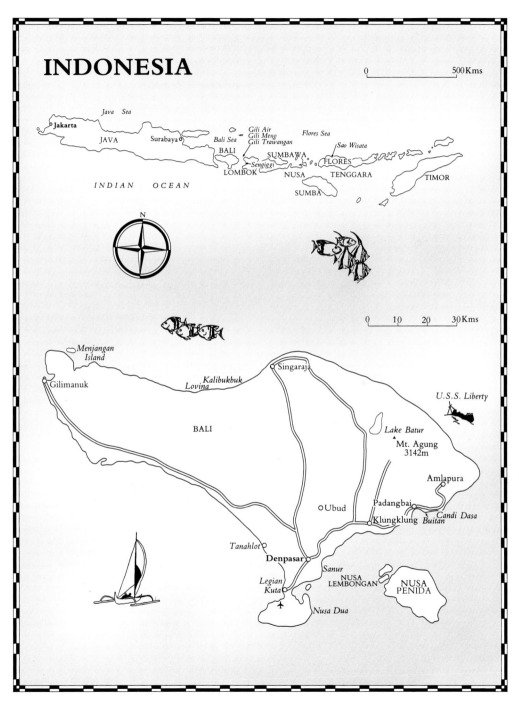

INDONESIA

0   500 Kms

Java Sea

Jakarta

JAVA   Surabaya   Bali Sea

Gili Air
Gili Meno
Gili Trawangan

Flores Sea

Sao Wisata

BALI   SUMBAWA

Sengiggi   FLORES

LOMBOK   NUSA   TENGGARA   TIMOR

INDIAN   OCEAN

SUMBA

N

0   10   20   30 Kms

Menjangan
Island

Gilimanuk

Singaraja

Kalibukbuk
Lovina

U.S.S. Liberty

BALI

Lake Batur

Mt. Agung
3142m

Amlapura

Ubud

Padangbai

Candi Dasa

Klungklung   Buitan

Tanahlot

Denpasar

Sanur

NUSA
LEMBONGAN

NUSA
PENIDA

Legian
Kuta

Nusa Dua

explore Bali will be rewarded with vivid images of Bali's bright green sculpted rice paddies and smiling people.

GENERAL INFORMATION

Time
GMT + 7 hours

IDD Code
62 + area code + number

Currency
Indonesian rupiah (Rps)
UK£1 = 2,900 Rps
US$1 = 1,600 Rps

A ceremony on Kuta

Hotels:
Some rates are subject to tax and service.
Doubles from:
Deluxe: US$70-150
Expensive: US$40-70
Moderate: US$10-40
Budget: under US$10

PUBLICATIONS
Indonesia Handbook

Bill Dalton (Moon Publications, 1988). Paperback, 900 pp, US$14.95. The fourth edition of this eclectic handbook covers the whole of the Indonesian archipelago in depth.

WEATHER
The dry season in Bali is from mid-April to October, the wet season from November to March. January and February get the heaviest rains. Bali is most crowded at Christmas and during May, July and August, which are the Australian school holidays. The mean annual temperature is around 80°F/27°C.

HEALTH
Yellow fever vaccinations required if coming from an infected area. Cholera, typhoid and gamma globulin recommended. Malaria precautions essential for Lombok and Flores.

VISAS
No visas required for stays of up to two months as long as you have a valid passport and onward ticket.

TOURIST BOARDS
Head Office: Jakarta, tel: 348 480; Frankfurt, tel: (069) 233 677. Information can also be obtained from the offices of Garuda Indonesian Airways: London, tel: (01) 486 3011; Los Angeles, tel: (213) 387 3323; Sydney, tel: (02) 232 6044; Frankfurt, tel: (069) 238 0688; Paris, tel (1) 45 62 45 45.

SANUR

Protected by the reef, Sanur is free of the surf which can prove so dangerous (or exciting, depending on your point of view) at Kuta, but because of the shallowness of the back-reef lagoon swimming isn't possible at low tide. Most people here spend their time around the hotel swimming pools rather than on the beach for this reason: the beach at Nusa Dua is better for swimming. Watersports at Sanur are similarly restricted by the tide.

The best part of Sanur to stay on is the north end: the southern half of the beach is badly eroded and strewn with concrete blocks. All the hotels listed here are at the north end and they all have swimming pools.

Sanur has dozens of restaurants spread out behind the beach so it's a better choice than Nusa Dua if you want to save money by eating outside your hotel.

WATERSPORTS★★
Windsurfing, sailing (catamarans and outriggers) and water ski-ing.

DIVING
• *Baruna Watersports*: Branches at the Bali Beach Hotel, tel: (0361) 8511, extn 764, and the Hyatt, tel: (0361) 8271, extn 93.
• *Aquanaut*: At the Sanur Beach Hotel, tel: (0361) 8011, extn 8483.

ACCOMMODATION
• *Bali Hyatt*: Deluxe **R**. Well-established, attractive hotel. Pool, sauna. Rooms from single/double US$105-115. **A** PO Box 392, Sanur, tel: (0361) 8271.
• *Hotel Bali Beach*: Expensive. Bali's only high-rise hotel, one of the first here, now frayed around the edges. Select the garden wing or cottages if possible. Three swimming pools Rooms from single/double US$60/80. **A** Jalan Pantai, Sanur, tel: (0361) 8511.
• *Segara Village*: Expensive **R**. Large complex spread over 11 acres of tropical gardens, terrific pool. Rooms from single/double US$35/40, bungalows from US$50/70. **A** PO Box 91, Denpasar, tel: (0361) 8407.

Sanur

• *Baruna Beach Hotel*. Moderate **R**. Small, good value. Single/double from US$25/35. **A** Jalan Pantai Sidhu 17, Sanur, tel: (0361) 8546.
• *Tandjung Sarui*, Expensive **R**. Outstanding, stylish combination of Balinese atmosphere and modern comforts. Single/double from US$80/100. **A** PO Box 25, Denpasar, tel: (0361) 8441. Reservations: UK, tel: (01) 995 3642.
• *Hotel Sanur Beach*. Expensive. Single/double US$60/70. **A** PO Box 279, Denpasar, tel: (0361) 8011.
• *Santrian Beach Cottages*. Moderate **R**. Bungalows from single/double US$40/50. **A** PO Box 55, Denpasar .

137

• *Ananda Beach Hotel*. Budget. North of the Hotel Bali Beach, the only decent budget accommodation in Sanur. Rooms from 15,000 Rps (US$10). **A** Jalan Pantai, Sanur, tel: 8327.

ACCESS
Twenty minutes from the airport. There are regular *bemos* (public jeep taxis) to and from Denpasar.

NUSA DUA

The beach at Nusa Dua is better for ocean swimming than either Kuta (heavy surf) or Sanur (shallow lagoon) and the hotels here are terrific, but it is rather cut off from everyday Balinese life. If you want a little of the magic of Bali to rub off during your holiday you'll have to hire a car and escape Nusa Dua – you'll need one anyway if you want to eat outside the hotels.

The two top hotels here are the Nusa Beach Hotel and the Bali Sol, both with gigantic, impressive swimming pools set amidst luxuriant tropical gardens. Numerous windsurfers further down the beach betray the presence of Bali's Club Med, which has its own Olympic-size pool. The other hotel here, the Putri Bali, doesn't come up to scratch compared to these three.

WATERSPORTS
Suitable for beginner's sailing for most of the year with stronger winds in July and August. Rentals at the *Nusa Dua Beach Hotel* (Mistral boards) and the *Bali Sol*. Tiga equipment. Lasers, F-Cats and free tuition at Club Med.

DIVING
Aquanaut (Nusa Dua Beach Hotel, tel: (0361) 71210, extn 680) and *Baruna Watersports* (Bali Sol, tel: (0361) 71350) both offer a similar menu for divers, including trips to the USS *Liberty* (US$50-65), Padangbai (US$50-65) and Menjangan Island (US$60-95). Menjangan is a tiny island on the north-west coast which is said to have the richest reefs of all Bali's dive sites. Intro dives and certifications available.

ACCOMMODATION
• *Nusa Dua Beach Hotel*: Deluxe **R**. Imaginatively designed hotel echoing the shapes and textures of a Balinese temple with stone carvings, intricate woodwork and contrasting sculpted grey sandstone and orange brickwork. Fitness centre, sauna, squash, tennis. An interesting option if you're staying here would be to spend a few days at the *Senggigi Beach Hotel* on Lombok (p 142), which is under the same management. Single/double from US$80/85, suites from US$150-1,200. **A** PO Box 1028, Nusa Dua, tel: (0361) 71210. Reservations: UK, tel: (01) 995 8211.
• *Bali Sol*: Expensive **R**. As impressive as the Nusa Dua but more modern in style. Fitness centre, sauna, tennis, squash. Single/double from US$90/100, suites from US$550. **A** PO Box 148, Nusa Dua, tel: (0361) 71510. Reservations: UK, tel: (01) 995 8211.
• *Club Med*: Expensive/moderate **R**. Chinese, European, Japanese and Indonesian buffets. Squash, aerobics, jacuzzi, tennis, sauna. One week fully inclusive from £450-540, two weeks

with flights from London, £1,560-1,750.
A PO Box 7, Nusa Dua, tel: (0361)
71520. Reservations: Club Med.

ACCESS
Seven miles/11 km from the airport.
Bemos run regularly from Nusa Dua to
Denpasar.

KUTA

Kuta and its neighbour Legian are really one and the same beach, stretching for several miles along the isthmus to the north of the airport. The beach is a constant flow of Australian surfies, tourists, Balinese beach boys and travellers of all nationalities. However, with over 300 – yes, that's right, 300 – registered masseuses in Kuta and Legian, don't expect to be left alone to sunbathe in peace. Tranquillity on the beach is achieved by choosing one person for your daily massage and sticking with her but off the beach your patience might well be stretched to breaking point by the non-stop cries of 'Hello *bemo?*' or 'Hello cold drink?' around the busiest parts of Kuta.

Kuta and Legian are good value and good fun but anyone who thinks Bali is a 'spiritual utopia' has yet to see a Balinese gigolo on a motorbike with a T-shirt which says 'Life's a C★nt' on the back.

There are literally hundreds of places to stay here, many of them enchanting bungalows hidden away down the little lanes which run perpendicularly back from the beach. There are so many bungalows for rent here that you shouldn't have trouble finding somewhere you like and I've given only a very limited selection. Prices are incredibly competitive (from around US$5 per person) and the cost usually includes tea and fruit brought to your verandah in the mornings.

Lots of people hire motorbikes in Kuta to explore Bali, and if you plan to do this bring an international driving licence with you. If you haven't got one you'll have to go into Denpasar and take a test.

Kuta's a great place to pick up cheap beach clothes and accessories since quite a few international chains manufacture stuff here for export to beach shops in Hawaii, Ibiza and so on. Bootleg cassettes and Indonesian crafts are also good value but watch out for rip-offs with Balinese art: a good piece of advice is never buy anything on your first few days here.

Kuta's Sea Goddess claims the lives of several victims every year so if you're not confident in heavy surf only swim in areas supervised by lifeguards. Great beach for body-surfing.

139

BARS AND RESTAURANTS

There are almost as many restaurants here as there are bungalows, and you can eat well for US$3-6. As well as Indonesian restaurants there are cheap eateries specializing in everything from Japanese to Swiss to Mexican food, although fresh, reasonably-priced seafood is harder to track down. *Poppies Restaurant* is one of Kuta's best, still popular after all these years. Nightlife is mostly aimed at the hordes of young Australian holidaymakers with huge, barn-like discos providing the backdrop for pick-ups, all-night raging and occasional fights between the Aussies and the young Balinese gigolos.

ACCOMMODATION

- *Poppies Cottages*: Moderate **R**. Enchanting, secluded cottages at two different locations. Everyone's idea of a slice of Balinese heaven, and with 24-hour room service as well! Cottages from US$25-40. **A** PO Box 378, Denpasar, tel: (0361) 51059.
- *Bali Oberoi*: Deluxe **R**. Balinese grace combined with Oberoi service and style, a unique hotel. At the end of Legian, the Oberoi is far from the madding crowds. Cottages from single/double US$105/115, sumptuous private villas complete with tropical gardens in the bathrooms for US$225-400. Pool, tennis, sauna. **A** PO Box 351, Denpasar, tel: (0361) 51061. Reservations: UK, tel: (01) 995 8211 or (01) 995 3642.
- *Kuta Beach Hotel*: Expensive. One of Kuta's original hotels, handy to the centre. Single/double from US$40/50. **A** PO Box 393, Denpasar, tel: (0361) 5305.
- *Yasa Samudra Bungalows*: Moderate. Central. Single/double cost

US$25-30. **A** PO Box 53, Denpasar, tel: (0361) 5305.
- *Bali Intan Cottages*: Expensive **R**. Very popular. Single/double from US$50/70. **A** PO Box 1002, Denpasar, tel: (0361) 51770.
- *Legian Beach Hotel*: Moderate. Great pool. Bungalows from US$40/50. **A** PO Box 308, Kuta, tel: (0361) 51711.
- *Bali Mandira Cottages*: Moderate. Single/double from US$35/40. **A** PO Box 1003, Denpasar, tel: (0361) 51381.

ACCESS

Ten minutes from the airport, 30 minutes from Denpasar.

Diving the USS Liberty

Tank porterage, Bali-style

CANDI DASA

On Bali's east coast, Candi Dasa (pronounced Chandy Dasa), has acquired a reputation as the in place away from the hurly-burly and crowds on the south coast. The beach is very narrow and almost non-existent at high tide and, although it's not a great beach, at least it's peaceful.

Most of the bungalows here are within a few paces of the beach and there are numerous bars above the beach with views over to Nusa Penida and Lombok on a clear day. Because of reefs and strong cross-shore currents, the swimming conditions here are lousy. Local people collect coral from the sea by the bucketful every day and this is contributing to erosion at such a rate that there soon won't be much beach left here at all.

Buitan is two miles/three km outside Candi Dasa, a much bigger beach with just two hotels on it.

SNORKELLING

Snorkelling trips are organized to the off-shore rocks or the 'blue lagoon', a shallow bay half-an-hour away by boat. Day trips are also organized from here to the wreck of the *USS Liberty* at Tulamben on the north coast (5,000 Rps/US$3 per person including **MSF**). To get there by motorbike, take the coast road to Singaraja and turn down to the beach at the Paradise Palm Beach Bungalows (about one hour from Candi Dasa). Walk down the pebble and volcanic sand beach around 800 ft/245 m to the left until you come to some white, angular buildings. Snorkel straight out from here and the wreck of the *USS Liberty* is about 130 ft/40 m off-shore. To stay in the Paradise Palm Beach Bungalows costs 15,000 Rps (US$15) double.

DIVING★

● *Abdi Padingga's Balina Diving*: at the Balina Beach Hotel. One-tank local dives US$25, Two-tanks US$40; Tulamben and the *USS Liberty*, one-tank US$35, two-tanks US$50, all inclusive. Good value – nearby sites such as Gili Tepekong which are used by all Bali dive operators cost around US$20 less with Abdi Padingga. The *USS Liberty* was torpedoed by the Japanese in 1942 and is now covered in anemones, sponges and corals. **A** Balina Beach Hotel, Buitan, tel: 8777.

BARS AND RESTAURANTS

Candi Dasa has a wide range of places to eat from *warungs* (small food stalls) where you can get a generous *nasi campur* (rice, eggs, vegetables, fish and meat) for under 1,000 Rps to smarter beachside restaurants where you can splurge on lobster. Crab, squid and gurami fish are often on menus at reasonable prices.

ACCOMMODATION

● Budget cottages here range in price from 3,000 to 10,000 Rps (US$2-6). Amongst the cheaper ones are *Homestay Ayodya, Homestay Segara Wangi, Liliberata, Homestay Natya* and *Puri Bali* **R**. In the smarter places such as *Candi Dasa Beach Bungalows, Pandan Bungalows* **R**, and *Pondok Bamboo Cottages* **R**, expect to pay around US$15 for a double room.

● *Balina Beach Hotel*: Moderate **R**. Set amongst the paddy fields on Buitan Beach, single/double from US$6/8 to US$22/25 including breakfast. The superior rooms are excellent value. **A** Balina Beach Hotel, Buitan, tel: (0361) 8777.

Lombok, west coast

ACCESS

One-and-a-half hours from Denpasar. Locals know Candi Dasa as Karangasen, which is useful to know when catching a *bemo*. From Denpasar, take a *bemo* to Klungklung and change for one going to Amlapura.

SENGGIGI

As more and more people discover the attractions of Lombok, *losmen* (guest houses) are springing up to meet demand and now, at Senggigi beach, so has the island's first decent resort hotel.

Senggigi is a double beach with the new resort on a promontory in the middle. Conveniently, the southern half of the beach is good for swimming and the northern half for snorkelling. Senggigi enjoys extensive views over Lombok's dramatic west coast as well as Nusa Penida and, on a clear day, Bali's holy volcano Mount Agung.

An excellent choice for a beach off the beaten track at whatever level you can afford to stay here, although for independent travellers it doesn't have such extensive snorkelling as the outer islands to the north-west (Gili Air, Gili Meno or Gili Trawangan, below). However, this is the only place on Lombok with diving facilities and you can dive the three coral cays from here. ·

WATERSPORTS★★
Mistral boards and outriggers available at the hotel.

DIVING
Two-tank dive including boat, lunch and all equipment US$85 (min two, max four people). Qualified divers only, no instruction.

BARS AND RESTAURANTS
The resort has a restaurant overlooking the pool. Outside the hotel, the grandly named *Holiday Inn* has a simple menu with tasty Indonesian and Western food.

ACCOMMODATION
• *Senggigi Beach Hotel*: Expensive **R**. Comfortable a/c bungalows with private bathrooms. All rooms have balconies and superb sea views. Large pool, tennis. Single/double from US$45/55, deluxe US$60/65. **A** PO Box 2, Mataram, Lombok, tel: (0364) 23430.

Reservations: UK, tel: (01) 995 8211.
• *Mascot Cottages*: Budget **R**. Simple, clean bungalows right on the beach, doubles 10,000 Rps/US$6.
• *Pondok Senggigi*. Budget **R**. Just over the road from the beach, run by an Australian-Indonesian couple. Doubles 6,000 Rps/US$4.
• *Holiday Inn*. Budget. Right on the beach, rooms costing 12,500-15,000 Rps (US$8-9).

ACCESS
Five flights daily from Bali on Merpati, flight time 20 minutes (o/w fares around 20,000 Rps/US$12.50). Senggigi is 20 minutes from the airport by taxi. The ferry from Padangbai (Bali) to Lembar (Lombok) takes four hours (3,000 Rps/US$2 o/w) with two or three crossings daily. From Lembar take a *bemo* to Ampenan and change for Senggigi; from the ferry to the beach takes roughly an hour-and-a-half.

GILI AIR, GILI MENO, GILI TRAWANGAN

Three islands off the north-west shore of Lombok. Gili Meno has the best beach,

Gili Trawangan the best snorkelling, but all three can easily be reached in a day from Bali. There's very little to do here apart from snorkelling and walking around the islands. Accommodation, plumbing and food are all basic, but if you don't mind no electricity and a limited diet you can be a castaway here in a way that isn't possible anywhere on Bali. However, at the time of writing the foundations were being laid on Gili Meno for a new 'international class' hotel.

SNORKELLING★★★★

Good snorkelling but bring your own mask and fins – all the equipment here leaks. On Gili Air the most accessible reef is on the south-east corner, near the Losmen Paradiso, with a gentle drop-off around 100 ft/30 m out from the beach. There are also large, untouched coral formations in 15 ft/4.5 m of water further off-shore. On Gili Meno the reef is on the south side, directly opposite the losmen, with a drop-off around 50 ft/15 m from the beach. Gili Trawangan has a dramatic little drop-off within just 20 ft/6 m of the beach opposite the Danau Hijau. Another good location is off-shore between Gili Trawangan and Gili Meno, known as the 'blue coral area'. Take a small *prahu* (outrigger) from either island (around 5,000 Rps/US$3).

Moderate to strong currents run parallel to the beach on all three islands, sufficiently powerful to propel you along at an exhilarating pace.

BARS AND RESTAURANTS

Food is limited to Indonesian staples such as fish, rice, eggs, fruit and *gado-gado* (cooked vegetables and beansprouts in a spicy peanut sauce). All the prices given below for accommodation include three meals a day.

ACCOMMODATION

• On Gili Air the most popular place is *Hans Losmen* **R** on the north-east corner of the island (doubles from 3,000 Rps/US$3). *Gili Indha* on the south of the island is of a similar standard, but minus friendly Hans. *Paradiso* (south) and *Sunset* (north) both have simple huts. New places here include *Fantasi* **R** and *Doa Bersama*.

• On Gili Meno there are three *losmen* and standards are slightly higher than on the other two islands. The oldest is *Mallia Child Bungalows* **R** but all three cost about the same (from around 6,000 Rps/US$4 per person).

• On Gili Trawangan the two oldest *losmen* are *Pak Majid's* and *Homestay Maktum*, about 10 minutes apart on the east coast (from around 5,000 Rps/US$3 per person). In between the two is the newer *Danau Hijau* **R**.

ACCESS

See under Senggigi (page 142) for how to reach Lombok. All three islands are reached by boat from the beach-port of Bangsal, one-and-a-quarter miles/two km outside Pemanang, on the north coast of Lombok.

From Sweta or Ampenan take a *bemo* to Rembiga and then change (locals will tell you where to get off if you say you want Pemanang). From Pemanang you have to walk to Bengsal, or take a horse-drawn cart.

If you're going to either Gili Trawangan or Gili Meno you have to get to Bangsal early in the morning: the boat leaves between 9 a.m. and 12 a.m. and if you miss it you'll have to 'charter' one, which is much more expensive (around 10,000 Rps/US$6). The normal fare is 600-700 Rps.

143

FLORES: SAO WISATA

Part of the rugged, volcanic Nusa Tenggara group of islands, Flores was given its name, Island of Flowers, by early Portuguese explorers because of the coral 'gardens' surrounding the island. It's these reefs which now draw divers to this remote spot, two hours' flying time east of Bali.

On the north coast of Flores there is one small, low-key hotel, the Sao Wisata Resort, with a diving operation run by Dive Indonesia's André Pribadi, a pioneer of diving in this country. Once underwater it's not hard to see why Flores has recently been identified as one of Asia's top dive destinations.

Dramatic wall diving is a feature of Flores and the reefs boast an enormous variety of huge sea fans, barrel sponges, organ pipes, filigree fans, sea whips and everything else you might expect to find in a flourishing, untouched environment such as this. Diving here is in its infancy and there is very little dive traffic, so reefs and walls are in virgin condition. Pelagic encounters are common. On my first dive here we came across a school of eagle rays as well as mantas and leopard rays and each subsequent dive provided new discoveries in warm, crystal-clear water. At the right time of year visibility averages 150-200 ft/45-60 m.

This is adventure diving at its best, high-voltage stuff and it's good value too: the cost per day for diving, accommodation and meals is the same as the price just for diving to some sites in Bali.

However, there are two drawbacks to this dive resort. Firstly, it takes up to two hours to get to some of the best sites; the dive boats are large and comfortable but they *are* slow. Secondly, the beach is horrible. The manager has promised a second boat to ferry non-divers to nearby white-sand beaches during the day, but quite frankly non-diving friends or partners would be better off in Bali.

Crinoids, Flores night dive

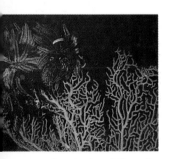

Gorgonia and crinoid, Flores night dive

DIVING★★★★★

The diving season is from the end of April to November. Water temperatures average 84°F/29°C. Photographers should bring plenty of film and batteries. It's important to monitor your depth closely on wall dives (the nearest recompression chamber is in East Java, 500 miles/800 km away). Check with *Dive Indonesia* in Jakarta before deciding to come here – the resort is quite small and at the time of writing there was no permanent divemaster but the amiable and exuberant André Pribadi is also a professional underwater photographer and you can expect video replays of the diving at the end of the day.

ACCOMMODATION

● *Sao Wisata Resort*: Expensive/ moderate **R**. Basic by international standards for dive resorts but efficiently managed and comfortable. Dive packages cost US$75 per person per day, including accommodation and three meals. **A** J1 Don Thomas 17, Maumere, Flores, tel: Maumere 342. Reservations: Dive Indonesia, c/o Hotel Borobudur International, J1 Lap Bateng, Jakarta, tel: (021) 370 108.

ACCESS

Flights on Merpati or Boraq from Bali take two hours and cost around 90,000 Rps (US$56) rtn. The resort is seven miles/10 km from the airport.

THE

Pacific

Queensland

Queensland is bisected by the tropic of Capricorn just below the town of Rockhampton and has three international airports, Brisbane, Townsville and Cairns. Townsville and Cairns are the most convenient gateways for reaching the Great Barrier Reef and island resorts. Out of Queensland's 24 island resorts, three are coral cays on the Reef itself – Green, Lady Elliott and Heron – and the rest are situated between the coast and the Outer Reef.

At the Barrier Reef's southernmost tip is **Lady Elliott Island★★★★**, just south of the tropic of Capricorn. This small, friendly resort has low-cost accommodation in safari tents and cabins, which makes it an appealing option for divers on a tight budget. **Heron Island★★★★★**, 43 miles/70km off the coast at Gladstone, is also a good choice. Heron has a worldwide reputation for diving and facilities for divers and non-divers alike are totally geared toward the Barrier Reef.

Unwinding with the help of large quantities of alcohol is the main objective of many guests on **Great Keppel★★★★★+**, just off the coast of Rockhampton. Great Keppel's reputation as a non-stop party-island is legendary but what comes as a surprise is that the island is mostly National Park and that there are no less than 17 terrific beaches to explore when you've had enough booze and boogie. As well as the resort there's a youth hostel, a campsite, and moderately-priced cabins. Great Keppel has diving and watersports facilities and there is plenty of scope for snorkelling too. A great island whatever your budget.

Between Mackay and Townsville are the Whitsunday Islands, one of Australia's most popular yachting areas. There are seven major resorts in the Whitsundays, including the new deluxe Hayman Island Resort. Unfortunately, with the exception of Whitehaven Beach (where you can camp) the beaches in the Whitsundays aren't good. We stayed at two resorts, neither of which I particularly recommend. The first we tried was Daydream, and this is definitely one to avoid. Tacky resort, dreadful beaches. What do you make of a resort which runs boat snorkelling trips and calls them 'Drive 'n' Snork'? A nightmare rather than a daydream.

We also stayed on Hamilton Island, Queensland's largest resort. More of a city-complex than an island retreat, Hamilton has its own international-size runway, a harbour for 200 yachts, accommodation for 1,500 people, and full diving and watersports facilities. Accommodation varies from Polynesian-style *bures* to high-rise blocks and butler-serviced penthouses, and this is complemented by numerous restaurants and chic shops. A motorized bar cruises the beach with cocktails on tap and a fleet of golf buggies is on hand to cart you around the island's tarmac tracks. Plans are in hand for an oceanarium, a golf course, a racing track, a vintage motorcycle museum and yet more restaurants and hotel rooms.

Hamilton has extremely high standards of accommodation and ser-vice and a great deal of attention is (and has been) paid to detail in the design and planning of the resort, but despite this it left me cold. The high-rise blocks on one side of the island and the artificial, fake-historic harbour area on the other side could be anywhere in the world. Throw in golf carts, yachts and helicopters and it feels more like America than Australia. And none of this comes cheap: if your idea of relaxation is parting with your money, you certainly won't find it hard to unwind completely on Hamilton.

Just off-shore from Townsville is Magnetic Island, which is consi-dered almost a suburb of the city (people commute to work from here). It's tame as islands go but it does have the advantage of being handy and cheap, with plenty of low-cost accommodation. Radical Bay and Horse-shoe Bay are two of the island's best beaches; other more secluded ones (such as Balding Bay, clothes optional) can only be reached on foot. The most convenient backpacker's accommodation for these beaches is Geoff's Place, two minutes' walk from Horseshoe Bay. Magnetic has over 13 miles/20 km of bush-walking tracks which take you from beach to beach or into the interior, all of them well-signposted and well-used.

From November/December to March/April you can't swim here (except in netted areas) because of box jellyfish. There are two dive operations.

In 1988 the world's first floating hotel was opened 44 miles/770 km off-shore from Townsville but it hasn't been a great success. Occupancy rates haven't risen above ten per cent and by early 1989 they were planning to tow this luxury, seven-storey hotel up to Cairns and beach it near the shore. Not only was it expensive to stay at (three times the cost of other reef resorts) but it had all the disadvantages of a boat (guests staying above the third floor were liable to sea-sickness) with none of the benefits – such as mobility. Another factor may have been that is was moored in the middle of a dead lagoon, a boat ride away from living reefs. An artificial 'dessert island' was also constructed nearby, but unfortunately it sank! Access to the hotel is by helicopter, seaplane or high-speed catamaran from Townsville.

Heading north, there are a cluster of resort islands between Townsville and Cairns. Bedarra and Orpheus are both very small and very exclusive. **Dunk★★★★★** is a larger resort, although still up-market and smart – silver service in a luxuriant tropical setting more or less sums it up. You can camp here too. Just to the south, **Hinchinbrook★★★★** is a different kettle of fish altogether. The resort here is deliberately low key and nature, in the form of several hundred square miles of thick jungle, plays the dominant role. The resort holds just 30 people, so come here with someone you know unless you're the solitary type. There's also a campsite on Hinchinbrook, on the opposite side of the island.

Cairns has undergone an enormous boom since the airport went international in the mid 1980s and there are direct flights into Cairns from the UK, west-coast USA and Japan. Cairns is a typically easy-going tropical city and perfectly congenial for a short stay at either the beginning or the end of your trip. In the last five years the number of hotel rooms available in Cairns has trebled, so whatever your budget you won't have difficulty finding suitable accommodation. Port Douglas, an hour's drive to the north, has likewise been enveloped by the tourist boom, transformed from the archetypal sleepy port where the petrol pump was part of the general store into an up-beat resort complete with

The Outer Barrier Reef

bijou boutiques and smart cafés. Port Douglas has the added advantage of Four Mile Beach (Cairns has no beaches) just outside of town. In 1988 a fabulous new hotel, the five-star Sheraton Mirage, opened on this beach.

Diving in Cairns and Port Douglas is booming, with dozens of day and overnight trips to the *Great Barrier Reef* (page 166) on offer, certification courses churning out newly-qualified divers literally by the hundreds and live-aboard dive boats departing for the Outer Reef and the Coral Sea on a regular basis. Snorkellers are also well catered for.

Green Island, 17 miles/27 km north-east of Cairns (40 minutes by boat) is the closest coral cay to the mainland. It's a popular day-trip destination and, with over 300,000 annual visitors, probably one of the most heavily-used coral cays of its size in the world. If you've been to any other island in Australia there's no reason to come here unless you need a

Reef walk, Heron Island

breather from the city or you want to go snorkelling. It's just about passable for snorkelling (fish life is good) but the reefs have been heavily damaged by crown of thorns starfish, pollution, and tourist traffic. Interestingly, Green Island is now being used as a working laboratory for creative new techniques in reef management – a field in which Australia leads the world – and is the first place in the world where they've

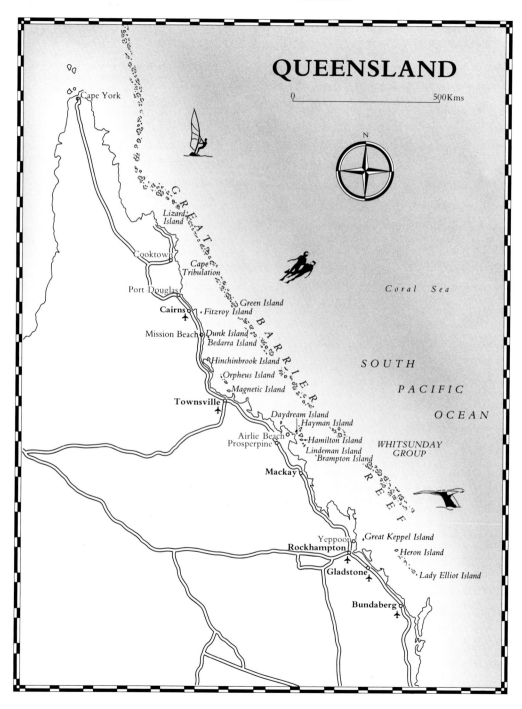

QUEENSLAND

0   500Kms

N

Cape York

Lizard Island

Cooktown

Cape Tribulation

Port Douglas

Coral Sea

Green Island

Cairns   *Fitzroy Island*

Mission Beach *Dunk Island*
Bedarra Island

Hinchinbrook Island

Orpheus Island

Magnetic Island

Townsville

Daydream Island
Hayman Island

Airlie Beach
Prosperpine   *Hamilton Island*
Lindeman Island
Brampton Island

WHITSUNDAY GROUP

Mackay

SOUTH

PACIFIC

OCEAN

Yeppoon   *Great Keppel Island*
Rockhampton
Heron Island
Gladstone
Lady Elliot Island

Bundaberg

GREAT BARRIER REEF

artificially transplanted coral to regenerate damaged areas.

Reef-oriented facilities on Green include an underwater snorkelling trail, an underwater observatory and a semi-submersible. You can also visit it as part of a Hayles Outer Barrier Reef Safari Cruise, which would give you two hours on Green and three hours out at Norman Reef for snorkelling or diving.

A better choice for an island to stay on near Cairns is **Fitzroy****, 14 miles/23 km to the east. Covered in forest, it has a small, friendly resort and a fully-equipped dive shop. Ideal for a budget break from Cairns.

These are the only islands in the immediate vicinity of Cairns; if you want to visit them a Reef Jet service takes in both in the same day.

The most remote island resort is **Lizard*****+, an hour's flight north-east from Cairns. The resort (which is faultless in almost every respect) houses a maximum of 64 people and between them they share around two dozen sparkling beaches and coves. You can take a motorized dinghy any time you like to go beach-hopping, snorkelling or diving and, as well as this, Lizard is just a short distance away from the Outer Reef and one of Australia's most exciting dive sites, the Cod Hole. If money is no object you couldn't choose a better resort.

The only mainland Queensland beach area covered in this chapter is **Cape Tribulation****, to the north of Port Douglas.

Remember that it isn't possible to swim (except in netted areas) on mainland Queensland beaches between December and March because of the danger from box jellyfish. With the exception of Magnetic (which is close in-shore) Queensland islands are not affected (see page 305).

GENERAL INFORMATION

Time
GMT + 10 hrs

IDD code
61 + area code + number

Currency

Australian dollar (A$)
UK£1 = A$2
US$1 = A$1.3

Hotels
Rates are per person
Deluxe: US$132-242

Expensive: US$75-132
Moderate: US$23-76
Budget: US$4-23

PUBLICATIONS

Australia Down Under – Exploring Australia's Underwater World

Christine Deacon with photographs by Kevin Deacon (Doubleday 1986). Hardback, 272pp, 300 colour plates, A$45. Lavishly illustrated guide to Australia's coastline, informative, non-technical text. US$35 from Helix (page 315).

Australian Sea Fishes North of 30° South

Neville Colman (Doubleday 1986). Hardback, 297pp, 300 colour photos, A$45. This is a heavy book to lug around and quite expensive, but it's the best fish ID book for Queensland and more practical than Marshall's guide. US$32.95 from Helix (page 315).

Australian Tropical Reef Life

Clifford and Dawn Frith (Tropical Australia Graphics 1987). Softback, 70pp. Well-illustrated, comprehensive and cheap (A$10).

Dive Australia

Peter Stone (Ocean Enterprises 1987). Softback, 420pp. A comprehensive compendium of dive sites with information on dive shops and charter boats.

Great Barrier Reef Fishwatcher's Field Guide

(Seahawk Press 1985). Underwater card, your best bet for easy, quick reference. Not widely available in Australia (US$4.95 from Helix, page 315).

Reef Report

Quarterly 20-minute video news programme produced by the Great Barrier Reef Marine Park Authority. A$25 including domestic postage from: GBRMPA, PO Box 1379, Townsville, Qld 4810.

Tropical Fishes of the Great Barrier

Reef

Tom Marshall (Angus & Robertson London and Sydney, revised edition 1982).Softback, 261pp, A$18. 500 species illustrated, many with delicate colour drawings. Full of scientific information but impractical as a fish ID book.

WEATHER

There are roughly four seasons in Queensland. The wet and humid one, and therefore the time to avoid, is usually December to March (their summer and early autumn). April is a good month to visit, but the coolest and driest season is during their winter (the northern hemisphere's summer). June, July and August are therefore prime diving months.

HEALTH

No vaccinations required unless coming from a yellow fever area. There are few major health hazards in Australia except hangovers.

VISAS

Visitors of all nationalities must obtain a visa prior to arrival. Short-term visitor visas are valid for up to six months. Return or onward tickets and sufficient funds to cover your stay are also required on arrival. Note that the telephone numbers below are for tourist information only, not visas.

The Cod Hole

Lizard Island

TOURIST BOARDS
Head Office: Brisbane, tel: (07) 833 5400; UK, tel: (01) 836 1333; Los Angeles, tel: (213) 465 8418; Tokyo, tel: (03) 201 7861; Singapore, tel: 253 2811.

LADY ELLIOTT ISLAND

Lady Elliott is one of three coral cays in Australia on the Outer Reef. Both divers and non-divers will enjoy this informal resort on a wild and natural coral cay.

Lady Elliott is at the southernmost extremity of the Great Barrier Reef, in the Capricornia section of the Marine Park. The island is 50 miles/80 km north-east of Bundaberg, 35 minutes' flying time with Sunstate Airlines.

Turtles nest on the cay from November to January and the hatchlings make their dash for the sea from January to March. As with Heron, humpbacks are occasionally sighted off the coast from July through to October. A ranger visits the island to take people on reef walks and give audio-visual shows.

Compared to Heron Island, Lady Elliott is nearly three times the size and holds just over half as many people. It covers 110 acres/45 hectares, and takes about two-and-a-half hours to walk around. There are no luxury amenities here, just simple cabins, a lively bar and restaurant, and a dive shop.

DIVING★★★

You can go shore diving whenever you like and on the opposite side of the island to the resort there's a clearly-marked underwater trail. Other popular dive sites (such as the Blow Hole and Hiro's Cave) are a short boatride away. Lady Elliott is famous for mantas but you might also come across wobbe-gong sharks and turtles and there are several pet morays. Staff and equipment are well up to the sort of standard you might expect from a dedicated dive resort such as this and you couldn't choose a better place to learn. Diving costs A$15 (US$11) for the first two dives, A$10 (US$8) per dive after that, full equipment hire AS$27 (US$20) per day extra. Five-day open-water courses cost A$395 (US$299) (bring medical certificate and passport photos), start Mondays.

BARS AND RESTAURANTS

The room rates are fully inclusive of three meals a day, the food is good, with fresh fruit and veggies flown in daily. Evenings tend to be informal and lively.

ACCOMMODATION

• *Lady Elliott Island*: Expensive/moderate **R**. Room rates are inclusive of air fares from Bundaberg, and therefore tend to be cheaper the longer you stay. Package deals for four days/three nights cost A$385 (US$300), each extra night A$120 (US$92). Reef cabins with private facilities cost from A\$100 (US\$77) per night per person. **A PO Box 6, Bundaberg, Qld 4670.** Reservations: Intasun, 355 Queen Street, Brisbane 4000, tel: (07) 221 5301; UK, tel: (01) 242 9433.

ACCESS
Tariffs normally include the air fare

from Bundaberg. Note that the free baggage allowance on these flights is just 10 kg. Bundaberg can be reached by bus or train from Brisbane and there are direct flights to Bundaberg from Brisbane and Gladstone with connecting flights from Rockhampton and Townsville.

HERON ISLAND

Heron covers just 40 acres/16 hectares and although the resort can hold over 200 people, most of them seem to be busy all day doing something reef-related, so it's not hard to find an empty part of the beach to relax on.

Everything here is kept deliberately simple and natural, with the main emphasis on the marine world. The resort is comfortable enough by most people's standards but it isn't in the luxury league. Rooms are for the most part housed in simple buildings connected by sand paths. It's a great island for nature lovers but one caveat is necessary: Heron is a breeding ground for millions of migratory sea birds so if you're allergic to the smell or noise of birds, choose somewhere else.

Due to its position on the Barrier Reef, Heron is one of Australia's most famous dive resorts but it doesn't necessarily follow that Heron is the best that the Barrier Reef has to offer. Two shortcomings on which most people seem to agree is that visibility at Heron is often considerably lower than you might expect (it averages only 50 ft/15 m) and most dives here are fairly shallow (46-60 ft/15-18 m). However, the majority of divers who come here seem satisfied with what Heron has to offer despite these conditions, and photographers in particular will be kept happy by the swarms of tame tropicals around the cay.

For guests not so enthusiastic about actually getting wet, a semi-submersible makes twice-daily trips outside the reef. Blue-spotted eagle rays lift off the harbour floor as it approaches and clouds of fish follow the craft out of the harbour, waiting to be fed. Reef walks, another means of gaining some insight into the inhabitants of this complex world, take place every morning.

Around a thousand green turtles and 250 loggerheads feed around Heron's reef, and both species nest here. In the turtle-nesting season (October/November to January/February) a ranger takes people on to the beach at night to watch the huge beasts haul themselves up the beach to lay their eggs. Hatchlings leave the nests and rush for the sea from mid-January until late March. Ironically, in the 1920s there was a turtle soup factory on the island. As the turtles came up the beach they were turned over and left to die of dehydration, after which they would be chopped up for soup, turtle extract and jewellery.

Humpback whales are sometimes sighted off the coast from July through to October as they make their way north after spending the (antipodean) summer months in Antarctic waters.

Heron holds an annual Dive Festival in November. Specialists in all aspects of the underwater world participate in the festival, during which, to quote one diver, 'divers are either diving, thinking about diving, talking with other divers about diving, or listening to an expert talk about diving while looking at underwater pictures' (so that's what they call saturation diving!).

SNORKELLING****
The area in the harbour around and beyond the wreck of the HMS *Protector* is the easiest place to start and, since visibility worsens along the outer reef, you'll find the best snorkelling on the inside. It's not far to snorkel out to Heron's best known dive site, the Bommie, but watch out for currents (check with the dive shop if unsure).

DIVING****
Heron is well known for its prolific fish life and there are numerous fish-feeding stations. Most dive sites are just a short boatride away and some of the better known ones are literally within a minute of the dock. One of these is the Bommie, a coral pinnacle just outside the harbour entrance which is home to pet morays Harry and Fang. One diver accurately described this as 'just one great big aquarium' but due to its popularity the coral cover is substantially damaged. The word 'bommie', which is widely used as a description for this type of coral pinnacle everywhere in Australia, comes from the aboriginal word 'bombura', meaning a sunken mountain.

Heron's other main dive sites, most of which are self-descriptive, are Gorgonia Hole, Plate Ledge, Coral Grotto, Hole in the Wall, Staghorn Bank, Blue Pools and Canyons.

As elsewhere on the Reef, June, July and August are the best months for visibility; January, February and March the worst.
- *Heron Island Divers*: NAUI, PADI.

Retail sales. Seven-day open-water courses start Sundays, A$280 (US$215). Prior booking essential, plus you must bring a medical certificate and passport photos with you. One-tank boat dives around A$30 (US$18) including equipment, three-day packages A$132 (US$100).

BARS AND RESTAURANTS
Accommodation is on a full-board basis and the food here is excellent (particularly the lunchtime buffets). Entertainment in the evenings is 'home-grown' (no, not that type of home-grown) and a bit noisy and amateur for some people's tastes.

ACCOMMODATION
- *Heron Island Resort*: Expensive **R**. The most basic accommodation units are Lodge rooms with shared bathrooms, from A$90 (US$68) per person twin share. Reef suites are the next grade up, single/double from A$140/240 (US$106/180). The best rooms are the Heron suites, from A$160 (US$114) per person twin share. All rates are fully inclusive. **A** P & O Resorts, 482 Kingsford Smith Drive, Brisbane, Qld 4007, tel: (07) 268 8224. Reservations: UK, tel: (0420) 88724 or (0345) 010900 or (01) 636 3524; USA, tel: (714) 786 0119.

ACCESS
Heron is 43 miles/70 km off Gladstone and it can be reached by either launch or helicopter. The chopper ride takes 25 minutes and costs A$160 (US$123) o/w, A$268 (US$206) rtn. A new 35-

knot high-speed catamaran, the *Reef Adventurer*, cuts the sea-crossing time down to 90 minutes. The fare is A$65 (US$50) o/w, A$130 (US$100) rtn.

Australian Airlines and Ansett services connect Gladstone with Brisbane, Melbourne and Sydney. Gladstone can also be reached by train or coach from Brisbane and Cairns.

GREAT KEPPEL ISLAND

The resort here is well known for its party atmosphere ('Get wrecked on Great Keppel' is one of their more successful marketing slogans) but there are also several quieter (and cheaper) options if you're thinking of coming here, and there are plenty of reasons for wanting to do so apart from dusk-till-dawn night life. The beaches are terrific and, with 17 of them scattered around the island, often empty. The island covers 3,460 acres/1,400 hectares and is criss-crossed by trails for bush-walking.

The resort (owned and run by Australian Airlines) is on Fisherman's Beach. At the north end of this beach there's a youth hostel and the Wapparaburra Haven, which rents cabins and tents. Just around the corner is another enormous stretch of sparkling sand, Putney Beach.

Middle Keppel, a short boatride away, has an underwater observatory.

SNORKELLING★★★
The most popular snorkelling spot is Monkey Beach, near the resort. A lot of the coral close in-shore has been damaged but further out there's a small drop-off and turtles are sometimes seen here.

Green Island

There are extensive reefs around neighbouring islands such as Halfway Island (to the south) and Middle Island (to the north). The best way of exploring these is to get a small group together and hire a motorized dinghy. You could combine a snorkelling trip with a picnic on one of the beautiful, deserted beaches on these islands. Reef charts are available from the *Wapparaburra Haven* shop. **MSF:** around A$5 (US$4)/day.

Chopper trips to snorkel on the Outer Reef cost A$155-195 (US$120-150) per person, min two people.

DIVING
Great Keppel is 25 miles/40 km from the Outer Reef. Haven Diving on Putney Beach is an NAUI and FAUI facility specializing in courses for beginners. The island is surrounded by fringing reef and is well known for its olive sea snakes (I'm told these attractive but venomous beasts have a disturbing habit of coming up and peering at their reflection in your mask!). There's a small wreck on the north side of Barren Island (the *Gallivant*) which is home to

potato cod, turtles and wobbegongs.
• *Haven Diving*: One-tank dive including equipment A$35-40 (US$27-31). Open-water courses start every Monday (bring a medical certificate). **A** Great Keppel Island, via Rockhampton, Qld 4700, tel: (079) 394 217.

9 p.m.) and a small shop.

ACCOMMODATION
• *Great Keppel Island Resort*: Expensive **R**. Twin rooms cost from A$140 (US$108) (garden) to AS$167 (US$128) (beach) per person in high

Heron Island

WATERSPORTS★★★★★
There are two watersports facilities on Fisherman's Beach and resort guests have free use of all non-fuel-powered watersports.Conditions are suitable for beginner to intermediate sailors, tuition and board rental available. Cat sailing, para-sailing, water ski-ing, yachting.

BARS AND RESTAURANTS
All meals at the resort are included in the room cost. Snack bar, pool-side barbecue and disco open to non-residents. The *Wapparaburra Haven* has a café and restaurant (both close at

season (September-December). Fully inclusive of all meals and 20 land-based sports. **A** PO Box 108, Rockhampton, Qld 4700, tel: (079) 391 744. Reservations: UK, tel: (01) 636 7315, or (0345) 010900, or (0420) 87423.
• *Wapparaburra Haven*: Moderate **R**. Self-catering cabins from A$60 (US$46) for two, A$80 (US$62) for four. Tents A$12 (US$9) per person. **A** Great Keppel, Rockhampton, Qld 4700, tel: (079) 391 907.
• *YHA*: Budget. A$12 (US$9) per person. Pre-book from the Rockhampton Youth Hostel, tel: (079) 275 288.

157

• Camping: Tents can be rented from the beach shed.

ACCESS

Twice-daily flights on Sunstate Airlines from Rockhampton, flight time 25 minutes, A$110 (US$85) rtn. There are several boat departures daily from Rosslyn Bay Harbour, with connecting coach services from Rockhampton. Day trips to Great Keppel are also operated by McCafferty's, tel: (079) 272 844. If you buy a ticket over on the *Victory*, which is operated by Great Keppel Island Tourist Services, it includes a three-hour tour around the Keppel Islands (A$28/US$22 per person).

HINCHINBROOK ISLAND

'Hinchinbrook looks like a piece of New Guinea that broke off and floated south' says the Cadogan *Australia* guide, and what's even more remarkable is that it's just 14 miles/22 km from the coast at Cardwell. This gigantic slab of jungle wilderness, which covers 250 square miles/647 sq km, is the largest island national park in the world.

Perched on the north-east corner of the island at Cape Richards, Hinchinbrook's only resort blends unobtrusively into the forest background. Beneath the resort there is a magnificent beach where nothing disturbs the illusion (or the reality) of natural wilderness except, perhaps, the occasional seaplane or helicopter dropping off guests. Although it's easy to get to (30 minutes by launch from Cardwell or 60 minutes by seaplane from Townsville) once on the island you're more or less cut off (no phones, no TV) and left to enjoy an 'unstructured retreat'.

Wallabies and goannas are regular visitors to the terrace at the resort and the wallabies sometimes venture boldly into the open-air restaurant. Sea eagles and kites circle high above the beach and the presence of at least another 250 winged species on the island will no doubt keep ornithologists happy. The mangrove swamps on Hinchinbrook are as dense as those in the Amazon basin.

Hinchinbrook isn't a five-star resort, and doesn't try to be. Most of what they do (which isn't much anyway – you're left to your own devices here) they do well, except for the accommodation, which I thought was of poor quality.

There is a campsite on a superb beach at Macushla, facing the elusive, cloud-shrouded Mount Bowen. It looked like an absolutely wonderful place to live on the beach for a few days or weeks and the people I met here (a mere handful) said it was just that. This is much more remote than campsites on Great Keppel, Dunk or Magnetic and the only other campsite I saw which matched it for 'castaway feel' was on Lizard. The launch to the resort will drop you off at Macushla and pick you up again when it's time to go. You can also camp at Haven, on the north-west of the island.

Hinchinbrook has a limited and specialized appeal, not the least reason for which is that there are no Barrier Reef trips available and no snorkelling or diving around the island. Snorkelling trips operate to the neighbouring Brook Islands when weather permits, but although they're only 15 minutes away it'll cost you A$30 (US$23) every time you want to go there.

WATERSPORTS★★
Sailboards, Topper dinghies, canoes and surf-skis free to guests, no tuition.

BARS AND RESTAURANTS
The restaurant serves plentiful, imaginative meals. There is a convivial bar area where you can't help but meet and get to know other guests (the resort only holds 30 people). This out-of-the-ordinary island tends to be appreciated by off-beat types.

ACCOMMODATION
• *Hinchinbrook Island Resort*: Expensive. Small pool. The resort has 15 cabins scattered through the forest but these were the worst resort rooms we came across in Australia. The management say they like it that way, but I can't see how it adds to the 'natural appeal' to be staying in a gloomy pre-fab which resembles a cross between a Porta-kabin and a dismal motel room. Cabins cost single/double from A$175/330 (US$135/254), half cabins single/double from A$145/270 (US$112/208), four sharing A$120 (US$92) per person. Rates include all meals. **A** PO Box 3, Cardwell, Qld 4816, tel: (070) 668 585.
• Camping: The *Macushla* has fireplaces and toilets but campers must bring their own fresh water. Seven-day permits obtainable from QNPWS, Cardwell Information Centre, Esplanade, Cardwell, tel: (070) 668 601.

ACCESS
Sea Air Pacific flies from Townsville five times weekly (A$202/US$155 rtn), from Cairns daily except weekends (A$230/US$177 rtn). The *MV Reef Venture* leaves Cardwell daily (except Monday) at 9 a.m., tel: (070) 668 539.

DUNK ISLAND

Dunk is the most 'tropical' of Queensland's continental islands and has a literary claim to fame as the island where E.J. Banfield, Australia's answer to David Thoreau, once lived. Banfield's life on the island and his nature observations were first chronicled in *Confessions of a Beachcomber*, published in 1908, in which he described his 20 years hacking a living out of a farm in the jungle. Banfield's heavy-going prose isn't exactly exciting beach reading but, serious though the old codger was, the inheritors of his island are dedicated to nothing but pleasure.

Dunk is a luxury resort with a reputation for fine food and wine, and it also boasts an impressive land-based sports and activities centre (tennis, squash, archery, etc.), two swimming pools and a well-equipped watersports centre.

There is a campsite just next to the best section of beach. Three-quarters of Dunk is a National Park and there are numerous trails across the island which can be explored on horseback or on foot.

159

SNORKELLING
Daily trips on the *MV Quick Cat* to Beaver Reef and Cay, A$60 (US$38).

WATERSPORTS★★★★★
All non-fuel-powered watersports are free to resort guests. Conditions are suitable for beginners and intermediates, tuition available. Regattas are held regularly. Hobie cats, surf skis, water ski-ing, sailboards, para-sailing and speedboats available.

DIVING
Daily trips on the *MV Quick Cat* to Beaver Reef and Cay, One-tank A$82 (US$63) including the cat fare. Intro dives, resort courses and open-water certifications can be arranged through Phil May of the *Great Barrier Reef Dive In*, tel: (070) 687 289.

BARS AND RESTAURANTS
All daily meals (breakfast, lunch, dinner) for resort guests are included in the price and taken in the *Beachcomber Room*, and the food is excellent. There is also an à la carte gourmet restaurant, *Banfields*, which costs extra. Down on the spit there's a snack bar, bar and grill area for campers and day-trippers.

ACCOMMODATION
● *Dunk Island Resort*: Deluxe/expensive **R**. Set amidst lush gardens, the resort's bright and cheerful rooms and suites all have balconies, mini-bars and tea and coffee facilities. Banfield

units are the most reasonably priced and cost from single/double A$203/336 (US$160/260). Luxury beachfront cabanas cost from single/double A$262/448 (US$201/334). All rates are fully inclusive. **A** PO Box 28, Townsville, Qld 48110, tel: (070) 688 199. Reservations: UK, tel: (0420) 87423 or (01) 636 7315 or (0345) 010900; USA, tel: (800) 551 2012; CA, tel: (800) 445 0190.
● Camping: Three-day permits obtainable from the QNPWS, Cardwell Information Centre, Esplanade, Cairns, tel: (070) 668 601.

ACCESS
Air Queensland flies direct to the island from Cairns and Townsville. The *MV Quick Cat* operates from Cairns and picks up at Clump Point Jetty near Mission Beach on the mainland. You can also get a speedboat taxi from Mission Beach. From Mission Beach there are coach services to Cairns or Brisbane.

FITZROY ISLAND

Fitzroy is a large island, covered in tropical rainforest and surrounded by reefs, just 45 minutes out of Cairns. Beaches are mainly coral (hard on the feet) but the splendour of the island more than compensates. Fitzroy is not only an economical choice of resort if you're looking for a quick escape from city life in Cairns but it's also a much better place to learn to dive.

The resort has been thoughtfully designed and was recently upgraded under new management. It has a swimming pool and accommodation options include bunks in shared rooms, camping or more comfortable villa-type units. Two bars, a restaurant and snack bar, a watersports shed and a fully-equipped Peter Boundy Dive Centre complete the inventory of facilities here.

The island is surrounded by fringing reef and there's plenty of scope for snorkelling (Bird Rock, where there are a dozen or more giant clams as well as a tame moray, is one of the best locations) and, of course, diving.

For those who feel so inclined there are some fairly taxing walks through the rainforest and the island's only sandy beach, Nudie Beach (clothes optional, as the name implies) is just 20 minutes away from the resort.

WATERSPORTS★★★★★

The *Fitzroy Beach Hire and Sailing School* runs one- and two-week sailing courses and part-owner Des Grummit is a thorough, enthusiastic teacher. The protected conditions of Fitzroy are perfect for learning to sail and for improving light- and heavy-weather techniques for the more experienced sailor. Sailboard tuition and rentals, canoeing and surf ski-ing.

DIVING

Worth considering as an alternative venue to Cairns for an open-water course: not only is it nearer to the Outer Reef but there is shore diving too. Four- or five-day NAUI or PADI open-water courses cost A$225-300 (US$173-230).

Qualified divers will find that there is some rewarding diving to be had around the island (shore dives cost A$30/US$22 including equipment) and they can also join the *Fitzroy Flyer* every day for the trip to the Outer Reef. Dive shop, tel: (070) 519 588.

BARS AND RESTAURANTS

You have the choice here of cooking your own meals or using the snack bar or restaurant. The restaurant has an à la carte menu and a budget menu. If self-catering, bring some supplies from the mainland, since the selection in the shop is limited. The communal kitchen is frequently visited by Wonga the kangaroo in search of scraps. At the time of writing camping facilities were poor, with no hot showers or cooking area. Weekly disco.

ACCOMMODATION

• *Fitzroy Island Resort*: Moderate/budget **R**. Villa units from A$99/US$76 per person twin or A$90/US$70 per person triple share, breakfast and dinner included. Beach house budget units with shared bathrooms from A$23 (US$18) per person, A$80 (US$62) for four people. **A** PO Box 2120, Cairns, tel: (070) 519 588.
• Camping: A$9 (US$7) per couple, no tents for hire. For permits, tel: (070) 515 644.

ACCESS

The Fitzroy Flyer leaves the Marlin Jetty in Cairns at 9.30 a.m. daily, crossing time 45 minutes, A$26 (US$20) rtn.

Cape Tribulation

161

Radical Bay, Magnetic Island

LIZARD ISLAND

Lizard is one of a kind among Queensland islands. Just under a hour's flying time north of Cairns, it has had a long history of remoteness and even now human contact is low key.

On the island there is an airstrip, a first-class resort (the Lizard Island Lodge), a marine biology station and a campsite. There are over twenty immaculate beaches scattered around Lizard and if you're staying at the resort you'll be given a dinghy (free) to go off and explore them with. They'll also provide a magnificent picnic with chilled wines to take with you: beach-hopping was never like this before.

The Outer Reef is 10 miles/16 km away and one of the Barrier Reef's most famous dive sites, the Cod Hole, is just 12 miles/19 km from Lizard. Although it has been the subject of numerous articles in diving magazines the Cod Hole isn't widely known outside of these circles, which is a pity, since the excitement of this unique wilderness location can be shared by anyone willing to get in the water with a mask and snorkel – most of the action takes place at depths of 30 ft/9 m or less. Around a dozen potato cod live here, and every day of the year they're ready and waiting when divers and snorkellers arrive, playful as puppies and eagerly swimming up to be fed and petted. It's quite something to be snorkelling next to a fish that weighs over 250 lb and is over six feet long. They look a bit like miniature Volkswagens, nipping round from person to person looking for a hand-out. To quote one anonymous diver, 'the Great Barrier Reef is the best in the world and one of the best things in the Barrier Reef is the Cod Hole, where divers can go down and hand-feed potato cod, morays and Napoleon wrasse. It's a zoo down there and it's an absolute must for any diver who comes to Australia.'

Lizard was named by Captain Cook, seeking an escape through the reef for his troubled ship the *Endeavour*. Many illustrious visitors since then (including Prince Charles – it's said to be one of his favourite islands) have followed Cook's footsteps to the top of the island's highest peak, now known as Cook's Lookout, for a panorama of the surrounding reefs, coral cays and richly-coloured lagoons. There are numerous walking trails over the island.

Apart from a small *bêche-de-mer* (sea cucumber) collecting enterprise, which ended tragically in the 1880s, Lizard had few visitors until the Lodge was built in the early 1970s. The Lizard Island Research Station, which now provides facilities for up to 150 visiting marine scientists from a dozen different countries each year, was established during the same period.

Lizard is a remarkable island and the price tag of course reflects this, but you can still enjoy Lizard's natural beauty by camping. The campsite is on Mrs Watson's Beach, over the hill from the resort; curiously, it seems to have been omitted from at least one current list of campsites provided by the QNPWS. Incidentally, Lizard is a continental island and has very few palm trees.

SNORKELLING

Popular snorkelling spots on the surrounding reefs include Trout Cave, Chinaman's Alley, Mermaid Cove and the Clam Gardens. The highlight, however, has to be the Cod Hole, although it does cost A$85 (US$65) per person.

WATERSPORTS★★★★★

From March to August/September the south-easterly trades blow a consistent 15-20 knots/4-5 Beaufort. From October through to March winds become lighter and more variable, with long periods of calm or light north-westerlies.

Sailboards, paddleboards, canoes, catamarans and water ski-ing complimentary, including tuition. There are 14 outboard dinghies which can be used at any time, also free.

DIVING★★★★★

The Cod Hole is unique because it's so predictable. Although the Cod Hole is also home to numerous coral trout, angelfish and other gorgeous reef fish they tend to pale into insignificance beside the spectacle of the tame potato cod – not forgetting the Napoleon wrasse who also live here.

Rated by *Skin Diver* as one of Australia's top five dive sites, the Cod Hole was first discovered by Australian diving celebrities Ron and Valerie Taylor in 1973. It was designated as a marine reserve by a special Act of Parliament long before the rest of the Barrier Reef became protected.

Late August through to December is the best diving season. This is the only time when you can expect to do wall dives on the outside of the Outer Reef (a wall dive followed by the Cod Hole would be a hard combination to beat). Outer Reef dives are, however, expensive at around A$100 (US$75) including equipment.

The island is surrounded by fringing reefs and divers who want to set off to explore will be charged around A$20 (US$15) for full equipment hire and use of a dinghy. The main local sites around the island are Batfish Point, Cobia Hole, Crystal Caves and the bommies at Entrance No 1 and Entrance No 2 to the Lagoon. With a guide, local dives cost A$40 (US$31), night dives A$55 (US$42).

BARS AND RESTAURANTS

The Lodge has an open-plan dining and bar area and the service and food here receive almost universal acclaim. There is a full choice of cooked breakfasts and a gourmet picnic lunch is provided if you wish to go off exploring far-flung beaches for the day. The only criticism which can be made is that the evening menu is too ambitious and falls short of expectations. The bar is at its liveliest during the cocktail hour (when videos of the day's diving are shown). This definitely isn't a late-night island.

ACCOMMODATION

● *Lizard Island Lodge*: Deluxe **R**. Rooms overlook the gardens and the sea, and are spacious and well-appointed with twin king- or queen-size beds, marble bathrooms and mini-bars. Swimming pool and tennis. Deluxe suites from single/double A$385/578 (US$320/480) per day, standard suites A$330/495 (US$275/412), fully inclusive. **A** PO Box 40, Cairns Mail Centre, Qld 4870. Reservations: Australia Airlines, tel: (070) 503 777; UK, tel: (0420) 88724 or (0345) 010900 or (01) 636 7315.

● Camping: 14-day permits from the QNPWS, 41 The Esplanade, PO Box 2066, Cairns 4870, tel: (070) 519 811.

ACCESS

150 miles/240 km from Cairns, daily flights on Australian Airlines A$230 (US$177) rtn.

163

CAPE TRIBULATION

Cape Tribulation's beaches are masterpieces of creation: this is where the jungle meets the sea and one complex, diverse eco-system adjoins its underwater counterpart, the meeting point of the Cape Tribulation National Park and the Great Barrier Reef National Park, both World Heritage Areas.

Until a few years ago Cape Tribulation (or Cape Trib, as it's referred to) was isolated and inaccessible, and few people bothered to make the effort to get here. Those that did were rewarded with a rare wilderness experience and they kept it pretty much to themselves. However, a few years ago the dirt track to Cape Trib was pushed further through the jungle all the way up to Cooktown and the area is gradually beginning to open up. This is not to everyone's liking, since the road itself was the subject of a fierce environmental battle when it was built and is already suspected of causing soil run-off which is damaging the off-shore reefs. With a huge increase in the number of four-wheel drive vehicles now churning up this unsealed road, it's easy to see how this could happen.

There are several low-cost options for staying at Cape Trib, including a very popular lodge with shared dormitories, a campsite, and basic cabin-type units.

Once you've got to Cape Trib (which is sometimes no mean feat, with the state of the road as it is) activities revolve around the wilderness. Bush walks through forests dripping with ferns and orchids, horse-riding and night-time croc spotting expeditions are all popular. As well as this there are snorkelling trips to untouched reefs, or you can just laze around contemplating moody Mount Sorrow which dominates the hinterland.

During the marine stinger season (November to March) it's only safe to use swimming holes in the forest or the pool at the Jungle Lodge. Myall Beach is 10 minutes' walk from the Jungle Lodge, with other beaches (Coconut Beach and Nos 1, 2 and 3 beaches north of the actual Cape) within walking distance.

The Cod Hole

SNORKELLING
Cape Trib being so far north, the off-shore reefs here are in virgin condition. Nick Balsdon of *Rainforest Reef Experience* takes small groups on day trips to Mackay Reef, a fragile little cay for which he is the only permit holder. 'It's a mid-shelf reef with a good selection of hard and soft corals,' says Nick. 'Groups of giant clams are a feature of the cay. Depths vary from 3 to 35 ft/1-10 m with no currents. Quite regularly we see turtles, eagle rays and small sharks, but it just depends on what's moving through.' Nick is also planning to start two-day trips to the Hope Islands, camping overnight on the islands and diving and snorkelling on Escape Reef.

• *Rainforest Reef Experience*: Contact Nick Balsdon at the Jungle Lodge or write: PO Box 2, Cape Tribulation, Qld 4873.

BARS AND RESTAURANTS
Provisions can be bought at the hostel or at the Cape Trib shop, but it's a good idea to bring as much as you need with you from Cairns or Port Douglas. The *Drysdale Arms*, at the hostel, serves filling meals for a few dollars and then degenerates into a party at night.

164

Heron Island

ACCOMMODATION

● *The Jungle Lodge*: Budget **R**. Beds in shared rooms cost from A$11 (US$8) per night, cooking facilities available. Book ahead if possible, since the Lodge is deservedly popular and fills up quickly. Credit cards accepted. Reservations: through Caravalla's Hostel, 77-81 The Esplanade, Cairns, tel: (070) 512 159.

● *Pilgrim Sands Holiday Camp*: Moderate/budget. Self-contained cabins from A$45 (US$35) for two; A$6.50 (US$5) per extra person (up to five). Campsite vehicle rates from A$7 (US$5) per day. **A** PO Box 3, Cape Tribulation, Qld 4873. Reservations: 41 Shield Street, Cairns, tel: (070) 517 366.

ACCESS

There are at least three daily bus services from Cairns or Port Douglas to Cape Trib, journey time two to four hours. Accommodation/coach packages are also available.

The Great Barrier Reef : Diving and Snorkelling

The Great Barrier Reef is the largest and most complex reef system on the planet and covers a total area of 100,000 square miles/260,000 sq km. It consists of 2,900 individual reefs, divided up into a complex set of usage zones administered by the Great Barrier Reef Marine Park Authority in conjunction with the Queensland National Parks and Wildlife Service. The area surrounding the Barrier Reef is the world's biggest marine park, home to over 1,500 species of fish and 400 species of coral.

Since the Reef is situated between 30 and 45 miles (48 to 72 km) off-shore, most people visit it on a day trip unless staying on one of the three reef islands (Heron, Lady Elliott and Green). These excursions are well organized and widely publicized. You'll normally travel on a large, comfortable twin-hulled catamaran which moors at a pontoon on the Outer Reef. From the pontoon, inflatables take divers off to one part of the reef and snorkellers off to another. There are also glass-bottom boats and semi-submersibles to hand.

Day trips are available from most resort islands as well as from Cairns, Port Douglas and Townsville. For divers the cost is A$90-150 (US$70-115) including two-tanks, all equipment and lunch. Snorkellers can expect to pay from A$70 (US$54) for Outer Reef day trips.

You can also go snorkelling with marine biologists for a small extra charge. This gives you a 'hands-on' experience of the reef and an opportunity to look at and safely touch corals and other marine life. Each marine biologist takes a small group for an hour's tour of the reef, explaining the habits and lives of the creatures they come across and bringing some of them up to the surface for a closer view or encouraging people to dive down and touch others. Divers might also find these tours worthwhile, mostly because when you're diving it's impossible to ask questions and by the time the dive is finished you've probably forgotten what it was you were trying to identify anyway.

Jim and Jo Wallace were the first to initiate guided tours with the experts when they invited Wendy Richards of Reef Biosearch to set up shop on board their big *Quicksilver* catamarans. Reef Biosearch has been so successful that they now employ eight marine biologists full time, making them the largest private employer of marine biologists in Australia. The income generated by snorkelling tours subsidizes their long-term research work on the reef.

Reef Biosearch operates on both the *Quicksilver* catamarans (daily trips to Agincourt Reef from Port Douglas) and the *Reef Express* (daily trips to the Low Isles, also from Port Douglas). A similar operation is run by Marine Bio Logic on the *Quick Cat*, with daily trips to Beaver Cay from Cairns.

Enormous numbers of people learn to dive in Cairns – over 7,000 people annually learn to dive with just one of the city's dive schools – earning it the reputation as the Dive Factory of the southern hemisphere. It's a convenient base for round-the-world travellers to gain their open-water qualifications so that they can go diving on their onward travels through Asia or the Pacific.

Prices are incredibly competitive but the 'churn 'em out' factory mentality does mean that you might not get the personal attention you would elsewhere. Most NAUI or PADI five-day courses include a minimum of two days' pool and theory and the rest of the course diving on the reef. Check exactly how many dives you're going to get on the Outer Reef, and find out which different parts of the reef you're going to see – a common complaint from newly-qualified divers is that they didn't get all the Outer Reef dives promised in the brochures.

A medical certificate is required by most schools but a few will allow you to sign a waiver, which means that you don't get a medical check-up and any subsequent accidents are your sole responsibility. This isn't a wise thing to do anywhere in the world (you might have an unforeseen condition which could result in a fatality underwater) so if even they don't insist, get a medical. Four-, five- and six-day courses cost A$200-300 (US$154-230). Aus Dive, Coral Sea Diving Services, Peter Tibbs, South Pacific Dive Centre and Deep Sea Divers Den all received recommendations from recently qualified divers we spoke to.

It's worth noting that open-water courses are available on all the islands we've covered (with the exception of Hinchinbrook) and not only will you probably get more personal attention at one of these dive centres but you'll also be learning in the sea rather than a swimming pool.

Occasionally, qualified or experienced divers express disappointment with the Barrier Reef, saying that it hasn't lived up to their expectations. I believe this is partly due to the fact that non-Australians tend to visit during the northern hemisphere's winter (when visibility is at its worst). Secondly, it's undoubtedly true that some reefs (particularly 'school reefs' near Cairns) are over-dived.

As always, the further you go the better the diving is going to be. There is a wide selection of live-aboards operating out of Cairns and Port Douglas, most of which head up to northern reefs such as the 10 Ribbon Reefs (including the Cod Hole). These trips usually last between two and eleven days and the average cost works out at around A$150 (US$114) per day fully inclusive.

Some of the best diving in Australia is not on the Barrier Reef at all, but in the remote Coral Sea, which is 100 miles/160 km further to the east. The diving here is said to be superlative, featuring virgin reefs and atolls, visibility which averages 200 ft/60 m, and everyday encounters with large pelagics. Write to the addresses below for more information or see *Skin Diver*, which runs regular up-dates on live-aboards operating in the Coral Sea.

DIVE SCHOOLS

- *Ausdive*: NAUI, PADI. **A** Sheridan Street, Cairns, tel: (070) 514 388.
- *Coral Sea Diving Services*: NAUI, PADI. **A** Princes Wharf, PO Box 122, Port Douglas 4871, tel: (070) 985 254.
- *Deep Sea Divers Den*: PADI. **A** 319 Draper Street, Cairns, tel: (070) 512 223.
- *Pro-Dive*: PADI. **A** Marlin Jetty, Cairns, tel: (070) 519 915.
- *Peter Boundy's Dive Centre*: See Fitzroy Island (page 160).
- *Peter Tibbs Dive Centre:* PADI, NAUI. **A** Tobruk Baths, 370 Sheridan Street, Cairns, tel: (070) 512 604.
- *Port Douglas Dive Centre*: PADI. **A** Ashford Avenue, Port Douglas, tel: (070) 995 327.
- *Cairns Underwater Camera Centre*: Two-day underwater photography courses start Tuesday and Wednesday A$200 (US$150). Three-day Cod Hole trips, A$550/US$423; Coral Sea trips during August, September, October. Large range of new and used underwater photo equipment, camera hire, E6-processing, underwater video hire and sales. **A** Corner Lake and Aplin Streets, Cairns, tel: (070) 518 662.

Cape Tribulation

LIVE-ABOARD DIVE BOATS

- *Reef Explorer Cruises*: Coral Sea trips aboard the *Reef Explorer*, Northern Barrier Reef trips aboard the *Auriga Bay*. **A** PO Box 1588, Cairns, Qld 4870, tel: (070) 331 899.
- *Coral Sea Diving Services*: Daily Outer Reef trips plus three-day trips to the Cod Hole and Lizard on board the *Aquanaut* (from A$598/US$460). **A** PO Box 122, Port Douglas, Qld 4871, tel:

(070) 985 254.
- *Pro-Dive*: Two- and three-day Outer Reef trips on board the *Stella Maris*. **A** Marlin Jetty, Cairns, Qld 4870, tel: (070) 519 915.
- *Seaboard Charters*: Seven-day Northern Barrier Reef trips on board the *Esperance Star*. **A** 14 Roslyn Close, Cairns, Qld 4870.
- *Scheherazade*: Eight-day trips to the Coral Sea and the Northern Barrier Reef (from A$1,850/US$1,425 per person fully inclusive). **A** 26 Abbot Street, Cairns, Qld 4870, tel: (070) 514 056.
- *Fantasy Dive Charters*: Six-day Northern Barrier Reef trips on board the *Si Bon* (from A$1,050/US$808 per person fully inclusive). **A** PO Box 241, Port Douglas, Qld 4871, tel: (070) 985 195.
- *Barrier Reef Cruises*: Six-day Northern Barrier Reef trips (from A$1,440/US$1.108) and eight-day Coral Sea trips on board the *Coralita* (from A$2,145/US$1,650). **A** PO Box 6605, Cairns, Qld, tel: (070) 537 377.
- *Bali Hai*: Seven- and ten-day Northern Barrier Reef and Lizard Island trips on board the *Bali Hai*. **A** 26 Abbot Street, Cairns, Qld 4870, tel: (070) 514 055.
- *Nimrod 111*: Five- and ten-day Coral Sea and Northern Barrier Reef trips. **A** PO Box 1458, Cairns, Qld 4870.
- In the USA information and bookings for many of the above can be made through: *Dive in Australia/See & Sea*, 50 Francisco Street, Suite 205, San Francisco, CA 94133, tel: (415) 421 5588 or Tropical Adventures, 170 Denny Way, Seattle, WA 98109, tel: (800) 247 3483.

Fiji

F iji is one of the best bargains in the South Pacific and despite
political upheavals Fijians still extend a warm welcome, a wide
smile and the traditional greeting of *'Bula!'* to overseas visitors.

Fiji can easily be visited as a side trip from Australia (where in fact
most visitors come from) or on a Pacific stop-over, and there are
numerous beach resorts suitable for everyone from round-the-world
travellers to divers to globetrotting jet-setters.

The gateway for international flights is Nadi airport, on the main
island of Viti Levu ('Great Fiji'). Comfortable transit hotels are within
reach of the airport and more moderately-priced accommodation is
available in the town of Nadi (pronounced Nandi) just a short distance
away. Viti Levu is the most populous and economically-important island
in Fiji (sugar and tourism are – or were – the principal industries) and it's
also home to the country's vibrant capital, Suva.

Between Nadi and Suva is Fiji's main tourist strip, the Coral Coast.
There are numerous hotels and beach resorts along this 50-mile/80-km

Soft corals, Fiji

Qamea

169

coastline, the best of which is the **Fijian Resort★★★★**, owned and operated by the Shangri-La International Group. It has all the facilities you would expect of a first-class resort hotel, including diving.

The Fijian is on a small island-peninsula and has a west-facing beach, which gives it a considerable advantage over other resorts on this coast (including the Hyatt) where the south-facing beaches are generally poor and move often than not diabolical.

The two newest and smartest resorts on Viti Levu, the Regent of Fiji and the recently completed Sheraton, share Denarau beach just outside Nadi on the west coast. Unfortunately the beach is terrible and, even if they do import several tons of fine white sand as planned, I suspect that it is much too close to nearby industrial facilities for the sea ever to be completely clean.

There is one huge, spectacular natural beach on Viti Levu, which is Natandola. Twenty-seven miles/43 km eastwards from Nadi, Natandola is a good beach for picnics and body-surfing but it has a terrible reputation for thefts, as I discovered after my hire car was broken into here. If you're visiting for the day, don't leave valuables unattended in your car.

For back-packers the best hotel on the south coast is the **Hideaway Resort ★** . The beach isn't exactly what you expect of the South Pacific but you can dive and surf at the Hideaway and it's relatively easy to reach from the airport. The Tubakula Beach Resort (near Sigatoka) has also been recommended.

If you've got more time, genuine dream beaches and cheap, locally-run bungalows can be found on the island of **Nananu-I-Ra★★★★★**, a short boatride off the north coast. I have also heard good reports about Kandavu, an island 55 miles/90 km south of Viti Levu, which is close to the famous Astrolabe Reef. Kandavu has budget accommodation, camping, good snorkelling and diving facilities.

Many of Fiji's most successful tourist resorts are in the Mamanuthas, a group of islands to the west of Viti Levu. Most are family-oriented and the beaches are a considerable improvement to those on Viti Levu.

Beachcomber and Treasure Islands★★★★ are twin resorts just a few minutes apart. While Treasure is similar to other mainstream family-oriented resorts here, Beachcomber is the only island in the Mamanuthas specifically aimed at a younger crowd. This dot in the ocean has quite a reputation as a party island (it's sort of a cross between Great Keppel and a Maldivian atoll, if you can imagine that) and it has dormitory accommodation as well as the usual beach cottages.

Mana**** is the biggest resort but with four beaches on the island it's by no means crowded. In the bay at **Malololailai***** there are two beach hotels, Musket Cove and the Plantation Resort. Nearby Club Naitasi is one of the smaller resorts, good value for watersports and the only island with para-sailing, but I found it too claustraphobic.

Other resorts in the Mamanuthas not covered here include Castaway, Matamamanoa and Turtle Island.

You can dive from most islands in this group. The surrounding reefs vary widely in quality but there are good facilities for beginners or qualified divers who want a combined diving/family holiday. Snorkellers might be lucky enough to come across exceptionally beautiful areas of shallow coral such as Sunflower Reef near Malololailai.

The top diving near Viti Levu is around Beqa (pronounced Benga) Island and Lagoon, an atoll off the south coast with 40 miles/64 km of surrounding reef featuring lush displays of soft corals, gorgonians and black coral as well as abundant pelagics and reef fish. There are dozens of potentially exciting sites around Beqa and it's much more accessible than Fiji's more famous reefs in the northern group of islands.

Beqa is half-an-hour away by fast catamaran from the Pacific Harbour Resort, 28 miles/43 km west of Suva, and your options include staying at the Pacific Harbour Resort (expensive) or the nearby Christian Coral Camp (cheap) or coming out for the day from Suva. The cost of diving here is slightly higher than elsewhere in Fiji but it's worth it (contact: Beqa Divers, PO Box 777, Suva, tel: 361 088).

Fiji's second largest island is Vanua Levu. One of the best-known resorts here is Namale Plantation, which has an unusual beach framed by sculpted rocks. Vanua Levu's newest hotel is the Na Koro Resort in Savu Savu Bay. Na Koro has all the usual watersports and resort facilities as well as a PADI school and dive trips on board the 42 ft/13 m yacht *Walk Tall*. The beach is unfortunately not that good, but if you're passing through there is one particular location close to the resort, known as Fantasy Crack, where snorkellers will find a patch of those brilliantly c̶ʳ̶ ̶̶ed soft corals which divers spend so much time raving about in ̶ji. For some reason they're not normally found this close to the surface.

Beachcomber

South of Vanua Levu there is a small resort on the island of **Namena** which will appeal to wealthy back-to-nature freaks, and the surrounding reefs have the potential for good snorkelling and diving. Although only 15 miles/24 km from Vanua Levu, Namena has no regular transport links and you need to charter a yacht or seaplane to reach it.

The northern group of islands, a short flight away from Vanua Levu, is Fiji's best-known diving area. On **Taveuni★★** the diving is spectacular and options for accommodation include old-style plantation resorts, camping, or locally-run guest houses. The diving is worth the journey but don't come to Taveuni for the beaches.

The neighbouring islands of **Qamea★★★★★** and **Mataqi★★★★** have better beaches, with just one resort per island, and the potential for diving reefs of a similar calibre to Taveuni's. Although each is different in its own way, both of these islands are small and exclusive compared to mainstream beach resorts in the Mamanuthas.

Travelling around Fiji is enjoyable and easy, and it's one of the few Pacific countries where extensive island-hopping and adventure travel is a reality for even those on modest travel budgets.

GENERAL INFORMATION

Time
GMT + 12 hours

IDD code
679 + 5 or 6 digit number

Currency
Fiji dollar (F$)
UK£1 = F$2.6
US$1 = F$1.45

Hotels
Rates given don't include tax.
Single/double:
Deluxe: US$150/180
Expensive: US$60/90
Moderate: US$30/60
Budget: US$5/10

PUBLICATIONS
Blue Lagoons and Beaches – Fiji's Yasawa Islands
James Siers (Millwood Press 1985).
128pp. Glossy guide to this popular yacht cruising area.
Finding Fiji,
David Stanley (Moon Publications 1986). Paperback 127pp, £6.95/ US$6.95. Budget travel guide.

WEATHER
The climate is dry and comfortable during the southern hemisphere's winter from May to October. The wet season (summer) is from November to April, with the most rainfall occurring during January, February and March. Winter temperatures average 68-78°F/20-26°C, summer temperatures 76-86°F/24-30°C.

The best season for diving is from May to October, with peak visibility in September and October. During December the sea starts to warm up and
visibility deteriorates until March, when it begins to clear up again. Ocean temperatures average 78°F/25.5°C (winter), 82°F/28°C (summer).

The best sailing months are during the south-east trades from April/May through to October/November, with winds often reaching 20 knots/6 Beaufort plus. During these months it's possible for waves generated by high altitude storms from the south and south-west to be as big as those in Hawaii.

HEALTH
Fiji is free of most tropical diseases, including malaria. No inoculations are required. Water is safe to drink in all the resorts and cities.

VISAS
Onward tickets and passports valid for at least three months required. Visas are issued on arrival for stay of up to 30 days, extendable for up to six months.

TOURISTS BOARDS
Head Office: Suva, tel: 22867; Representatives: UK, tel: (01) 242 3131; Los Angeles, tel: (213) 417 2234; Sydney, tel: (02) 358 4055; Tokyo, tel: (03) 587 2038.

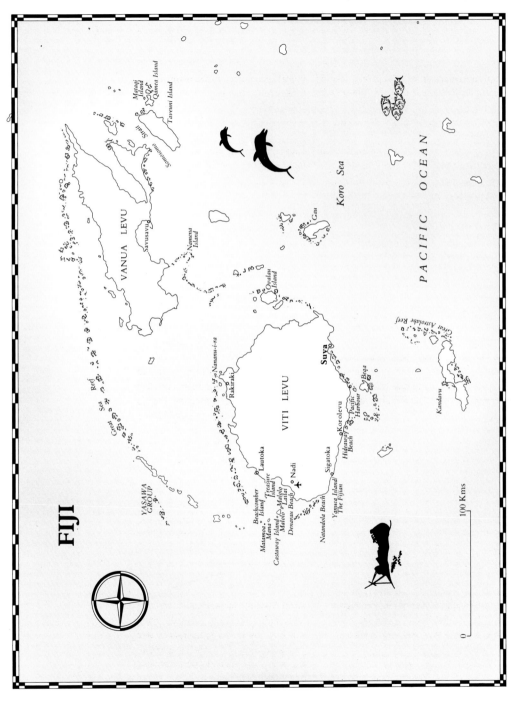

FIJI

PACIFIC OCEAN

Koro Sea

VANUA LEVU

Somosomo Strait

Matagi Island
Qamea Island
Taveuni Island

Savusavu

Namena Island

Ovalau Island

Gau

VITI LEVU

Nananu-i-ra

Rakiraki

Great Sea Reef

YASAWA GROUP

Lautoka

Beachcomber Island
Treasure Island
Matamoa Island
Castaway Island
Mana
Malolo Malolo
Lailai

Denarau Beach

Nadi

Sigatoka

Natandola Beach

Yanuca Island
The Fijian

Korolevu

Hideaway Beach

Pacific Harbour

Suva

Beqa

Great Astrolabe Reef

Kandavu

100 Kms

0

FIJIAN RESORT

The Fijian is an enormous, rambling resort spread over 105 acres/42 hectares of tropical gardens on its own private island (Yanuca) connnected to the mainland by a causeway. Because the hotel's beach faces west rather than south it is the most protected and therefore one of the most pleasing beaches on this coast. The hotel also has two swimming pools and the large, sheltered lagoon is ideal for watersports.

The resort is one of several on this coast where qualified or potential divers are taken care of by the friendly, professional staff of Dennis Beckman's Seasports. Most dives take place on the gentle slope of the outer reef and although it is neither as dramatic as the sheer walls further up the coast at the Hyatt nor as extensive as the untouched reefs of Beqa, the diving here is good value and certification courses are reasonably priced.

Owned and operated by Shangri-La International, the Fijian has a wide range of activities on tap (including golf and tennis with resident pros) and, however you choose to spend your time here, the cheerful, attentive staff take good care of you.

SNORKELLING★★★

The shallow reefs directly off the beach have been badly damaged by snorkellers and people going reef-walking but fish populations seem to be quite healthy. Amongst the more colourful small reef tropicals to look out for here are the splendid yellow, orange and black ornate butterflyfish, delicately-coloured moon wrasse, and the almost unbelievably cute yellow sweetlips. There are also graceful lionfish here too, which of course shouldn't be touched. There are other snorkelling locations nearby (such as Kaba Island) where the coral is less damaged and motorized long-boats make regular trips to these sites. **MSF**: free.

WATERSPORTS★★★★★

Good conditions for beginners wind-surfing inside the lagoon, tuition available. Hobie cat rentals. Dinghies and canoes free. Water ski-ing with tuition.

DIVING★★★

Dive sites on the outer reef are reached by a 20-minute boat ride. One of the most popular is Golden Reef, where they have been feeding fish (including the normally shy clown triggerfish) for several years. This is a 60-ft/18-m dive amidst massive colonies of table and plate corals, and common reef fish such as fusiliers and sergeant majors will mob you as you descend. Other popular sites include Barracuda Wall and the Pinnacles (the latter is a deep dive to 120 ft/36 m on the edge of the island shelf where it plunges off to 3,000 ft/900 m).

• *Dennis Beckman's Seasports*: One-tank dives F$50 (US$34) including equipment; PADI open-water certification F$237 (US$166). **A** PO Box 65, Korolevu, Fiji, tel: 50598.

BARS AND RESTAURANTS

Fijian, Indian, Chinese and European food, four restaurants, 24-hour room service, disco. Entertainment also includes regular *mekes* (Fijian dances), fire-walking performances and *lovos* (Fijian feasts).

ACCOMMODATION

• *The Fijian*: Deluxe/expensive **R**. All rooms have private balconies and sea views, and are comfortable and well-appointed. Twin rooms from F$135 (US$93), deluxe rooms and suites from F$170-260 (US$117-228), self-contained beach cottages from F$330 (US$228). **A** Private Mail Bag, Nadi airport, Fiji, tel: 50155. Reservations: UK, tel: (01) 581 4217 or (0345) 010 900.

ACCESS

Forty-five minutes from Nadi airport.

HIDEAWAY RESORT

Thirteen miles/20 km east of Sigatoka, the Hideaway is set amidst flourishing tropical gardens and although the beach isn't brilliant they do have a swimming pool. Free activities include snorkelling trips, guided reef walks and guided treks into the mountains.

There is a branch of Dennis Beckman's Seasports at the hotel for divers (see under the Fijian Resort for details).

For surfers Hideaway has a perfect right-hand break within an easy 330-ft/ 100-m paddle from the beach. The surf runs year round with the peak season between May and September, says Hideaway's manager Andrew Wade, adding that the reef is very shallow and you should be experienced.

Three Quarter Mile Beach,
Nananu-I-Ra

evening meal costs from F$20 (US$14). Entertainment includes regular *mekes* (Fijian dances), live bands, limbo-dancing, BBQ nights and *lovos* (Fijian feasts).

ACCOMMODATION

Hideaway: Moderate/budget **R**. Dormitory beds from F$10 (US$7), self-contained *bures* for up to three from F$70 (US$50), for up to six from F$92 (US$63). **A** PO Box 233, Sigatoka, tel: 50177. Reservations: UK, tel: (01) 828 4585; Australia, tel: (02) 902 700.

BARS AND RESTAURANTS

Sociable bar and large dining hall. Full breakfast and four-course à la carte

ACCESS

One hour from Nadi airport.

NANANU-I-RA

Just 3 miles/4 km off-shore from the burnished hills of Viti Levu's north coast, Nananu-I-Ra is the best island to head for if you're travelling around Viti Levu and looking for relaxation on some real South Pacific-style beaches.

The jumping-off point for Nananu-I-Ra is the town of Rakiraki. Although you can get to Rakiraki from either Suva or Lautoka, the road from Lautoka is sealed for most of the way and therefore much quicker whether you're travelling by local bus or hire car.

A 10-minute boat ride from the mainland brings you to Nananu-I-Ra's main beach, where there are several guest houses. Just a minute's walk away on the other side of the island is Three Quarter Mile Beach, strewn with coconut husks and backed by a long line of sea-grape bushes and palm trees. Yet another practically empty beach is within 10 minutes' walk – you won't find beaches like this on mainland Viti Levu. The only drawback to this particular slice of heaven is that on most beaches swimming is only possible at high tide.

SNORKELLING★★
In the main bay the reef is just a short swim through the boat channel with a small wall dropping off to right and left. Moorish idols, butterflyfish and blue angelfish are amongst the more colourful small reef fish you'll find scooting about between the corals. On Three Quarter Mile beach there is a gentle slope with small coral heads scattered over the seabed.

BARS AND RESTAURANTS
All the beach cottages are self-catering, so bring supplies from Rakiraki before catching a boat. Once on the island, boats go daily for shopping.

ACCOMMODATION
• *Bethams Beach Cottages*: Moderate/budget **R**. Self-contained cottages on the beach, single/double from F$20/25 (US$14/17), extra person F$5 (US$3.50). Cottages for up to seven people from F$7.50 (US$5) per person. **A** PO Box 1244, Suva, tel: Suva 362 892, 382 013; Rakiraki 94320.
• *Nananu Beach Cottages*: Moderate/

budget **R**. Self-contained cottages from single/double $F30/35 (US$20/24). **A** PO Box 40, Rakiraki, tel: Suva 22672; Rakiraki 94174.
• *Charlie MacDonald's*: Budget **R**. Shared bungalows from F$6 (US$4) per person, on the hillside overlooking the beach.
• *Kon Tiki Island Lodge*: Budget **R**. On its own beach with the advantage of day-long swimming. Twin bungalows from F$17 (US$12), shared dormitory from F$8.50 (US$6) per person. **A** PO Box 87, Rakiraki, tel: Nadi 72844, Rakiraki 94174.

ACCESS
Rakiraki is just over 60 miles/100 km from Lautoka and 100 miles/160 km from Suva. Express buses take two hours from Lautoka, up to three-and-a-half hours from Suva. In Rakiraki, contact Empire taxis, tel: 94275 or 94320, who will book a boat (this costs around F$18/US$12 per group). Coach and ferry transfers from Nadi cost F$20 (US$14) per person through PVV Tours, tel:70600.

Diving Beqa

177

BEACHCOMBER and TREASURE ISLANDS

Originally known as Tai (Beachcomber) and Elevuka (Treasure), these twin islands are just off-shore from Lautoka. Beachcomber, which is the smaller of the

two, is geared towards a young crowd and has a large, sand-floored bar with live bands at night. Facilities are simple (no hot-water showers) and this is not the island to choose if you're looking for acres of space or privacy on the beach. It's very small and, I would imagine, quite crowded when full. Treasure is larger and more expensive to stay on, with facilities aimed at families and an older clientele.

There is a PADI dive centre on Beachcomber, good value if you're considering learning to dive (people staying on Treasure can get to the dive centre in five minutes by boat) but these aren't the islands to choose if diving is your main motivation. However, the High Chief (Tui Vuda) who owns both islands has renounced his traditional fishing rights around them and the National Trust of Fiji are hoping to create Fiji's first national marine park here.

WATERSPORTS★★★★★
On Beachcomber windsurfing, sailing, canoes and water ski-ing cost extra. On Treasure Island all watersports are free but water ski-ing is extra. Para-sailing.

DIVING★
On the south side of Beachcomber there is a shallow underwater trail between the coral heads, suitable for novices.
● *Dive Centre (Fiji)*: Beach dive F$30 (US$20), boat dive F$35 (US$24), two-tank boat dive F$55 (US$38), all inclusive of equipment. PADI open-water certification F$250 (US$172). **A** PO Box 13416, Suva, tel: 314 599.

BARS AND RESTAURANTS
On Beachcomber meals are included in the daily tariff, with plentiful buffets. Treasure Island has an à la carte restaurant.

ACCOMMODATION
● *Beachcomber*: Moderate **R**. Dormitory beds with shared bathrooms from F$55 (US$39) per person, rooms with shared bathrooms from F$109 (US$77), self-contained *bures* from F$124 (US$100). All rates are fully inclusive of meals but not drinks.
● *Treasure*: Expensive. Self-contained *bures* from F$150 (US$105) per day. **A** PO Box 364, Lautoka, Fiji, tel: 61500. Reservations: UK, tel: (01) 828 4585; USA, tel: (800) 624 6163; Australia, tel: (008) 221 318.

ACCESS
Boats leave Lautoka twice daily and take 75-90 minutes, F$50 (US$35) rtn including transport from Nadi area hotels or Nadi Airport.

MANA ISLAND

Twenty miles/32 km off-shore from Viti Levu, Mana is the oldest and, some would say, still the best of the Mamanuthas resorts. This well-managed resort has a good range of facilities and activities for families (kids can learn to net fish Fijian-style, amongst other things) and all the rooms have recently been refurbished. There is a fully-equipped, Australian-run dive shop and the island has two huge sandy beaches (one on each side, so there's always somewhere sheltered).

WATERSPORTS****

Windsurfers, canoes, and Hobie cats free, water ski-ing extra.

DIVING***

At Mana resident instructor Graham Deanes and Fijian dive guide Api are on hand to show you the best that the surrounding reefs have to offer. Forests of gorgonians, caves, soft corals and deep walls on the outer reef frequented by pelagics are just some of the features of the diving here. A good place to learn.

• *Mana Divers*: One-tank boat dive F$30 (US$20); FAUI open-water certification F$250 (US$172). Dive packages through Mana Divers, Sydney, tel: (02) 212 3833; or Dive Adventures Australia, tel: (02) 233 5976.

BARS AND RESTAURANTS

Three restaurants including a new Japanese one, the *Suehiro*. Beach bar with daily BBQ. Resident band, weekly *mekes* and Polynesian dance nights.

ACCOMMODATION

• *Mana Island*: Expensive **R**. Comfortable *bures* with fans and fridges from F$130 (US$90) per double. Tennis, swimming pool. **A** PO Box 610, Lautoka, Fiji, tel: 61210, 61333. Reservations: UK, tel: (01) 828 4585; Australia, tel: (02) 233 5967, (02) 212 2833.

ACCESS

Speedboat launch leaves the Regent Beach twice daily (F$44/US$30 o/w). Ten minutes' flight by Turtle Island Airways seaplane from the dock near Nadi Airport, tel: 72988.

MALOLOLAILAI

Malololailai ('little Malolo') is just across the causeway from Malolo, the biggest island in the Mamanuthas. There are two resorts on the island, one either side of the airstrip, both sharing a scenic setting in Malololailai's westward-facing bay.

The Plantation Island Resort is the bigger of the two properties, with a good location on a fine white sandy beach which curves endlessly around the island to the east. At Musket Cove low tides leave guests high and dry by several hundred yards, but it's not far to walk around the end of the airport runway if you want to go for a swim. Malololailai is big enough to allow for some long walks.

The diving at both resorts is run by Aquatrek, who specialize in certifications. Some of the nearby reefs have been badly damaged by cyclones and crown of thorns starfish but the diving here is fairly reasonable.

SNORKELLING***

There is some very fine snorkelling in the vicinity of the island, such as Sunflower Reef, a short boatride off-shore, which is as perfect an underwater landscape of overlapping hard corals as you're likely to find. **MSF**: Free.

WATERSPORTS***

At Plantation an activity pass costs F$36 (US$25) per week and covers windsurfers, Hobie cats, sailing dinghies, kayaks and water ski-ing. At Musket Cove windsurfing and water ski-ing are complimentary but dependent on the tides.

DIVING**

• *Aquatrek*: One-tank boat dive F$45 (US$31) including equipment; PADI certifications F$310 (US$213). **A** PO Box 9176, Nadi Airport, Fiji, tel: 72333. Reservations: USA, tel: (415) 728 5955; Australia, tel: (02) 371 0731.

BARS AND RESTAURANTS
At Plantation there is a restaurant,

snack bar and poolside bar . Musket Cove is the livelier and cheaper of the two resorts and has a band playing six nights a week. All *bures* at Musket

Cove are self-catering (there is a small general store on the beachfront).

ACCOMMODATION
● *Plantation*: Expensive. Twin beachfront *bures* from F$195 (US$137), garden *bures* from F$170 (US$120), standard rooms from F$145 (US$100). They also have comfortable dormitories with beds from F$20 (US$14). Tennis, small swimming pool. **A** PO Box 9176, Nadi Airport, Fiji, tel: 72333. Reservations: UK, tel: (01) 828 4585.
● *Musket Cove*: Expensive **R**. Beachfront *bures* from single/double F$85/105 (US$58/72), standard *bures* from F$75/95 (US$51/65) deluxe villas from F$150/US$103. Rates include free air transfers from Nadi for stays of six nights or more. Swimming pool. **A** Private Mail Bag, Nadi Airport, Fiji, tel: Nadi 72077, 72488, Malololailai 62215, 62878.

ACCESS
Ten minutes by air from Nadi Airport, seven flights daily on Sunflower Airlines. One-and-a-half hours by boat from the Regent Hotel Beach.

NAMENA ISLAND

Small resort on a wild, untouched island 15 miles/24 km south of the Vanua Levu coast. The island has jungle trails, six beaches, free snorkelling and windsurfing.

There are shallow reefs just off-shore for snorkelling and the whole island is surrounded by a barrier reef with deeper drop-offs for divers. Divers must bring their own regs, BCs, and gauges (one-tank dives cost F$36 (US$25) including tanks, weights, boat and guide). The best time for diving here is December, January, February and March, they say.

Turtles nest on the main beach by the resort from December to January, and you can watch the hatchlings struggle from their nests and dash for the waves during February and March. Red-foot boobies nest from April and May onwards, with their eggs hatching in June.

I haven't visited Namena but considering its isolated position and the care which I'm told is taken of the surrounding reefs, it should be worth a try for diving and snorkelling (if you can afford it).

ACCOMMODATION

• *Moody's Namena*: Expensive. Self-contained *bures* with hardwood floors and woven bamboo walls, from single/double F$217/275 (US$150/190) including all meals (US$600 deposit required). Guest numbers are limited to 8-10 people, resort closed 15 March to 15 May annually. **A** Private Mail Bag, Suva, radiophone via Suva operator: 906 388M Namena Island.

ACCESS

Sunflower Airlines flies from Nadi to Savusavu twice daily, and from here you have to charter a yacht (one hour under power, four hour's sailing) or a seaplane. Regular seaplane charters every Saturday cost F$260 (US$180) per person (min three).

TAVEUNI

Arriving in a light plane on Taveuni's grass airstrip you soon realize that this is a different Fiji to the one most visitors see on Viti Levu. Gone are the endless fields of sugar cane, the hustle and bustle of Suva and Nadi, the duty-free shops and the traffic. Driving along the unsurfaced road which snakes along the coastline, there's nothing in sight here except hillsides blanketed with coconut plantations, sloping off gently into the sea. Deep in the interior, rare flowers such as the Tajimancia can be found, and treks into the hills of Fiji's 'Garden Isle' are popular.

For divers, however, Taveuni is primarily the jumping-off point for the 19-mile/30-km long Rainbow Reef and one of Fiji's most talked about dive sites, the Great White Wall. The diving season is from April to December.

DIVING★★★

Iridescent soft corals are the main drawcard of Taveuni diving, as well as abundant fish. There are around a dozen regularly-visited spots on Rainbow Reef (including Blue Ribbon Eel Reef, Cabbage Patch and Pandora's Box) but by far the most spectacular is the Great White Wall itself. On this dive you enter a tunnel at 40 ft/12 m, emerging on the drop-off at 80 ft/24 m to find it solidly covered in soft white corals feeding in the currents. This is a unique and quite spectacular sight, resembling a massive field of snow-drops tipped over on its side. The wall plunges on down to around 240 ft/73 m but when I dived here our contemplation of this extraordinary mass of vibrant white coral was interrupted by a too-curious mako, so we slid back to the top of the reef. Here, the soft corals were no longer white but a fabulous *mélange* of purples, mauves and blacks, a scene of untouched primal beauty no less impressive than the White Wall itself.

• *Dive Taveuni*: Run by a laconic Kiwi, Ric Cammick. Tanks, back-pack and weightbelts are provided but no hire gear is available, so you must bring a reg, wetsuit, fins and mask. Ric's big cat (the *Lelewai II*) is comfortable and spacious and most dive sites are within half-an-hour's boat ride. Two-tank dives cost F$94 (US$65). Dive packages through Tropical Adventures in the USA, tel: (800) 247 3483. **A** c/o Matei Post Office, Taveuni, Fiji, tel: 406-M.

Malololailai

ACCOMMODATION

• *Maravu Plantation Resort*: Expensive/moderate **R**. Eight modern *bures* set amidst a working copra plantation. Free horse-riding and windsurfing. Mountain treks and jeep safaris. Five minutes' walk from the beach, swimming pool. Friendly management, bar, restaurant. Single/double from F$50/90 (US$35/60). **A** c/o Matei Post Office, Taveuni, Fiji, tel: 401-A.

● *Dive Taveuni*: Expensive. Comfortable *bures* on the cliffs overlooking the Somosomo Strait. Small beach at the bottom of the cliff. No separate dining room, meals are taken in the Cammicks' home: boarding school atmosphere' complained one dive magazine, and it is true that the Maravu resort is more sociable. Accommodation costs F$102 (US$70) per person inclusive of meals and transfers. **A** c/o Matei Post Office, Taveuni, Fiji, tel: 406-M.

● *Matei Plantation Lagoon Resort*: Moderate. Over the road from the airport, bungalows from F$60 (US$42). **A** c/o Matei Post Office, Taveuni, Fiji, tel: 87 401G.

● Camping: Divers can camp with the hospitable and friendly Valentine family on the beach five minutes' walk from Dive Taveuni (from F$3/US$2).

● *Kaba's Motel and Guest House*: In the town of Somosomo, 30 minutes from the airport. Self-catering rooms from single/double F$12/20 (US$8/14), new motel section from single/double F$25/30 (US$17/20). Dive Taveuni will collect from here. **A** Box 4, Taveuni, tel: 87, extn 233.

ACCESS
Sunflower Airlines flies daily from Nadi (90 minutes) and Savusavu (25 minutes); Fiji Air flies daily from Suva (45 minutes).

QAMEA BEACH CLUB

One step beyond Taveuni, Qamea (the Q is pronounced as a G) is even more remote from the civilized world. It is not, however, remote from civilized comforts, since the island is home to the small but stylish Qamea Beach Club run by Americans Frank and Jo Kloss.

Ploughing across the channel from Taveuni in a small boat, your first glimpse of the resort will be the enormously tall roof of a *bure kalou* nestled into the tropical foliage on the hillside. A *bure kalou* is traditionally a Fijian chief's house but here it serves as bar, restaurant and social focus for the resort instead, with voluble hostess Jo Kloss in the chief's role.

Built from lacquered bamboo and thatch, the *bure kalou* is a fine setting for the memorable meals which they somehow manage to conjure up in this remote spot.

The beach isn't brilliant for swimming, although there is always one channel which is swimmable on either tide.

WATERSPORTS**
Windsurfers, Hobies and outriggers complimentary.

DIVING****
The shallow- to medium-depth reefs in

the immediate vicinity of Qamea are typical of diving in the Northern Group, with the potential for untouched areas similar to neighbouring Taveuni. There are never more than 10 divers at the Beach Club at any one time and the staff here offer their usual attentive service when it comes to transporting and rinsing gear. One-tank dive F$58 (US$40), two-tanks F$80 (US$55). PADI/CMAS certifications available.

BARS AND RESTAURANTS
The *lali* (Fijian drum) summons guests like bees to the hive around the *bure kalou* at meal times. Superb food .

ACCOMMODATION
• *Qamea Beach Club*: Deluxe **R**. Ten spacious *bures*, all beach-facing, with lacquered bamboo interiors, tiled bathrooms, king-size beds, fans, fridges, and tea and coffee facilities. Single/ double F$218/247 (US$150/170). Dive packages US$170 per person double occupancy including food, accommodation, transfers from Taveuni airport and two dives per day. **A** PO Taveuni, Fiji, tel: 87 and ask for 220 Taveuni. Dive packages through Tropical Adventures, USA, tel: (800) 247 3483. Reservations: UK, tel: (0345) 010900.

ACCESS
See under Taveuni (page 181). Transfers from Taveuni (taxi and boat) cost US$25 rtn per person.

MATAQI ISLAND

Six miles/10 km off the coast of Taveuni, Mataqi is the next island on past Qamea. The resort is unsophisticated compared to its neighbour at Qamea but that's part of the attraction: set in a coconut grove on the edge of the beach, it is simple and low key. Mataqi has a good beach and the island's 240 acres can be explored on horseback or on foot.

Noel Douglas and his family have been on the island for five generations and they originally ran it as a fishing camp: diving is a new activity here but the nearby 16 mile/25 km-long Heemskercq Reef has enormous potential and is so far almost totally unexplored. The Douglas' large, comfortable twin-engined diesels (the *Lady Christene* and the *Chicane*) mean short journeys to dive sites.

WATERSPORTS★★★
Windsurfers, Hobie cats and Fijian canoes complimentary.

BARS AND RESTAURANTS
Plentiful, tasty food in outdoor setting.

ACCOMMODATION
• *Mataqi Island*: Expensive. **R**. Simple *bures* underneath the palm trees. Single/double from F$90/130 (US$62/90), meal plan F$49 (US$34), per person per day. Dive packages from single/ double F$135/230 (US$93/160), includes accommodation, weights tanks, two boat-dives per day and unlimited shore diving. **A** PO Box 83, Waiyevo, Taveuni, Fiji, tel: Taveuni 87-260. Reservations: Suva, tel: 27384. Dive packages through Aquarius Dive Travel in Australia, tel: (008) 338 409.

ACCESS
See under Taveuni (page 181). Mataqi is a further 30-40 minutes from Taveuni by boat (F$30/US$20 rtn).

Cook Islands

Diving Rarotonga

Almost at the centre of the South Pacific's Polynesian triangle, the 15 Cook Islands are scattered over two million square kilometres of ocean. Although there are regular airlinks with Australia, New Zealand, Fiji, Hawaii, Samoa and Tahiti, tourism in the Cooks is still in its infancy.

'Visit Heaven while you're still on Earth' urges the publicity, omitting to mention that you need a pre-paid reservation. Altogether there are only enough hotel rooms for a thousand people here and it's not good enough just to give the name of a hotel when you land at the airport (unlike the Seychelles, which also officially requires pre-booked accommodation, where you can get away with doing just that).

A substantial number of Round-the-World travellers stop off here on their way across the Pacific. Quality self-catering rooms cost around NZ$30 (US$20) per person and there are a number of locally-run lodgings where you can stay for much less. Compared to Tahiti these islands are good value for money, but it's not as cheap here as it is in Fiji.

The largest island in the group, Rarotonga, is where most visitors end up staying. Rarotonga is a scenic, mountainous island with just one road which runs all the way around its 18-mile/32-km circumference.

The main township of Avarua is in the north of the island and although there are numerous resorts on the north and north-west coasts, most of the beaches on this side of the island were whipped away by Hurricane Sally in 1987.

The only beaches which are left are in the south, between **Muri Beach★★★★★** and the **Rarotongan★★**. Near Muri Beach there are a number of small hotels and the Rarotongan is the country's main resort.

Rarotongan is small enough to whizz round on a moped in under an hour and, apart from trekking into the mountains, there's not much to do here except laze around and let the world slip by.

The next most popular island is **Aitutaki**, an hour's flight away, yet one stage further from civilization. The beaches here are extremely disappointing but this is compensated for by the fact that Aitutaki is surrounded by a series of stunning little off-shore islands (known as *motus*) which you can visit on day-trips. For many visitors a *motu* trip will provide them with their most vivid memories of the South Pacific.

Very few people venture further than these two islands.

Muri Beach

On Rarotonga the damage wrought by Hurricane Sally has been quickly repaired above water but the damage to the surrounding reefs will take longer to heal, largely because the hurricane more or less finished off the job started by a crown-of-thorns-starfish plague 10 years earlier. The island also relies heavily on nitrogen-based fertilizers and the run-off from agricultural land has further damaged the reefs. In addition, marine life has been heavily depleted by overfishing and spearfishing and this is one of the few countries in the world where dive operators allow people to spearfish on scuba. On Aitutaki the marine life is in slightly better shape, but only just. There are two marine parks in the Cook Islands but they are so remote you need a yacht to get to them. Although

Muri lagoon

185

the visibility is often exceptional, there's not a lot here for divers and snorkellers. Fiji is a better choice.

Cook Islanders are staunchly Christian and toplessness is not permitted on the beaches.

GENERAL INFORMATION

Time
GMT – 10 hours

IDD code
682 + 5 digit number

Currency
New Zealand dollar (NZ$)
UK£1 = NZ$2.8
US$1 = NZ$1.5

Hotels
Single/double:
Deluxe: US$87/150
Expensive: US$43/63
Moderate: US$33/37
Budget: US$8/23

PUBLICATIONS
The South Pacific Handbook
David Stanley (Moon Publications, fourth edition, 1988). Paperback, 578pp, US$13.95.
Rarotonga & The Cook Islands – a travel survival kit
Tony Wheeler (Lonely Planet 1986). Paperback, 117pp, £4.95 US$7.95.

WEATHER
The best time to visit is between March and November. The rainy season is from December to March. Seasonal variations in temperature, humidity and rainfall are slight: from June to October the average temperature is 70°F/22°C, from December to March 78°F/26°C. The visibility for diving and snorkelling is best from June to October.

HEALTH
No inoculations required. No major health hazards.

VISAS
Pre-booked accommodation and onward flight required. A 31-day visa is granted on arrival, can be renewed three times up to a total of four months. Applications must be made 14 days before expiry of the previous visa.

TOURIST BOARDS
Head Office: Rarotonga, tel: 29435. Representatives: Sydney, tel: (02) 232 7499; Auckland, tel: (09) 794 314. Elsewhere: Air New Zealand, Ansett, Cook Islands International or Polynesian Airlines offices.

MURI BEACH

On the far side of the island from Avarua and the airport, Muri beach fronts on to a shallow lagoon with the islands of Koromiri, Taakaoka, Oneroa and Motutapu a few hundred yards off-shore inside the reef. The island on the right, Taakaoka, is a volcanic plug and hence doesn't have any beach. The first island on the left, Koromiri, is a popular lazing and picnic spot since its beach is protected, and is warmer and less windy than the main beach when the south-east trades blow during the winter.

This is undoubtedly Rarotonga's best beach. The lagoon positively invites you to take to the water and there are a dozen different ways of doing so.

COOK ISLANDS

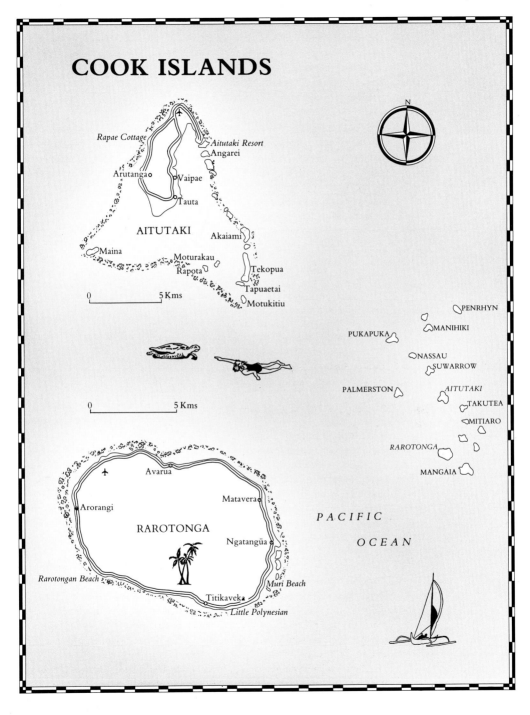

Rapae Cottage

Aitutaki Resort
Angarei

Arutanga

Vaipae

Tauta

AITUTAKI

Akaiami

Maina

Moturakau
Rapota

Tekopua

0   5 Kms

Tapuaetai
Motukitiu

PENRHYN

MANIHIKI

PUKAPUKA

NASSAU
SUWARROW

0   5 Kms

PALMERSTON

AITUTAKI

TAKUTEA

MITIARO

RAROTONGA

Avarua

MANGAIA

Matavera

Arorangi

RAROTONGA

PACIFIC

Ngatangüa

OCEAN

Rarotongan Beach

Muri Beach

Titikaveka

Little Polynesian

At the centre of Muri Beach is the Rarotonga Sailing Club which has a comprehensive and well-maintained range of watersports equipment for hire to day visitors or guests staying nearby. The Sailing Club (which is open every day except Sunday) is flanked by a new resort, the Pacific, to the left and the Muri Beachcomber to the right: further on (2 miles/3km away) are the Little Polynesian and Moana Sands, both of which have similar beaches.

SNORKELLING

Most of the coral in the lagoon is dead. If you want to have a look around underwater anyway, the Sailing Club has two Aquascooters which haul snorkellers through the water at about four knots but are notoriously unreliable.

Snorkelling, Aitutaki

WATERSPORTS★★★★★

The Sailing Club has a huge range of equipment including outriggers, kayaks, dinghies, canoes and sailboards (long boards, semi- and fullfloating short boards and F2 Strata with a choice of sails). No cat sailing – the lagoon is too shallow.

BARS AND RESTAURANTS

The Sailing Club has a bar with balcony overlooking the lagoon and islands serving snacks and drinks from 10 a.m. to 6 p.m. Portofinos Restaurant has opened a new branch in the old Marine Zoo next door, and there are also facilities in the hotels listed below.

ACCOMMODATION

● *Muri Beachcomber Motel*: Expensive **R**. Next door to the Sailing Club, pool. Self-contained units from singles/double NZ$75/90 (US$50/60). **A** PO Box 379, Rarotonga, tel: 21022.

● *The Pacific*. Deluxe **R**. New resort. Self-contained one- and two-bedroom suites with kitchens from NZ$110 (US$73). Tennis, swimming pool, free windsurfing. **A** PO Box 790, Rarotonga, tel: 20427. Reservations: New Zealand, tel (074) 89709.

● *Little Polynesian*: Expensive **R**. Two miles/3 km from Muri Beach, on its own well-kept beach. Small pool. Self-catering rooms from NZ$80 (US$53). **A** PO Box 366, Rarotonga, tel: 24280.

● *Moana Sands*: Expensive **R**. Next to the Little Polynesian. Self-catering rooms from NZ$95 (US$63). Good beach. **A** PO Box 1007, Rarotonga, tel: 26189.

ACCESS

Six miles/10km from town around the north coast road, buses run to and from town every hour.

RAROTONGAN BEACH

The Rarotongan is the Cooks' top resort hotel, although modest by international standards, and the beach isn't as good as Muri Beach or those near it. The hotel has a busy activities programme with South Pacific touches you might not find elsewhere (lessons in island dancing, shell-hunting, coconut-husking and reef walks during which they'll show you local ways of eating seafoods).

A few minutes down the road from the hotel is the Rarotonga Dive Hostel, aptly known as 'the Dive', and if you're staying there you can use the Rarotongan's beach.

SNORKELLING

Despite following every tip-off and recommendation neither I nor any of the other numerous aquatic-fanatics at the Dive Hostel could find anything underwater around here which merited the trouble of getting wet.

WATERSPORTS★

Canoes and outriggers free to guests at the Rarotongan. Windsurfers are also available but using them in front of the hotel is tricky because of reef and rocks in the lagoon: Muri Beach is better for windsurfing.

Avarua. One-tank dive NZ$35 (US$24). No certifications. Good selection of reasonably-priced diving equipment. **A** PO Box 38, Rarotonga, tel: 21873.

● *Greg Wilson*: NAUI certification courses NZ$330 (US$220). Bring a medical with you from overseas (also applies to Aitutaki). **A** Tropical Garden Bar, tel: 22483, 20501.

BARS AND RESTAURANTS

Two restaurants in the Rarotongan, regular floor shows. The evening's entertainment on Raro revolves around

DIVING

All dives are boat dives from Avarua Harbour – no shore diving.

● *Dive Rarotonga*: Next to the Ministry of Public Works on the main road out of

set nights at various bars: Polly's on Wednesdays, for instance, when a big Polynesian lady rips open coconuts with her teeth, the Banana Court for late nights on Fridays, and so on.

Little Polynesian Beach

ACCOMMODATION

• *The Rarotongan*: Deluxe. Doubles from NZ$145-165 (US$97-110). **A** PO Box 103, Rarotonga, tel: 25800. Reservations: UK, tel: (0420) 88724.

• *Dive Hostel*: Budget shared rooms from NZ$12.50 (US$8.50). Heavily-booked – write to Barry and Shirley Hill at Dive Raro well in advance if possible. **A** Dive Rarotonga, PO Box 38, Rarotonga, tel: 21873.

ACCESS

Twenty minutes from the airport, hourly buses from town.

AITUTAKI

The Cook Islands' second major destination for visitors after Rarotonga, Aitutaki is a smaller, even less hurried version of the main island, if you can imagine that.

The beaches on Aitutaki itself are a write-off but the outlying *motus* (small uninhabited islands perched on the edge of the reef) are fabulous.

There are a handful of guest houses and two hotels on the main island. All the guest houses are clustered just outside the village of Aruntanga and the better of the two hotels is the Rapae Cottage, which is about half a mile/one km from the village. The government-run Aitutaki Resort Hotel, on the other side of the airport, is dreadful.

The lagoon around Aitutaki is so shallow in-shore that it's impossible to go swimming, so people tend to go out to the *motus* every day. Most excursions go to those on the east side of the lagoon – Akaiami, Tekopua, Moturakau, Rapota, Tapuaetai and Motukitiu. Tapuaetai ('One Foot') is the most popular and is one of the best for swimming, with a deep lagoon. Trips run by the Rapae Cottage and Josie's are good value and cost around NZ$20-25 (US$14-17) including lunch.

On the other side of the lagoon there is just one *motu* all on its own, Maina, and trips here are run by amiable young Captain Ben of Lagoon Sailing Tours, who sails out with a fleet of Hobie cats. Captain Ben's tours are more expensive (around NZ$55/US$37) but well worth it for the sumptuous feast of fresh fish and baked fruit provided for lunch on the beach. Any of these excursions can be booked at Maina Trader's on the way into the village. Sometimes locals on their way out fishing will drop you off on a *motu* with a few pineapples and coconuts, and pick you up later (the usual charge is around NZ$10-15 (US$7-10).

Like Rarotonga, Aitutaki shows a strong missionary influence. All the guest houses are run by either Mormons or Seventh Day Adventists (no smoking or drinking is allowed) and although the room prices include breakfast you have to bring your own tea or coffee! Aitutaki is extremely quiet – in fact it's so quiet that people have been known to run screaming on the first plane back to Rarotonga – but the *motus* are well worth the journey from Rarotonga, which has nothing to compare. Whatever you do, don't miss a trip to one of these little islands, surrounded by vanilla-coloured beaches and turquoise lagoons.

SNORKELLING★★★

Aitutaki is surrounded by a barrier reef and on most of the trips to the *motus* you'll be snorkelling on the inside of the wall, where the seabed is not more than 10-20 ft/3-6 m deep. Clams of every conceivable colour are clustered along the ridge walls, interspersed with small tube worms throwing out their spider-like webs to trap small planktonic animals around the clams. Large fish aren't abundant but the visibility is often exceptional and you should come across common reef fish such as Moorish idols, parrotfish, snapper, wrasse and so on.

It's also possible to snorkel on the drop-off on the outside of the reef where it arcs around the end of the airport runway in the north of the island. This is a favourite spot for local spear-fishermen hunting in the 30 ft-/9 m deep canyons that cut into the wall. Delicately coloured, white-spotted surgeonfish and the striking black-and-orange Achilles Tang (known locally as blood tail), both of which are spearfishing targets, inhabit the surge zone. If there's any swell you'll need diving gloves and wetsuit boots to get over the reef edge here and back in again – it can be tricky. An easier option is to locate the sandbar which runs out to the reef edge from directly in front of the Rapae Cottage Hotel and walk out across this. Once over the reef snorkel round to the harbour entrance about 300 yards to the left and you should find plenty of marine life.

A locally available map (NZ$6/US$4) of Aitutaki shows the location of coral ridges inside the lagoon if you want to explore elsewhere.

WATERSPORTS★★★
Lagoon Sailing Tours: Five Hobie cats (NZ$25/US$17/hr), tuition available. Windsurfers NZ$14/US$9/hr. A Opposite Aitutaki Scuba, tel: 197U.

DIVING★
A good place to learn – certifications are cheap. Most dives are on the northwest reef.
● Aitutaki Scuba: On the main road between the Rapae Cottage and the village. One-tank dive NZ$50 (US$33) including all equipment; NAUI open-water certification NZ$320 (US$214). A Neil Mitchell, Aitutaki.

BARS AND RESTAURANTS
There are just two restaurants here, one at the Rapae Cottage and the other at Big Jay's bar, over the road. Big Jay's has island-dancing on Thursdays, the Rapae Cottage on Fridays. Guest houses charge around NZ$10 (US$6.50) for an evening meal.

ACCOMMODATION
● The Rapae Cottage: Moderate R. Basic but comfortable, single/double NZ$50/55 (US$33/37). Tends to be heavily booked, reserve as far in advance as possible from Rarotonga.
● Budget guesthouses include Josie's, the Tiare Maori and Tom's Seaside Cottages, all of which provide simple rooms and shared bathrooms: singles/doubles around NZ$25/40 (US$17/27). When you book a flight to Aitutaki the airline will book your guest house.

ACCESS
Air Rarotonga, tel: 22888, and Cook Islandair, tel: 26304, both fly twice daily from Rarotonga (55 minutes) for around NZ$165 (US$110) rtn.

191

Tahiti

I t's easy to knock Tahiti: one travel industry boss went so far as to say that the arrival of a tourist here is purely accidental. Those visitors that do come here are chagrined to discover soon after they arrive that the fantasy of Tahiti turns out to be just that – a fantasy. The *Tahiti Sun Press* feels obliged to tell its readers that 'Tahiti occasionally has to be rudely reminded not to take too seriously its own tourist brochure descriptions about what life in paradise ought to be like as it desperately tries to get its struggling tourist development back on track.' Tourism in Tahiti is facing a crisis, says the paper. 'What separates the Tahiti of today from the promised tourist land of tomorrow looks more like a mine field than a gold-paved road to paradise.' The head of Club Med is reported as saying, 'the country is dirty, the people are inhospitable, the service is deplorable and the infrastructure is totally insufficient.'

Tahiti's negative image overseas has not been helped by the continued French nuclear-testing programme in the Tuamotus. After 20 years of testing on Muroroa, the atoll is badly cracked and leaking large amounts

Cook's Bay, Moorea

of radiation into the sea and the government has now had to transfer tests back to the original test site at Fangataufa, 25 miles/40 km away.

Given this official lack of concern for the marine environment perhaps it shouldn't come as a surprise to find tourist board literature which

says 'Come to Tahiti – jump in with a speargun.' This is an invitation for divers to take themselves off to another country, to spend their money elsewhere. High-performance spearguns are widely available in shops and spearfishing competitions (which devastate fish populations) take place regularly.

None the less, Tahiti is offered as a stop-over on many Round-the-World or cross-Pacific tickets and despite all these drawbacks it would be a shame not to take advantage and have a look around if you have the opportunity to do so, even at the cost of a large hole in your bank balance.

Most people tend to refer to this part of the world as 'Tahiti', a convention I have followed, but in fact Tahiti is just one island in the Society Islands group, which is one of five different archipelagos in French Polynesia (the other four are the Marquesas, the Gambiers, the Australs and the Tuamotus).

Most visitors arrive at Faaa International Airport on Tahiti, 20 minutes from the busy, cosmopolitan capital of Papeete. Jacques Cousteau visited French Polynesia as part of his five-year long 'Rediscovering the World' project and, having docked in Papeete, declared it dirty, polluted and crowded. You might well end up agreeing with him, although it also has to be said that the capital buzzes with vitality and the

193

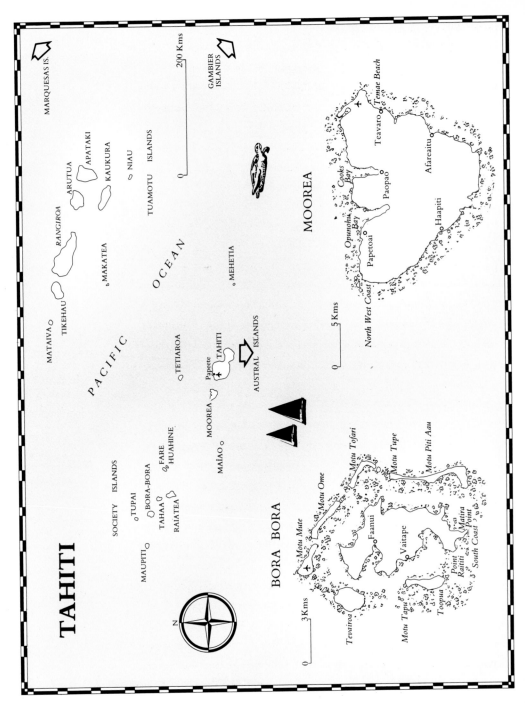

TAHITI

SOCIETY ISLANDS

MAUPITI

TUPAI

BORA-BORA

TAHAA

RAIATEA

FARE

HUAHINE

MAÏAO

MOOREA

TETIAROA

Papeete

TAHITI

AUSTRAL ISLANDS

MEHETIA

MAKATEA

MATAIVA

TIKEHAU

RANGIROA

ARUTUA

APATAKI

KAUKURA

NIAU

TUAMOTU ISLANDS

MARQUESAS IS.

GAMBIER ISLANDS

PACIFIC   OCEAN

200 Kms

0

N

3 Kms

0

BORA BORA

Motu Mute

Tevairoa

Motu Ome

Motu Tofari

Motu Tupe

Motu Piti Aau

Faanui

Vaitape

Motu Tapu

Toopua

Point Raititi

Matira Point

South Coast

MOOREA

Temae Beach

Teavaro

Afareaitu

Cooks Bay

Paopao

Haapiti

Opunohu Bay

Papetoai

North West Coast

5 Kms

0

restaurants are superb.

On the island of Tahiti there is only one beach which isn't black volcanic sand, and I wouldn't recommend staying at any of the resort hotels here if you can help it. Even for a short stop-over for a day or two, it's worth making the effort to get out to another island and for a holiday you definitely wouldn't want to be based on Tahiti.

The nearest island to Tahiti is Moorea, just seven minutes away by a regular air shuttle or under an hour by launch. Moorea is famous for the scenery of Cook's Bay, and for many people the jagged volcanic peaks and vertical cliffs surrounding this inlet represent the essence of the South Pacific. There are several hotels on the shoreline here (including the famous Club Bali Hai) where you can relax and absorb this photogenic panorama but regrettably beaches in Cook's Bay are either non-existent or small, man-made efforts.

Moorea's main beach area is on the **North-West Coast****. There are a number of beach resorts here, including a Club Med, and there is also a campsite. The snorkelling and diving are poor, but watersports such as windsurfing and water ski-ing are popular. This isn't an exceptional beach area but it's not bad if you're looking for a quick and easy escape from Papeete.

If you can afford it, a better choice would be **Temae Beach****** on the south side of Moorea. The Sofitel Kia Ora Moorea has this terrific white sand beach all to itself.

A new deluxe resort has recently been completed on Moorea, the Sofitel Tiare Moorea. This enormous, lavish complex comprises over 140 rooms and bungalows (including 50 overwater bungalows) but it appears to have been built facing a rather shallow mud flat. When I asked them about this they agreed that major engineering of the coastline might be necessary to create a proper beach, so until that is accomplished (and goodness knows how they'll do it) I suggest giving it a miss.

The next most popular island after Moorea is Bora Bora. Perhaps the most famous of them all, this island of legends was first settled by the Polynesians in the ninth century. Bora Bora is surrounded by a stunning lagoon with several smaller islands, most of them uninhabited, perched

195

on the outside. As elsewhere in the Pacific, these satellite islands on the fringing reef are known as *motus*.

The only beach area on Bora Bora (not counting the *motus*) is on the **South Coast**★★★★★+. There are one or two exceptional beach hotels here (principally the Hotel Bora Bora and the new Bora Bora Moana Beach) but you can also camp or stay in a moderately-priced family room. Accommodation here is in great demand and if possible I suggest making an advance reservation from Papeete or overseas. However, that isn't always practicable and many people end up staying in Vaitape and making their way out to the beach by day.

Bora Bora is the only place in the world where snorkellers can go and watch wild sharks being fed by hand, an event which definitely shouldn't be missed. In the tropics, shark-feeding is common for divers, but for snorkellers this is unique. The Shark's Breakfast takes place every morning on the far side of the Bora Bora lagoon and, once you've been ferried over by outrigger, the local lads will position everyone in the water behind a rope before they start dishing out the food. A mass of brightly-coloured reef tropicals cluster around and within a minute or two, the sharks have started to shoulder their way through. On most days, between six and twelve will turn up (mostly blacktips) swooping back and forth within yards of your mask.

The lagoonarium is another Bora Bora special. This is a private underwater park stocked with tropical fish, harmless nurse sharks and several types of rays including giant mantas. To be able to snorkel so close to giant mantas is a thrilling experience, a privilege worth travelling long distances for.

It doesn't make any difference where you're staying on Bora Bora in terms of going on these trips. Excursions to outlying *motus* are also highly recommended.

North West Coast, Moorea

There's more guaranteed action snorkelling on Bora Bora than there is diving. There is one dive operation on the island but due to cyclones and over-fishing, the diving is poor.

Experienced divers will be better off heading out to locations such as **Rangiroa**★★★★★+, a remote atoll in the Tuamotus. Rangiroa is an unusual and particularly interesting atoll and although the coral is poor, a profusion of marine life inhabits the nutrient-rich passes into and out of Rangiroa's gigantic lagoon. Cousteau was diving and filming here for exactly that reason (as well as to test the bathyscaphe before surveying Muroroa, also in the Tuamotus). Rangiroa has one first-class resort, the Kia Ora Rangiroa, and there are several other moderately-priced options for divers and anyone else who feels like escaping the world.

Manta ray, Bora Bora

Despite having described it as both remote and far flung, I must admit that Rangiroa is the same distance away from Tahiti as Bora Bora. The contrast, however, couldn't be greater, and there is a sense of isolation to Rangiroa which Bora Bora doesn't have. Because the atoll is so huge and so low-lying, you really do feel as if you're lost in the middle of millions of square miles of ocean. However, air links have recently improved considerably and there are now regular flights to Papeete (60 minutes) and Bora Bora (70 minutes), so it's easy enough to reach.

Neighbouring Manihi, a smaller atoll with just one hotel, is said to be similarly rich in marine life and also suitable for diving.

197

If you want to explore off the beaten track in the outlying archipelagos such as the Marquesas or the Gambiers you'll need plenty of time, since the main form of inter-island transport is copra supply boats. However, the tourist office (OPATTI) on the quayfront in Papeete can supply you with a list of boat timetables as well as details on family *pensions* on islands where they exist.

GENERAL INFORMATION

Time
GMT – 10 hours

IDD code
689 + 6 digit number

Currency
French Pacific Franc (CFP)
UK£1 = 180 CFP
US$1 = 105 CFP

Hotels
Rates don't include tax. The more expensive hotels in French Polynesia normally quote prices in US$ only. Single/double:
Deluxe: US$125/200
Expensive: US$75/120
Moderate: US$30/60
Budget: US$15/30

PUBLICATIONS
Sharks of Polynesia
R.H. Johnson (Les Editions du Pacifique, Papeete 1987). 170pp. Comprehensive, readable introduction to shark biology and behaviour, covers all species found in the tropical Pacific between the Cook Islands, Hawaii and French Polynesia. Particularly useful on shark encounters, 'shark sense' and countermeasures. Available locally in English and French for around 1,650 CFP (US$15).

South Pacific Handbook
David Stanley (Moon Publications, third edition, 1987). 580pp, US$13.95.

Underwater Guide to Tahiti,
R Bagnis, photographs by E Christian (Les Editions du Pacifique, Papeete 1985). 152 pp. A general guide to marine life, no specific information about diving or snorkelling sites.

WEATHER
The warm, humid season with the most rainfall is from November/December through to February/March. Temperatures average 81°F/27°C. From March/April through to October/November the climate is cool and dry, with average temperatures of around 75°F/24°C. The outlying atolls are generally cooler and less humid than mountainous islands such as Bora Bora and Moorea. For windsurfing the best time to visit is between June and September when the south-east trades are working.

HEALTH
Cholera and yellow fever vaccinations required if coming from an infected area, otherwise no inoculations required. French Polynesia is malaria-free and there are no major health hazards.

VISAS
Valid passports and onward tickets required. No visas required for citizens of the EEC, Australia and New Zealand for stays of up to three months. For most other countries (including North America) no visas are required for stays of up to one month but are mandatory for longer periods. Extensions for up to six or 12 months are possible.

TOURIST BOARDS
Head Office, Papeete, tel: 429 626; Los Angeles, tel: (213) 207 1919; Sydney, tel: (02) 235 0703; Tokyo, tel: (03) 586 6599; Paris, tel: (01) 46 34 50 59.

MOOREA: NORTH-WEST COAST

Moorea's main resort area, consisting of a series of beaches facing the off-shore islands (*motus*) on the outside of the lagoon. There is a Club Med here, several medium-grade beach hotels, and a handful of 'budget' bungalows.

Club Med is roughly in the middle of the beach area. With over 700 people squeezed onto a small beach it's a bit of a zoo, even by Club Med standards. They do have a regular boat shuttle to one of the off-shore islands but this too seems overcrowded – not the place to be if you're looking for your own South Pacific desert island.

None of the resort hotels here are particularly special. Those with the best beaches are to the north of Club Med (these include the Hotel Hibiscus and the Moorea Village). Those to the south aren't quite so good (these include the Tipaniers and the Climat Moorea Beach Club). Hotels are listed below starting from the south.

Next to the Hibiscus hotel there's a popular campsite set in a coconut grove overlooking the lagoon. This is one of the most convenient beach locations for budget travellers within easy reach of Papeete.

WATERSPORTS★★★
Sailboard rentals and tuition are available at several hotels, plus water ski-ing. Club Med's main activity is water ski-ing and they have five resident instructors. For surfers there are excellent right and left reef breaks, just off Club Med, driven by north-west swells (October to March).

DIVING
Lousy diving .
• *Club Med*: One free dive per day, no diving below 100 ft/30 m. Club Med clients can also gain CMAS one-star certifications (also free) but the ratio of instructors to pupils is low.
• *Scubapiti*: At Linereva, just up the coast. One-tank dives around 4,000 CFP (US$38) including equipment, tel: 56 15 35.

ACCOMMODATION
• *Hotel Résidence Tiahura*: Moderate/budget **R**. Not on the beach but reasonable value. Twin bungalows from 3,500 CFP (US$33), with kitchen from 5,500 CFP (US$52). Restaurant and small pool. **A** PO Box 1068, Moorea, tel: 56 15 45.
• *Climat Moorea Beach Club*: Expensive/moderate. Bungalows cost 7,000-10,000 CFP (US$67-95) for three to six people. **A** PO Box 1017, Moorea, tel: 56 15 48.
• *Hotel Résidence Les Tipaniers*: Expensive. Bungalows cost 7,500-9,000 CFP (US$71-95). **A** PO Box 1002, Moorea, tel: 56 12 67.
• *Club Med*: Expensive. Aerobics, tennis. One week fully inclusive from 7,000-10,000 CFP (US$670-950). **A** PO Box 1010, Moorea, tel: 56 15 00.
• *Hotel Hibiscus*: Expensive/moderate. Bungalows cost 7,500-9,000 CFP (US$71-86). **A** PO Box 1009, Moorea, tel: 56 12 20.
• *Chez Josiane Camping*: Moderate/budget **R**. Large camp ground, pitches right next to the beach from 500 CFP (US$5). Basic facilities, cold showers, no cooking facilities. No tents for rent.

199

Two garden bungalows with kitchens and bathrooms cost 5-6,000 CFP (US$48-58). **A** Chez Josiane, Moorea, tel: 56 15 18.

• *Moorea Village Hotel*: Expensive. Bungalows cost 9,000-12,000 CFP (US$86-114). **A** PO Box 1008, Moorea, tel: 56 10 02.

• *Billy Ruta Bungalows*: Moderate/budget **R**. Just a few yards past the end of the beach. Twin bungalows from 4,000 CFP (US$38), with kitchenette 5,000 CFP (US$48), extra person 500 CFP (US$5). Bar and restaurant overlooking the water. **A** Billy Ruta, Moorea, tel: 56 12 54.

ACCESS
Ten miles/15 km from Cook's Bay. Nineteen flights daily from Papeete on Air Moorea, tel: 42 44 29. Air Tahiti flies from Papeete, Bora Bora and Huahine. Daily departures by ferry from Papeete, around 500-1,100 CFP (US$5-11) o/w.

TEMAE BEACH

Temae is a white sandy beach on the south side of Moorea with views of Tahiti in the distance. There is just one resort here, the Sofitel Kia Ora Moorea.

The Kia Ora has an enormous pier for swimming and sunbathing and there is a huge range of aquatic activities for guests including gourmet snorkelling trips complete with clam tasting and white wine (although the snorkelling here, as

The public half of the beach is grubby compared with the well-groomed sections near the hotel but if you're staying in Cook's Bay it's worth the hike or bike ride to come out here for the day.

Bora Bora

SNORKELLING★★
Snorkelling here you'll be able to see evidence of the extensive damage which occurred throughout Moorea in the 1983 cyclones, with upturned and smothered corals visible all over the bottom of the lagoon. Some new growth is starting to come through. Fish life tends to be more prolific on the inside wall of the fringing reef, and the hotel provides free outriggers so you can paddle yourself out. However, currents here are very strong and people often have to be rescued by the hotel speedboat (myself included). Complimentary snorkelling equipment and outriggers, underwater camera rentals. The cost of snorkelling excursions is 10,000-50,000 CFP (US$10-50).

WATERSPORTS★★★
Sailboard rentals and tuition (at extra cost), water ski-ing. For surfers there's an excellent right-hand break driven by heavy south-south-east swells (April to September).

DIVING

By arrangement with *Moorea Underwater Scuba-Diving Tahiti* (MUST), a small dive operation based at the wharf in Cook's Bay. Two dives daily, shark feeding every week. Well-equipped dive shop with a high ratio of instructors to students.

• *MUST*: One-tank dive 5,500 CFP

(US$53) including equipment. **A** PO Box 13, Moorea, tel: 56 17 32.

BARS AND RESTAURANTS

Over-water bar and two restaurants. The food here is better than the service, which is friendly but deplorable. Tahitian night on Fridays.

ACCOMMODATION

• *Kia Ora Moorea*: Deluxe **R**. Garden bungalows from US$140, beach bungalows from US$170. Stop-over packages through UTA French Airlines from single/double US$205/264. Tennis. **A** PO Box 28, Moorea, tel: 56 12 90. Reservations: UK, tel: (01) 724 1000; USA, tel: (800) 221 4542; Sydney, tel: (02) 290 1933; Tokyo, tel: (03) 432 2161; Frankfurt, tel: (069) 742 598; Paris, tel: (01) 47 76 55 55.

ACCESS

One mile/one-and-a-half km from the airport. Flight time from Papeete is just seven minutes and there is a regular air taxi shuttle.

Moana Beach Hotel, Bora Bora

BORA BORA: SOUTH COAST

There are several beaches on this part of the coast, the first of which are at the Hotel Bora Bora on Point Raititi. This first-class resort has three beaches surrounding it and bungalows are set in well-tended, flourishing tropical gardens. It also has a number of bungalows on stilts over the water, which is typical of many of the better Polynesian hotels.

The 200-metre zone around the Hotel Bora Bora pier has been (unofficially) declared a protected area by its American owner Monty Brown, who has been encouraging fish feeding here for some time. Guests staying in the overwater bungalows can get out of bed and walk straight down the steps to find a mesmerizing variety of fish waiting to greet them beneath the surface. Visitors to the hotel can snorkel off the pier and although they discourage casual visitors they're hardly going to object if you come for lunch or a drink at the beach bar. Many tropical species – including the ever-curious butterflyfish, nibbling at your face and fingers – will appear if you take down some bread and I'm told that mantas sometimes come into this area. This is the only rewarding place to snorkel on Bora Bora without getting a boat.

The Hotel Bora Bora has a long-standing reputation and is hard to fault from the point of view of accommodation, beaches, and standards of service (which seem to be noticeably higher than in many French-managed resorts). Next to the hotel is Moana Adventure Tours, Bora Bora's main dive operation, which is run by the well-known underwater photographer Erwin Christian.

Across the bay from the Hotel Bora Bora is Matira Point, on the west side of which is the island's main public beach. This is where people normally come for the day from Viatape and, although sometimes crowded, it's a superb sandy beach, shallow and calm for swimming. There are several options for staying here, including one *pension* with double rooms from 5,250 CFP (US$50) (this is the cheapest accommodation directly on a good beach that you'll find in Bora Bora and even at that price it's hard to get rooms – book in advance or phone from Papeete if possible).

On the east side of Matira Point a new hotel recently opened, the Bora Bora Moana Beach. Despite having stayed in over 160 beach hotels whilst writing this book, and inspected hundreds more, I have never seen bungalows quite like these. Thirty of the forty here are built on stilts over the water with glass-topped tables set into the floor so you can see through to the lagoon beneath. Each bungalow also has two private sun decks and low-set windows so you can see the lagoon from in bed. The interiors have been imaginatively designed using bamboos from the Philippines, African Iroko wood and local ironwoods; Japanese sliding doors separate the living and sleeping areas. Each bungalow has its own CD player. Of course, they also have the standard trappings such as IDD phones and mini-bars. Decadent just isn't the word for it.

In an area between the bungalows nearest the beach they've fenced off part of the lagoon and stocked it with turtles and lobster and you can go snorkelling here and catch a lobster for your supper (at a price, of course, since the lobsters have to be replaced). I feel sorry for the turtles but it's better that the locals bring them here to sell rather than kill them for food or jewellery.

Down the track at Matira Point you'll find Matira Point Excursions, who run the best snorkelling and outrigger trips on Bora Bora.

Past Matira Point is another bay with a smaller beach shared by the Sofitel Marara and the Ibis. The Sofitel Marara also has overwater bungalows but it's not in the same class as either the Hotel Bora Bora or the Bora Bora Moana Beach. The Ibis is part of a low-cost, French-run chain and although we stayed here as a guest of the Ibis chain I thought it was sloppily-managed. The beach here is good. Just near these two hotels there's a campsite.

SNORKELLING******

As mentioned in the introduction, Bora Bora is the only place in the world where snorkellers can go and watch wild sharks being fed at shallow depths. On one of the off-shore islands there is also a privately-run lagoonarium stocked with mantas and other rays (primarily southern stingrays and spotted or butterfly rays) as well as nurse sharks and tropical fish.

Most hotels (including those in Vaitape) run trips to the Shark's Breakfast or the lagoonarium or both. The cost is normally 2,000-3,000 CFP (US$19-29) and the cheapest at the time of writing was run by the *Hotel Oa Oa*. The most action-packed trip is run by *Matira Point Excursions*, with stops for shark-feeding, snorkelling with rays in the lagoonarium and diving for mussels. The cost (around 4,000 CFP/US$38) includes a fabulous Tahitian-style lunch on a *motu*. Reservations advisable, tel: 67 70 97.

WATERSPORTS***
Windsurfers and outriggers are free to guests at most hotels and can also be hired by day visitors. The strongest winds here are during July and August. Water ski-ing is available at the *Bora Bora Moana Beach* and the *Sofitel Marara*.

DIVING**
You're likely to see as many – if not more – fish snorkelling around the pier as you are diving in the Bora Bora lagoon, but a lagoon dive will be memorable for other reasons. The rolling underwater sand dunes, for instance, look so much like virgin snow fields in the clear blue waters that you feel more like you're skiing than diving as the current sweeps over and around their undulating slopes.

Sharks and rays are the main drawcards inside the lagoon (when I dived here one blacktip and three small rays obligingly appeared and they say sharks are seen on 70 per cent of dives). Maximum depths are around 50 ft/15 m and fast speedboats take five minutes or less from the pier to the dive sites.

Diving outside the lagoon is disappointing; the gradual slope of the outer reef is almost barren of life and there is no definable drop-off. It takes slightly longer to get to the outer reef but I thought the cost of this dive was outrageous, at 8,000 CFP (US$75) for one tank. When I complained to *Moana Adventure Tours* they justified the high cost on the basis that only the latest equipment is used. This is total rubbish. Although there were only six divers on our outer reef trip they didn't have enough BCs to go round and, to my astonishment, I was given a snorkeller's flotation collar instead. On both dives I had short fills and paying this kind of money you certainly shouldn't be expected to lug your tank around. I requested a night dive but they said they never offer night dives because 'the type of divers who come here aren't up to coping with it'. To me this says more about the quality of the guides and divemasters than anything else. A rip-off at these prices. An instructor at the *Hotel Sofitel Marara* called Claude was offering dives for a much more reasonable cost (4,000 CFP/US$38) but at the time of writing he had disappeared from the scene.
• *Moana Adventure Tours*: One-tank lagoon dives 6,800 CFP (US$65), outer reef 8,000 CFP (US$75). **A** Hotel Bora Bora, tel: 67 70 33.

BARS AND RESTAURANTS
As well as the bars and restaurants in the hotels there are two restaurants on either side of Matira Point: a simple Vietnamese restaurant (refectory tables and benches outside) open for lunch only, and *The Matira Chinese Restaurant*, overlooking the sea, open for lunch and dinner (good but very expensive).

ACCOMMODATION
South Coast
• *Moana Beach Hotel*: Deluxe **R**.

203

Overwater bungalows half-board rates on stop-over packages through UTA French Airlines from single/double US$372/422 per night, beach bungalows from single/double US$283/334. **A** PO Box 6008, Faaa, Tahiti, tel: 42 60 70. Reservations: UTA French Airlines, UK, tel: (01) 493 4881; Paris, tel: (01) 47 76 55 55.

Matira Beach, Bora Bora

Shark's Breakfast, Bora Bora

• *Hotel Bora Bora*: Deluxe **R**. Twin bungalows cost US$233-420. **A** Nunue, Bora Bora, tel: 67 70 28. Reservations: Papeete, tel: 48 11 22; UK, tel: (01) 686 5242 or (0345) 010900; USA, tel: (800) 421 1490; CA, tel: (800) 262 4220; Sydney, tel: (02) 298 356.
• *Hotel Sofitel Marara*: Deluxe **R**. Twin bungalows cost US$245-370. **A** PO Box 6, Bora Bora, tel: 67 70 46. Reservations: UK, tel: (01) 724 1000 or (0345) 010900; USA, tel: (213) 649 2121; Paris, tel: (01) 60 77 27 27.
• *Hotel Ibis*: Expensive. Twin bungalows cost US$130-150. **A** PO Box 252, Bora Bora, tel: 677116. Reservations: UK, tel: (01) 724 1000 or (0345) 010900; USA, tel: (800) 221 4542, CA, tel: (213) 649 2121; Paris, tel: (01) 60 77 27 27.
• *Chez Robert et Tina*: Moderate/budget **R**. Rooms with shared kitchen from

single/double 3,000/5,000 CFP (US$29/48). **A** Point de Matira, Bora Bora, tel: 67 72 92.
• *Chez Nono Leverd*: Moderate. Rooms with shared kitchen from single/ double 4,000/7,000 CFP (US$38/67). On a popular part of the beach. **A** PO Box 12, Vaitape, Bora Bora, tel: 67 71 38.
• *Hotel Matira*: Expensive. Twin bungalows cost 10,000-12,500 CFP (US$95-118). **A** PO Box 31, Vaitape, Bora Bora, tel: 67 70 51.
• *Chez Pauline Youssef*: Budget **R**. No beach at high tide, limited facilities. Camping from 700 CFP (US$7), beach cabins from single/double 1,500/2,500 CFP (US$14/24). **A** PO Box 15, Vaitape, Bora Bora, tel: 67 72 16.

Vaitape
• *Yacht Club de Bora Bora*: Expensive **R**. Twin bungalows cost 8,000-11,000 CFP (US$76-105); they also have floating bungalows anchored between two small islands in the north of the lagoon, from 16,000 CFP (US$150) for up to four people. **A** PO Box 17, Vaitape, Bora Bora, tel: 67 70 69.
• *Club Med*: Expensive. Ten minutes by boat (regular shuttle) to their beach on Motu Tapu. Windsurfing with instruction, sailing, canoeing. One week fully inclusive 8,000-10,000 CFP (US$770-980). **A** PO Box 34, Vaitape, Bora Bora, tel: 67 70 57.
• *Royal Bora Bora*: Expensive. Twin bungalows from 11,000 CFP (US$104). **A** PO Box 202, Vaitape, Bora Bora, tel: 67 71 54.
• *Hotel Oa Oa*: Expensive **R**. Small, American-run hotel, artificial beach. Sailing and windsurfing free. Shark-feeding and snorkelling excursions 2,000 CFP (US$19). Yacht anchorage, favourite watering hole for yachties

and other itinerants. Bungalows from single/double 10,000/12,000 CFP (US$95/115). **A** Greg & Elaine Claytor, PO Box 10, Vaitape, Bora Bora, tel: 67 70 84. Reservations: USA, tel: (800) 521 7242; CA, tel: (800) 621 1633.

• *Chez Denise and Fariua*: Moderate/budget **R**. Dormitory projecting out over the water, kitchen facilities. 1,050 CFP (US$10) per person. Good value for trips to the *motus*. **A** PO Box 128, Vaitape, Bora Bora. Denise and Fariua also run an extremely popular waterfront hostel in Papeete, tel: 43 54 90.

• *Bungalows Marama*: Moderate. Bungalows cost 6,000-8,000 CFP (US$57-76). **A** PO Box 11, Vaitape, Bora Bora, tel: 677297.

• *Chez Fredo Doom*: Moderate/budget. Twin bungalows from 5,000 CFP (US$48), rooms with shared facilities from 1,200 CFP (US$12) per person. **A** Chez Fredo Doom, tel: 677031.

ACCESS

Air Tahiti flies eight times daily from Papeete (50 minutes). Flights also connect Bora Bora with Raiatea, Huahine, Moorea, Rangira, Manihi and Maupiti.

The airport is on an outlying island and some hotels offer express launch transfers but otherwise boats go to Vaitape. From Vaitape, the south coast is 15 minutes away on *le truck* or, if you're visiting for the day, 20-25 minutes by bicycle.

Ferries to Bora Bora from Papeete take 18-20 hours. The most comfortable is the *Raromatai*, which goes twice weekly via Huahine, Raiatea and Tahaa. Seats cost from around 3,600 CFP (US$34) o/w, cabins or berths from 5,000 CFP (US$48). The other ferries are the *Taporo IV* and the *Temehani II* and tickets for all three can be purchased on the quay. Timetables are available from OPATTI.

Avatoru pass, Rangiroa

RANGIROA

In the Tuamotos archipelago an hour's flying time from Papeete, Rangiroa is the largest closed atoll in the world. In the local dialect Rangiroa's name (*puamotu*) means Boundless Sky, and as you fly over the immense expanse of this atoll, you realize how apt that is: the whale-shaped lagoon is 43 miles/70 km long and 14 miles/22 km wide. Although there are three other atolls in the world as big or bigger than Rangiroa, none of them are 'closed' in the way Rangiroa is, with only two passes into or out of the atoll.

The passes are called Avatoru and Tiputa, and each has a village next to it which bears the same name. Trading schooners come through the passes to load copra and bring supplies but Avatoru and Tiputa also have an important – if less vital – function which draws divers from all over the world. Twice a day the tide flushes the nutrient-rich waters of the lagoon through the narrow confines of the two passes and this attracts large numbers of pelagics including mantas, eagle and leopard rays, barracuda and shark.

Rangiroa is famous for sharks and no less than 3,000 are said to live in and around the atoll. Cousteau was here in 1987 on board the *Calypso*, filming for his five-year long 'Rediscovering the World' project.

Apart from the diving, Rangiroa's appeal lies in its remoteness, a chance to escape the world totally. But it isn't a 'desert-island' retreat: the shoreline consists

205

mostly of rocks and coral beaches rather than sand. From the shore the passes are fascinating to watch, great heaving mill-races expressing elemental power.

There are several options for staying here. The main hotel is the Kia Ora Rangiroa, a charming collection of thatched-roof bungalows in a coconut grove beside the lagoon. Owned and run by three Frenchmen (all ex-Club Med) the hotel provides all the necessary facilities for guests to take advantage of the fact that they are on a unique atoll in the middle of the Pacific Ocean and boats are on hand for snorkelling, diving, picnic trips to uninhabited islands, sailing trips or deep-sea fishing. Considering its remote position, the hotel is remarkably comfortable.

A short way down the coast from the Kia Ora is the Bouteille à la Mer, which, as you might guess, is a diving resort. Being considerably cheaper than the Kia Ora, the Bouteille à la Mer tends to attract a younger crowd and although it shares many of the same simple natural qualities, the beach is poor by comparison. There is a third hotel, the Rangiroa Village, but it appeared to be closed at the time of writing. There are also several *pensions* on the island and although none of them is on a beach as such, several are located on the edge of the ocean.

The diving here is jointly run by Eric Jullian and Yves Lefèvre, both of whom are competent and enthusiastic divemasters. Eric is based at the Kia Ora and Yves can be found in a beachside building further down the road towards Avatoru, but when I spoke to them they were planning to merge their separate operations into one. If you want to go diving it doesn't matter too much where you stay but evidently the Kia Ora and the Bouteille à la Mer are the most convenient. Yves also rents rooms in his house.

SNORKELLING

Drift snorkelling trips on the racing tides are popular. Guest houses run trips to the smaller islands for snorkelling (1,500 CFP/US$15 per person) and every afternoon the Kia Ora has a boat out to Motu Nohi Nohi, just inside the Tiputa Channel.

DIVING ★★★★

Pelagic encounters are more or less guaranteed for divers but the reefs are no good, as both Eric and Yves will point out: Rangiroa is poor in coral species, and those that do exist are not extensive. However, the cost of diving here is about half what it is on Bora Bora and I thought it was good value. They say that the diving season here is year-round, since Rangiroa is not subject to the same weather patterns as the main islands.

Every morning there is an ocean diver for qualified divers, and this is usually a drift dive going back through one of the channels into the lagoon at a depth of around 100 ft/30 m. On the east reef at Avatoru they feed Napoleon wrasse and in both passes sharks and rays are common. 'Mobbed by fish, three giant mantas' says my logbook of the first dive in Avatoru. They also do regular shark feeds at a location known as Gorgonia Caves, and although I didn't go on one of these they assure me that the presence of at least 20-30 sharks is common. Hammerheads are also apparently found in Tiputa pass.

For beginners there is a dive every afternoon on the shallow reefs around Motu Nohi Nohi where they feed tame morays. There are plenty of small reef tropicals here too, but none of the bigger species found outside the lagoon.

● *Kia Ora Raie Manta Club*: the diving is well supervised and the equipment here is good. One-tank dives cost around 3,500-4,500 CFP (US$35-45); night diving at no extra charge; CMAS courses available; Nikonos rentals. **A** Kia Ora Raie Manta Club, Avatoru, Rangiroa, tel: 480.

ACCOMMODATION

● *Kia Ora Village*: Deluxe **R**. Terrific location. All bungalows face the lagoon and there is also a long pier and an overwater bar. Complimentary windsurfers, dinghies, bicycles and snorkelling equipment. The bungalows are as good as you'll find anywhere in the Pacific and they cost from single/double US$190/250 half-board. Stop-over packages on UTA French Airlines from single/double US$166/240 half-board per night. **A** PO Box 706, Papeete, tel: 42 86 72. Reservations: UK, tel: (01) 724 1000 or (0345) 010900; USA, tel: (800) 221 4542; Australia, tel: (800) 221 4542; Tokyo, tel: (03) 432 2161; Frankfurt, tel: (069) 74 25 98; Paris, tel: (01) 60 77 27 27.

● *Bouteille à la Mer*: Expensive. Free outriggers, bicycles and snorkelling equipment. Bungalows from single/double 9,500/16,000 CFP (US$95/160) half-board. **A** PO Box 17, Avatoru, Rangiroa, tel: 334.

● *Pensions* cost from 2,500 CFP (US$25) half-board and 4,000-5,000 CFP (US$40-50) full-board per person. For a couple this can work out at US$100 per day for a basic room which is sometimes no bigger than a cupboard, and with no amenities. US$100 per day for a shack and there isn't even

a beach here! No wonder people are put off travelling around French Polynesia: you have to be a millionaire to be a beach bum and you have to pay cash too. Half-board is better value and you can normally choose whether to take lunch or an evening meal. *Pensions* on Rangiroa include *Chez Teina Richmond and Marie Bellais* (good waterfront location, good food), *Chez Glorine To'i* (next to the above), *Chez Nanua Tamaehu, Chez Iris Terorotua* and *Chez Yves Lefèvre*.

● The tourist office (OPATTI) in Papeete has a full list of *pensions* so that you can make an advance reservation. We flew out here with no reservation but undoubtedly we would have got a much better room with one.

● *Village Sans Souci*: On a *motu* at the west side of the lagoon, 45 minutes from the airport. Fifteen bungalows and one restaurant. Minimum stay three nights, from around 30,000 CFP (US$300) per person full board for three nights (includes round-trip boat transfer from the airport). **A** Avatoru, Rangiroa. Reservations: Papeete, tel: 42 48 33.

ACCESS

Air Tahiti fly from Papeete daily Tuesday to Sunday and twice on Friday. There are also flights to Bora Bora (twice weekly) and Manihi (four times a week). It's important to reconfirm your reservation out as soon as you arrive at Rangiroa airport, otherwise it will be cancelled. Divers should note that the free baggage allowance on Air Tahiti flights is only 10 kg.

Boats from Papeete to Rangiroa take one week.

Hawaii

Hawaii welcomes you with a fantastic climate and the warm spirit of *aloha* and there can be few countries in the world with such an incredible diversity of beaches. Hawaii has beaches for everything from windsurfing to boogie-boarding and from people-watching to whale-watching. You can go from a snorkelling beach to a body-surfing beach within just a few minutes and, if neither of these turns you on, there's bound to be a beach around the next headland which does.

The hub of this 1,500-mile/2,400-km long volcanic chain is the island of Oahu, the crossroads of the North Pacific and home to the state capital of Honolulu. Oahu is also where you'll find one of the oldest and most famous beach resorts in the world, **Waikiki★★★★**. The first beach hotel, the Royal Moana, was built here in 1901 and it still graces the waterfront amidst the high rises which now dominate the Waikiki skyline. Although the total area of Waikiki is under a square mile, there are no less than 177 hotels and condominiums squeezed into this space. On an average day there are 60,000–80,000 tourists in Waikiki; sandwiched between tanned bodies on the beach and watching a constant procession of jets descending into Honolulu airport to disgorge yet more people, you wonder where on earth they're going to put them all.

Accommodation ranges from YHA hostels to butler-serviced penthouses and there are probably as many restaurants and food outlets as there are days in the year, so whatever your budget Waikiki can deliver. You can do just about everything imaginable on the beach from learning to surf to taking outrigger canoe rides and all this is just 20 minutes from Honolulu airport. As well as the fact that Waikiki is simply a lot of fun, it's also a convenient base from which to explore the rest of Oahu, which can easily be done by hire car or local buses.

Twelve miles/19 km to the east of Waikiki is **Hanuama Bay★★★★**, Oahu's top snorkelling and diving beach, incredibly popular and almost as crowded as Waikiki. Don't let this put you off since beneath the waves it is equally as crowded with tropical fish.

Past Hanuama Bay to the east you come to two of Oahu's most famous body-surfing beaches, **Sandy Beach** and **Makapu'u Beach★★★★**. Like Hanuama Bay, either of these is easily reached from Waikiki or Honolulu for the day. At Makapu'u there is the added attraction of the Sea Life Park with its regular dolphin shows.

The next main beach on this coast is Waimanalo, three-and-a-half miles/five km of soft, pure white sand sloping off into the translucent waves. Waimanalo is a great beach to escape to (except at weekends, when it becomes very crowded) and it's also good for beginners' body-surfing; if you're not confident enough to try Makapu'u or Sandy Beach, practise here first. Waimanalo is 40-60 minutes from Waikiki.

You'll find a similar quality beach at Kailua Bay, 25 miles/40 km from Waikiki, which is popular with body-surfers and windsurfers. This large, sheltered bay has reliable on-shore winds and is a good location for beginners' windsurfing as well as intermediates.

209

For divers, Oahu's south and south-west coast features lava tubes and wrecks, and the island has numerous professionally-run dive shops. See *Oahu: Diving* (page 220).

Oahu's **North Shore★★★**, a refreshing contrast to Honolulu and

Kaewakapu, Maui

Waikiki, is renowned in surfing circles the world over for sites such as the Banzai Pipeline. The three principal beaches where the action takes place during the winter months (October to April) are Waimea Bay, Ekuhai Beach and Sunset Beach. Surfies rent beach houses for the whole season but even if you're just passing through Honolulu it's worth driving over to the north coast to witness the spectacle of surfers pitting themselves against the dramatic, towering waves. During November and December (actual dates depend on wave conditions), Oahu's North Shore is the locale for the annual Triple Crown competition. During the summer (from mid-May to September) the sea is calm and suitable for swimming and snorkelling.

Another famous surfing beach on Oahu is Makaha, 37 miles/60 km west of Waikiki. In the 1960s Makaha hosted Hawaii's first international competitions and is now the annual venue for the Buffalo Big Board Surfing Classic. This is a rare chance to find out what surfing was like in its early days in Hawaii. Early surf boards, known as 'Tankers', were 12-16 ft long and weighed up to 75lb. And the competition is based on the surfers' abilities to put these enormous boards through a variety of trick manoeuvres. The event usually takes place in February or March.

The north and west coasts of Oahu have their biggest waves from October to April, and the south and east coasts are at their best for surfing from May through to September. However, conditions are changeable; if you want to find out exactly what's going on, ocean conditions are broadcast daily by most radio stations or you can call the National Weather Service's recorded forecast.

Residents of Maui, the second largest island in the Hawaiian chain, have a saying: 'Maui no ka oi' – Maui is the best! Just 30 minutes' flying time away from Honolulu, Maui is as famous for whale-watching and windsurfing as Waikiki and the North Shore are for surfing.

The best sandy beaches on Maui are on the leeward (west) coast. **Kaanapali**★★★ is Maui's biggest and busiest beach. Like Waikiki, Kaanapali has practically every conceivable watersport to keep you amused but, unlike Waikiki, the beach here is natural.

The most reasonably priced accommodation on Maui is on the Kihei

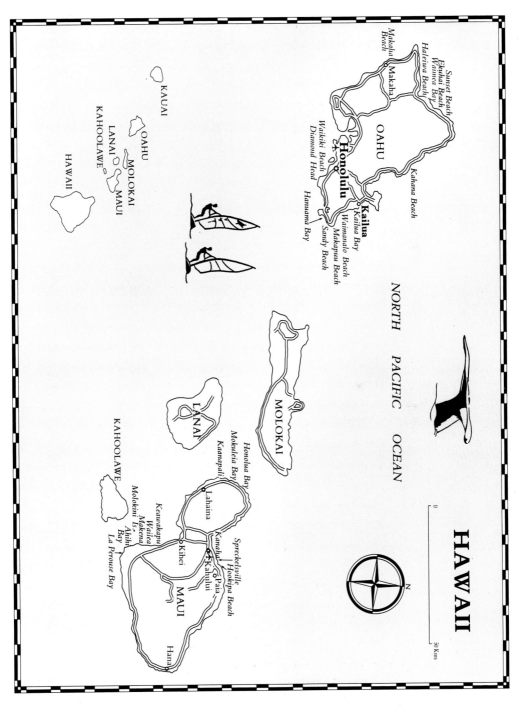

Makaha
Beach

Makaha

Sunset Beach
Ekukai Beach
Waimea Bay
Haleiwa Beach

KAUAI

OAHU

OAHU
MOLOKAI
LANAI
MAUI
KAHOOLAWE

HAWAII

Kahana Beach

Waikiki Beach
Diamond Head

Honolulu

Kailua
Kailua Bay
Wainanalo Beach

Hanauma Bay

Makapuu Beach
Sandy Beach

NORTH   PACIFIC   OCEAN

MOLOKAI

LANAI

KAHOOLAWE

Honolua Bay
Mokuleia Bay
Kaanapali

Lahaina

Keawakapu
Waitea
Makena
Molokini Is.
Ahihi
Bay
La Perouse Bay

Kihei

Kanaha
Kahului

Spreckelsville
Hookipa Beach
Paia

MAUI

Hana

N

0

50 Kms

HAWAII

section of the coast, to the north of Wailea. Although we haven't listed them, there are over 50 condos around Kihei so you should be able to find something within your budget. There is also reasonably-priced accommodation at the Surf 'n' Sand Hotel at Kaewakapu, just passed Kihei. Next along is Wailea, a series of small sandy coves with a sprinkling of first-class hotels. This coast is popular with speed and slalom sailors.

Makena is a long, wild – but never deserted – beach at the end of the road, four miles/6.5 km past Wailea. Next door, Little Makena is an unofficial nudist beach. It is reached by a track at the north end of Makena.

On the other side of the coast there are several moderately priced hotels in Kahului, south of Paia. Paia itself is a fabulous old town which still has a frontier-type atmosphere (despite the trendy boutiques springing up) but the hotels in Kahului are the pits. This is really the worst place you could be on Maui, as I learnt from bitter experience when a travel agent in Waikiki booked us into one of these hotels with the assurance that this was 'a good beach'. As I found out, this is basically an industrial area and there is no beach. Hotels to avoid here include Maui Palms, the Maui Beach Hotel, the Maui Hukilau and the Maui Seaside. If you're on a budget, Kihei (or even Paia) is the place to be.

The hub of Maui is the old whaling town of Lahaina, now stuffed to the gunwales with trendy boutiques and restaurants of every description. **Diving** on Maui (page 222) is well organized and reasonably competitive and there is also some excellent **snorkelling** (page 222). Maui is of course internationally famous as a **windsurfing** Mecca (page 223).

Whale-watching is a major attraction for anyone coming to Maui in the winter (November to May), when North Pacific humpback whales visit Maui and the surrounding islands to mate and give birth, travelling here on a 5-7,000 mile/8-11,000 km round trip from their summer feeding grounds in Alaskan waters. Prior to the destruction wrought by commercial whaling there were an estimated 15,000 humpbacks in the North Pacific: today the estimate is around 1,500 and between 600 and 700 of them visit Maui each winter to breed and play in the shallow underwater shelf that surrounds Maui, Molokai, Lanai and Kahoolawe.

Sandy Beach, Oahu

Although the majority are seen in this area, in recent years sightings have increased off Kauai, the coast of Hawaii, and windward Oahu.

The odd-looking humpbacks indulge in spectacular displays of tail-slapping, breaching or head-slapping. They start arriving in late

November, with the maximum numbers seen during February and March. Dozens of boats run whale-watching specials in season and on dive boats during this period, whale-watching is an integral part of the trips to the dive sites. Lucky divers might hear the whales' haunting songs underwater.

Breaching humpback whale

Specialized whale-watching tours are run by the Pacific Whale Foundation, a non-profit research organization based in Kihei. Researchers from the PWF interpret the whales' behaviour and tell you exactly what is going on and why. Adopt a whale and they'll let you know what your whale gets up to over the years (see page 312).

The movement to save the whales, says the PWF, is possibly one of

213

the greatest conservation success stories of the twentieth century and they estimate that the income from whale-related activities now totals nearly US$100 million annually.

Hawaii, the Big Island, is famous for its drive-in volcanoes and lava wastelands. The majority of beach resorts on Hawaii are located to the south of Kailua and they are almost without exception catastrophic. One hotel brochure is candid enough to describe their property as being located on 'a volcanic rock beach'. That ain't no beach, that's rocks! Even Hawaii's newest and most extravagant resort, the US$360-million Hyatt Regency Waikoloa, is on a lousy beach. The hotel has a gigantic man-made lagoon where you can swim with Atlantic bottlenose dolphins (for a fee).

The only decent resort beach on the Big Island is at Kuanaoa, on the north-west coast, an oasis of white sand, palm trees and tropical luxuriance in the midst of the otherwise arid and bleak volcanic landscapes; the only hotel here is the very expensive Manu Kae Beach Hotel. Just south of Kunao there's also a superb beach at Hapuna.

All Hawaiian beaches are open to the public; toplessness is illegal.

GENERAL INFORMATION

Time
GMT – 11 hours

IDD code
1 + 808 + number

Currency
US dollars (US$)
UK£1 = US$1.8

Hotels
Deluxe: US$200-2,000
Expensive: US$100-200
Moderate: US$40-80
Budget: US$10-15

PUBLICATIONS
● *Most of the publications listed here can be found either in branches of Waldenbooks in Waikiki, the Waikiki Aquarium Bookshop or at the Sea Life Park*

General
An Underwater Guide to Hawaii
Ann Fielding and Ed Robinson (University of Hawaii Press 1987). 150pp, US$14.95. Superb guide to Hawaiian marine life, crammed with colour underwater shots.
Bodyboard Handbook
Ben Severson (GrubbStake Media 1986). 24pp, US$5.95. Excellent introduction to this fast-growing sport by a

world champion body-boarder, hard to find.

Diving and Snorkelling Guide to Hawaiian Islands
Doug Wallin (Pisces Books, New York 1984). 95pp, US$9.95. Clear, concise descriptions of 30 top sites: ten on Oahu and Maui, five on Hawaii and Kauai.

Fishwatcher's Field Guide to Hawaii
(Seahawk Press, Miami 1983). US$5 Underwater fish card, valid for the whole of the Pacific. Available locally.

Fishwatching in Hawaii,
Russell and Blyth Carpenter (Natural World Press, California 1981). 120pp, US$7.95. Readable introduction to fish behaviour.

Guide to Hawaiian Reef Fish
(Natural World Press, California 1983). US$2.95 Underwater fish card, not as good as the Seahawk Press version.

Hawaii Handbook
JD Bisignani (Moon Publications 1987). 790pp, £14.95. The definitive budget-travellers' guide to the islands.

Hawaiian Marine Invertebrates
(Seahawk Press, Miami 1987). US$2.95 Underwater card with Hawaiian shells on the reverse.

Hawaii's Humpback Whales
A Complete Whalewatcher's Guide by Gregory Kaufman and Paul Forestell (Pacific Whale Foundation Press 1986). 175pp. Covers the known spectrum of whale behaviour from sleep to social dynamics, illustrated with many previously unpublished photos. Includes tips for whale-watching.

Underwater Guide to Hawaiian Reef Fish
John E Randall (Harrowood Books 1981). 36pp, US$11.95. Waterproof.

The Windsurfing Guide to the Islands
(US$8.95, annual magazine) covers Maui well as Oahu, Kauai and Hawaii.

Oahu
A Guide to Beach Survival
Ken Suiso and Rell Sunn (Honolulu Water Safety Consultants Inc 1986). 70pp, US$3.95. Witty booklet written by two lifeguards, tells you all you need to know to avoid being drowned, robbed, or knocked out by the surf on Oahu's dozen most popular beaches.

The Beaches of O'ahu
John Clarke (The University Press of Hawaii 1977). 190pp, US$5.95. One of a series written by an ex-lifeguard

Maui
The Beaches of Maui County
John Clarke (The University Press of Hawaii 1985). 160pp, US$9.95.

Maui Handbook
JD Bisignani (Moon Publications 1986). 235pp, US$8.95. Budget-travellers' guide, packed with facts and opinions on every nook and cranny on the island.

Windshopping Maui – a Serious Sailor's Guide to the Valley Isle
by Arleone Dibben Young (1987, US$12.95). Covers board and sail makers, shops, schools, contests, practical facts and analyses of conditions at top Maui sites.

WEATHER
The average daily temperature on the islands is 71-80°F/21-27°C. On Oahu, November to March is the cool, wet season with the Kona winds stirring up the surf on the west coast and North Pacific storms creating similar conditions on the north coast. Beaches on the southern coast have the highest surf in the summer months from May to September. The prevailing winds are from the north-east and since the Hawaiian chain lies perpendicular to the north-east, half the coasts in Hawaii are on the lee side for most of the year, with calm conditions for diving.

215

HEALTH
No formal health requirements.

VISAS
US visas required for all non-US citizens except Canadians. For British visitors visa requirements depend on which airline you fly with.

TOURIST BOARD
Head Office: Honolulu, tel: 923 1811; Representatives: London, tel: (01) 323 3288; New York, tel: (212) 986 9203; Los Angeles, tel: (213) 385 5301; Sydney, tel: (02) 235 0194; Tokyo, tel: (03) 597 7951.

WAIKIKI BEACH

Famous as a beach resort since the end of the nineteenth century, Waikiki's ageing façade recently underwent a massive facelift, with over US$330 million being spent on improvement projects for its hotels, parks and boulevards.

In fact there's no such thing as Waikiki Beach – this is merely the collective name given to a series of eight different beaches spread out along two miles/three km of coast. Over 170 condominiums and hotels are squeezed into this space and there are a total of over 33,000 rooms for rent ranging from US$1,000-a-night penthouse suites to small self-catering apartments costing under US$30 a day.

Despite the acres of tanned bodies there are less crowded patches (principally Sans Souci, Fort de Russy and Queen's Surf in front of the Honolulu Zoo) but it doesn't really matter where you stay since it's only half-an-hour's walk from one end of Waikiki to the other.

We've given a selection of top hotels and a few more modestly-priced options; a comprehensive accommodation guide is available from overseas offices of the Hawaii Visitors Bureau. Studio-apartments are good value if you're staying for more than a few days (see under Hotels in the Yellow Pages).

Since the beginning of the century numerous attempts have been made to halt erosion here but most of the beaches are now made from imported sand. This too is seeping out to sea, causing changes in the currents and altering Waikiki's famous surfing breaks – wave patterns have changed radically since Hawaiian royalty first surfed here over a century ago on their 75-lb wooden planks.

Waikiki's name is, of course, synonymous with surfing, and tuition is available from the beach-boys. If you haven't got the time or inclination to try surfing, body-boarding is an easier alternative. Body-boards (also known as boogie-boards) are smaller and lighter than surf boards and you don't need the same sense of balance (or perseverance) necessary for learning to surf.

The most popular spot for body-boarding is between Kuhio Beach Park and Queen's Surf near a projecting breakwater known as The Wall. Every day crowds of people are out practising from early morning through until sunset. All you have to do is rent a board, paddle out (special short fins are provided) and watch how the regulars try to catch the waves.

There is no diving off-shore from Waikiki but dive organizations collect from Waikiki hotels free of charge for dives anywhere around the coast (see *Oahu: Diving and Snorkelling,* page 220). The nearest snorkelling is at Hanuama Bay (page 218). The Waikiki Aquarium (behind Sans Souci beach) is well worth a visit.

WATERSPORTS★★★★★

Surfing lessons cost US$10-20/hr. International pro surfer Nancy Emerson runs a school for beginners (US$40 for a group lesson) and clinics for advanced surfers (US$75 for private tuition), tel: 732 1944. Boogie boards and fins cost around US$3-5/hr, US$7-10/day. Hobie cats, windsurfers, jetskis, outriggers and para-sailing.

BARS AND RESTAURANTS

Waikiki has literally hundreds of restaurants and food outlets. Free holiday guides such as *Oahu Star Vacation Guide, Spotlight Hawaii, This Week, Guide to Oahu* and the *Waikiki Beach Press* will give you numerous ideas about where to go for seafood, *sushi*, traditional Hawaiian *luaus* and more.

ACCOMMODATION

• *Outrigger Reef Hotel*: Expensive/moderate **R**. Rooms cost US$80-160. Bar and disco on the beach. **A** 2169 Kalia Road, Honolulu, HI 96815, tel: 923 3111. Reservations: USA, tel: (800) 367 5170.

• *Sheraton Waikiki*: Deluxe **R**. Rooms cost US$115-200. Two pools. US$50 million recently spent on improvements. **A** 2255 Kalakaua Avenue,

Honolulu, HI 96815, tel: 922 4422. Reservations: UK, tel: (0800) 353535; USA, tel: (800) 325 3535.

• *The Royal Hawaiian Hotel*: Deluxe **R**. One of the original Waikiki hotels, now managed by Sheraton, recently renovated. Rooms cost US$140-225, suites US$230-1,200. **A** 2259 Kalakaua Avenue, Honolulu, HI 96815, tel: 923 7311. Reservations: As above.

• *Outrigger Waikiki*: Expensive **R**. Rooms cost US$95-185, suites US$240-415. **A** 2335 Kalakaua Avenue, Honolulu, HI 96815, tel: 923 0711. Reservations: USA, tel (800) 367 5170.

• *Sheraton Moana*: Expensive. Built in 1901, Waikiki's oldest hotel, recently renovated. Rooms cost US$65-140, suites from US$130. **A** 2365 Kalakaua Avenue, Honolulu, HI 96815, tel: 922 3111. Reservations: See Sheraton Waikiki.

• *The New Otani Kaimana Beach Hotel*: Expensive/moderate **R**. Located at the more peaceful end of Waikiki (towards Diamond Head), this hotel is small, informal and good value for Waikiki. Rooms cost US$70-90, suites from US$135-305. **A** 2863 Kalakaua Avenue, Honolulu, HI 96815, tel: 923 1555. Reservations: UK, tel: (01) 731 4231; USA, tel: (212) 308 7491.

Off the Beach

• *Outrigger Surf*: Expensive/moderate **R**. One of the most reasonable hotels in Waikiki if you can get a room. Rooms cost US$50-75, suites US$80-100 (four people). **A** 2280 Kuhio Avenue, Honolulu, HI 96815, tel: 922 5777. Reservations: USA, tel (800) 367 5170.

• *Waikiki Surfside Hotel*: Moderate **R**. Good value, heavily booked, reserve in advance. Rooms cost US$40-60. **A**

Skimboarding, Hawaii

217

2452 Kalakaua Avenue, Honolulu, HI 96815, tel: 923 0266. Reservations: UK, tel: (01) 637 7961; USA, tel: (800) 367 5124.

• *Waikiki Marina Hotel*: Moderate. Rooms with kitchenettes US$40-80. **A** 1956 Ala Moana Boulevard, Honolulu, HI 96815, tel: 955 0714. Reservations: USA, tel: (800) 367 6070.

• *Network International Hostel*: Budget. From US$12 per person. **A** 2413 Kuhio Avenue, Honolulu, tel: 924 2636.
• *Waikiki International Youth Hostel*: Budget **R**. From US$10 per person (YHA members only), close to beach. **A** 2417 Prince Edward Street, tel: 946 0591.

ACCESS
Twenty minutes from Honolulu airport.

HANUAMA BAY

Hanuama Bay is an enormously successful marine park which draws over one million snorkellers and divers annually. It used to be a favourite fishing ground for Hawaiian royalty and was fished out until made a reserve in 1967. Now the fish here are quite tame and will boldly approach snorkellers to be fed.

Due to the number of snorkellers kicking up the sand, visibility near the beach isn't good so you should go through the reef (just follow the trans-Pacific telephone cable which is visible on the seabed). You might come across the fish with the longest name in the world, the *Humuhumunukunukuapuaa* (Hawaii's state emblem), as well as many other beautiful reef tropicals including hordes of tangs and jacks, surgeonfish, butterflyfish, wrasse, bullethead parrotfish and bold filefish bearing their teeth to grab a bite.

You may also occasionally see turtles. However, thousands of people visit Hanuama each week, all of whom are given plastic bags of bread to feed the fish with and a lot of these plastic bread bags are left floating in the water after the bread is finished. Turtles mistake the plastic bags for jellyfish, eat them, choke, and die, so take them back to the beach.

There are numerous tours available from Waikiki, the cost of which is usually US$6-12 including snorkelling equipment. Hanauma Bay starts to fill up around 9.30 a.m. and for most of the day the beach is as crowded as the water, so come as early as possible.

DIVING
The inner areas of the bay are suitable for intro dives or beginners, although most of what there is here can be seen from the surface, snorkelling. Near the mouth of the bay the outer reef slopes down to 70 ft/21 m but due to the turbulence and currents it is restricted to experienced divers.

ACCESS
Twenty to thirty minutes from Waikiki.

SANDY BEACH, MAKAPU'U BEACH

Sandy Beach is the south coast's premier body-surfing and boogie-boarding location for the more experienced, a great beach for just hanging out and watching how it should be done – but if you're a beginner practice your skills elsewhere before attempting to tackle the surf here.

The Guide to Beach Survival (see Publications) says, 'the shorebreak at Sandy Beach breaks in shallow water, often causing strong currents and causing the highest incidence of broken necks at any of Hawaii's beaches. If the waves are big, if you are inexperienced, and if you have no fins on, you have no business being in the water'. More rescues take place here than on any other Oahu beach except Makapu'u. Bring boogie boards from town – no rentals on the beach. Bring lunch – no concessions or snack bars. The sea here is too rough for normal swimming.

Tucked beneath the volcanic cliffs opposite the Sea Life Park, Makapu'u is as popular as Sandy Beach for body-surfing and body-boarding and just as danger-ous. The pounding shorebreak and strong off-shore currents present death-traps for the unwary but experienced boogie- and body-surfers will relish the powerful waves and outside peaks which carry them all the way into the shore.

If you come here and there's no beach left, don't be surprised. The strong currents often carry the whole of the beach out to sea, leaving nothing but rocks, only to return it to its original condition a few weeks later. Board-surfing is prohibited; swimming is only safe in the summer.

Just across the main road from the beach is the Sea Life Park which has daily dolphin shows and a Hawaiian reef tank with some beautiful little hammerheads cruising amongst the rays and fish. They've also got the world's first captivity-bred 'wolphin', a natural hybrid from a female dolphin and a male whale (the wolphin can only be seen on a 'Behind the Scenes Tour'). Admission is US$8.25

ACCESS
Half-an-hour from Waikiki by car, 45
minutes by bus (No 58).

NORTH SHORE

Waimea Bay, Ekuhai Beach and Sunset Beach
The main reason to come to Oahu's north shore can be summed up in one word – surf. In winter all the surf pros will be here but if you're merely mortal and just want to watch the action you can easily visit for the day from Waikiki or Honolulu. Accommodation on the north shore is limited – most people rent beach houses for the season.

Unhampered by a continental shelf the winter swells approach this coast with tremendous energy and speed, rising up abruptly on the shallow reef and pitching forward to form almost perfect cylindrical tubes. This produces some of the most perfectly-shaped but dangerous waves in the world and resulted in the break at Ekuhai being named the Pipeline in the late 1950s.

The main township on the north coast is Haleiwa, where there are numerous restaurants and shops for supplies. Waimea Bay is the first beach you come to heading out of Halewai, a deep curve of sand in the crook of the main highway, by summer a popular diving and snorkelling site, and in winter home to the largest ridable waves in the world. Sunset Beach and the nearby Ekuhai Beach Park,

219

with their ever-changing sands sculpted by the ocean, are a few miles further on.

WATERSPORTS★★★★★
In Haleiwa there are numerous surf shops including *Race Surfboards* (tel: 637-SURF), *Hawaii Surf and Sail* (tel: 637 5373) and *Beach Scene*; *XCEL Wetsuits* (tel: 637 6239) are on the outskirts of town. *Surf'n'Sea* (tel: 637 9887) have a selection of over 150 used surfboards from US$30 up and offer board repairs in 24 hours. Personalized videos through *Surfers Video Service*, tel: 637 5297.

ACCOMMODATION
• *Vacation Ends*: Accommodation agency. Beach studios and houses cost US$50-150 per day. **A** PO Box 716, Haleiwa, HI 96712, tel: 638 7838.
• *Turtle Bay Hilton and Country Club*: Deluxe/expensive. Four miles/6.5 km north of Sunset Beach. Rooms cost US$100-750. **A** PO Box 187, 57-091 Kamehameha Highway, Kahuku, HI 96731, tel: 293 8811. Reservations: Hilton worldwide.

ACCESS
Haleiwa is just over one hour by car from Waikiki, two hours by bus (No 52 from the Ala Moana centre).

Hanuama Bay

OAHU: Diving and Snorkelling
Most of Oahu's dive sites are on the south and west shores and all the dive shops provide a pick-up service from Waikiki. The island's volcanic formation provides numerous underwater lava tubes and caverns to explore as well as several wrecks including the *Mahi*, the *Kahala Barge* and a plane wreck near the Makaha Caves. Other popular spots include Turtle Canyon, Big Eel Reef, and Hanuama Bay (see page 218). The average cost of a two-tank dive is US$60–65 fully inclusive. Intro dives average US$45, certifications US$250.

• *Aloha Dive Shop*, tel: 395 5922; *Blue Water Divers*, tel: 955 1066; *Elite Divers*, tel: 637 9331; *Leeward Dive Centre*, tel: 696 3414; *Ocean Adventures*, tel: 487 9060; *Pacific Quest Divers*, tel: 235 3877; *South Sea Aquatics,* tel: 538 3854; *Steve's Diving Adventures,* tel: 947 8900; *Vehon Diving Ventures,* tel: 396 9738; *Waikiki Diving*, tel: 922 7188.

KAANAPALI BEACH

Kaanapali is one of Maui's biggest resort areas, four miles/six km of sandy beach just a short distance from Lahaina. On this meticulously landscaped beach numerous ostentatious hotels compete for attention.

The old Maui Surf Hotel was recently remodelled at a cost of US$155 million and has emerged from the ashes as the new Westin Maui, complete with a 650,000-gallon swimming pool complex featuring water slides, swim-through rock grottos, and no less than five separate swimming areas and no less than five separate swimming areas and four waterfalls. Two million dollars' worth of oriental art has been scattered around the grounds of the hotel for good measure. At the southern end of Kaanapali, the Hyatt Regency Maui features an impressive atrium complete with classical art works, parrots and a penguin pool. At the next door Maui Marriott, guest rooms are decorated with original works of art depicting the lifestyles of old Hawaii.

Whatever else it may lack, Kaanapali isn't short of opportunities for rubber-necking and pool-hopping between hotels.

At the north end of the beach, Black Rock is one of Maui's best-known (although not necessarily best) on-shore snorkelling sites.

SNORKELLING★★★

Black Rock (right in front of the Sheraton Maui) is a safe and convenient beginner's spot with plenty of fish life. The rock is a small volcanic peninsula which drops down to a sandy seabed at 30 ft/9 m. Fish here are accustomed to snorkellers and divers so it's a good spot for photos (underwater still and video cameras can be rented in the hotels). You should come across the *Humuhumunukunukuapuaa* (the Hawaiian reef triggerfish) as well as numerous small reef tropicals. **MSF** US$5/hr, US$10/day.

WATERSPORTS★★★★★

Hobie cats and sailboards can be rented, tuition available. Jetskis, water ski-ing, para-sailing.

DIVING★★

All the hotels (except the Westin, where they charge US$10) offer free demo dives: one-tank dives at *Black Rock* cost US$50-60.

ACCOMMODATION

• For Information on condo rentals contact the Maui Visitors Bureau (tel: 871 8691) or overseas offices of the Hawaii Visitors Bureau.

• *Hyatt Regency Maui*: Deluxe **R**. Rooms from US$195, suites US$250-900. **A** 200 Nohea Kai Drive, Lahaina, Maui, HI 96761, tel: 667 7474. Reservations: USA, tel: (800) 233 1234.

• *Westin Maui*: Deluxe **R**. Rooms from US$180, suites US$400-1,500. **A** 2365 Kaanapali Parkway, Lahaina, Maui, HI 96761, tel: 667 2525. Reservations: USA, tel: (800) 228 3000.

ACCESS

Kaanapali is five miles/eight km north of Lahaina, free trolley bus service.

MAUI: Diving

There are numerous dive shops on the island with comprehensive facilities for every level of diver, and dive charter boats with daily departures to the outer islands. Molokini is one of the most popular spots (too popular, according to some), with the cathedrals at Lanai – huge lava grottoes with caverns and tunnels to explore – a close second. There are also off-shore sites around the neighbouring islands of Kahoolawe and Molokai (all part of Maui County).

Although Molokini has deteriorated considerably, divers will probably get more out of it than snorkellers. The clear, fresh water brings in pelagics of every description (including whale sharks on rare occasions) and there are several pet morays to be photographed as well as white tip sharks at Shark Ledges.

The cost of a two-tank dive to Molokini and/or Lanai varies between US$65 and US$90; Aquatic Charters of Maui and The Dive Shop had good deals at US$65 including all equipment and lunch, although the best value by far was Steve's Diving Adventures with a two-tank dive for US$49.95 (inclusive of equipment) or two people together for US$90. Central Pacific Divers' three-tank dives at three different locations is also a good deal at US$82.

Open-water certifications cost US$225-300.

Lahaina

• *Captain Nemo's Ocean Emporium*, tel: 661 5555; *Central Pacific Divers*, tel: 661 8718; *Dive Maui*, tel: 667 2080; *Extended Horizons*, tel: 661 5555; *Scuba Schools of Maui*, tel: 661 8036; *Hawaiian Reef Divers*, tel: 667 7647; *Lahaina Divers*, tel: 667 7496; *Tropical Hydro*, tel: 871 2686

Kihei

• *Aquatic Charters of Maui*, tel: 879 0976; *Hawaiian Watercolours*, tel: 879 3584; *Maui Dive Shop*, tel: 879 3388; *Maui Sun Divers*, tel: 879 3631; *Mike Severns*, tel: 879 6596; *Steve's Diving Adventures*, tel: 879 0055; *The Dive Shop*, tel: 879 5172.

MAUI: Snorkelling

Maui's best known snorkelling location is the dramatic, sunken volcanic crater of Molokini, off the west coast. Spectacular aerial shots of Molokini sell Maui as a destination in glossy magazines such as Condé Nast's *Traveler* and all the guide books will tell you that this is 'the best'. Whether or not it's the best, Molokini is certainly the most popular snorkelling and diving location here and probably ranks as one of the world's most economically successful marine parks – one boat operator estimates that it generates around US$10-20 million per annum.

For many people, a snorkelling trip to Molokini will be a highlight of their stay in Maui. There are plenty of tame fish and the underwater visibility is a consistent 150 ft/45 m or more. Unfortunately, Molokini is becoming a victim of its own success. On some days there are as many as 30-35 boats here, disgorging up to a thousand snorkellers a day into the water. The dense coral which previously covered the seabed is completely finished and although there are still plenty of fish, the number of species has dwindled to the bread-eaters. The *Humuhumunukunukuapuaa*, for instance, is no longer to be seen here. 'People still love it, but the attraction for seasoned divers and snorkellers just isn't there,' one operator said.

'It's not a reef anymore, it's a fish show.'

If you still want to snorkel at Molokini, opt for an afternoon trip, when it will be less crowded. The average price for a half-day trip is US$40-60, although you can find some boats offering no-frills trips for as little as US$30-35. The journey takes 40-60 minutes.

There are plenty of snorkelling sites along Maui's coast which will prove just as rewarding as Molokini, and you don't need to fork out for the boat trip either. Mokuleia Bay and Honolua Bay, for instance, are part of a marine reserve at the top of the west coast. Coming from Lahaina, Mokuleia Bay (commonly referred to as 'Slaughterhouse') is the first of the two, with reef along the left-hand side of the bay. At Honolua there are reefs on both side of the bay but fish are plentiful in both locations. The only problem with these two bays is that the visibility is either extremely good or appalling. However, by some quirk of nature when one bay is so murky you can't even see your fins, the other is often crystal clear.

Slaughterhouse and Honolua are just over eleven miles/seventeen km from Lahaina, heading north on Highway 30. Keep going past Kaanapali, Napili and Kapalua until the highway becomes a narrow, winding road: half-a-mile past here you'll see the sign at the top of the cliff for the Honolua – Mokuleia Marine Preserve. Park here and walk down the cliff. Honolua is just a little further on.

Another good coastal location is Ahihi Bay, to the south of Makena beach (continue down the dirt track for another mile past Makena until you see the signs for Ahihi-Kinau Natural Area Reserve). The reef is in depths of 20 ft/6 m or less over most of the bay, dropping off to a sandy seabed at 50 ft/15 m further out where there are scattered coral heads. The reefs here are home to dozens of yellow tangs, wrasse and butterflyfish, as well as enormous parrotfish and bluefin trevally.

With initiative, it's easy to find places as good as Molokini. The boat operators are realizing this too, so if someone offers you a trip to somewhere apart from Molokini, don't turn your nose up at it. It will undoubtedly be less crowded and the chances are that the marine life will be more prolific too.

MAUI: Windsurfing

Maui is the island that the experts head for and although there are a couple of beaches for the less experienced, it's the breaks of Ho'okipa and Spreckelsille that pull in the best from all over the world.

The narrow shape of Maui, formed from two volcanoes with a narrow isthmus in between, creates a *venturi* effect which speeds up the trades and ensures 20-25 knots/5-6 Beaufort winds for 80 per cent of the year. For slalom and speed sailors the best area is on the south-west coast at Kihei, Ma'alaea or Wailea. On the south coast the most consistent winds blow from April/May through to September, and during this season you can expect to sail every day. Winter winds are more sporadic but this is when the north shore comes into its own for wave sailing.

The most demanding of Maui's northern beaches is Ho'okipa, where the outer reef builds up mast-high waves and more on the outside and two footers on the inside. Currents abound and some of the rips have had even the best swimmers wondering whether they'll ever make another payment on their credit card.

Ho'okipa is a contest venue and a great place to go and watch those who can master the combination of cross-shore winds and perfection in water origami.

West of Ho'okipa is Spreckelsville, possibly the windiest spot on the north shore. Kanaha, the least daunting place to sail on the north shore, is enclosed by an outer reef which allows only the gentlest of waves to find their way to the inside on most days. It's primarily a novice-intermediate spot but it does get busy – the greatest danger comes not from the waves but from other sailors.

• *Hi-Tech Sailboards of Hawaii*: Complete rental fleet with 80 Hi-Tech custom boards and production boards. Private tuition available. **A** 230 Hana Highway, Kahului, HI 96732.

• *The Maui Windsurfing Company and Maui Magic Windsurfing Schools*: The closest shop to Kanaha beach and the airport. Top quality equipment inclu-ding Fanatic, Ultra-Protech, Carbon and Angulo custom boards. Rentals and tuition available. **A** 520 Keolani Place, Kahului, HI 96732.

• *Paia Beach Centre*: Budget **R**. Shared accommodation from US$125 per person per week, US$400-500 per month. Private or group tuition, beginner to advanced. Board rental. On the beach in Lower Paia. **A** PO Box 118, Paia, HI 96779.

• *Second Wind*: Five minutes from Kanaha beach. Specialists for Maui used equipment although new gear is also available. Rental boards and tuition. **A** 111 Hana Highway, Kahului, HI 96732.

• *Hawaiian Island Windsurfing*: Close to the airport, one mile/1.6 km from Kahana, 200 rental boards available including F2, Mistral, Jimmy Lewis customs, Tiga and Hifly.

• *Freedom Maui*: Wide variety of custom boards available. **A** 555 Kaahumana Avenue, Kahului, HI 96732.

THE

Caribbean

Jamaica

The third largest island in the Caribbean, nearly half of Jamaica is mountainous wilderness and all of it can be explored by hire car, motorbike or local buses. Most of the beach resorts are spread out along the north coast, so unless you need to go via Kingston you're better off flying directly into Montego Bay's international airport. Jamaica's most famous beach is **Negril*****+, right on the island's westernmost point. With tourism now back on the increase new hotels are springing up here rapidly to cope with demand and the range of accommodation is enormous, with rooms and beach bungalows costing anything from US$15 to US$150 a night. If you can drag yourself away from the sound systems in the beach bars there's plenty to do on, under or even above the water, such as windsurfing, diving, para-sailing, snorkelling and water ski-ing. Originally discovered by hippies in the 1970s, Negril is too busy to be an escapists' beach but it's certainly a lot of fun, with a young and laid-back atmosphere.

Between Montego Bay and Ocho Rios the coast is liberally sprinkled with smart beach hotels, many of them with long-standing reputations for good food, good service and high standards of accommodation. The only problem is that a lot of the beaches along here are awful. Some beach resorts (such as the Club Caribbean) are suffering from erosion to such an extent that they've had to call in oceanographic engineers to try and alter the currents which are carrying away their sand. No less than eight beaches along the north coast are currently under intensive care by oceanographers, with sums as high as J$2.2 million (US$440,000) being spent in an effort to halt the damage.

Montego Bay is the largest resort (and the largest town) on the north coast but the sea here is polluted by the Montego River, which carries the

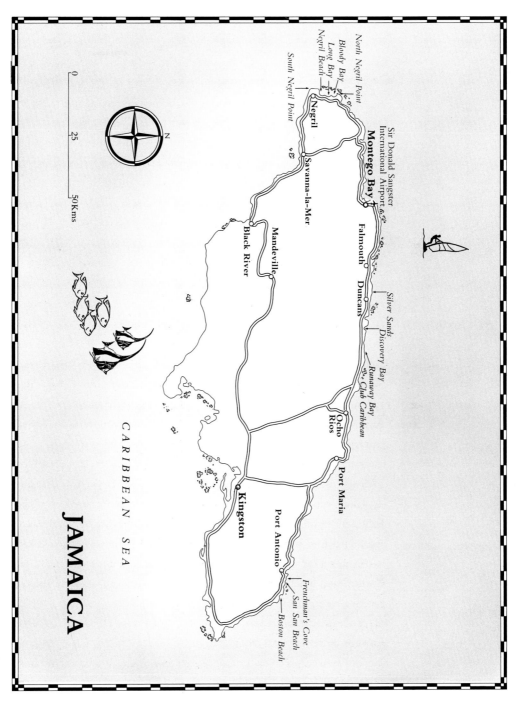

North Negril Point
Bloody Bay
Long Bay
Negril Beach
South Negril Point
Negril

Sir Donald Sangster
International Airport
Montego Bay
Falmouth
Duncans
Savanna-la-Mer
Silver Sands
Discovery Bay
Runaway Bay
Club Caribbean
Black River
Mandeville
Ocho Rios
Port Maria
Kingston
Port Antonio
Frenchman's Cove
San San Beach
Boston Beach

0
25
50Kms

N

C A R I B B E A N   S E A

JAMAICA

outflow from a major sewage treatment plant, and from the airport's swamp drainage channel, which carries dirty water and oil into the sea in considerable quantities after heavy rains.

Ocho Rios is one of the worst beach resorts in the Caribbean. It overlooks a disused bauxite works, the beach is crowded and the sea is choc-a-bloc with noisy jetskis and motor boats. There is one small dive operation (plus a multitude of glass-bottomed boats for snorkelling) but divers and snorkellers can save themselves a lot of effort and all that troublesome business of putting on equipment and getting wet since a large proportion of the reef is for sale on the beach.

One of the best beaches on this coast is at **Silver Sands★★★★**. This is a great beach for windsurfing and there are facilities on tap for day visitors or there are villas to rent for anyone considering a complete windsurfing holiday. High Winds Jamaica, who recently established themselves here, have a fleet of 24 boards including the full range of Mistrals and a number of custom boards. A day's rental includes the full use of the Silver Sands beach facilities (showers, open-air restaurant and beach-side bar) and tuition is of course available.

Jamaica Jamaica★★★★ is on a passable beach in Runaway Bay. This is one of four 'Super Clubs' on the north coast, an American all-inclusive resort concept similar to Club Med. Jamaica Jamaica is primarily geared towards singles, although couples and families are also welcome. Beach activities and watersports tuition at all Super Clubs are extensive and included in the cost, as is diving. A feature of the Super Clubs is that casual visitors can pay a day entrance fee (J$125/US$25) and use all the facilities as well as eat and drink as much as they wish – reasonable value for a day out if you're staying somewhere else.

East of Port Antonio there are one or two good beaches including **Frenchman's Cove★★★★**, one of the most peaceful and isolated in Jamaica, and probably the prettiest too.

A short distance past Frenchman's Cove you come to the **Blue Lagoon and San San Beach★★**, which is worth visiting for snorkelling. Boston Beach, a few miles past San San, is famous for its jerk pork (seasoned and pit-barbecued pork) which is sold at stands near the beach.

Diving at Negril

It is also one of four good surfing spots in Jamaica, with 16-ft/5-m waves breaking across the mouth of the bay during December.

You can reach these beaches for the day from Port Antonio, where there is a selection of local guest houses, and it's just feasible to come for the day from north coast resorts or even Kingston.

Monkey Island, San San

Jamaica is currently promoting itself as a diving destination but unfortunately, as many divers already know, all is not well underwater. The situation is outlined by Dr Jeremy Woodley of the Discovery Bay Marine Lab: 'Jamaica's reefs are in a sad state, smashed by hurricanes, polluted, deprived of fishes and overgrown with algae,' he says. 'Deforestation of the watersheds has led to soil erosion and the loss of thousands of tons of sediment into the sea, carrying fertilizers which encourage algae and smother the coral.'

Spearfishing, shell and coral collecting and damage by anchors have all contributed to the catalogue of disasters and fish populations are extremely overfished and diminished in size and numbers. 'The consequences are especially severe on the north coast where the submarine shelf is very narrow and the impact of reef fishing has been concentrated into a small area,' says Dr Woodley.

Ironically, this is the area currently being promoted for diving, with glossy, full-colour adverts selling Jamaica as a diving destination in the diving press. Given the catastrophic problems on Jamaica's reefs, one wonders whether the money wouldn't be better spent on marine parks so that divers would have some fish to look at when they get here.

Although Jamaica was one of the first countries to introduce marine parks (Ocho Rios was declared a reserve in 1966, Montego Bay in 1974) they have never had the means – that is, the money – to protect them. However, the Jamaican Association of Dive Operators (JADO) and the government have recently embarked on a programme to establish a series of eight new marine parks on the north coast, the first of which is likely to be around Airport Reef (visible out of the window as your plane comes in to land) in Montego Bay. This area is unique because it is practically the only reef which wasn't damaged by Hurricane Allen in 1980; the effects of 1988's Hurricane Gilbert, however, are not yet known.

Coupled with the marine parks initiative, an important new fisheries management project has been started by the Discovery Bay Marine Lab, with the help of funding from Canada.

Experienced divers who normally go to Caribbean destinations such as the Caymans, Belize or Cozumel won't be coming to Jamaica for a few years yet. However, that shouldn't deter anyone from learning to dive here or from going diving as part of their holiday, especially if you haven't dived in the tropics before. There are several reliable dive operations on the north coast (if you're a novice choose only a licensed operator who is a member of JADO), and underwater there are plenty of caves, canyons, gullies and photogenic sponges and sea whips to look at. And who knows, you might even come across a fish or two.

Jamaica is one of the few Caribbean countries where it's possible to travel around independently on a reasonable budget by catching local mini-buses (always jam packed and with reggae on full blast) and staying in guest houses. Jamaica can be a lot of fun but it isn't the place for inexperienced or timid travellers unless you're going straight to a resort.

Food and accommodation are reasonable value for money but car rental is very expensive – around J$360 US$65 per day with unlimited mileage. Despite being the country's largest foreign exchange earner, *ganja* is illegal.

GENERAL INFORMATION

Time
GMT – 5 hrs

IDD code
1 809 + 7 digit number

Currency
Jamaican dollar (J$10)
UK£1 = J$10
US$1 = J$5.5

Hotels
Most hotels quote prices in US$.
Deluxe: US$130-140
Expensive: US$80-130
Moderate: US$30-80
Budget: US$5-30

PUBLICATIONS
Guide to Jamaica
Harry Pariser (Moon Publications 1986). Paper-back 175 pp, £5.95/ US$6.95. Invaluable for independent travellers.

WEATHER
The dry season is from November/ December through to March. The wettest months are May, early June and September, October and early November. The hurricane season is from June to October and they're most common during August and September. Year-round temperatures average 89-90°F/27-32°C on the coast.

HEALTH
No vaccinations required.

VISAS
Visas issued on arrival, valid passport and onward ticket required.

TOURIST BOARDS
Head office: Kingston, tel: 929 9200; London, tel: (01) 499 1707; New York, tel: (212) 688 7650; Los Angeles, tel: (213) 304 1123; Tokyo, tel: (03) 578 9012; Frankfurt, tel: (069) 597 5674.

NEGRIL

More of an experience than a beach, Negril sums up Jamaica: reggae, *ganja*, always the hustle, and hot. Seven sandy miles/11 km of sybaritic indulgence, Negril is the Caribbean's answer to Goa.

In terms of beach 'extras', there's very little that you can't get: coconuts, cocaine, coconut oil, fresh prawns, pineapples, mangoes, avocados, ice-cream, *sensimillia*, fresh-squeezed orange juice, peanuts, *indica*, banana bread, hash oil, mushroom tea, patties, *aloe* massages . . . all these will come your way within a few hours of being here. Lie back and enjoy it would be the appropriate phrase except for the fact that with so many people selling on the beach (in local parlance they're known as 'higglers') beach life is far from peaceful. 'But we're just trying to go for a walk' is the plaintive cry of tourists cornered on the edge of the sea by fast-talking Rastas flogging reggae cassettes and everything else in sight. A Walkman and a pair of shades come in very handy for deflecting higglers.

In Negril the more expensive beach hotels have their own roped-off sunbathing areas for guests (Hedonism even has sentry boxes stuck out on piers in the sea – ucch) but most of Negril is not like this and it would be unusual if you hadn't made local friends after a few days.

The beach slopes off gently into the sea with no reefs, rocks or other obstacles underwater, perfect for swimming and watersports. The western end (nearest the shopping centre and the river outlet) does suffer from some pollution but all the hotels and guest houses listed here are on a good part of the beach.

There are also dozens of small hotels and guest houses strung out along the cliffs at the west end of Negril in the direction of Rick's Café; if you're booking a holiday from abroad and you want to be directly on the beach (and who doesn't?), check with your travel agent that your hotel is *not* on the west end cliffs. If it is, you'll need a motorbike to get to the beach every day.

For independent travellers guest houses cost from J$66 (US$12) per person per day; always negotiate for weekly rates, especially in off-season. Camping is also available (from J$22-27/US$4-5 at Sammy's Place and Root's Bamboo).

Bloody Bay, beyond the last headland to the east, used to be the beach to escape to away from the hustle of Negril, but with a new Super Club resort recently built next to Hedonism this is no longer a virgin beach. There is also a new Sandals resort to the west of Hedonism.

Negril is perfectly safe by day or night but don't leave valuables unattended. There are probably as many rip-offs here (particularly with coke) as there are grains of sand on the beach, so don't say you haven't been warned. In high season (late December to April) Negril can get very crowded.

Hurricane Gilbert caused more damage at the west end of Negril than it did on the beach itself, but most of it has now been repaired. Some palm trees have gone and parts of the beach lost a few yards of sand, but otherwise Negril is back to normal.

SNORKELLING*

There are numerous snorkelling excursions but sadly most of Negril has been

speared out. As one local fisherman explained, 'It don't make no sense to go out there and try and spear fish, buddy. There are just little baby fish living out there right now. There are no more to spear.'

The two most frequently-visited reefs are to the west of Booby Cay, offshore from Hedonism, and in the mouth of Bloody Bay. Local boatmen charge between J$20-75 (US$4-15) depending on how gullible or how far down the beach you are.

Joseph's Caves, beneath the cliffs at the western end of Negril, is a popular snorkelling area. You don't need a boat – steps go down the cliffs at a bar called Aweemaway Village, 2 miles/3 km west of the shopping centre. **MSF:** from J$45 (US$9) day.

WATERSPORTS****

Sailboards cost from J$44-55 (US$8-10)/hr, mostly beginners' boards and not in very good condition. Certification courses are non-existent and with instruction it's pot luck. Catamarans cost around J$110 (US$20)/hr, Sunfish J$44-55 (US$8-10)/hr, para-sailing J$110-137 (US$20-25), water ski-ing J$55-82 (US$10-15).

DIVING*
Local dive sites are just five to ten minutes out from the beach.

• *Blue Whale Divers*: Run by Cecil Brown with his assistant Paul, who will happily free dive down to 80 ft/24 m while you're on scuba and, what's more, hang around to pose for photos while he's there! One-tank dive J$192 (US$35); resort course J$275 (US$50); PADI open-water certification J$1,650 (US$300). **A** Norman Manley Blvd, Negril, tel: 957 4438.

• *Negril Scuba Centre*: Run by Karen McCarthy at the Negril Beach Club and the Negril Inn. One-tank dive J$165-190 (US$30-35); resort course J$275 (US$50); three dives J$440-522 (US$80-95). **A** Negril Beach Club, tel: 957 4425.

• *Hedonism II*: Two dives daily for guests (free), plus complimentary resort courses and certification courses. No night dives. Day guests to the resort may dive (free) if there's space available on the 11.30 a.m. shallow dive, 'C' card (and preferably also a logbook) required. Book in advance.

BARS AND RESTAURANTS
With around 20 beach bars and restaurants along the length of Negril there's no shortage of places to eat, knock back the Red Strip and listen to reggae. *Alfred's Ocean Palace* is the liveliest meeting place on the beach, with regular live bands even in the off-season. I have yet to find a restaurant in Negril where it's worth splashing out

on a meal: most of the up-market ones are a waste of money, with food which varies from the mediocre to the execrable and with service to match in most cases. Negril is a beach for connoisseurs of other pleasures besides food.

Jamaica Jamaica

ACCOMMODATION
• Where no address is shown write c/o Negril Post Office.

• *Negril Beach Club*: Expensive **R**. Lively hotel, young clientele. Tennis, pool. Double studios from US$65 (LS) to US$95 (HS), double rooms from US$75 (LS) to US$110 (HS). **A** PO Box 7, Negril, tel: 957 4220. Reservations: UK, tel: (01) 486 3560; USA, tel: (800) 526 1422.

• *T-Water Beach Hotel*: Expensive. Rooms and studios for US$80-100. **A** PO Box 11, Negril, tel: 957 4270. Reservations: USA, tel: (800) 654 1592.

• *Sammy's Place*: Moderate. Simple bamboo cabins and rooms for US$40-50. **A** c/o Negril Post Office.

• *Tambo Villa*: Moderate. **R**. Fairly sophisticated. Rooms for US$35-40 (LS), US$50-70 (HS), two-bedroom

233

cottages with kitchen from US$85 (LS) to US$145 (HS). **A** PO Box 6, Negril, tel: 957 4282.

• *Arthur's Golden Sunset*: Moderate/budget. Rooms from US$25-50. **A** PO Box 21, Negril, tel: 957 4241.

• *Gloria's Sunset and Carl's*: Budget **R**. Doubles from US$12-25. **A** c/o Negril Post Office.

• *Sunbeam Cottages*: Moderate. Double bedroom attic, US$40. **A** c/o Negril Post Office.

• *Negril Inn*: Expensive **R**. Pool, gym, tennis. One week from US$720 (LS) to US$840 (HS) fully inclusive of all meals, watersports and diving. **A** Negril, tel: 957 4209. Reservations: USA, tel: (800) 221 4588.

• *Whistling Bird*: Expensive **R**. Garden cottages (sleep four) from US$100. **A** Negril. Reservations: USA, tel: (303) 442 0722.

• *Westlea Cabins*: Budget. Cabins from US$20 (LS) to US$30 (HS). **A** Negril, tel: 957 4422. Reservations: USA, tel: (415) 647 9045.

• *Rondel Village*: Deluxe/expensive. Self-catering villas from US$90-100 (LS) to US$140-150 (HS). **A** Negril, tel: 957 4413. Reservations: UK, tel: (01) 486 3560.

• *Silver Sand Villa*: Moderate. Rooms and studios from US$30-65. **A** Negril, tel: 957 4207.

• *Negril Palm Beach Hotel*: Moderate. Rooms from US$40-50 (LS) to US$60-80 (HS). **A** Negril, tel: 957 4218.

• *Firefly Cottages*: Expensive/moderate. Self-catering cottages from US$45-55 (LS) to US$75-90 (HS). **A** Negril, tel: 957 4358. Reservations: USA, tel: (800) 221 8830.

• *Negril Tree House Cottages*: Expensive **R**. Rooms from US$55-85 (LS) to US$80-105 (HS). **A** PO Box 29, Negril, tel: 957 4287. Reservations: UK, tel:

(01) 486 3560; USA (800) 633 0045.

• *Foote Prints on the Sands Hotel*: Expensive. Self-catering rooms and studios from US$60-85 (LS) to US$90-125 (HS). **A** Negril, tel: 957 4300.

• *Mahogany Inn Beach Hotel*: Expensive. Double rooms from US$70-80 (LS) to US$90-110 (HS). **A** Negril, tel: 957 4401. Reservations: USA, tel: (614) 221 0014.

• *Poinciana Beach Hotel*: Expensive **R**. Pool, gym, sauna, Hobie and sunfish sailing, windsurfing, tennis. Rooms from US$40 (LS) to US$75 (HS), villas from US$105 (LS) to US$140 (HS). **A** Negril, tel: 957 4256. Reservations: UK, tel: (01) 486 3560; USA, (800) 468 6728.

• *Our Past Time Villas*: Moderate **R**. From US$50-100 (LS) to US$65-180 (HS). **A** Negril, tel: 957 4224. Reservations: UK, tel: (01) 486 3560.

• *Sundowner Hotel*: Expensive. Rooms from US$110-160. **A** PO Box 5, Negril, tel: 957 4225. Reservations: USA, NY, tel: (800) 243 9420.

• *Hedonism II*: Expensive. Around US$1,000 per week fully inclusive of all meals, drinks, sailing, windsurfing, tennis, squash, gym, water ski-ing and diving. Sports clinics with tuition by top pros in tennis, squash, bodybuilding and windsurfing are held during September. **A** PO box 25, Negril, tel: 957 4200. Reservations: USA, tel: (800) 858 8009.

ACCESS
Negril is 45 miles/72 km from Montego Bay airport, just under two hours' drive. Frequent mini-buses run along the coastal road or to Kingston (four hours).

SILVER SANDS

Home to High Winds, Jamaica's first professional windsurfing school, Silver Sands is the only real sandy beach between Negril and Runaway Bay. It is exposed to the north-east trades which get progressively stronger from January through to June, peaking in June and July, when they reach a consistent 18-22 knots daily. Challenging wave jumping for the experienced, with more sheltered conditions inside the reef for beginners.

Behind the beach there's a large estate of private villas for rent, or alternatively you can stay in a friendly establishment called the Sober Robin half-a-mile back up the hill on the main road.

WATERSPORTS★★★★★
Top-quality equipment, repair service. Boards cost J$55-80/US$11-15/hr. Beginners' courses and advanced instruction for beach and water starts available.

ACCOMMODATION
• *Silver Sands*: Deluxe. Villas from US$800-900 (LS) to US$1,200-1,900 (HS) per week for up to eight people. **A** Duncans, Trelawny, tel: 954 2001. Reservations: UK, tel: (01) 486 1301.

USA, tel: (800) 327 6511.
• Windsurfing packages through High Winds cost from US$450-600 per week, including accommodation, meals, board hire and instruction. **A** PO Box 143, Kingston 11, tel: 9262 485.
• *The Sober Robin*: Budget **R**. Just outside Duncans. Rooms from J$100 (US$20). **A** Duncans, Trelawny.

ACCESS
Thirty-one miles/50 km from Montego Bay, 36 miles/57 km from Ocho Rios.

RUNAWAY BAY: JAMAICA JAMAICA

Jamaica Jamaica is the liveliest of the all-inclusive 'Super Clubs', open to singles or couples. The beach is one of the better ones on this coast (it even gained five feet of sand after Hurricane Gilbert) and activities include sailing, windsurfing, diving, snorkelling, aerobics, tennis, and beach parties. This is a good swimming beach and there are also three swimming pools. The 'clothes optional' section of the beach has its own self-service bar and secluded jacuzzi.

Day passes cost J$125 (US$25), include buffet lunch and drinks, sailing, windsurfing, catamaran and snorkelling trips and all other activities except diving.

235

SNORKELLING
Boats leave twice daily for off-shore sites such as the sunken remains of a banana boat on a nearby headland, and there should also by now be a marked underwater snorkelling trail on the outside of the reef. Plenty of small reef fish, canyons, gullies, and healthy growths of staghorn and elkhorn corals. **MSF**: free.

WATERSPORTS★★★
Mistral school, three qualified instructors. Suitable for intermediate sailors. Sunfish sailing. No water ski-ing.

DIVING★★
Free boat dives twice a day for certified divers. A good place to learn, and with no less than seven dive guides on tap the ratio of guides to divers is high. Resort courses free. Certifications extra, (PADI five-day course, J$1,100 US$200). Top-of-the-line equipment.

ACCOMMODATION
• *Jamaica Jamaica*: Expensive. **R**

Rates from US$1,000 (LS) to US$1,200 (HS) for one week, fully-inclusive. Night club and disco. **A** PO Box 58, Runaway Bay, tel: 973 2436. Reservations: USA, (800) 858 8009; NY, (516) 868 6924.

ACCESS
Forty-five miles/72 km from Montego Bay airport, 60-90 minutes.

FRENCHMAN'S COVE

Frenchman's Cove is in a class of its own – you won't see a beach like this anywhere else in Jamaica. It is a small and perfect beach, surrounded by rocky cliffs and skirted by a stream from the Blue Mountains which creates cool, inviting pools of clear water in the sand. The hotel on the cliffs above the beach has seen better days and now has a rather derelict air to it, but Frenchman's Cove is a brilliant retreat from the hassles of Jamaica and also makes a good base from which to explore this un-touristy part of the coast. Day admission for outside visitors is J$10/US$2, and there's a small bar with waiter service on the beach. Frenchman's Cove is handy for San San and the Blue Lagoon. The hotel was badly damaged by Hurricane Gilbert in 1988 and was closed for rebuilding as we went to press.

DIVING★
A safe, easy beginners' spot for beach dives. The reef is just a short way out, dropping off gradually from 30-60ft/9-

Frenchman's Cove

18m. Diving can be arranged through Janet Lee, tel: 993 3481. Resort dive US$50; One-tank dive US$27.

BARS AND RESTAURANTS
Beach bar open from 10a.m. to 5p.m. Unfortunately the food in the main restaurant is terrible.

ACCOMMODATION
• *Frenchman's Cove*: Expensive **R**. Large, comfortable rooms cost from B&B US$50 (LS), full-board US$200 (HS). Cottages cost from US$100 (LS) to US$300 (HS). **A** Port Antonio, tel: 993 3224. Reservations: USA, (512) 625 1030.

ACCESS
Port Antonio to Frenchman's Cove is 5 miles/8 km, ten minutes by car or mini-bus. Port Antonio is two hours from Kingston and 65 miles/104 km miles from Ocho Rios (two-and-a-quarter hours by car).

THE BLUE LAGOON and SAN SAN BEACH

San San Beach is one half of a double-bowed bay, the other half of which is the Blue Lagoon: this dreamy location was first discovered by Errol Flynn in the 1950s, who popularized river-rafting down the nearby Rio Grande. Today, the elegant waterfront villas in the middle of the 'w' of the two bays are fit for film stars and accordingly cost a fortune to rent.

San San itself is open to the public and fills up with as many as 300 people at weekends but during the week it's okay. Independent travellers can 'commute' to the beach from guest houses in Port Antonio.

From San San you can swim or snorkel out to Monkey Island, where there is a little sandy beach with jungle towering directly above it on the rocks. Mind out for sea urchins in shallow areas.

To see or swim in the Blue Lagoon, take a track several hundred yards east of San San (signposted Blue Lagoon Restaurant & Bar). Partially enclosed by a semi-circular wall of jungle, the lagoon is nearly 200ft/60m deep and is fed by over thirty underground springs. There is a pier for swimming, handily located next to the bar. For ethnic locomotion around the lagoon you can hire bamboo rafts.

SNORKELLING★★

The most rewarding areas are on the outside arms of the reef where they curve inwards, directly opposite San San. The quickest way to get there is straight out from the right-hand end of the beach towards Monkey Island, and then hang a left. This will place you at the beginning of the deeper sections with the minimum of travelling across boring turtle grass. Follow the reef wall as it curves round to the right, eventually dropping from 20ft/6m down to 60ft/18m. Ravines, mini-walls and some impressive, undamaged elkhorn corals on the wave-washed edge of the reef are the main features.

On the Blue Lagoon side of the bay you'll come across thermoclines while snorkelling: these occur whenever different temperatures of water mix, and the effect is like swimming through petroleum jelly or 3-D clingfilm. Don't panic, your mask is not out of focus! Put your head under further and the separation of the two can be seen as a horizontal slice – the colder water is from the Blue Lagoon.

BARS AND RESTAURANTS

Snack bar at San San. The *Blue Lagoon Restaurant and Bar* serves reasonable but expensive food in a cinematographic setting.

ACCOMMODATION

Port Antonio

• *DeMontevin Lodge*: Budget. **R.** Rooms from J$100-150 (US$20-30). **A** 21 Fort George Street, tel: 993 2604.

• *Sunnyside Guest House* (overlooking the bay at 18 Fort George Street), *Rose Guest House* (25 Fort George Street) and *Nova Scotia Guest House* are all clustered around the DeMontevin, with rooms for J$30-60 (US$6-12).

ACCESS

San San is twenty minutes east of Port Antonio by bus or car.

237

St Lucia

S t Lucia is a wild, untamed island with some of the finest mountain scenery in the Caribbean. The island's most recognizable and spectacular landmarks, the twin peaks of Gros Piton and Petit Piton, are easily seen as your plane banks before landing at Hewanorra international airport. The majority of St Lucia's beach resorts are clustered on the north-west coast near the capital of Castries (over 40 miles/64 km from the airport) so be prepared for long transfers.

St Lucia's best beach is **Reduit Beach★★★★★** to the north of Castries. Here you have the option of staying in the enormous St Lucian Hotel, which is on the beach, or the much smaller Islander Hotel, which is self-catering and set back several hundred yards from the sea. This is the liveliest beach on the island and it has a number of restaurants within easy reach of the hotels.

The northern-most hotel on the island is Le Sport at Cariblue Beach. This is the old Cariblue Hotel relaunched as an all-inclusive resort offering clients a 'Body Holiday' with spa therapies in tropical surroundings. The concept is that you check your body in knackered and defunct and check it out restored and feeling like a million dollars. Meals, drinks, land-based sports and diving, windsurfing and water ski-ing are included in the cost. When I stayed here work had just begun on remodelling the resort and it certainly merits consideration, as long as you don't mind a grey volcanic beach. The only other resort on this coast which I recommend is the Halcyon Beach Club.

Apart from these hotels, I wouldn't bother with any of the others on this coast. Club St Lucia, which is near the Cariblue on the north of the island, has now been converted into yet another all-inclusive resort. St Lucia regulars will know this as the old Smuggler's Village but it has now

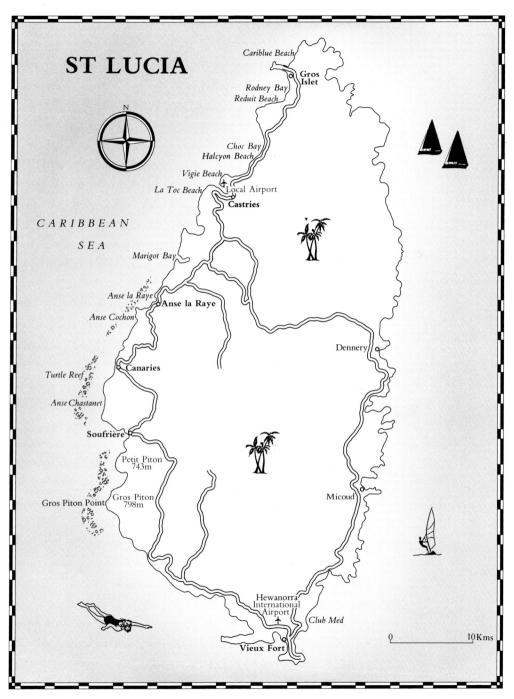

ST LUCIA

Cariblue Beach

Gros Islet

Rodney Bay
Reduit Beach

N

Choc Bay
Halcyon Beach

Vigie Beach
La Toc Beach   Local Airport

Castries

CARIBBEAN

SEA

Marigot Bay

Anse la Raye   **Anse la Raye**

Anse Cochon

Dennery

Turtle Reef   **Canaries**

Anse Chastanet

Soufrière

Petit Piton
743m

Gros Piton Point   *Gros Piton*
798m   Micoud

Hewanorra
International
Airport   *Club Med*

Vieux Fort

0   10 Kms

gone horribly down-market (a sort of Butlins in the tropics) and none of the bungalows has ocean views.

Vigie Beach is the nearest beach to Castries, right alongside the inter-island airport. The main property on the beach is the all-inclusive Couples, with the tatty Vigie Beach Hotel at the northern end. The latter has recently been acquired by the owners of the Halcyon Beach Club, who plan to spend EC$1 million (US$400,000) on redevelopment. It needs it. Couples has all usual free amenities of the franchised Super Clubs (including unlimited food and wine, continuous entertainment, sports and watersports) but unfortunately the beach is suffering badly from erosion and is narrow and crowded. Their brochure says 'We believe the bond between men and women who choose to be together is the kind of magic that deserves a special celebration all of its own. There's something happily guileless about your Couples holiday which is reminiscent of French philosopher Jean Jacques Rousseau's "noble innocence". Everything is included because Adam and Eve didn't have pockets in paradise, so why should you?' If that makes you want to vomit, wait until you see the people who booked in after reading it. The resort is next to a cemetery.

Heading down the coast in the other direction from Castries brings you to the Cunard La Toc, one of St Lucia's best-known hotels.

The road from La Toc southwards takes you through banana plantations to Marigot Bay, a photogenic natural harbour and 'hurricane hole' with extensive mooring facilities and one hotel, the Marigot Bay Resort. Alas, the small beach (on a peninsula in the middle of the bay) is only kept in place by concrete blocks and you have to clamber over these to swim here. Not recommended for a beach holiday, but it makes a pleasant lunch stop.

Two-thirds of the way down St Lucia's south-west coast is the diving resort of **Anse Chastanet****, hidden away around a winding cliff road just north of the town of Soufrière. For potential or qualified divers this is the obvious choice on St Lucia and there's enough to see and do in the surrounding area to make it a suitable base for non-divers too. Although there are reefs elsewhere around St Lucia they're less well developed than at Anse Chastanet and in the north most of them have been destroyed by dynamite fishing. Scuba St Lucia, who are based here, organize resort courses and dive trips to Anse Chastanet from most of the hotels in the north.

Near the southern tip of the island is St Lucia's Club Med, just five minutes from the airport. The beach here is on the exposed side of the island and normally covered in seaweed. However, wind and waves provide excellent conditions for intermediate to advanced windsurfing. As with neighbouring Barbados, the most consistent winds are from November to March/April, with the peak (20-25 knots/5-6 Beaufort daily) in December and January. Club Med has a range of well-maintained boards and all the usual activities for guests.

You'll need a car to get out and about from the hotels and explore St Lucia's rich natural surroundings – tourism still takes second place to bananas in the island's economy. There are well-organized island-hopping excursions to neighbouring countries such as Martinique and the Grenadines (from US$135-150 for the day including flights). Over the Whitsun weekend every year St Lucia holds the Aqua Action watersports festival with an international yacht race, dinghy and windsurfing races and water polo and water ski-ing events.

Toplessness and nudity are illegal.

Tube sponges, Anse Chastanet

GENERAL INFORMATION

Time
GMT – 4 hours

IDD code
1 809 45 + 5 digit number

Currency
Eastern Caribbean dollar (EC$)
UK£1 = EC$4.9
US$1 = EC$2.5

Hotels
Hotel rates don't include 18 per cent tax

Frogfish, Anse Chastanet

241

and service. Most hotels quote prices in US$.

Single/double from:
Deluxe: US$120/140 (LS) to US$160/200 (HS)
Expensive: US$80/100 (LS) to US$100/160 (HS)
Moderate: US$40/45 (LS) to US$70/80 (HS)

WEATHER

The driest and coolest period is from January to April, with the rainy season being June to October. Daytime temperatures average 80-82°F/27-28°C from November to February and 88-90°F/29-30°C from April to October. Water temperatures average 78°F/26°C from November to January and 82°F/28°C for the rest of the year.

HEALTH

No formal health requirements unless coming from an infected yellow fever area.

VISAS

Valid passport required except for nationals of the UK, USA and Canada, providing length of stay does not exceed six months. Onward ticket required.

TOURIST BOARDS

Head Office: St Lucia, tel: 24094; London, tel: (01) 370 0926; Homburg, tel: (06172) 304431; USA, tel: (212) 867 2950.

REDUIT BEACH

Big, busy beach just over 6 miles/10 km north of Castries, with the St Lucian Hotel situated right on the beach. Behind the St Lucian is the Islander Hotel, a good choice for a moderately-priced hotel as long as you don't mind not having the beach right outside your doorstep.

This is the best beach on St Lucia despite the fact that it's shored up at intervals with netted rocks close to the hotel. The hotel also pulls a younger, more lively crowd than elsewhere and this is practically the only beach on the island (apart from Anse Chastanet) which isn't clogged up with inactive couch-potatoes.

At the St Lucian most watersports are free and it's the only hotel on the island to offer para-sailing. Diving courses plus trips to Anse Chastanet for qualified divers can be arranged from here through Scuba St Lucia.

A big advantage of this beach is that there are a number of restaurants within walking distance. In most of the other resorts you need transport to go out in the evening.

The owners of the St Lucian are planning to build a new multi-storey block, the Royal St Lucian, on a small piece of land adjacent to the present hotel: whether or not this will spoil St Lucia's prettiest beach remains to be seen.

SNORKELLING

Free snorkelling trips twice a day to reefs around the headland. Five-hour trips to Anse Chastanet (US$45 per person, includes lunch and sightseeing) through Jacob's Watersports; if you just want to go snorkelling it's cheaper to book through Scuba St Lucia (tel: 47355), who charge US$25.

WATERSPORTS★★★★★

Free watersports for St Lucian guests

except parasailing (EC$50-75/US$20-30), windsurfing lessons (EC$85/US$35/3hr), and high performance sailboards (EC$350/US$140/week). Conditions are suitable for beginner to intermediate sailors and there is a Mistral school with a good selection of up-to-date equipment. For visitors board rental costs EC$25 (US$10)/hr, EC$62.50 (US$25)/day, Sunfish EC$20 (US$8)/hr and water ski-ing is EC$25 (US$10).

DIVING

Diving is by arrangement with *Scuba St Lucia* (tel: 47354). Pool demos on Mondays and Thursdays, resort courses and dive trips to Anse Chastanet on Tuesdays and Fridays. Resort courses cost EC$162.50 (US$65) including an open-water dive at Anse Chastanet (second dive, add EC$62.50/US$25); two-tank dives cost around EC$200 (US$80) including equipment and transport.

BARS AND RESTAURANTS

The St Lucian has two restaurants and five bars, including the *Hummingbird Bar* (mini-steel band every night, jazz on Sundays), the *Sunset Bar* (live bands every night), the *Surf Club Bar* (overlooking the beach), and *Splash Disco* (St Lucia's biggest and best disco, open to non-residents). There is also a small, well-stocked supermarket on the premises.

ACCOMMODATION

• *The St Lucian*. Expensive **R**. Recently expanded to 222 a/c rooms, single/double from US$80/100 (LS) to US$130/160 (HS). Swimming pool, tennis. **A** PO Box 512, Castries, tel: 28351-5. Reservations: UK, tel: (01) 589 0144; USA, tel: (201) 488 7788 or (800) 221 1831.

• *The Islander*: Moderate **R**. Small self-catering complex. Studios from single/double US$40/45 (LS) to US$75/85 (HS), apartments with kitchenettes from single/double US$45/55 (LS) to US$85/95 (HS). **A** PO Box 907, Castries, tel: 28757. Reservations: USA, tel: (212) 840 6636 or (800) 223 9815.

ACCESS

Seven miles/11 km (15 minutes) north of Castries, 60-90 minutes from the international airport.

ANSE CHASTANET

Anse Chastanet is a small, informal resort in a sheltered cove not far from Soufrière and the Pitons. The setting is typically tropical and, although the pace is relaxed, the hotel is totally geared to the needs of divers at any level. Right on the beach there is a PADI five-star dive centre, Scuba St Lucia, which is managed by two Brits, Chris and Joyce Huxley. The diving service is personalized and efficient and the attitude of the staff at Scuba St Lucia to the marine world on their doorstep is as enthusiastic as it is fanatically protective. You couldn't choose a better place to learn to dive.

243

Anse Chastanet is famous for its beach diving and the nearest reefs are literally within a minute or two of the dive shop. Most other dive sites are just a short boat ride away. There's certainly enough variety here to satisfy all but the most choosy of divers, although the reefs are limited by comparison with more famous

Caribbean destinations and large fish aren't common (despite the fact that Anse Chastanet is officially a marine park, fishing boats pull in here twice a day to cast their nets and local spearfishermen wander freely down to the beach). However, Anse Chastanet is still home to an enormous variety of marine life.

The visibility averages around 50-70ft/15-21m. This is good in comparison to temperate waters but it isn't exceptional for the tropics (St Lucia is a very lush island and coastal areas are subject to considerable amounts of fresh water run off). I'm told it can sometimes reach 100ft/30m and it will of course be best in the dry season (November/December to April/May).

Because of the proximity of the reef to the beach this is a good place for snorkelling but (as with the diving) don't expect anything too dramatic. When a northerly wind is blowing the main snorkelling area around the headland is sometimes invaded by small jellyfish (known locally as sea ants) which can inflict a nasty rash, so if it's at all windy check with the dive shop before going out. You might need a bodysuit or wetsuit.

The beach consists of grey volcanic sand and, as is normal with volcanic beaches, it tends to be scorchingly hot. If you're just coming to St Lucia for a beach holiday and prefer white sandy beaches it would be better to choose another hotel.

The resort is owned by Canadian architect Nick Troobitscoff and all the rooms and bungalows are individually designed. Accommodation ranges from enormous suites on top of the hill (with terrific views of the Pitons) to more recently-built, but no less spacious, beach-houses. Except for the beach units all rooms and suites involve a long climb to get to and from the beach.

The resort is just around the corner from Soufrière, which was the original French capital of St Lucia. Many of the old gingerbread-style houses in this historical settlement are currently being restored and if you can tear yourself away from the diving its worth exploring.

Anse Chastanet

Reduit Beach

WATERSPORTS*
Sunfish and sailboards free (visitors US$10/hr).

DIVING****
The first dive for everyone who arrives here is an orientation dive off the beach. Although there are twice daily boat dives to other areas many people find themselves going back again and again to the reef right off the beach. *Undercurrent* comments 'this rates among the best, most beautiful, easy beach dives in the Caribbean.' It includes a good shallow section, a cave that goes back 80ft/24m and a wall that drops down to 120ft/36m, so there's plenty of interest.

Around the corner from the resort, Fairy Land is a reef area on the headland which jumps with colour and variety, normally dived at around 50ft/15m. Numerous boulders and cubby holes provide hiding places for fish to lurk in, and strong changeable currents ensure consistently good visibility.

Further afield, the Pinnacles is a dramatic site with volcanic seamounts coming right up to the surface, covered in soft corals and black and orange gorgonia. At the base of the dramatic Petit Piton – the nearest of the twin Piton peaks – are two of Chris Huxley's favourites: the spectacular Piton Wall, and Superman's Flight, a cliff face with some very unusual currents. 'I've seen it when one group of divers is travelling in one direction at 30ft/9m, without finning, and another group is travelling in the opposite direction at 60ft/18m, also without finning,' says Chris. 'I've had a dive there where the current changed on me five different times, quite dramatically.' Emerging from the underwater domain to find the Pitons towering vertically for hundreds of feet above you is a highlight of a dive at the Pitons.

On the Gros Piton Point they have a new site, the Piton Terrace, which features solid beds of sponges concealing a number of unusual sargassum trigger fish. Just north of the resort is Turtle Reef, which is frequented by many schooling fish such as jacks, rainbow runners, grunts, yellowtails, Bermuda chubb, and southern sennet. You'll also come across the remains of a Porsche 911 on Turtle Reef, sunk by Nick Troobitscoff as an artificial reef after it caught fire in 1985.

Thirty-five minutes' boat ride to the north is the wreck of the *Lesleen M*, a freighter which was put down as an artificial reef in 1986. Home to French angelfish and Nassau grouper, the wreck is already starting to be covered with hydroids and soft corals.

Beyond the *Lesleen M* are Anse La Raye and Anse Cochon, both areas where the coral is less well developed than at Anse Chastanet but with a boulder-terrain featuring sponges with plenty of fish hiding in nooks and crannies. This is one of the few areas where turtles are regularly seen.

• *Scuba St Lucia*: One-tank dive EC$62.50 (US$25) not including equipment; resort course EC$125 (US$50); PADI open-water certification EC$812.50 (US$325); underwater photography courses EC$375 (US$150) (own camera), EC$500 (US$200) (hire

camera); Sea & Sea 35mm EC$50 (US$20) per dive; E6 processing EC$20 (US$8) per film. Diving packages for 3-7 nights including accommodation and transfers cost from EC$950 (US$380) (3 nights/4 dives) to EC$2,150 (US$860) (7 nights/12 dives), double occupancy. **A** PO Box 216, St Lucia, tel: 47354.

BARS AND RESTAURANTS

Meals cost EC$87.50 (US$35)/day and food is plentiful; as well as the main restaurant there's a beach bar with a varied and interesting lunchtime menu (the fish kebabs and home-made soups and ice-creams are particularly good). Weekly Creole buffets.

Reduit Beach

ACCOMMODATION

• *Anse Chastanet*: Expensive **R**. Single/double from US$60/80 to US$100/120 (LS); US$115/130 to US$175/210 (HS). **A** PO Box 216, Soufrière, St Lucia, tel: 47354. Reservations: USA, tel: (800) 223 5581; NY, tel: (212) 535 9530 or Go Diving, tel: (800) 328 5285, 328 0734.

ACCESS

40-50 minutes by taxi from the airport.

245

Barbados

B arbados is the most easterly of the Windward group of Caribbean islands and for beachgoers it has a little of everything, including some of the best windsurfing conditions in the Caribbean and several world-class surfing spots.

Barbados has a very distinct pattern of beaches. The island is pear-shaped, 21 miles/34 km from north to south and 14 miles/22 km from east to west, and every part of the coast has a different facet.

The **West Coast★★★** is the main 'Caribbean' beach area, with white sand beaches and calm, azure-coloured seas. This is where most of the better hotels on Barbados are located and the sheltered conditions provide plenty of opportunities for watersports. There are also facilities for diving and snorkelling.

Going anti-clockwise around the island, immediately to the south of Bridgetown there is a fine white sandy beach in Carlisle Bay, quite unexpected so close to the town centre. This beach is perfectly suitable for a swim or a lunch break when you're duty-free shopping in town but Carlisle Bay is essentially a boat harbour and I wouldn't recommend the hotels here for a holiday.

On Needham's Point at the end of Carlisle Bay the Barbados Hilton has had to import an artificial beach, and although it's a decent-sized expanse of white sand most of it is held in place by rock walls, which is not attractive.

Barbados' southern resort area (from Needham's Point round the Grantley Adams International Airport) was the first to be developed for tourism on the island. Unfortunately, pollution has destroyed the off-shore reefs and led to the loss of most of the beaches along here. This spiral of decline has affected many of the hotels, which can no longer afford to renovate their facilities. Ribbon building along the roadside, including fast-food outlets and supermarkets, has further added to the over-development of this coast and turned it into one of the least desirable beach areas.

Further east, in the direction of the fishing port of Oistins, there are several beaches and bays which are ideal for intermediate and advanced windsurfing. The first of these is **Benston Beach****** in Oistins Bay, home to the largest Club Mistral on the island and a small selection of moderately-priced hotels if you want to stay longer than just for the day.

Several miles past here you'll find **Silver Sands*******, a superb little beach which also happens to be the island's hottest windsurfing spot. This is experts-only territory but, whereas you would only want to stay on Benston if you were a keen sailor, Silver Sands merits consideration for a non-sailing holiday too. The only drawback is that like most of the beaches east of Oistins Silver Sands is a long way from shops or restaurants and you'll need to rent a car to get out and about.

On the **South East Coast*******+ there are a series of small coves and beaches which are considerably more isolated and less developed than either their south or west coast counterparts. Swept clean by the Atlantic breakers, with fine white sand and almost constant surf, the three principal beaches in this area are Crane Beach, Ginger Bay Beach and Long Bay. The first two in particular are good beaches to escape to with a picnic for the day.

Barbados' east coast is directly exposed to the Atlantic Ocean and subject to strong winds and tides. Although swimming is dangerous at most of the beaches along here the area is worth visiting for its rural landscapes and the dramatic views of the coastline which can occasionally be glimpsed from the road. It takes about 30–40 minutes to drive to across the middle of the island from the west coast.

The focal point of the east coast is the small fishing community of Bathsheba, with, just below it, a small beach and surfing area known as the Soup Bowl: this is Barbados' most well-known surfing break (see *Surfing*, page 258).

Beyond Bathsheba is the east coast's main beach, over three miles/

five km of pounding breakers. It's almost impossible to swim along here and extreme care should be taken because of heavy surf, currents and dangerous submerged rocks in the surf-zone.

Barbados' wildest and most isolated beach, Morgan Lewis Beach, can be found without too much difficulty by continuing on from here into the parish of St Andrew. Once you arrive at St Andrew's Church (which is well signposted), take the north-east fork at the junction and follow the road until you see and old windmill on the hillside in front of you. Before you draw level with the mill you'll see a track flanked by a double row of palms going off to the right. Follow this for about a mile until you come to the beach. It's sometimes grubby with washed-up debris from ships but there is over two miles of sand and it's the only place on the island where you can hope to get an all-over tan. Officially, toplessness and nudity are illegal in Barbados.

East Coast

On all Barbados beaches you should be careful of the indigenous Manchineel trees, which has a fruit like a small green apple. This is toxic and can produce blisters if touched; it should never be eaten. When it's raining the drips from the tree can produce allergic skin reactions, so never shelter underneath one. Most Manchineel trees are clearly marked with warning signs.

Almost every square inch of Barbados is either built up or under cultivation (in complete contrast to its jungly neighbour, St Lucia) and it's a very tame and safe country to visit.

Beach-hopping is easy: buses and mini-buses operate all over the island for a flat fare of 75 cents. Mini-mokes and cars cost from B$80 (US$40) per day and from B$300-400 (US$150-200) a week. Driving is on the left, and the main roads are both busy and narrow, with motorists

making frequent and unpredictable stops to say hello to friends or to pick up and drop off passengers – you really need ESP to drive here.

Barbados has never been known as a serious diving destination and visiting snorkellers and divers shouldn't expect too much (see *Diving and Snorkelling*, page 260). However, Barbados does have a hi-tech passenger submarine, *The Atlantis* which will take anyone down into the depths (see page 261).

GENERAL INFORMATION

Time
GMT – 4 hours

IDD code
1 + 809 + 7 digit number

Currency
Barbados dollar (B$)
UK£1 = B$3.7
US$1 = B$2

27°C, with the highest averages in August and September (81°F/29°C) and the lowest in January (77.5°F/24°C). June/July to November is the rainy season.

HEALTH
No major health hazards. Water drinkable everywhere.

Sandy Lane

Hotels
Hotel rates quoted do not include 10 per cent service charge and 5 per cent government tax. Most hotels quote prices in US$.
Single/double from:
Deluxe: US$130/150 (LS) to US$180/300 (HS)
Expensive: US$90/120 (LS) to US$150/200 (HS)
Moderate: US$30/40 (LS) to US$60/80 (HS)
Budget: US$10/20 (LS) to US$20/40 (HS)

WEATHER
Year-round temperatures average 80°F/

VISAS
Passports only necessary for citizens of countries other than the UK, USA and Canada. Nationals of these three countries must however carry valid ID and be in possession of an onward or return ticket. Visas are not necessary for citizens of most other countries for stays of under three months.

TOURIST BOARDS
Head Office: 427 2623, 427 2624; London, tel: (01) 636 9448; New York, tel: (212) 986 6516 or (800) 221 9831; Los Angeles, tel: (213) 380 2198, 2199; Toronto, tel: (416) 979 2137 or (800) 268 9122; Frankfurt, tel: (069) 280982.

249

WEST COAST

Paradise Beach, Payne's Bay, Sandy Lane, Discovery Bay, Cobbler's Cove

With the demise of the south coast this is now Barbados' main holiday beach area, several continuous miles of beach curving in and around the headlands with dozens of hotels and restaurants, from the glitzy to the grotty, lining the shore.

Since this is the Caribbean side of the island the turquoise-coloured sea is normally calm with only light winds, suitable for beginners' windsurfing and water ski-ing. There are numerous small watersports shacks for rentals and tuition and the local lads zoom up and down on the beaches on their jetskis all day to try and get you to have a ride.

The first resort on the west coast is Paradise Beach, where there is a Cunard Hotel. The hotel is about as tasteful as the QE2 and almost as dull, but the beach is good. Next along is Payne's Bay, a spacious beach with five hotels and holiday apartment blocks (the Buccaneer Bay, Tamarind Cove, Treasure Beach, Smuggler's Cove and the Beachcomber Apartments). The beach is okay and you can swim along most of it.

The next beach is Sandy Lane, one of the west coast's finest and home to one of Barbados' big-name hotels, the Sandy Lane Hotel, host to many famous jet-set and showbiz personalities during the early 1960s and now managed by the Trusthouse Forte Group. The beach is normally calm but sometimes there is an unexpected and very powerful shorebreak.

At the end of Sandy Lane beach is the Divi St James Resort, which has a dive shop attached. This is a convenient hotel on the west coast for potential or qualified divers and it also has the largest range of free watersports (windsurfing, water ski-ing, Sunfish and Hobie sailing) of any hotel. Unfortunately, ocean swimming directly in front of the hotel is limited because of shallow reef, but it's not far to Sandy Lane on one side or Discovery Bay on the other.

The next beach is Discovery Bay, the busiest and liveliest, a constant mêlée of jet skis and speedboats and also the stopping point for the *Jolly Roger* booze-cruise pirate ships. Not the place to choose if you want a quiet life. Several hotels here have self-catering rooms and there is a large, well-stocked supermarket just the other side of the road.

At the end of Discovery Bay there is a small marine museum in Folkestone Park. This is due to be renovated in the near future as part of the new management plan for marine parks.

Beyond here the Coral Reef Club and the Colony Club share a good beach with safe swimming: both these hotels tend to attract an older clientele. Next along is the Royal Pavilion, a ritzy revamp of the old Miramar Hotel, also on a reasonable beach. Finally, Cobbler's Cove is a small hotel on a good beach just south of Speightstown.

Some of the beaches along here are becoming eroded; resorts to avoid on the west coast include the Barbados Beach Village (cramped, ugly beach, swimming restricted to one channel in the rocks), the Coconut Creek Hotel (no beach at high

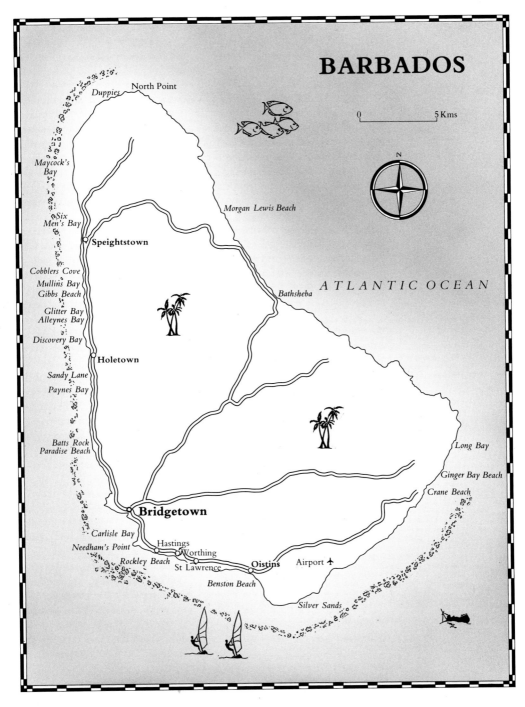

BARBADOS

0 _____ 5 Kms

North Point

Duppies

Maycock's Bay

Six Men's Bay

○ **Speightstown**

Morgan Lewis Beach

ATLANTIC OCEAN

Cobblers Cove
Mullins Bay
Gibbs Beach

Glitter Bay
Alleynes Bay

Discovery Bay

○ **Holetown**

Bathsheba

Sandy Lane
Paynes Bay

Batts Rock
Paradise Beach

Long Bay

Ginger Bay Beach

Crane Beach

Bridgetown

Carlisle Bay
Needham's Point
Rockley Beach
Hastings
○ *Worthing*
St Lawrence
Oistins
Benston Beach
Airport ✈

Silver Sands

tide), Sandy Lane Beach Apartments (no beach frontage), the Sandridge Beach Hotel (dismal beach, impossible swimming) and Heywood's (narrow beach, swimming restricted to one channel because of beach rock and shallow reef).

SNORKELLING★

There is a marine preserve and underwater trail in between the Divi St James and Discovery Bay, half-a-mile/.8 km south of Folkestone Park and the Marine Museum. This is the west coast's main snorkelling area but it's in a sad state: the buoys which mark the trail have drifted off or been damaged and the underwater plaques which are supposed to tell you what to look for are no longer visible. Spearfishing still takes place and there's not a lot to see. Okay for beginners. **MSF**: rentals on the beach.

WATERSPORTS★★★★★

Rates run at around B$20 (US$10)/hr for windsurfing, B$20-30 (US$10-15)/hr for Sunfish, B$25 (US$12.50) for water ski-ing, B$25-30 (US$12.50-15)/hr for Hobie cats and B$25 (US$12.50)/

Benston Beach

15 minutes for jetskis. Para-sailing B$50 (US$25).

DIVING★★

The most dramatic local dive site is the wreck of the 365 ft/111 m *Stravonikita*, a Greek freighter which was sunk off Fitt's Village in 1978. Unfortunately, it was sunk just downstream from a river outlet which pumps large amounts of fine silt and chemicals into the sea whenever there is heavy rainfall, so visibility here rarely exceeds 30-40ft/9-12m. It is, however, one of the biggest and most dramatic wrecks in the Caribbean, with its top structure within 55ft/17m of the surface and the prop at around 140ft/42m. Fish life around the wreck isn't prolific but you can explore the entire wreck (holds, cabins, etc) in safety.

Some of the best dive sites on the coast are up towards the north end of the island where the reefs are much less affected by sewage pollution from the hotels and, although dynamiting is still a problem up here, the destruction is confined to the shallow and medium depth reefs. Marine biologists from the Bellairs Research Institute in Folkestone Park say that these are the only reefs in Barbados with a 100 per cent coral cover.

On average one-tank dives cost around B$60-70 (US$30-35) including all equipment, resort courses US$50, certifications US$300.

● *Underwater Barbados*: tel: 428 3504: *Dive Barbados/Jolly Roger Watersports*, tel: 432 7090; *Blue Reef Watersports*, tel: 422 4177; *The Dive Shop*, tel: 426 9947; *Shades of Blue*, tel: 422 3215; *Sandy Lane Dive Shop*, tel: 432 1311, ext. 278; *Willie's Watersports*, tel: 425 1060.

BARS AND RESTAURANTS

There are numerous tourist restaurants along the coast and plenty of cheap local eateries. Of the hotel restaurants, the best of the many that I tried were at *Treasure Beach* (tel: 432 1346) and the *Cobbler's Cove* (tel: 422 2291). At Cobbler's Cove the imaginative menu is supervised by an English chef and the four-course *table d'hôte* menu (around US$35 per person) would please all but the most critical gourmet.

Hotels provide live entertainment throughout the winter season, with calypso, steel bands and other shows. The best two nightspots on the island are the *Warehouse* (on the quay in Bridgetown, tel: 436 2897) and *Harbour Lights* (on the beach south of Bridgetown, tel: 436 7225).

ACCOMMODATION

• *Treasure Beach*: Expensive **R**. Small pool. Double suites from US$105-135 (LS) to US$205-245 (HS). **A** St James, tel: 432 1346. Reservations: UK, tel: (0244) 41131; USA, tel: (800) 223 6510

or (212) 832 2277.

• *Smuggler's Cove*: Expensive/moderate. Small pool. Apartments and studios from single/double US$50/70 (LS) to US$100/120 (HS). No sea views, dull hotel. **A** St James, tel: 432 1741.

• *Beachcomber Apartments*: Expensive/moderate. Apartments with kitchens from US$150 (LS) to US$250 (HS) for up to four people. Studios from US$55 (LS) to US$110 (HS). **A** St James, tel: 432 0489.

• *Sandy Lane Hotel*: Deluxe **R**. Single/double from US$115/140 (LS) to US$390/430 (HS), suites from US$230 (LS) to US$810 (HS). Swimming pool, 18-hole golf course, floodlit tennis. Windsurfers and Sunfish free to guests. **A** St James, tel: 432 1311. Reservations: UK, tel: (01) 567 3444; USA, tel: (800) 225 3050.

• *Divi St James*: Deluxe/expensive **R**. Adults only. Single/double from US$95/110 (LS) to US$170/190 (HS), suites from US$130/140 (LS) to US$205/225 (HS). Tennis, Nautilus gym, squash, sauna, free windsurfing, sunfish and Hobie sailing and water ski-ing. **A** St James, tel: 432 7840. Reservations: UK, tel: (01) 631 4797; USA, tel: NY (800) 367 3484.

• *Inn on the Beach*. Moderate **R**. Modest hotel, simple, clean rooms all a/c with sea-facing balconies and fully-equipped kitchenettes. Single/double from US$45/60 (LS), double/triple from US$110/130 (HS). **A** St James, tel: 432 0385. Reservations: USA, tel: (800) 545 8437.

• *Na-Diesie Beach* Apartments. Moderate. Studios with kitchenettes from US$40 (LS) to US$70 (HS), not as good as its neighbour, the Inn on the Beach. **A** St James, tel: 432 0469.

• *Palm Beach Hotel*: Expensive/moderate. Studios and apartments

Cobbler's Cove

Paradise Beach

253

with kitchenettes, reasonable value. Studios from single/double US$40/45 (LS) to US$90/100 (HS), apartments from single/double US$50/60 (LS) to US$155/165 (HS). These rates are for the beach-block. **A** St James, tel: 432 1384.

• *Discovery Bay Beach Hotel*. Expensive **R**. Friendly, informal and popular with British tourists. Small pool. Mistral school, windsurfing (including instruction) and Sunfish free to guests. Rooms from single/double US$90/100 (LS) to US$180/195 (HS), seafront from single/double US$105/120 (LS) to US$210/225 (HS). **A** St James, tel: 432 1301. Reservations: USA, tel: (800) 223 6510, NY, tel: (212) 262 1870.

• *Coral Reef Club*: Deluxe/expensive. English-run, loyal and somewhat ageing British clientele, quiet atmosphere. Single/double from US$90/110 (LS) to US$180/290 (HS). **A** St James, tel: 422 2372 Reservations: UK, tel: (01) 631 4797; USA, tel: (800) 223 1108.

• *Royal Pavilion*: Deluxe **R**. Oceanfront rooms from US$200 (LS) to US$390 (HS), suites and villas from US$350 (LS) to US$780 (HS). **A** St James, tel: 422 4444. Reservations; UK, tel: (01) 631 4797; USA, tel: (800) 223 6510 or NY, tel: (212) 832 2277.

• *Cobbler's Cove*: Deluxe/expensive **R**. Free watersports, small pool. Good beach. Comfortable suites with kitchens from single/double US$95/130 (LS) to US$140/180 (HS), ocean view from US$116/150 (LS) to US$164/200 (HS). **A** St James, tel: 422 2291. Reservations: UK, tel: (01) 631 4797; USA, tel: (800) 223 6510 NY, tel: (212) 832 2277.

ACCESS

Thirty-five to 40 minutes from the airport (taxi B$30-35/US$15-17). There are regular bus and mini-bus services along the coast road.

BENSTON BEACH

First class beach for intermediate to expert sailors in the Bay of Oistins. The soft white sand beach is small and busy all the time with an international crowd enjoying the first class sailing conditions. Benstons is not recommended for beginners except in the summer when winds are light. On the beach there's a Club Mistral attached to the Barbados Windsurfing Club Hotel; there are several other hotels within convenient distance of the beach, most of them moderately-priced.

WATERSPORTS★★★★★

The serious sailor's bible for this part of the world, *The Boardsailors Guide to the Caribbean* (Derek Wulff and Toozie Dyck, Associated Sailing Publications, 1987), describes this bay as super for learning water starts, carving gybes, and generally blasting. This is not a spot for beginners when the wind is strong. It does get choppy, and there is a small but powerful shorebreak (1-3 feet) which we watched eat up quite a few sailors who appeared to have some knowledge of the sport. It is great for freestyle (both longboard and shortboard) when you go about 40 metres off-shore, where the wind usually starts to pick up.

Winds here are side-shore, averaging 10 knots/3 Beaufort on a quiet day and up to 30-35 knots/7-8 Beaufort during the winter, with the most consistent conditions during December and January.

- *Club Mistral*: the biggest windsurf centre in Barbados, with 100 boards (including Diamond Head, Ventura, Equipe, Pandera, and Challenge Flex) and 300 sails; harnesses are included in the hire costs. Rates are around B$26 (US$13)/hr, B$80 (US$40)/full day, B$330 (US$165)/week, with waist and seat harnesses included in the cost. They also run courses for beach/water starts, gybing and speed-sailing (B$80/US$40/two hours), three-hour brush-up courses (B$120/US$60), and six-hour advanced courses (B$296/US$148). Ten-hour beginners' courses (summer only) cost B$340 (US$170). **A** Benston Beach, Christ Church, tel: 428 9095. Information and reservations: Munich, tel: (089) 338 833.

ACCOMMODATION

- *Barbados Windsurf Club Hotel*: Moderate **R**. Basic rooms, some with kitchenettes, from US$30 (LS) to US$80 (HS), suites from US$70 to 150 per day. Very popular – book by August or September at the latest for peak season. **A** Benston Beach, Maxwell, Christ Church, tel: 428 7277, 428 9095. Reservations: UK, tel: (0293) 519151, USA, tel: (800) 22 LATH.

- *San Remo Beach Hotel*: Moderate/budget **R**. Friendly, family-run hotel on the beach next to the Club Mistral, cheap and convenient. Single/double from US$25/30 (LS) to US$50/55 (HS), apartments US$40 (LS) to US$60 (HS), four-person rooms US$45 (LS) to US$75 (HS). **A** Benston Beach, Maxwell, Christ Church, tel: 428 2816, 428 2822. Reservations: USA, tel: (800) 227 7002, MA, tel: (617) 262 9200.

- *Golden Sands*: Expensive/moderate. Over the road from the beach, small pool. Studios from single/double US$50 (LS) to US$75 (HS), apartments from US$60 (LS) to US$85 (HS). **A** Benston Beach, Maxwell, Christ Church, tel: 428 8051. Reservations; USA, tel: (800) 223 9815 or (212) 545 8437.

ACCESS

Seven miles/10 km from Bridgetown, 3 miles/5 km from the airport (15 minutes, B$16/US$8 by taxi).

SILVER SANDS

Silver Sands is a perfect powder-sand beach ten miles/16 km outside Bridgetown and is one of the best small beaches on Barbados. There is none of the aggravation or constant disturbance from jetskis found on the west coast, and if you're looking for a quiet holiday and I would recommend it for that reason alone. However, the main appeal of Silver Sands is for advanced windsurfing – this is where all the pros come. The Club Mistral here only rents Hookipas and Diamond Heads and you must be able to gybe and water start properly or they'll send you down to Benston Beach to practise first.

The beach has one resort hotel, the Silver Sands, which is modest by west coast standards but perfectly adequate – there is tennis and a large, double swimming pool. Even though it attracts a much younger crowd than most hotels on the island, evenings are quiet: for entertainment in the evenings you have to make your way into St Lawrence Gap or Bridgetown.

A hundred yards or so to the east of Silver Sands is a much bigger beach, Round Rock Beach, which is packed with sailors during the winter season and if you're not confident launching a shortboard the shorebreak is less powerful than at Silver Sands. There is a new windsurf centre here, the Atlantic Sails Windsurf Club, and if you're on a tight budget the Round Rock Apartments (on a small cliff at one end of the beach) are cheap.

Silver Sands

WATERSPORTS★★★★★

The most consistent winds are from late November through to February and March, when they blow between 15-25 knots/4-6 Beaufort, reaching 30-35 knots/7-8 Beaufort on a good day: December and January are the prime months. There is a heavy 2-4 ft shorebreak. *The Boardsailor's Guide to the Caribbean* says: 'This area has a very nice sideshore breeze with a port tack jump on a reef about 150-200 metres off-shore. The reef is pretty deep, and the waves can be from 5 ft to mast high when it's really windy. For the advanced intermediate this is an excellent spot to practise in the waves without worry of ripping off skegs or coral cuts. But, there is a current running from east to west (with the wind) of about 3 knots, so you should be able to hit 85-100 per cent of your gybes if you're on a shortboard, or you may be blown downwind, where the shore is rocky. This is a spot for very good sailors.'

● *Club Mistral*: 15 Diamond Heads and 15 Hookipas, 35-40 harnesses and 60-70 sails. Boards cost from B$80/ (US$40)/day, B$330(US$175)/week (longer rates negotiable). No tuition was available at the time of writing but they were planning to start advanced courses sometime in the future. Closed from July to November, but if you bring your own board the summer is a good time for beginners to practise speed sailing. **A** Silver Sands, tel: 428 6001.

ACCOMMODATION

● *Silver Sands Resort*: Expensive/ moderate **R**. Single/double from US$45 (LS) to US$80 (HS), studios from US$47 (LS) to US$92 (HS), ocean front studios from US$52 (LS) to US$100 (HS), suites from US$60 (LS) to US$115 (HS). **A** Christchurch, tel: 428 6001. Reservations: UK, tel: (0293) 519151; USA, tel: (800) 635 9900.

● *Round Rock Apartments*: Budget. Grotty but cheap. Rooms with kitchenettes from double US$30 (LS) to US$40 (HS) per day, US$180 (LS) to US$250 (HS) per week, two-bedroom studios for four people from US$40 (LS) to US$55 (HS) per day, US$245 (LS) to US$345 (HS) per week. **A** Christchurch, tel: 428 7500.

ACCESS

Ten miles/16 km from Bridgetown, 15 minutes from the airport .

SOUTH EAST COAST

Crane Beach, Ginger Bay Beach, Long Bay

Beaches on this coast are wild and windswept with fine white sand and almost constant surf. The sea here goes through an alluring range of colour changes as it slopes off into the depths and although the shorebreak looks wicked it is actually quite safe. Because of the surf there are no watersports on this coast – this is body-surfing and body-boarding territory.

The first beach heading east is Crane Beach, 12 miles/19 km out of Bridge-town, which is overlooked by a superb resort perched on the clifftop, the Crane Beach Hotel. Converted from an eighteenth-century mansion built of hewn coral stone the resort is one of the island's oldest properties, an oasis of serenity and luxury. The hotel's Roman-style swimming pool right on the cliff edge is the sexiest on the island but don't be fooled by the photography in the brochures – it's a long walk down to the beach from the pool. With the double bonus of a beautiful pool and a beautiful beach, the Crane Beach Hotel is highly recommended if you can afford it.

The beach itself is the island's most popular body-boarding location. The break is right up under the cliff at the hotel end; this is a classic body-boarding break, a short and sweet ride on a wave which picks up quickly and dumps you almost as fast.

Ginger Bay Beach is just a mile or so further on, a small cove framed by volcanic cliffs with the Ginger Bay Beach Club perched on the cliffs above it. There is even less to do here than at Crane Beach; either bring a stack of novels or a typewriter and write one yourself.

At Long Bay there is a Marriott resort surrounding Sam Lord's Castle. Completed in 1833, the 'castle' features fine plasterwork ceilings and Georgian woodwork built by English and Italian craftsmen. The castle rooms themselves (of which there are ten) would be fun to stay in, but the rest of the resort is disastrous.

Crane Beach

If you're visiting this area for the day from the west or south coasts the best place to have lunch is Crane Beach, where they serve a selection of seafood and local dishes in the clifftop restaurant. On Sundays the Crane holds a Bajan Buffet Luncheon with a steel band and free use of tennis courts and swimming pool ($B35 /US$17.50 per person). I haven't tried the other restaurants at Sam Lord's Castle but I suggest you avoid eating at the beach snack bar, where the food is revolting.

257

ACCOMMODATION

● *Crane Beach Hotel.* Deluxe/expensive **R**. Rooms have fans (no a/c) and fridges and most have balconies overlooking the sea. Tennis. Rooms from single/double US$100/110 (LS) to US$180/225 (HS), suites from US$145-235 (LS) to US$300-400 (HS).

Rooms in the annexe (250 yards from the main building, with its own pool) are much cheaper: single/double from US$45/65 (LS) to US$70/90 (HS). **A** St Philip, Barbados, tel: 423 6220. Reservations: UK, tel: (01) 387 1555; USA, tel: (800) 387 3998.

● *Ginger Bay Beach Club*: Expensive

R. Spacious and well-furnished rooms from single/double US$55/105 (LS) to US$140/180 (HS). Small pool, tennis. A St Philip, Barbados, tel: 423 5810. Reservations: USA, tel: (212) 545 8439.

• *Sam Lord's Castle*. Deluxe/expensive. Castle rooms from US$115 (LS) to US$245 (HS), standard rooms from US$95 (LS) to US$190 (HS). A St Philip, Barbados, tel: 423 7350. Reservations: UK, tel: (01) 434 2299; USA, tel: (800) 248 0215; NY, tel: (212) 603 8200.

ACCESS

All three beach hotels are within 10-15 minutes of the airport, around B$20 (US$10) by taxi. You can also easily reach them by bus.

Surfing

As well as numerous breaks for beginner/intermediate surfers Barbados has several world-class surfing locations, the most famous of which is the Soup Bowl at Bathsheba. The other two prime spots are Brandon's near the Hilton Hotel, and Duppies, at the far north of the island. Comments in the following résumé are by ex-national longboard champion Bill Thomson.

The Soup Bowl is the most popular spot on the island and although it breaks year-round it's at its best in the summer and autumn, which is when most of the national and international competitions are held here. You'll never find it empty, but a crowd is thirty at most. ('An excellent wave: we've never yet postponed a contest at Bathsheba. The Soup Bowl faces east/north-east and the whole of the swell focuses right in on the reef, which has just the right configuration so when it's breaking well, wave after wave comes in, all breaking the same way. At weekends it's crowded with locals who are very jealous of Bathsheba and sometimes can be a little aggressive and not willing to share their waves; but during the week it's quite possible to find only six to eight people out.') Surfers coming here for long-term stays can rent cottages in Bathsheba for 5-6 people for as little as B$250/US$125 a week.

The island's second top site is Brandon's, which is also easy to find. Go east past the Hilton until you come to the Garrison Savannah racetrack. Immediately opposite is a police station with a road leading down behind it to the beach. Brandon's breaks from November through to June. ('Again, this is a world-class break. You can surf it from waist height up to 12-15 ft and on a good day you can get a 250-yard ride. The biggest danger at Brandon's is getting out to the break because the reef is full of what we call 'cobblers', or black sea urchins. It's difficult to get over the reef without stepping on something, but once over the reef it's safe even when it's big.')

The other main south coast spot is at South Point Lighthouse, just past Oistins Bay. This is a small beach break, close to the shore, suitable for beginners.

There are several locations for beginner/intermediate surfing along the west coast, all of which break with the northerly swells during December, January, February and March. The first is at Batt's Rock, just north of Paradise Beach, easy to see as you drive along the road ('a beautiful wave with an off-shore reef that is very forgiving. A lot of people learn here'). The next is at Sandy Lane, on a shallow little reef at the south end of the bay ('a fabulous little wave').

Further north is a wave known as Tropicana, opposite the beach hotel of the same name. The local name for this break is John Moore's, after the nearby rum shop ('extremely shallow and very, very dangerous. When it's breaking it doesn't get big, probably no more than 5-6ft at its best, but it throws out huge tubes and when you're surfing it you're probably not more than 12-18 inches off the coral').

The next break up the coast is Gibbs, an off-shore reef 300 yards out to the left of Mama Leone's Pizzeria on Mullin's Beach, two-and-a-half miles/3 km north of the Royal Pavilion Hotel ('a nice wave, very popular').

Just before the cement plant on the other side of Speightstown is a break known as Hulls or Six Men's Bay. Go through Six Men's Village and then take a cart road that winds down the side of the hill to two private houses, park here and walk through the wood to get to the beach ('a small break, very well protected by the cliff, a long, peeling wave, a real fun wave. One of the reasons it's called Hull is that there are always ten or twenty 'hullers' – body-board riders – in the water, so it can be crowded').

After the cement plant is Maycock's Bay. Finding this beach isn't that easy, although it is signposted at various points. During 1988 there was a new villa estate under construction on top of the cliff here: go through the estate and take a grass track down the cliff to the right. ('A shallow reef about 400 yards off-shore takes some of the power off the swell so when the waves get inside they're only around 5-6ft. A very relaxing place to surf').

Finally, you come to Duppies, the island's third world-class site. To find Duppies, follow the road from the Heywood's Resort to Six Men's Village and then through a rock canyon as it takes a right swing. You'll come to a left turn signposted Maycock's Bay and Checker Hall. Take this turning and then go straight over a major junction on the tarmac road. Continue down this road, and one mile/1.6 km past Rennie's Mini Mart you'll come to a left fork signposted Archer's Bay via Crab Hill. A third of a mile further on, where the road curves to the right, there is a track leading off to the left (past a small shack) and this will take you to the cliff edge. You have to scramble down the cliff to a pocket-handker-chief-sized beach, and the break is around 300-400 yards off-shore ('Duppies is a wave of real quality. It's a big wave, it doesn't break when it's small. You have to paddle across a deep-water channel, which is quite scary because it's one of the few places on the island where you can expect to find sharks. It's been ridden at 12-15 ft and, more so than anywhere, this is not a place for beginners. There's a constant south-to-north current of about 2-3 knots, so you have to be constantly paddling to maintain position').

If you're bringing a board into Barbados you have to pay a customs bond of 25 per cent on the value of the board, so make sure you undervalue it (the same applies to windsurfers).

● *Lazy Days & Island Waves*: Stockists of quality surf wear, American boards and accessories, locally-made Flying Fish boards and boogie boards. **A** Hastings, Christ Church, tel: 436 0633.

Diving and Snorkelling

Although Barbados is surrounded on the west and south coasts by a fringing reef, the stark facts are that all of the fringing reefs on the south coast and over 50 per cent on the west coast are dead. This means that snorkelling or diving on shallow reefs here is a waste of time except for beginners.

Beyond the fringing reef there are a series of three barrier reefs (known locally as 'bars', they drop off progressively to around 100ft/30m) and the situation here is marginally better. However, I found myself surfacing after 30 minutes out of sheer boredom from a dive on one of these low-profile bars.

To be fair, no one claims that the diving here is much good anyway. Local instructors such as Mike Young are the first to admit that they've got problems: 'I'll be honest with you, I just can't say that it's a fantastic place for diving. There are no laws governing what can be taken, spearfishing is permitted, and people just take whatever they like from the reefs,' he says. 'But you can have good diving', he adds, 'as long as the divemasters show you what life there is on the bottom.' Indeed, Mike has a reputation as a wizard for finding stuff to show divers but in my experience not many other dive guides here take such care to provide their clients with a rewarding dive.

The reefs are in a poor state due to a number of factors including uncontrolled spearfishing, dynamite fishing, clumsy anchoring, the harvesting of coral to sell to tourists, and the release of swimming-pool effluent and sewage from hotels into the sea. In addition, rivers release large amounts of silt, chemicals and other pollutants from agricultural land into the ocean. Although the government is attempting to tackle some of these problems as part of their new National Environmental Plan and the Eastern Caribbean Safe Divers Association is also hoping to set up a number of reserves and fish sanctuaries, it will be years before they recover.

However, Barbados does have plenty of wrecks to dive on. The best of these is the MV *Stravonikita* (see page 252). Carlisle Bay just outside Bridgetown is a popular area for snorkelling and beginners' shallow diving because of the presence of at least three wrecks, foremost amongst which is the *Berwyn*. Scuppered by its crew sometime around 1919, the *Berwyn* is a French tug which reaches to within 7ft/2m of the surface. If you want to snorkel on the *Berwyn* there's no need to pay for a boat trip: just look for the Prime Minister's Office behind Carlisle Bay beach and head straight out for 200-300 yards.

Diving for antique bottles is a popular and unusual underwater activity which often yields hand-blown beer bottles dating back to the seventeenth century, which you are allowed to keep.

The diving in Barbados is mostly only suitable for beginners but if you're planning on learning to dive here be selective about your choice of instructor. Although standards have risen considerably in recent years, there are still a few Mickey Mouse operations around. It's worth bearing in mind that at least three or four tourists every year are treated for diving accidents in the recompression chamber at the Barbados Defence Force Medical Unit and I'm told that until recently very few of the locals offering lessons were qualified divers, let alone instructors.

260

During the winter, heavy swells and run-off from the land can often reduce the visibility to as low as 20-30ft/6-9m. Visibility is said to be best from April/May through to October/November, with August and September the best months.

The Atlantis

Based in Bridgetown harbour, the *Atlantis* is one of a new generation of passenger submarines which are proving enormously popular all over the tropics in giving people a chance to glimpse the marine world in complete safety at depths usually reserved for scuba divers. The *Atlantis* is owned and operated by Sub Aquatics of Canada, who launched their first submarine in Grand Cayman in 1985. This proved so successful that they immediately built a second, which started up in Barbados in 1987. Since then, Sub Aquatics have gone on to build even bigger submarines capable of holding up to 46 people; certified to depths of 300ft/90m these are the largest passenger submarines in the world and currently operate in St Thomas, Guam and Hawaii.

In Barbados, passengers are taken on an hourly shuttle to the sub's dive site, which is 2 miles/3 km up the coast opposite the Cunard Paradise Beach. By chance, this happens to be one of the reefs on the west coast which is in better condition than most and on this particular site there is also a large wreck, the *Fort Willoughby*, which is as big as the sub itself. At night, powerful lights are used to illuminate the colours of the coral.

The *Atlantis* has a small response-support vessel which always stays at the dive site and is in constant contact with the sub via an underwater communication link. The response vehicle also keeps surface traffic away when the sub's going up or down and alerts the pilot if there are divers in the area (divers tend to ham it up like mad when they see the sub coming by at 100ft!). The whole journey is narrated by the pilot and co-pilot as you descend down the reef (it has eight of each). Dives take place ten times daily (on the hour from 9 a.m. to 6 p.m.) and cost US$58 for adults, children half price. Reservations advisable, tel: 436 8929.

261

Cozumel

T his small island, just 12 miles/19 km off the Yucatan peninsula, has recently become an international Mecca for divers and offers an unbeatable combination of value for money and world-class diving.

Cozumel is divided from the mainland by a deep channel (the Cozumel Trench) which is swept by rich currents, providing Cozumel not only with flourishing marine flora and fauna but also with guaranteed visibility in excess of 100ft/30m. Once underwater it's not hard to see why divers keep coming back: the terrain is unique in the Caribbean, with colossal buttresses riddled with huge caverns and tunnels, and because of the strong currents drift diving is the norm, which further adds to the interest and excitement.

Cozumel has so many outstanding dive sites it's almost impossible to have a disappointing time here. There are numerous professionally-run dive operations and the reefs and the divers are both well looked after by enthusiastic and diligent local dive guides. Over half the visitors who come here are divers and the island is totally geared to their needs.

Although it used to be popular for diving as long ago as the 1960s, Cozumel went downhill in the 1970s because of uncontrolled spearfishing (which took care of the large groupers and sharks) and the harvesting of coral but, thanks to the foresight of the Mexican government in creating a marine park on Cozumel's west coast, the area is now fully-protected and rapidly recovering. Admittedly, the huge volume of divers now streaming through also causes problems, but maximum effort is made to diminish the impact.

The island has a wide range of accommodation to suit every budget, great restaurants, friendly people, and a warm, sleepy Mexican atmosphere. The cost of hotels is higher than on mainland Mexico, but by

Caribbean standards it's a bargain – especially compared with destinations like the Caymans. There is one slight drawback: Cozumel's coastline is mostly eroded limestone (known as ironshore) and there are very few good beaches. For beach holidays the mainland resort of Cancun is a better bet than Cozumel. You can learn to dive in Cancun and visit Cozumel for diving on day trips.

Cozumel's main town is San Miguel, the hub of which is the plaza, sleepy and unhurried by day, lively and full of strolling couples and families by night. Divers on a tight budget will find that there is a wide choice of places to stay in San Miguel (page 272) and it's just as convenient to be based here as it is at a resort beach. Around the plaza and the surrounding streets there are plenty of lively bars and you can eat out at anything from a cheap Mexican café to a ritzy seafood restaurant. The new Museo de la Isla de Cozumel (which has a series of well-presented displays on reef systems, micro-atolls, tropic networks and reef ecology) is just off the main plaza and worth visiting.

The busiest resort area on Cozumel is just a few miles outside of town near the international cruise ship pier. There are two minute beaches here squeezed between hotels and the area doesn't seem to have a name so I've just called it **Pier Beach★★★**. The best resort beach on the island is further past here at **El Presidente★★★★**. These are the only two accommodation centres to the south of town. To the north there are also a few resort hotels at Playa San Juan but they're rather out of the swing of things and a long way from the reefs (which are in the south).

There are two other beach areas to know about. The first is **Chankanaab★★** (2 miles/3 km past El Presidente, this is the island's most popular snorkelling location) and the second is **Playa Maya** and **Playa San Francisco★★★**. The last two are Cozumel's only Caribbean-style beaches.

Beaches on the windward coast (such as Punta Morena and Playa Chen Rio) tend to be debris-covered and fly-blown and people only usually go to them as part of the obligatory round-the-island trip. Exploring Cozumel is easily done by moped or hired jeep and taxis are cheap and plentiful.

263

Statue of Christ, Palancar

To a certain extent it doesn't matter where you stay since the island is quite small and dive operations service all the hotels. Most hotels also offer dive/accommodation packages which are excellent value (write for full details to the addresses given here or look out for advertisements in *Skin Diver*). For Cozumel business is booming, and although the dive scene is changing rapidly – one dive shop now has a sophisticated computer reservations service and others now offer dive computer rentals, to name but two recent innovations – the cost of diving here is still extremely competitive. See **Diving** (page 270).

With designer fashion shops starting to open up on San Miguel's seafront it's hardly a traditional Mexican town anymore and there are no intact ruins on the island if it's history you're after, but for divers Cozumel is now firmly on the international map. There are frequent flights from Miami and it's also easily reached from Mexico City and major US hubs such as Houston.

Hurricane Gilbert caused considerable damage to homes, hotels and dive shops on the island. Although the reefs are on the leeward coast, there has inevitably been some deterioration of the shallow reefs – shallow Colombia, for instance, is apparently ruined. There have been conflicting reports in the US diving press on the extent of the damage to the deeper reefs, and the jury is still out.

Just near Cozumel the small island of Isla Mujeres, the Island of Women, has long been famous for its snorkelling. However, the shallow

Deep Palancar

reefs of El Garrafon (the island's only marine park) are very limited in extent, considerably over rated and not worth the journey from Cozumel, let alone further afield. For divers Isla Mujeres has little to offer in comparison to Cozumel, although the shark caves on the north side of the island are unusual. Isla Mujeres' chief merit is as a cheap island for travellers. The island's main beach, Playa Los Cocos, is better than most on Cozumel and is just five minutes' walk from budget hotels in town.

GENERAL INFORMATION

Time
GMT-6 hours

IDD code
52 + 987 + number

Currency
Mexican peso. US dollars are used extensively
UK£1 = 4,000 pesos
US$1 = 2,200 pesos

Hotels
Rates do not include tax and service. Most hotels quote prices in US$.
Deluxe: US$70-90 (LS) to US$90-120 (HS)
Expensive: US$30-40 (LS) to US$50-70 (HS)
Moderate: US$15-30 (LS) to US$40-50 (HS)
Budget: Under US$15

PUBLICATIONS
Diver's Guide to Underwater Mexico
Michael and Lauren Farley (Marcor Publishing 1986), 288pp, paperback. Comprehensive source book covering most areas including Cozumel, the Sea of Cortez and the Pacific. US$14.95 + US$1 postage (surface USA) from: Marcor Publishing, PO Box 1072, Port Hue-neme, CA 93041, USA.
Diving and Snorkelling Guide to Cozumel
George Lewbel and Larry Martin (Pisces Books, 1987), paperback 95pp. Thorough, fully illustrated in colour. Around US$8 in local dive shops.
Hidden Mexico, Adventurer's Guide to the Beaches and Coasts
Rebecca Burns (Ulysses Press, 1987), paperback. US$12.95 + US$2 postage (surface USA) from Ulysses Press, PO Box 4000H, Berkeley, CA 94704, USA.
Insider's Guide Sheet – Cozumel Diving and Snorkelling
Free from Dive Paradise, full of useful tips on local dive sites.

WEATHER
The dry season on the Yucatan is from November through to April. May, June, September and October are the wettest months, with the heaviest rains in June and September. The annual average temperature is around 80°F/27°C, peaking in July and August. During the Christmas, New Year's and Easter holiday seasons resorts can be very crowded. Diving is year-round, with water temperatures between 75-85°F/24-28°C. Visibility is at its best during the dry months.

265

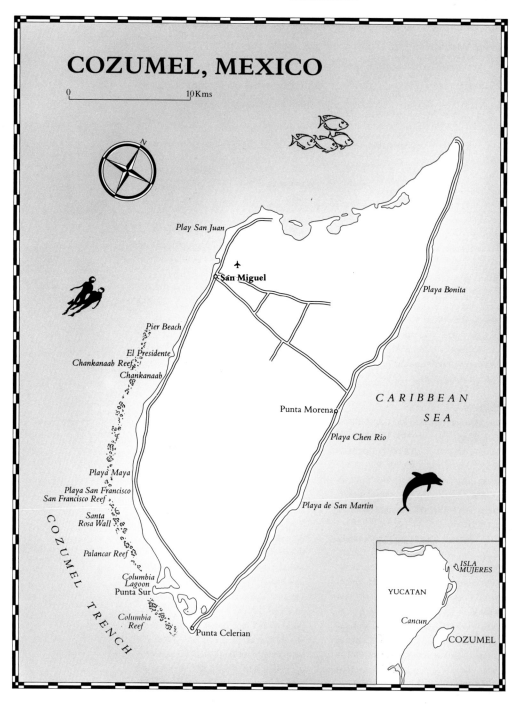

COZUMEL, MEXICO

0   10 Kms

N

Play San Juan

✈
San Miguel

Playa Bonita

Pier Beach

El Presidente

Chankanaab Reef

Chankanaab

Punta Morena

CARIBBEAN
SEA

Playa Chen Rio

Playa Maya

Playa San Francisco

San Francisco Reef

Santa
Rosa Wall

Playa de San Martin

COZUMEL TRENCH

Palancar Reef

Columbia
Lagoon

Punta Sur

Columbia
Reef

Punta Celerian

ISLA
MUJERES

YUCATAN

Cancun

COZUMEL

HEALTH
No inoculations required but tetanus and cholera/typhoid are recommended.

VISAS
All visitors are required to have a tourist card, obtainable at the border or overseas tourist offices.

TOURIST BOARDS
Head Office: Mexico City, tel: 250 8555; London, tel: (01) 734 1058; New York, tel: (212) 755 7512.

PIER BEACH

This small resort area 2½ miles/4 km south of San Miguel is a busy hub for dive boats. Three large hotels (La Ceiba, the Sol Caribe, and Casa del Mar) and one smaller one (the Diver's Inn) share a shoreline which mostly consists of piers and rocks, with two very small sandy coves sandwiched between the hotels, bars and dive shops. This is one of the better locations on the island because the hotels are close to the main reefs (only divers staying at El Presidente have shorter boat rides).

All three big hotels have decent-sized swimming pools and there's no shortage of reasonably-priced restaurants and bars serving Mexican, Yucatan and seafood meals. Ernesto's Fajita Factory (in front of the Diver's Inn) is cheerful and good value; for nightlife and a multitude of local restaurants San Miguel is just a short taxi ride away. Car and moped rentals are available but they're cheaper if hired downtown. E6 processing is available. One dive shop here, Del Mar Aquatics, has a new passenger submarine capable of taking divers or non-divers 1000 ft/300 m down into the depths of the Cozumel Trench on one-hour tours.

SNORKELLING★★★★
The area is famous for the sunken plane which can be found a short distance out from La Ceiba hotel. Located in 35ft/10m of water, the plane is a 40-passenger Convair which was sunk in 1977 as a prop for a Mexican disaster movie. Storms have long since turned it upside down, and most of the fuselage to the rear of the wings has fallen to pieces, but grouper, snapper, sergeant majors and angelfish will all come to greet you if you take some food. Hurricane Gilbert may have finished this plane off.

Normally only divers head out past the sunken airplane to the International Pier, but snorkellers will also find it interesting. The massive concrete pylons provide some spectacular, almost surreal, perspectives underwater when visibility is good, and the pier is also home to red sheet sponges and green-coloured fire coral growing on the vertical concrete walls. Be mindful of the ever-present currents when snorkelling in this area and watch out for cruise liners! **MSF:** US$6-10/day.

WATERSPORTS★
Northerly winds during November and December sometimes reach 25 knots/6 Beaufort. Tuition and board rental available opposite the Diver's Inn.

DIVING★★★★★
For beach diving the sunken plane is a popular site for beginners or refresher dives and the sponges and corals growing under the International Pier

are photogenic on night dives. *Dive Cozumel, Del Mar Aquatics* and *Fantasia Divers* all have dive shops in the beach area and offer dive packages in conjunction with the hotels here. The Del Mar Aquatics/La Ceiba inclusive dive packages, for instance, are excellent value: six days (five nights) with four boat trips, one night dive and unlimited beach diving costs from US$300 (double occupancy). Dive packages at the Casa del Mar (also in conjunction with Del Mar Aquatics) are even more competitive.

ACCOMMODATION
• *Hotel La Ceiba*: Deluxe **R**. Right on the seafront. Single/double from US$70-80 (LS) to US$90-110 (HS). **A** PO Box 284, Cozumel, Q.Roo, 77600, tel: 20844. Reservations: USA, tel: (800) 621 6830.
• *Hotel Sol Caribe*: Deluxe. High rise hotel, ugly but comfortable. Magnificent rambling swimming pool with swim-up bar. Rooms from US$80-90 (LS) to US$110-120 (HS). **A** PO Box 259, Cozumel, Q. Roo, 77600, tel: 20700. Reservations: USA, tel: (800) 223 2332.
• *Hotel Casa del Mar*: Expensive **R**. The area's newest hotel, owned by La Ceiba. Good value, although the rooms are basic. Single/double from US$40/50 (LS) to US$55/65 (HS). **A** PO Box 129, Cozumel, Q. Roo, tel: 21665. Reservations: USA, tel: (800) 621 6830.
• *Diver's Inn*: Moderate **R**. Doubles cost US$36 B&B. **A** PO Box 165, Cozumel, Q.Roo, 77600, tel: 20145.

ACCESS
Two-and-a-half miles/4 km from town, fixed-rate taxi fare.

EL PRESIDENTE

El Presidente not only has the best beach (for a hotel) on the island, it is also as close to the major reefs as you can get. Palancar Divers (Dive Cozumel) and Fantasia Divers both have branches at the hotel, or any downtown dive operator will pick you up here on their way out to the reefs. El Presidente has a large swimming pool and windsurfers, kayaks and Sunfish can be rented on the beach.

ACCOMMODATION
• *El Presidente*: Deluxe **R**. Single/double from US$80/85. Fitness centre, tennis. **A** Carretera a Chankanaab, 77600 Cozumel, Q. Roo, tel: 20322. Reservations: USA, tel: (800) 472 2427.

ACCESS
Four miles/6 km from town, fixed-rate taxi fare.

CHANKANAAB

Chankanaab ('small sea') is one of Cozumel's better known snorkelling areas, a well-organized state park with a lagoon, botanical gardens, a diving and snorkelling zone and a small beach. There are four dive huts on the beach, renting out tanks and equipment for qualified divers, snorkelling gear, underwater cameras and offering introductory dives ·

SNORKELLING★★★

Steps lead into the water where dozens of people are busy exploring wrecks, rocks, corals and cannons. To the left of the swimming platform is the wreck of an old fishing boat in 30ft/9m of water, in front of the platform several corals heads come up to within 15ft/4.5m of the surface. Closer in-shore you'll find purple sea fans, elkhorn coral, and a series of small caves and overhangs beneath which schools of striped grunts can be found hiding. French angelfish, large parrotfish, sergeant majors, chubs, spotted drum, butterflyfish and snapper all inhabit the near in-shore area. **MSF**: US$4/day.

ACCESS

Five-and-a-half miles/9 km south of San Miguel, fixed rate taxi fare.

French angelfish

PLAYA MAYA and PLAYA SAN FRANCISCO

These are Cozumel's real beaches, as opposed to the pocket-sized versions in the hotel zones. There are no hotels here, or indeed any buildings at all except thatched-roofed restaurants on the beach – just the forest creeping down to the water's edge.

Out to sea, dive boats of every size and description ply backwards and forwards on their way to the major reefs: if you're on a full-day dive trip the boat will most likely pull in at one of these beaches at midday for lunch, a game of volleyball and a rest before setting out again for the afternoon dive.

Playa Maya is the first one you come to driving from town, just under nine miles/14 km from the main square.

A quarter-of-a-mile further on, Playa San Francisco is the busiest and most

269

popular of the out-of-town beaches and gets very crowded at weekends. The two seafront restaurants pour out Mexican music all day while the waiters pour out pina coladas and margaritas to sunbathers lounging on the wooden deck-chairs on the edge of the sea.

The sea is mostly clear with a sandy bed on both beaches, and windsurfers and Hobie cats rentals are available with tuition. There is no point in snorkelling here, since the reef is much too far off-shore.

Playa Maya Divers (next to the Playa Maya Beach Club) is a PADI facility with the usual menu of options at similar prices to the down-town dive shops. If you book a dive here you'd be on the reefs in under fifteen minutes.

BARS AND RESTAURANTS
Paloma's Beach Club and the Playa Maya Beach Club, a hundred yards apart on Playa Maya, are open for lunch only. The two restaurants on Playa San Francisco (the Santa Maria and the San Francisco) are open until late afternoon.

ACCESS
Twenty to thirty minutes by car or bike from town, US$4-5 by taxi.

Diving

Cozumel's marine park covers 20 miles/32 km of reef on the west side of the island, running from Playa Paraiso southwards all the way down to Maracaibo reef on the tip of the island at Punta Celerian.

Possibly Cozumel's most famous dive site is Palancar, a massive reef system over three miles long with gigantic coral buttresses rising up towards the surface, interspersed with sand channels and caves. You could put in a couple of dozen dives on Palancar and still find it full of surprises.

Different sections of Palancar include the Big Horseshoe (a much-photographed semi-circle of coral heads rising up from 100 ft/30 m to within 20 ft/6 m of the surface), Palancar Gardens (a shallow dive with smaller buttresses), Palancar Caves, Little Palancar Caves and Deep Palancar (which starts at 100 ft/30 m and is not often visited). Near the Horseshoe, a statue of Christ is anchored to the bottom in 60-80 ft/18-24 m of water.

Colombia Reef is similar in nature to Palancar, with massive coral pinnacles rising up 70-90 ft/21-27 m towards the surface, covered in sponges, plate corals and anemones and interspersed with caves and caverns. Shallow Colombia is equally interesting with coral formations rising from just 40 ft/12 m to within 15 ft/4.5 m of the surface.

270

Santa Rosa is the most frequently-visited drop-off after Palancar, with a similar profile of enormous buttresses, cut through with sand channels and dropping off into the deep blue beyond: lots of big overhangs and caverns, over-sized sea fans, sponges and tame groupers.

Most dive boats leave dock between 9.30a.m. and 10a.m. for full day trips to the reefs but, this being Mexico, punctuality is not their strong point. Many of the older dive boats are converted fishing boats, and these usually take between 45-60 minutes to reach the dive sites. After the first dive they pull into one of the beaches for a surface interval and lunch, followed by a leisurely second dive in the afternoon before returning you to your hotel.

A recent development in Cozumel has been the introduction of smaller, faster boats which take fewer divers (usually six or less) and which allow you to have two dives in the morning and be back at your hotel by around 1p.m.

There is also some interesting shore diving here, and all you have to do is hire a taxi (which are cheap and diver-friendly) and load the tanks into the boot.

Local dive guides are extremely conscious of the need to look after their reefs; with this in mind they will make sure that you are completely in control of your buoyancy once down and not touching the reef at all with your fins.

Cozumel recently modernized its recompression chamber and ambulance boats are continually on patrol on the reefs. These safety precautions are financed through a US$1 levy on every dive. Treatment, should the need arise, is free.

Two-tank dives usually cost around US$35-40, resort courses around US$50, and open-water certifications US$250-300.

At the last count there were around 35 dive shops on Cozumel, so this is by no means a complete list. All operators offer daily trips.

• *Aqua Safari*: Full service PADI dive shop. **A.** PO Box 41, Cozumel, Q.Roo, tel: 20101; USA, tel: (800) 854 9334.

• *Blue Angel Scuba School*: Customized diving trips for small groups. PADI. **A** PO Box 280, Cozumel, Q.Roo, tel: 20730.

• *Caribbean Divers*: Full service dive shop (PADI, NAUI, YMCA, CMAS, SSI). Private charters to any reef. At the Mayan Plaza Hotel, tel: 20072; Cabanas del Caribe Hotel, tel: 20017; Cantarell Hotel, tel: 20144. **A** PO Box 191, Cozumel, Q.Roo, tel: 20180.

• *Clear Water Divers*: PADI, NAUI, YMCA. **A** PO Box 233, Cozumel, Q.Roo, tel: 20983; USA, tel: (800) 445 0953.

• *Deportes Acuaticos Dive Shop*: Fast trips with a maximum of eight people. Despite the shabby appearance of this shop they have a good reputation for personal service and it's the only place in Cozumel where you can get a Nikonos repaired.Underwater camera rentals. **A** Rafael Melgary Y Calle 8 Norte, Cozumel, Q.Roo, tel: 20640.

• *Discover Cozumel Diving*: Full PADI service dive shop. Underwater camera rentals. **A** Hotel Barracuda, San Miguel, Cozumel, Q.Roo, tel: 20280; USA, tel: (800) 328 5285.

• *Dive Cozumel*: PADI courses. **A** PO Box 165, Cozumel, Q. Roo.

• *Dive Paradise*, PADI, SSI. Small groups, personal service, recommended. **A** PO Box 222, Cozumel, Q. Roo, tel: 21007.

• *El Clavado/Tony Tate Scuba School*: Underwater video service. **A** PO Box 30, Cozumel, Q.Roo, tel: 21444.

• *Fantasia Divers:* **A** Ave 20 Y Calle 2 Norte, tel: 21258; Sol Caribe Hotel, tel: 20700; Hotel El Presidente, tel: 20322; La Ceiba Hotel, tel: 20844; USA, tel: (713) 558 9524.

• *Galapago Inn*: Diving hotel just outside of town. PADI. Underwater photography, equipment repair, on-site E6 processing. **A** PO Box 289, Cozumel, Q. Roo, tel: 20663; USA, tel: (800) 847 5708.

• *Neptuno Divers*: PADI. Dive packages with Hotel Meson San Miguel. **A** PO Box 136, Cozumel, Q. Roo, tel: 20999; USA, tel: (800) 282 4198.

• *Palancar Diving Company*: Small groups. **A** PO Box 384, Cozumel, Q.

271

Roo, tel: 21601.

• *Playa Maya Divers*: PADI. **A** Ave 10, Rosado Salas, Cozumel, Q. Roo, tel: 21615.

• *Scuba, Scuba!*: PADI. Fast trips, underwater camera rentals. **A** PO Box 137, Cozumel, Q. Roo.

• *Viajes Y Deportes Caribe*: **A** PO Box 72, Cozumel, Q.Roo, tel: 20923.

• *Yucab Reef Dive Shop*: PADI. **A** PO Box 85, Cozumel, Q. Roo, tel: 21439.

San Miguel Accommodation

• All of the hotels listed here are within a short walk of the main square. This is just a selection to give you some idea of the range available but be warned that prices are rising fast. Between the two visits which I made to Cozumel whilst writing this book the cost of some hotel rooms had trebled in just ten months.

• *Bahia Hotel*: Expensive **R**. Smart seafront hotel, a/c rooms with kitchenettes from single/double US$45/50 (LS) to US$50/60 (HS). **A** San Miguel, tel: 21387. Reservations: USA, tel: (800) 446 8343.

• *Bazaar Colonial*: Expensive **R**. Dou-bles with kitchenette from US$25 (LS) to US$60-70 (HS). **A** 5a Avenida Sur 9, tel: 20542.

• *Hotel Meson San Miguel*: Expensive/moderate. North of the square. Single/double from US$35/40 (LS) to US$40/45(HS). **A** Avenida Juarez, tel: 20238. Reservations: USA, tel: (800) 468 6224.

• *Villa Las Anglas*: Moderate **R**. Modern apartments with kitchens. Doubles from US$30 (LS) to US$40-50 (HS). Heavily booked, advance reservations necessary. **A** PO Box 25, Cozumel, Q. Roo, tel: 21403.

• *Hotel Vista del Mar*: Moderate. Sea-facing rooms from US$27. **A** Avenida Rafael Melgar 45, tel: 20545.

• *Hotel Aguilar*: Moderate/budget **R**. Spacious double rooms from US$15, swimming pool (not always usable). **A** 5a Avenida Sur Calle 22, tel: 20307.

• *Hotel Posada Cozumel*: Moderate/budget **R**. Rooms from US$15. **A** Calle 4 Norte No 3, tel: 20314.

• *Hotel Soberanis*: Moderate/budget. Sea-facing rooms from US$15. **A** Avenida Rafael Melgar 471, tel: 20246.

• *Hotel Mary Carmen*: Moderate/budget. Pleasant courtyard,double rooms from US$16. **A** Avenida 5a Sur 4, tel: 20581.

• *Hotel Lopez*: Budget. On the main square, single/double US$10/15. **A** PO Box 44, Cozumel, tel: 20108.

• *Hotel El Marques*: Budget. Rooms from US$10-15. **A** Avenida 5a Sur 4, tel: 20537.

THE

Red Sea

Egypt

Egypt automatically conjures up images of the pyramids and the Nile, but for divers Egypt means only one thing – the Red Sea. The Red Sea is the northernmost point in the world where reef-building corals grow and is unique in terms of the density and diversity of marine life to be found in its waters.

Although Israel, Jordan, Saudi Arabia, Sudan and even Yemen all have coastlines which border the Red Sea, by far the most convenient country from which to dive it (since the Sinai was handed back) is Egypt.

There are two major dive bases in Egypt. The first of these is at **Na'ama Bay*******, near the port of Sharm el Sheikh at the southern tip of the Sinai desert. Thousands of divers are now coming here on holiday from all over the world to discover (or rediscover in many cases) the Gulf of Aqaba's reefs and such world-famous dive sites as Ras Muhammed. Located at the extreme southern tip of the Sinai and the confluence of the Gulf of Suez and the Gulf of Aqaba, Ras Muhammed has spectacular, dizzying walls rich in reef-dwelling fish as well as pelagics such as barracuda, tuna and several species of shark. Other areas within reach of Na'ama Bay, such as the Tiran Straits, are equally exceptional.

In the region of Na'ama Bay and Sharm el Sheikh there are 40 miles/64 km of reefs to explore and the means to do so in whatever fashion you please, whether it's by boat, car, jeep or even camel.

Those with no inclination to dive will find that they can snorkel on many of the same drop-offs and reefs and find themselves face to face with a wealth of tropical fish. At Ras Nasrani, just a short distance from Na'ama Bay, enormous Napoleon wrasse will approach snorkellers to be fed. An encounter with one of these massive fish will certainly provide more than just average holiday memories.

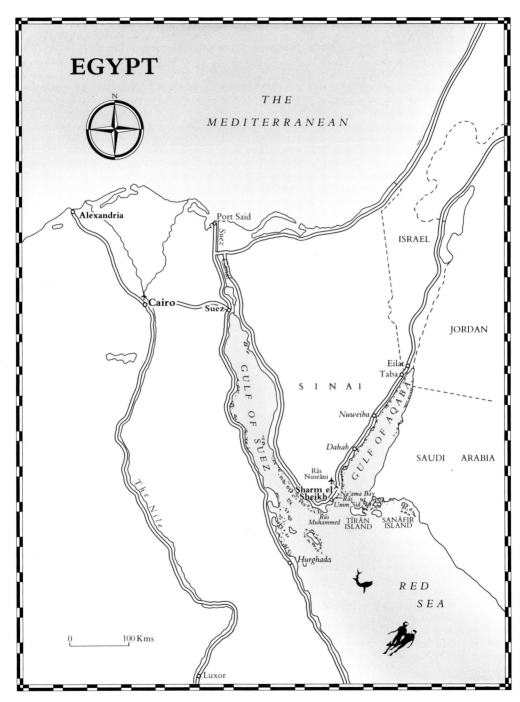

EGYPT

THE
MEDITERRANEAN

Alexandria

Port Said

ISRAEL

Cairo

Suez

Suez Canal

Suez

The Nile

GULF OF SUEZ

S I N A I

JORDAN

Eilat
Taba

Nuweiba

GULF OF AQABA

Dahab

SAUDI   ARABIA

Râs
Nusrâni

Sharm el
Sheikh

Na'ama Bay
Râs
Umm Sid

Râs
Muhammed

TÎRÂN
ISLAND

SANÂFIR
ISLAND

Hurghada

R E D
S E A

0   100 Kms

Luxor

For the beginner or experienced snorkeller the Sinai has the most accessible and exciting snorkelling within reach of Europe.

The choice of accommodation in Na'ama Bay ranges from luxury suites in the newly built Hilton to modest beach huts and tents which cost under US$5 a night.

Napoleon wrasse, Ras Muhammed

276

The only drawback to this apparently perfect destination is that the beach is coarse, brown desert sand and rather unpleasant. This is compensated for by the Gulf's rich underwater life and, to a lesser extent, by the surrounding scenery of mountains and desert, but if you're just looking for a beach holiday I wouldn't recommend it.

North of Na'ama Bay is **Dahab★**, an overlander's resort which also has excellent snorkelling and diving, although the same comments apply to the beach.

Egypt's second major dive base after Na'ama Bay is at Hurghada, on the other side of the Red Sea. Hurghada owes its popularity to the fact that from 1982 onwards (the year the Camp David agreement came into force) this was the only alternative for divers who could no longer reach Sharm el Sheikh. Hurghada does have some excellent diving but most people who've dived both locations seem to come down heavily in favour of the Sinai. An indication of the relative status of the two destinations is that whereas dive trips from Hurghada regularly visit Sharm el Sheikh, no one would dream of doing it the other way round.

This doesn't prevent hundreds of divers from visiting Hurghada, but there is no shore diving and no snorkelling from the beach: the nearest reefs are at least three-quarters-of-a-mile/1 km off-shore and all diving and snorkelling is by boat.

Hurghada is currently being promoted as a beach resort but the beach is truly awful. The only reason for coming here would be if you wanted to go diving before or after a visit to Luxor (which is relatively close, 161 miles/260 km to the east) and, for some reason, you couldn't get over to the Sinai.

At the northern tip of the gulf of Aqaba there is also the Israeli resort of Eilat, heavily promoted as a winter sunshine and diving destination. Eilat has several top-notch dive schools but the reefs and dive sites aren't comparable to what you can find down at Sharm el Sheikh.

Although almost two-thirds of the Red Sea does lie within the tropics (the Tropic of Cancer bisects Egypt 45 miles/70km south of Aswan), the Gulf of Aqaba is not in the tropical belt, so it's important to time your visit to coincide with warm sea temperatures. Winter may be the best time for sight-seeing holidays (cool and dry) but in January, February and March it's too cold for extensive snorkelling. Unless you're super-macho or impervious to the cold you might last about fifteen minutes without a wetsuit.

Although the water is warmest in summer, many people find landside temperatures unbearable (as high as 125°F/50°C) during this time. Spring (March, April, May) and autumn (September, October, November) are considered the optimum seasons with the right balance between land and sea temperatures, not forgetting the all-important underwater visibility.

Egypt is currently extremely good value and just a short flight away from northern Europe but it bears repeating that this is not really a beach destination. Pyramids and snorkelling or diving, definitely yes. Pyramids and beaches, no. But for divers this is guaranteed good quality, good value, convenient and accessible tropical diving.

GENERAL INFORMATION

Time
GMT +2 hours

IDD code
20+area code+number

Currency
Egyptian pounds (LE)
UK £1=LE 4.10
US$1=LE 2.25

Hotels
Single/double B&B
Deluxe: US$80/90
Expensive: US$60/70
Moderate: US$20/30
Budget: under US$10

PUBLICATIONS

Books listed below in the series from Immel can be ordered direct from: 37 Dover St, London W1X 3RB, tel: (01) 491 1799. Postage rates given are UK surface.

Red Sea Diver's Guide

Shlomo Cohen (Seapen Books, Tel Aviv, second edition 1988). Softback, 180pp. Guide to 18 shore diving sites from Eilat down to Ras Muhammed with aerial photos showing currents, depths and entry and exit points. Lavishly produced, but the long-awaited second edition will disappoint those who were hoping it might cover the Sinai in more detail; the only four new dive sites in it are all near Eilat. US$25 from Sinai Divers.

Red Sea Fishwatcher's Guide

(Seahawk Press, Miami). Underwater card, sometimes available locally. US$5.

Red Sea Reef Fishes

John E Randall (Immel Publishing, London, 1983). Hardback, 192pp. Large format, 446 colour photos, £32+£2 p&p.

Red Sea Safety

Peter Vine (Immel Publishing, London, 1986). Hardback,145pp. Covers marine life that is dangerous to eat, touch or merely encounter, with appropriate medical remedies. £16.75 + 77p p&p.

The Diver's Guide to Red Sea Reef Fishes

John E Randall (Immel Publishing, London, 1982). Softback, 50pp. Waterproof. Not as good as Seahawk Press waterproof books largely because of the author's preference for photographing dead fish on plain backgrounds out of the water. Also not as useful as Helmut Debelius' book (see below) for fish ID because information is restricted to the common and Latin names of fish. £20 + 30p p&p.

Underwater Guide to Red Sea Fishes

Helmut Debelius (Verlag Stephanie Naglschmid, Stuttgart, 1987). Softback, 160pp. The best Red Sea fish ID book available. Schematic diagrams illustrate exactly where on the reef and at what depths most of the fish live. Dual German-English text. Despite the title, not waterproof. US$20 from Sinai Divers.

Underwater Guide to Red Sea Invertebrates

Dr Peter Schmid and Dietmar Paschke

(Verlag Stephanie Naglschmid, Stuttgart, 1987). Softback, 168pp. Similar format to the above, US$20 locally.

WEATHER

Egypt has hot, dry summers and mild, dry winters. Rainfall is negligible. Nights are cool to cold, so some warm clothing is advisable in winter. In the middle of summer (June, July and August) it can be unbearably hot in the daytime (120-125° F/49-50° C) but if you can put up with the daytime heat this is a good time to visit because the water is at its warmest (79-80° F/26-27° C) and there are less people around. Land temperatures start to cool down again in late August. The optimum time in terms of water temperature, land temperature and underwater visibility is September, October and November. In January, February and March water temperatures are at their lowest (around 70-75° F/21-23° C) and even with a wetsuit you will probably be cold by the second dive because of the wind chill factor. From March onwards the water starts to warm up again and late March to May is also considered a good time to be here in terms of visibility and land and sea temperatures.

HEALTH

No vaccinations required except yellow fever if coming from an infected area. Typhoid, cholera, tetanus, polio and gamma globulin shots are advisable.

VISAS

Passports valid for at least six months required. British Visitors Passports not accepted. Visas are required by everyone. These can be obtained in advance or issued once you arrive in the country. One month tourist visas cost £17. Although visa requirements have recently been simplified (you no longer have to change

US$150 on entering Egypt, for instance) there are still complications in the Sinai because of the Camp David agreement.

If you enter Egypt from Israel at Taba, or if you fly in on a direct charter from abroad to Sharm el Sheikh, you will only be granted a seven-day visa. It's important to realize that these visas are NOT valid for Ras Muhammed. The reasons for this are historical and complicated, but at the minute all dive boats are strictly controlled and checked at the quays and although this is a considerable nuisance the diving organizations here are doing their best to get it changed. Until this happens it's vital to have the one-month visa if you want to dive Ras Muhammed. For people coming on charters, this means getting it in advance in Europe. If you're coming from Israel, it must be obtained in Tel Aviv.

All visitors must register with the police within one week of entering Egypt; this is normally done for you by your hotel.

TOURIST BOARDS

Head Office: Cairo, tel: (02) 3552600, 923000; London, tel: (01) 493 5282; New York, tel: (212) 246 6960; San Francisco, tel: (415) 781 7676; Tokyo, tel: (03) 589653; Frankfurt, tel: (069) 252319, 252153; Paris, tel: (01) 45 62 94 43.

NA'AMA BAY

Na'ama Bay is the Sinai's primary resort area, a crescent-shaped bay four miles/six km north of the port of Sharm el Sheikh with magnificent views of the eastern Sinai mountains.

After years of neglect following the Israeli withdrawal, Na'ama has bounced back as the Red Sea's number one diving destination and there are as many divers here now as there were during the peak years of the 1970s. Several new hotels and diving operations have recently opened, providing previously unheard of levels of comfort and diving services. Direct charters from Europe (principally Condor from Germany) have further fuelled this dive boom.

For the visiting diver at Na'ama there is the choice of shore diving, boat diving, live-aboards for extended trips from two to fourteen days and land-based diving safaris for those who want to sleep out under the stars in the desert at night and tumble over drop-offs during the day. Costs are low and the diving is exceptional value for money. For potential divers introductory dives and certification courses are available at a price which compares favourably with diving centres worldwide. Standards of equipment and instruction at the new dive bases here are good. Opportunities for snorkelling along this coast are almost limitless and this is unquestionably the most rewarding snorkelling destination within easy reach of Europe. For non-divers there are excursions to the ancient monastery of St Catherine's and desert safaris by jeep or camel, but otherwise there is very little to do, so think carefully before opting to join a diving friend or partner here on holiday unless you intend to learn to dive or spend all day snorkelling. Na'ama Bay is a diver's and snorkeller's Mecca but the beach itself is not attractive.

Shore diving, Sinai

SNORKELLING★★★★★★

There are some superb spots within walking distance of Na'ama Bay and many more which can be reached on

day trips. Within walking distance are Herb's Bay (the closest drop-off, 10-15 minutes over the cliffs to the south past the Marina Hotel), Near Gardens, Middle Gardens and Far Gardens.

Near Gardens is the most frequented site: walk north past the camp site and continue round the cliffs until you can no longer see Na'ama Bay (20-30 minutes). You'll find a small, triangular pebble beach and a drop-off zigzagging around the headland with its extremity marked by a buoy.

Middle Gardens is a further 15-20 minutes northwards, with two or three holes and canyons parallel to the beach (max depth around 13ft/4m). These canyons are easily visible from

the cliff-top two beaches before the headland curves out to sea again. Far Gardens is half-way along this last headland, and is marked by a buoy.

To go further afield, the accepted method is to hire a big seven-seater Peugeot taxi, with a Bedouin driver who will drive you across the desert just about anywhere you want to go for around LE 60-80 (US$15-20) for the car for the whole day. Including the hire of snorkelling equipment this works out at around US$9 per person ·

Ras Muhammed is a must (make sure you have the right visa, see page 279), as is Ras Nasrani (take boiled eggs for the Napoleon wrasse).

Another alternative is a snorkelling safari by jeep. These operate only in the summer and are run by a local character called 'Desert Fox' who can be contacted at the Sanafir Hotel. One-day trips usually take in two different snorkelling sites either north or south of Na'ama and cost around US$10 including lunch, snorkelling equipment and Fox's services as a guide (Ras Muhammed is an extra US$5).

Good quality MSF can be hired at most dive shops for around US$5-7.

WATERSPORTS★★
Windsurfers can be hired at Sinai Divers and DTM Diving. Water ski-ing and jet skis at the Hilton.

DIVING★★★★★★
This is one of the richest diving areas in the world, teeming with marine life of every description. As well as Ras Muhammed (one of the world's most famous dive sites) other spectacular locations include the reefs in the Straits of Tiran (Jackson, Gordon, Wood-house and Thomas) and numerous shore dive sites whose names will be familiar to many divers (Ras Umm Sid, Ras Nasrani, the Tower and many others).

Ras Muhammed is renowned for sharks but you won't necessarily see them here all year round. Their numbers have been greatly exaggerated, and many have left now that there are so many divers here.

Contrary to popular myth, sharks avoid humans and are nearly always the first to leave when divers swamp an area. Summer is a better season for sharks, because there are fewer divers and the tuna arrive, which they feed on. Hammerheads mate here during April, May, June and July. The manta season is from March/April through to June/July. Common reef sharks mate here from mid-December to the end of January.

In the Straits of Tiran (which is periodically closed for military reasons) the two best reefs are Thomas and Woodhouse, both done as drift dives. At Gordon or Jackson Reefs you might come across white-tip sharks.

One advantage of the Sinai being handed back to Egypt is that dive sites all over the Red Sea are once again accessible and divers are no longer restricted to the Gulf of Aqaba. For instance, on a fast boat from Na'ama you can dive the wreck of the Dunraven (used by Lawrence of Arabia to bring gold from India to Aqaba to fight the Turks) in the Gulf of Suez.

Despite the superlatives which are heaped on the Gulf of Aqaba, some coastal sites are clearly damaged along a divers' 'highway' between 17 and 65ft/5 and 20m. This is no longer a good area for divers who want virgin adventure diving. The reefs further down the Red Sea towards Sudan are much better if you're after untouched underwater wilderness. The number of divers now visiting Sharm is phenomenal – during 1989 no less than 25 dive boats were leaving the dock daily.

Photographers should bring the usual necessities for remote locations (batteries and films are of dubious quality and expensive). At the time of writing there were no E6 processing facilities (except on live-aboards such as the *Lady Jenny V*) but several dive shops promise them in the near future.

When it comes to gearing up you might not believe the advice given on weights and buoyancy but it's a fact that the Red Sea has a high salinity factor and this means at least two kilos over your normal requirements.

The average price of a one-tank dive is around US$20, two-tanks around US$35, full equipment hire around US$10 extra. Night dives work out at US$20-30, intro dives US$40, and five-day open water certifications US$175-200. Ras Muhammed and the Straits of Tiran, being slightly further away, cost more – on average, US$40 for an all day two-tank boat dive. Five- and ten-day dive packages are available at all the dive shops. The volume of divers coming here during 1989 started a price war, so if anything the cost of diving will be lower than quoted.

If you want to set off and explore local coastal sites on your own, this is easily arranged by simply hiring a big Peugeot taxi. Although they can take seven people, four or five is probably the comfortable limit with tanks and equipment. Taxis cost LE60-80 (US$15-20) a day, and will take you anywhere including Ras Muhammed.

All the dive clubs below offer full- and half-day trips for qualified divers and certification for beginners.

● *Sinai Divers:* The biggest operation in Na'ama, run by Rolf Schmidt and Petra Roglin, both of whom have been diving in the Sinai for over a decade. PADI, NAUI and CMAS certifications. **A** Ghazala Village, Na'ama Bay, tel: (062) 70217. Reservations: Cairo, tel: (02) 672441.

● *Oonasdivers:* New dive base at the north end of the beach, still under construction in March 1989. **A** Oonasdivers, Na'ama Bay. Reservations: UK, tel: (0323) 648924.

● *DTM Dive Tours:* One of the two largest dive operations. CMAS and PADI, German and English instruction. **A** Hilton Hotel, Na'ama Bay, tel: (062) 769400. Reservations: Munich, tel: (089) 2319080.

● *Camel Dive Club:* Small dive club, personalized service. Daily trips, certifications. One- or two-week land-based dive safaris from US$65 per person per day fully inclusive. **A** Sanafir Hotel, Na'ama Bay. Reservations: Cairo, tel: (02) 291 0380. Reservations: UK, tel: (0323) 648924.

● *Aquamarine:* PADI, NAUI and CMAS, French, English and German instruction. **A** Aquamarine Hotel, Na'ama Bay, tel: (062) 70474. Reservations: UK, tel: (01) 892 7606.

● Diving safaris and Sinai land safaris are organized from the UK by Oonasdivers, tel: (0323) 648924; Speedwing, tel: (01) 491 1734, 629 2268; and Twickers World, tel: (01) 892 7606.

● Live-aboards can be chartered in situ or complete packages are available from the UK through Virgin Divers World, tel: (0293) 515704 and Twickers World, tel: (01) 892 7606. Eight-day cruises on board the *Colona II* and *Colona IV* can be booked in the USA through See and Sea, tel: (415) 434 3400.

283

ACCOMMODATION

- *Fayrouz Hilton Village*: Deluxe/ expensive **R**. Restaurant, smart disco/ bar, poolside bar. Small pool. Well-appointed, comfortable, a/c chalets from single/double US$85/95 B&B, suites from US$120/130. **A** Na'ama Bay, South Sinai, tel: (062) 769400. Reservations: Cairo, tel: (02) 777444; UK, 0800 289 303.
- *Ghazala Holiday Village*: Deluxe/ expensive **R**. Solid and comfortable, German-managed. Large sheltered swimming pool. Single/double US$60/ 70 B&B. **A** Na'ama Bay, South Sinai, tel: (062) 649 602. Reservations: UK, tel: (0293) 515704.
- *Sanafir*: Moderate **R**. Designed with its desert location in mind, the Sanafir's Moorish/Arabic-style main building is complemented by a Bedouin tented area outside. Rooms in the main build-ing cost from LE40/45 (US$18/22), small bamboo huts from LE20/25 (US$9/11). Extremely popular, advance reservations advisable. Small pub, busy restaurant. **A** Na'ama Bay, South Sinai. Reservations: Cairo, tel: (02) 920489, 910873. UK, tel: (0323) 648924.
- *Aquamarine*: Closed for rebuilding until March 1990.
- *Marina Sharm Hotel*: Expensive/ moderate. Awful hotel, choose it only as a last resort. Single/double from US$35/45, bungalows from US$25/35. **A** Na'ama Bay, South Sinai. Reser-vations: Cairo, tel: (02) 770200.
- *Marsa Alaat*: Budget. Tents from LE5-7 (US$2-3).
- *Cafy Camp*: Budget **R**. Shared tents from LE7-30 (US$3-14), chalets from LE40 (US$18).

ACCESS

Egyptair flies daily from Cairo (except

Mondays and Wednesdays), flight time one hour, o/w fare around LE100/ US$45. Egyptair also connects Sharm with Luxor and Hurghada. Air-condi-tioned buses from Cairo (five a day) take six hours and cost around LE11/US$5.

It's possible to get a taxi direct to Cairo International airport from Sharm for around LE150/US$66; this takes around six hours and isn't too costly shared between four or more people, but I wouldn't guarantee that the reverse journey is as cheap.

There are twice daily buses from the Israeli border at Taba or you can get a shared taxi (from LE80/US$35 for six) which takes four hours. Buses also connect Sharm with Nuweiba, Dahab and Suez.

There is an erratic boat service to Hurghada (crossing time five-six hours) which costs around LE40/ US$18 per person.

Barracuda, Ras Muhammed

DAHAB

Sixty miles/100 km north of Sharm el Sheik, Dahab has always been popular amongst backpackers or overland travellers looking for a stint of cheap beach life after working or touring in Israel. The main attraction – as elsewhere in the Sinai – is underwater but even though there are plenty of opportunities for snorkelling in the immediate vicinity of the village, it is not the sort of place you'd want to come to specially.

The village itself has changed considerably in recent years, with most of the palm-leaf dwellings now replaced by scores of brick huts: Dahab draws large numbers of overlanders looking for the 'ethnic experience' of living in a Bedouin village but unfortunately there isn't anything terribly ethnic about concrete huts and fly-blown travellers' restaurants. However, it is incredibly cheap to live here (under US$5 per day).

DIVING★★★

Dahab is famous for two locations in particular, the Blue Hole and the Canyon. The Blue Hole, which is considered to be one of the Sinai's most spectacular dive sites, is a large crater in the reef top which disappears into the depths down to over 330ft/100m. There is a tunnel and arch at around 200ft/60m through which you leave the hole on to the reef wall. Since this is below the depth of normal sport diving even if you are a qualified diver you will (or should) have to do a series of progressively deeper dives at other sites before being allowed to dive here. There have been several fatalities.

• Egyptian-run dive centre at Dahab Holiday Village: two-tank dive US$35; full equipment hire US$10; CMAS/NAUI open water certifications US$170. In summer the dive centre runs a two-day camel safari to Ras Abu Galoum (US$45 per person per day fully inclusive).

BARS AND RESTAURANTS

There are over a dozen beach cafés at the Bedouin village serving cheap travellers' fodder (*falafel*, spaghetti, hamburgers and so on). Restaurant, bar and beach café at the Dahab Holiday Village.

ACCOMMODATION

• *Dahab Holiday Village*: Moderate/budget. Gloomy and stuffy. Single/double rooms from US$21/33 B&B. Dorm beds from US$7 per person, camping US$5 per tent. A Dahab, tel: (062) 70788. Reservations: Cairo, tel: (02) 770200.

• In the Bedouin village there are over a hundred basic huts to choose from, mostly costing under US$2.

ACCESS

Buses from either Sharm el Sheikh or from Taba (at the Israeli border) stop at the resort. The Bedouin village is one-and-three-quarter miles/two-and-a-half km north of here (US$2 per person in a shared taxi). Four buses a day from Sharm el Sheik, twice daily buses from Taba and Cairo.

Appendices

SUNTANNING

Everybody wants a glowing tan to show off when they come back from holiday but unfortunately the message now is that the short-term cachet of having a tan is acquired at the expense of long-term damage to your skin, premature ageing and skin cancers.

Sunlight is composed of three different types of ultraviolet radiation (UVR). The first of these, short wavelength UV-C, is potentially the most damaging but is mostly screened out by the ozone layer (one of the effects of the depletion of the ozone layer will be an increase in the penetration of UV-C causing widespread skin cancers). Medium-length UV-B rays cause sunburn, tanning and eventual ageing of the top layers of skin. Long-wave UV-A rays penetrate deeper into the skin than UV-B and add to the tanning effect, as well as causing ageing. Both types of rays may cause skin cancer but UV-B is considered the more dangerous of the two: UV-B rays are concentrated at midday, within two hours either side of the solar noon.

The risks of skin damage are considerably increased the nearer you are to the equator, where the sun is that much fiercer and the harmful rays more intense: sunburn on your first few days in the tropics could do more then just ruin your holiday.

The people most at risk from melanomas – the most dangerous form of skin cancer – are those who are exposed to short, sharp bursts of sun, particularly if they're not used to it. Fair-skinned people, especially office-workers who see the sun rarely, are the highest risk group, and a rising proportion of skin cancers occur in affluent travellers who can afford two or more holidays a year. Children below the age of fifteen are also particularly vulnerable, although the damage may not appear for many years.

The vital point to remember is that it's burning which is most likely to give rise to skin cancers. If you're on a short holiday, take it slowly and only gradually increase your exposure to the sun. Start with just 20 or 30 minutes per day for the first few days, building up to longer periods later. A slow tan is safer and tends to last longer, as well as reducing the risk of peeling and painful burning caused by initial over-exposure. A light tan is naturally preferable from the health point of view than a deep, dark tan. If you're travelling for a long time, it's better to develop a light tan and maintain it throughout your journey, topping up when necessary, to give you protection against burning.

Most sunscreens now have SPF (Sun Protection Factor) ratings marked on them on a scale from 0-15. This number indicates how much longer you can stay in the sun without burning compared to how your skin normally reacts when unprotected. For instance, if you normally start to burn after half-an-hour, a sunscreen of SPF 10 will theoretically allow you to stay in the sun for five hours before you start to burn (provided the sunscreen has been applied thoroughly and reapplied when necessary). Some sunscreens go up to a scale of 25; unfortunately there is no international standardization of SPF ratings.

Choose a high SPF factor to start with and work your way down the scale as appropriate. If you have a pale complexion and burn easily, start with SPF 12-15, moving on later to SPF 8-10. If you tan easily and don't burn, start with SPF 5-7 and switch to SPF 2-3 later. In the tropics the sun is much fiercer than it is in temperate zones, so choose a higher SPF than you would normally use. Also, use more of it: research shows that we don't apply enough sunscreen to protect ourselves properly.

• Stay out of the sun between 10 a.m. and 2 p.m. when starting a tan.

• Cloudy days are no protection against sunburn, and don't rely on the shade of a beach umbrella to protect you either: 70-80 per cent of UV rays penetrate clouds and you can still get burned by reflections off the sea, sand, concrete or other sufaces.

• UV rays reach to at least three feet underwater: when snorkelling or swimming wear a T-shirt or a waterproof blocker.

• Reapply sunscreen after swimming, preferably having taken a fresh water shower beforehand: salt water and chlorine both contribute to drying out your skin.

• If you start to burn, switch to a higher SPF, or a total blocker such as zinc cream or SPF 25, on affected areas. Use different SPF factors for different parts of your body as your tan progresses.

• If your children have the same complexion as you, apply double the SPF factor that you normally use.

• Avoid using coconut oil until your skin is sufficiently acclimatized, and even then use only for short periods of time. Be particularly careful of using coconut oil during peak tanning hours (10 a.m. to 2 p.m.).

• Watch out for vulnerable areas such as the face, lips, ears, the backs of hands and knees, and tops of shoulders. If you're going for an all-over tan, use a higher protection factor on areas not normally exposed to the sun and cover up sooner.

• Moisturize your skin after tanning with a commercial after-sun product, aloe vera or any lanolin-rich preparation.

• Some sunscreen products can cause allergies: choose those with the fewest unnecessary additives such as perfumes.

• The use of sunbeds has always been controversial. Recent studies show that even modern sunbeds, which emit UVA, could be dangerous. Not only does UVA damage the skin but it may also suppress the body's immune system. In California, all sunbeds must now carry health warnings by law. Britain's Institute of Dermatology recommends that fair-skinned people shouldn't use sunbeds at all. If you still want to pre-start your tan, only ever use a UVA sunbed and always wear protective goggles.

• Most skin cancers can be treated if caught in time. Malignant melanomas usually arise from moles: the danger signals are if a mole starts to itch, bleed, enlarge or change shape. The most common sites for malignant melanomas are on the back for men and on the legs for women.

289

SNORKELLING

It only takes a minute or two to learn how to snorkel, and once you've had a glimpse of the underwater world going on holiday without your mask and snorkel will seem as inconceivable as leaving without your swimsuit.

Snorkelling is often dismissed as an inferior alternative to diving but there's little justification for this. Although scuba gives you the freedom to explore deeper reefs, much of the colour and life on a coral reef is within the first few metres of the surface: reds and oranges, for instance, are filtered out of the spectrum below 30ft/10m. Part of the attraction of scuba is the opportunity it gives you for close encounters with the denizens of the deep but there are locations all over the world where snorkellers can meet them too: Napoleon wrasse in the Red Sea, giant potato cod on the Barrier Reef, sharks in Bora Bora, manta rays on Maldivian islands . . . all these magic encounters are possible just by snorkelling.

Snorkelling has other advantages. Apart from the outlay on hiring or buying a set of equipment, it's free. You can jump in when and where you want and go wherever you wish: you don't have to stick with a group or a diving partner and you don't have to return to your point of departure, as you almost invariably do when diving. There are none of the anxieties or even potential dangers of breathing compressed air at depth and, just as important, your time in the water isn't limited by the amount of air in a tank. Snorkellers can often get closer to fish which might otherwise be frightened away by the sound of a diver's noisy bubbles. Some reefs are so shallow, why bother going to the trouble of hiring and lugging scuba gear around when you can see the same stuff just as easily from the surface, and for nothing? What's more, if you've had a few Mai Tais in a beach bar you'll be absolutely forbidden to go diving, but there's nothing to stop you floating off for a relaxed post-prandial snorkel. You don't need to organize anything to go snorkelling, all you need to do is locate a good spot – and that's what this book is for.

For psychological, physiological or financial reasons some people never take up diving and prefer to snorkel instead; if you happen to be in that category there's no need to feel you're missing out.

290

EQUIPMENT

The two basic items you need are a mask, which will allow you to see underwater, and a snorkel, which will allow you to breathe whilst floating face down. Although you can hire snorkelling equipment almost anywhere, it's better to have your own. Rented equipment is often in poor condition and may leak, and there's nothing more aggravating than a mask which constantly fills up with water.

There are several different types of mask on the market, most of which now have frames made from clear silicone. These last longer and give you better peripheral vision underwater than the old black rubber type; they're also softer and more comfortable to wear. Thanks to the introduction of silicone most snorkelling equipment now comes in a range of bright and snazzy fluorescent and pastel colours.

The mask is the most important item you'll buy, so make sure you choose one which fits well. The mask is a good fit if it stays on your face without the use of the straps. Pull the straps around to the front of the mask and hold it to your face, inhale through your nose and let go. If it stays on and feels comfortable, it's okay.

Low volume silicone masks are ideal, since they take up less room when you're travelling and the lower volume of air inside means that they're more easily cleared of water. Some masks have purge valves on the nosepiece to help clear water trapped inside the mask, but this is a bit of a gimmick and the valves often leak. Quick-release buckles for easy adjustment of the mask strap are an asset.

Faceplates should be made of toughened glass. If you normally wear glasses or contact lenses you can get a prescription lens fitted to the mask (in London, Harrods, Lillywhites or any good diving shop offers this service) or else you can get armless frames which clip into your mask.

Most masks come with matching snorkels and ideally the snorkel should have a short, wide barrel. These are easier to breath through than long thin barrels. The snorkel should have a soft, pliable mouthpiece which feels comfortable when held in the mouth. Many snorkels now have a swivelling mouthpiece so that you can get the angle just right and some even have mouldable mouthpieces. Snorkels are also available with built-in self-draining valves at the base of the tube, which allow the water to run out when you surface, but purists consider these unnecessary and just another potential source of leaks, like purge valves on masks.

The snorkel can be kept in position by slipping it under the mask strap or by using a snorkel-keeper which attaches it directly to the strap. Traditionally, snorkels are worn on the left because this is the custom when diving (a diver always has his or her regulator on their right).

A mask and snorkel are all you need to get started, but for fast and easy propulsion through the water you'll also need a pair of fins. Again, these can normally be hired, but if you've got space in your luggage it's better to have your own. They'll fit better than hired equipment and be much more comfortable to use. Snorkelling with badly-fitting fins can be agony.

There are two basic types of fins: one-piece fins and open-heel fins. One-piece fins have built-in foot pockets and are smaller and less powerful than open-heel fins. They're lighter and more convenient to carry around but if you're thinking of learning to dive later on it's better to get open-heel fins.

Open-heel fins have an adjustable strap which goes round your heel and they're normally worn over a pair of reef boots. Reef boots are like seamless slippers covering your foot and ankle; sometimes they have zips to make putting them on easier. This combination of boot and fin has considerable advantages over one-piece fins. For instance, you can walk across reef, rocks or the beach with just the boots on and only put the fins on once in the water. This can be particularly important if you're trying to get in the water at a snorkelling location where waves are breaking over a shallow reef top, and it'll save your feet from being cut to pieces on the coral. If you're on the beach the easiest procedure is to go to the sea,

291

rinse the sand off your feet and put on the reef boots, and then return to collect your snorkelling equipment, camera, fish food, underwater fish books, or whatever.

Open-heel fins normally have more rigid blades than one-piece fins, which make them more powerful, giving you greater propulsion in the water.

Some open-heel fins have flow-through vents near the base of the blade which reduces resistance on the upstroke and some (such as NASA fins made by Technisub) also have the option of flexible vents which close on the downstroke for maximum power. Ribs down the side of the fin can also improve efficiency by channelling the water and preventing the blade twisting.

Fins are normally made from a blend of rubber and synthetic compounds. A recent development has been the use of thermoplastics, which weigh less and give greater thrust, but I sometimes wonder if 'fin technology' hasn't gone completely over the top. Take, for instance, this publicity blurb from Oceanic: 'From Oceanic's Diver Propulsion Labs comes the Fara Fin – X. Designed with a 31 per cent increase in the foward thrust component of the blade and an eight degree change in the blade/foot angle, this fin is made from a new elastomer compound and gives an extra 22 per cent thrust for the same kicking effort.' Diver Propulsion Labs? Do they mean the swimming pool?

All snorkelling equipment should be rinsed with fresh water after use and dried off in the shade. Don't leave silicone or neoprene equipment out in the tropical sun.

Underwater notebooks for snorkellers and divers from Hawkins and Mainwaring include the standard Aquascribe (150 × 105 mm, £3.38) or larger ringbinder notebooks – yes, the underwater Filofax is here – which cost £14.68 each. Prices include UK postage but not VAT. Hawkins and Mainwaring, Westborough, Newark, Notts NG23 5HJ, tel: (0400) 81492.

UNDERWATER CAMERAS
There are several underwater cameras on the market suitable for snorkelling, amongst them the Canon As-6 Aquasnappy (waterproof to 30ft/9m), the Fuji HDM (6ft/2m), the Minolta Weathermatic (15ft/4.5m), the Nikon AWF (10ft/3m) and the new Minolta WD-L 35 mm (16ft/5m with dual lens facility). The above maximum depths are what the manufacturers recommend but you can normally go quite a bit deeper. However, if there's a possibility you might want to learn to dive at a later stage you should consider the Sea & Sea Motormarine (waterproof to 140ft/43m), the Hanimex Amphibian (147ft/45m) or the big daddy of underwater cameras, the Nikonos V (164ft/50m). Naturally, these are much more expensive.

TECHNIQUES
Breathe through the snorkel before getting in the water if you're not confident about plunging straight in. Make sure that stray strands of hair aren't caught under the flange of the mask, since this will cause it to leak. The mask strap shouldn't be tight, since this increases wear on the strap and can give you a headache. Misting can be prevented by rubbing saliva on the inside of the lens and then rinsing with sea water before going in. There are anti-mist products on the market which have

the same effect but saliva is more practical, always available, and free.

Once in the sea, if your mask fills with water put your head above the surface and lift the bottom of the mask so that it runs out. If the snorkel fills with water, give it a vigorous 'phut' of breath to expel it. *Voilà* – you're all set to roam the ocean deep.

You can snorkel without fins if necessary (sometimes, setting off for a distant beach, it's easier to chuck just a mask and snorkel into a beach bag), but for easy propulsion they're essential. The technically correct finning technique is with your legs straight, since this gives the maximum propulsion. The 'incorrect' way is bicycling underwater with your legs (i.e., drawing your knees up to your waist before kicking out); although this is less efficient it doesn't really matter what technique you use as long as you're comfortable and going where you want.

If you get cramp while snorkelling, there are two ways of dealing with it. If it is in the calf muscles at the back of the leg or your instep, reach foward and grab the end of your fin(s) with one hand, straighten your leg, and pull the fin(s) towards you. If it's in the front, reach behind for your ankle and pull the leg up and back.

It's useful to know a few variations for finning so that you can change strokes and give your muscles a break, especially during extended or long-distance snorkelling.

Apart from just straight fin-kicking, other techiniques include the frog kick and the scissors kick. With the frog kick, start with your heels together and your knees apart and then kick out, bringing your legs back together to glide through the water. It's a bit like the leg action used in breaststroke except that your legs are apart when straight out behind. For a scissors kick start with your legs half-bent and splayed out, with fins sideways (rather than horizontal as they usually are). Bring your feet together for the stroke, slicing the fins up and out of the water afterwards to return to the original legs-apart position. You can alternate left and right with this stroke by twisting your body round before the fins slice back in the water again. The nearest equivalent is side-stroke. Both these techniques are much harder to describe than they are to do.

Snorkelling manuals normally tell you not to use your hands and arms when snorkelling and say that arms should be kept folded or against your sides. This is good practice for diving (novice divers are easily recognized by their flapping arms) but for snorkelling it really doesn't matter. By saying this they fail to take in to account the fact that the fastest way to travel on the surface is a crawl stroke with fins.

'Free diving' is sometimes used to describe snorkelling in general, but its more specific meaning is to refer to a dive beneath the surface without scuba tanks.

If you're fit, with practice you can reach depths of 20-30ft/7-9m or more when free diving. In many tropical countries locals can often dive down to 70 or 80 ft/21-24m with no problem at all. The record for a breath-hold dive is held by Jacques Mayol of France, who descended to an astonishing 344 ft/105m in December 1983 off Elba, Italy. Mayol used a sled and it took him 104 seconds to go down and 90 seconds to come back up. The women's record is held by Rossana Majorca of Italy, who descended to 246ft/75m off Sicily in July 1987 (source: Guinness Book of Records).

The most important thing about free diving is that you must equalize the pressure in your ears as you swim down. This is common knowledge for divers, and for snorkellers the same principle apply. Sometimes your ears will clear of their own accord, but if not simply hold the nosepiece of your mask and blow gently. If you feel pain in your ears when free diving it's because they haven't cleared properly (this also happens with a cold or bad sinuses). Come up and try again – don't continue down until your ears have cleared.

As you descend pressure will push the faceplate of the mask towards your face. This is called mask squeeze (or 'mask squidge' as one foreign instructor insisted to a friend of mine) and is easily dealt with simply by exhaling through your nose.

Hyperventilation is a means of staying underwater longer and involves making several deep inhalations and exhalations prior to free diving. It can be extremely dangerous because it can cause sudden loss of consciousness underwater, which is often followed by drowning.

The reason for this is as follows: 'By hyperventilating, the partial pressure of carbon dioxide in the blood is considerably reduced. Unfortunately, the chemical reaction between oxygen and haemoglobin is such that hyperventilation has little or no effect on the amount of oxygen in the blood. When the diver is finning hard underwater, oxygen is rapidly consumed, but it takes longer for the amount of carbon dioxide in the blood to reach a level at which it stimulates the desire to breath. The oxygen content of the blood may be reduced to dangerous levels and unconsciousness may occur before the carbon dioxide content is sufficient to stimulate the respiratory centre.

'This problem is exacerbated by an increase in depth. Occasionally, breath-holding divers become unconscious, as a result of hypoxia, a few seconds after surfacing and despite having taken a breath. This is because there is a lag of a few seconds between the blood picking up oxygen in the lungs and delivering it to the brain'. (from *Sport Diving*, Stanley Paul 1985).

Naturally, all diving and snorkelling manuals will tell you not to hyperventilate. However, the legendary swimming coach Fred Lanoue, author of the classic manual *Drownproofing*, carried out a series of tests on hyperventilation at the Georgia Institute of Technology in the 1960s. Of twenty-five thousand students who attempted to swim fifty yards underwater, about five hundred passed out. Of these five hundred, Lanoue claims that five times more students passed out without hyperventilating than with hyperventilating. In Lanoue's tests a teacher and a student lifeguard at the side of the pool ensured that the swimmers were pulled out within seconds after losing consciousness, and, he says, 'not one of our passouts underwater has ever taken in water, regurgitated, felt nausea or needed resuscitation'. He concludes that the ability to swim to the point of passing out is a measure of will power, adding that 'the important thing is never to extend yourself in underwater swimming unless under the exclusive, direct observation of a competent observer'.

Whether or not to hyperventilate while snorkelling is up to you. Personally I use this method all the time, especially when I want to stay down longer to get a particular photographic shot. Tom Hartdegen of Dive Paradise in Cozumel shares my view that people are going to do it anyway (whatever the risks) and recommends the following: Do not exceed four hyperventilations per dive and always rest on the surface for at least one or two minutes before diving again. To be on the safe side, don't hyperventilate when snorkelling on your own.

The easiest way to get beneath the surface is known as a pike or surface dive. Bend forward at the waist and lift your legs in the air perpendicular to the surface. The weight of your legs will cause you to sink downwards. Use your arms to breatstroke until your fins are beneath the surface.

As you come up from a dive, look upwards to make sure you don't crash into another snorkeller or the bottom of a boat. When you reach the surface, exhale forcefully to blast the water out of your snorkel and then take your first breath slowly. The first exhalation is unlikely to have cleared all the water from your snorkel and a small amount will probably remain in the bottom of the tube. Don't breathe in too sharply on the first breath or you'll swallow it: take a shallow breath and then give the snorkel a second blast to clear the remaining water.

A weightbelt is not necessary for free diving unless you're wearing a wetsuit or have excess body weight, both of which will add to your buoyancy and make it hard to descend.

Night diving can be a thrilling experience and there's no reason why you shouldn't snorkel at night too. I prefer to snorkel at night somewhere where I've already snorkelled during the day, so that I have some idea of the underwater terrain (I also prefer night snorkelling in shark-free areas!). It's a good idea to wear a wetsuit even if it's not cold, since there's more likelihood of bumping into nasties in the dark. Obviously an underwater torch (the more powerful the better) is essential. You can buy a mask from Tekna which has a compact but quite powerful light, the Tekna I-Beam, which clips on to the top of it. Finally, tell someone if you're going snorkelling at night, and don't go on your own.

LEARNING TO DIVE

Anyone who is reasonably fit can learn to dive and there is no better place to do it than in the tropics, where the water is warm and the beauty and diversity of the marine life will make you an instant convert.

Diving courses are run by most of the diving centres listed in this book. A good set of snorkelling equipment is a sound investment if you plan to take a course, but it's not absolutely necessary to have your own. Before leaving home have a medical check-up, and take the certificate with you. A form for your doctor to fill in is obtainable free from the British Sub Aqua Club. In many destinations it's easy enough to arrange a medical when you arrive (and people who spontaneously decide to take a scuba course will have to do that) but it may not be possible on remote islands and it's a drain on developing countries' resources to examine fit people. Any good diving school will require a medical exam, but some will let you get away with signing a waiver and doing the course without one. This isn't sensible, since you might have an unforseen physical problem which could prove dangerous or possibly fatal underwater.

For the beginner there are essentially three types of diving course: an introductory or resort dive, a novice diver course and an open-water certification course. The introductory dive usually involves a brief theory lesson followed by one or two dives under the supervision of an instructor and will provide you with a taste of the underwater world but no qualifications. Novice diver courses involve a greater degree of training and instruction and allow you to dive under the supervision of a dive guide until you upgrade to open water. An open-water certification covers lessons on the theory and practice of diving, medical and safety procedures, thorough instruction and practice in the use of equipment and a number of open-water dives. Open-water courses usually last four, five or six days, at the end of which you will be a qualified sport diver able to dive without supervision. You will be issued with a 'C' card from one of the regulatory bodies (such as PADI, NAUI or CMAS) which will allow you to hire scuba equipment. No reputable dive centre will hire equipment to unqualified divers. From sport diver you can move up the scale to advanced open-water diver, rescue diver, divemaster and beyond.

There are several good diving manuals on the market if you wish to find out more (see page 313).

It's also possible to learn to dive at home before travelling abroad. In Britain, courses are arranged through BSAC, which has branches all over the country. Once you've joined you can take part in weekly training sessions in a local swimming pool. However, whilst this might be suitable for some people it doesn't give you much motivation and it takes a long time to become qualified. BSAC say that with their method you can complete theory and pool training in six months and gain a sport diver qualification in twelve months. This is far too long for most people and rather pointless when you can gain a similar qualification in warm tropical waters in under a week.

There are certain medical conditions which preclude learning to dive, and these are epilepsy, heart disease or chest conditions, bronchitis, asthma, pneumothorax, head injuries or chronic ear and sinus diseases. Controversy surrounds the question of diabetics and diving: in Britain, diabetics are banned from holding BSAC membership although the medical evidence which suggests they are at risk is by no means conclusive. There are no age limits on learning to dive: you can still take a certification course at 70 and beyond.

Given appropriately-tailored training there is no reason why disabled people shouldn't dive. In Britain the best source of information is a booklet produced by BSAC entitled *Diving for Disabled People* (£1 inc. p & p from BSAC). This thorough and well-researched manual is primarily aimed at giving advice to BSAC instructors on the specific needs of novice divers with disabilities but will prove equally useful for the potential diver as well, with guidance tailored to different categories of disability.

In the United States the foremost authority is the Handicapped Scuba Association. The HSA is an independent training and certifying agency and in addition to issuing open-water certifications to students they also conduct special training courses for instructors. A documentary entitled *Freedom in Depth* features 19 divers with different kinds of disabilities (there is a captioned version for the deaf). It costs US$45 including domestic postage (US$60 overseas airmail) from HSA.

UK
• *British Sub-Aqua Club (BSAC)*, 16 Upper Woburn Place, London WC1H 0QW, tel: (01) 387 9302.

USA
• *Professional Association of Diving Instructors (PADI International)*, 1251 East Dyer Rd, Suite 100, Santa Ana, CA 92705, tel: (714) 540 7234.
• *National Association of Underwater Instructors (NAUI)*, PO Box 14650, Montclair, CA 91763, tel: (714) 621 5801.
• *National YMCA Center for Underwater Activities*, Oakbrook Square, 6083-A Oakbrook Parkway, Norcross, GA 30093, tel: (404) 662 5172.
• *The Handicapped Scuba Association (HSA)*, 116 West El Portal, Suite 104, San Clemente, CA 92672, tel: (714) 498 6128.

AUSTRALIA
• *Federation of Australian Underwater Instructors (FAUI)*, PO Box 246, Tuart Hill, WA 6060, tel: (09) 344 7882.

WORLDWIDE
• *World Underwater Federation/Confédération Mondiale des Activités Sub-aquatiques (CMAS)*, 34 Rue du Colisée, 75008 Paris, tel: (01) 42 25 60 42, 42 25 85 85.

TRAVELLING AND DIVING

What equipment you take with you on a diving holiday or an extended dive travel trip will depend on your personal preferences and the space available, but at the very least it should include your own mask, snorkel and fins.

What kind of wetsuit you carry if any will depend on your personal susceptibility to cold. Some people consider it unnecessary to wear a wetsuit at all in the tropics, and indeed many divers relish the freedom from having to wear wetsuits which warm sea temperatures allow. However, even though tropical waters are generally warm, prolonged submersion can have a considerable chilling effect on the body. In addition, some degree of protection from coral cuts and scratches is advisable.

Jeans and a T-shirt are perfectly suitable for diving if you don't want to go to the expense of buying a wetsuit or hiring one.

The normal recommendation for tropical diving is a 3 or 4mm 'shortie' wetsuit, which has short arms and legs. However, a full-length wetsuit will give you increased protection against marine hazards. You might find that one of the new generation of lightweight or nylon lycra bodysuits, which give some degree of insulation and total protection from coral scratches, is all that you need.

In remote tropical locations with small dive operations (often where the best diving is, far from civilization), the equipment isn't necessarily going to be as reliable as your own. In some cases, of course, it's probably going to be better, but if you're going way off the beaten track you might consider taking your own regulator. It's always comforting and makes for more comfortable diving if you know you can trust this vital item of equipment. Perhaps just as important, you'll be familiar with the gauges and their accuracy so there's no room for doubt about dive depths or air supply remaining. It's important to monitor your depth

297

frequently if you've not dived in the tropics before, since the increased water clarity can often lead you to greater depths than you planned for. Curled up in your luggage with other items stuffed in and around the hoses, a regulator needn't take up much space.

Dive gloves are essential and take up hardly any room, especially if they're the cotton kind with protective rubber bumps on them. Household rubber gloves make cheap and effective diving gloves.

What else you carry in addition to this will depend on your own preferences and might include a dive knife, underwater torch, underwater slate or cameras.

DIVING AND FLYING
Stepping off an aircraft onto a sultry tropical island and immediately going for a dive is a recipe for pleasure; unfortunately the reverse isn't true and flying after diving is dangerous.

After you've surfaced from diving there is still some nitrogen in your body tissues and if you get straight on to a plane the low pressure inside the aircraft is likely to cause the residual nitrogen to be released – in other words, you'll get 'bent'. Bends are unpredictable and there's no telling how bad it might be, so for the sake of cramming in a last dive or two it's not worth the risk.

The generally accepted rule now is that you shouldn't dive at all in the 12 hours preceding a flight. This period is doubled following a decompression dive: after a dive requiring decompression stops you must have a surface interval at sea level for 24 hours before flying. It used to be thought that two or three hours after a dive was enough, but diving medics have pushed this back since they've discovered that it takes considerably longer for nitrogen to desaturate than earlier research indicated. Some diving resorts don't allow diving on the day of departure for this reason, and it would be a foolhardy diver who ignored the rule.

TRAVELLING AND WINDSURFING

The standard of hire boards can vary quite considerably depending on where you stay in the tropics and while many centres offer excellent hire facilities, quite a few have dated and heavy equipment which doesn't fulfill the intermediate or advanced sailor's requirements. Also you may be used to a certain board/rig combination (such as a custom), in which case your holiday will not be the same with hired gear.

The answer is to take your own sail and board quiver with you. While it's not easy, it's not impossible; it just needs a little pre-planning. The stumbling block is the airline rather than the resort, so much of your efforts should be directed at them.

First and foremost tell your travel agent from the outset that you are taking your board with you. He or she will need to contact the airline to make sure that they have space on the flight for what will turn out to be a fairly bulky package. Some airlines refuse to take boards under any circumstances although they will take surfboards; others regard boards as freight and charge a very high kilogramme tariff. Some airlines will regard the board as part of your baggage and only impose charges on the extra weight (remember the weight of the hull alone can exceed your baggage allowance) and there are a small number of airlines who will let them through without quibble or charge. If you're going on a package holiday then you're unlikely to be able to choose the airline to suit your own needs, so take a look at other tour operators who offer holidays in the resort of your choice.

If the airline is one of those which accepts surfboards but not windsurfers it's probably because the aircraft can't accept the mast: length is a restriction on some aircraft in these days of containerized baggage handling. In this case buy a two- or three-piece mast and tell them you're taking a surfboard – the baggage handlers are unlikely to unwrap the whole thing at the airport.

Their objections may also be on the grounds of the length of the board itself, in which case take a shorter board such as a 3.20-metre or less. Winds in the tropics are such that short-board sailing is a reality at most times of the year.

Once you've decided on the airline, get them to telex your travel agent confirming the arrangement, and ask them to follow it up with a letter. Do NOT accept a letter from the agency itself as it's unlikely to cut any ice with an unhelpful airline official in some corner of the world who's never heard of your travel agent or the town they come from!

The next part is the packing. You may know the value of your board but airport staff neither know nor care what's in the package that drops from the conveyor belt just as it was about to enter the aircraft hold. Good packing will prevent damage to your board during transit, but you've got to strike a balance between weight and protection as every kilo of protection you add on is going to cost you extra in excess charges. There's another argument that says don't overpack . . . the heavier the total package the more likely the baggage handlers are to drop it. So the answer is two or three smaller bundles rather than one large one. The board should be packed in one, with sails, two-piece masts and booms in another and equipment such as the mast foot or a wet suit in a third. Packing the board is the most critical as it's the most vulnerable. Bubble pack is undoubtedly the best material – it's light, has good impact resistance if used in two or more thicknesses and is readily available.

Start by taping six-inch wide strips to the board's rails, nose and tail, having first removed the fin and daggerboard. The extremities are always the most vulnerble parts during transit and the more protection you can give the better. Next, put a layer across the whole board, wrapping the excess around the nose and tail, and finally a second full layer of bubble pack taped down exactly as before. As you're likely to want board straps at your destintion you might as well put them to some use now. Strap them onto the board about four feet apart using the free ends to tie them in to each other and prevent them slipping off. The end result is a well-protected board that can't be distinguished from a surfboard by airport staff and which has built-in carrying handles. Rigs are best kept in a quiver bag. These are quite cheap and usually take three or four sails plus two-piece masts but check that the one you are buying is long enough for your gear.

When travelling take a board repair kit with you, as well as tape for sealing up

299

the package again on your return. But most importantly regard the telex and letter from the airline as the board's passport and keep it accessible.

Some countries will expect you to pay an import duty on arrival, you can check with the local office of the tourist board before you travel. Other countries will stamp details of the equipment into your passport. The measures are there to prevent you from selling the board without paying the proper import duty. Expect hassles, you won't always get them, but be prepared for trouble somewhere along the way.

Perhaps the ultimate answer for the travelling sailor is the inflatable wind-surfer, a British idea recently launched on the market. Called the Airtec 2000, it's the same size as a conventional board except that it weighs just 7 kilos including fin, straps, daggerboard and sliding mast track. The board, mast, sail and boom pack into a large holdall and it takes between 10-20 minutes to inflate (pump supplied) and assemble. The Airtec 2000 costs £699 plus VAT from Richards Airtec, 827 Wilmslow Rd, Manchester M20 8RU (tel: (0483) 426295).

BODYSURFING

Bodysurfing is the ultimate natural water sport, something that can be done by anyone on any beach where there's enough surf. You don't need any equipment to go bodysurfing: it's down to just the waves and you, your mind and the energy of the ocean.

The best kind of beach for bodysurfing is one where the sand slopes off gradually and the waves are breaking some distance from the shore. If the beach is steep and the waves are breaking right on the shoreline you won't be able to ride far and you'll probably get wiped out. The best kind of wave is one which rolls in for some distance and maintains the same shape, with the foaming crest just burbling over itself on top of a gradual wave front. If the face of the wave is too vertical it will tumble over itself and form a pipeline or tube as it rolls in: exhilarating though it is to be inside the wave looking down a cylindrical tube of water, the circular motion of this kind of wave has a tendency to dump you unceremoniously upside-down on the beach.

In order to be powerful enough to carry you for any distance the waves should ideally be 4-5ft high or more and if they are anything like a decent size you'll have to go underneath them to get out to the right position. Dive into the base of the wave just before it reaches you and surface on the back of the crest – keep doing this until you're past where they start to break.

Now you're in place, hanging in the water and doing what bodysurfers spend most of their time doing: waiting, watching the waves, and waiting some more (a famous surfing quote says: 'Waiting for waves is okay – most people spend their lives waiting for nothing').

Watch how other surfers position themselves; when the wave you want is just behind you, swim like crazy until it lifts and carries you along with its own momentum.

The 'correct' basic bodysurfing position is with a slightly arched back, arms

300

out in front, feet together. The secret is to use your body as a surfboard and to make it hard and rigid so that you plane on the wave. The highest part of the wave is the fastest; if you get too near the bottom you'll slow down and the wave will swallow you and pound you down. Too high, and you either go over with the wave or get thrown back over the lip. The perfect position is in the top third or quarter of the wave on big waves; on smaller ones it won't make much difference.

And now comes the crunch – what happens when the wave ends? Hopefully you'll just get carried smoothly on to the beach but more than likely – to begin with anyway – you'll get wiped out. Wipe-outs from big waves can be frightening: your body is violently tossed around under the wave for what seems like an eternity in a maelstrom of sand and water, you won't know which way is up, and there's the risk of a broken neck from hitting the seabed, rocks or reef upside down.

If you do get wiped out, take a deep breath and stay calm. Don't panic – most wipe-outs only last a few seconds. If you're worried about hitting anything, curl up in a ball with one hand on top of your head and the other in front of your face. As soon as your feet or any part of you touches ground, spring up to get out of the wave. A good technique to learn to avoid wipe-outs is called the bodysurfer's pull-out: this involves simply jack-knifing back into the wave and going back underneath it, much as you did to get through them in the first place.

Bodysurfing takes a lot of practice and for some people it's practically an art form, with many different freestyle manoeuvres and techniques to perfect. Advanced tricks include spinning the body through 360 degrees, cutting back across the wave, or diving straight into the wave and arcing back into its towering face.

Regular bodysurfers use special, short fins to help them get through the waves and to manoeuvre. These include Viper fins with rails on either side to give an edge to bite the wave, longer fins for big waves and Churchills, which have a slanting blade – these are bodysurfers' most popular fins, extremely comfortable and easy to pull out of the water for manoeuvres like belly-spins, although they don't give much propulsion. Some bodysurfers also use a handgun or handplaner, a small wooden block which is strapped to the wrist to act as a steering mechanism. Incidentally, you can make do with bodysurfing fins for snorkelling but you can't use snorkelling fins for bodysurfing.

One of the world's most accomplished bodysurfers is Mark Cunningham, the undisputed king of the Banzai Pipeline, Hawaii's most famous wave. Working as a lifeguard at Ekuhai Beach Park on Oahu's north shore, he manages to combine earning a living with doing what he likes best – bodysurfing. How did this obsession start?

'I began boardsurfing before boards had cords attached, and seemed to spend more time bodysurfing after my board to catch it up than standing up and riding it, so a local lifeguard suggested I got a pair of fins. I just took to it naturally and ever since then putting on a pair of fins has been my first choice, as opposed to grabbing a surfboard. I feel comfortable and at ease with just a pair of fins on, I'm not attached to anything like surfers are. I know it sounds clichéd, but I feel I'm part of the ocean: instead of being on the waves, I'm in the waves. I like it because it's different too – everyone's on a board or body-board nowadays.'

Although Mark regularly takes on waves up to 12-15ft/4-5m high (in Hawaii they measure the back of the wave, not the drop, so by anyone else's standards that's a 25-30ft/8-10m wave), anything bigger is asking for trouble, he says. Even when they're that size, you're probably travelling at around 25-30mph. 'The sensation of speed is tremendous because your face is so close to the water,' he says, 'but I get just as much enjoyment from good conditions and little waves as I do on a 10-12ft/3-4m at the Pipeline where I'm probably risking my life.' At that kind of speed, how do you avoid getting wiped out? 'Stay on the beach – don't go in the water!' is the succinct reply. His advice for bodysurfers is to know your limits. 'Know how strong a swimmer you are and how familiar you are with the beach and the break,' he says. 'If other people are out, watch them for half-an-hour or so to get the feel for it. See how often the waves are coming in; are they coming every couple of minutes or every 20 minutes? Are they 2ft or 20ft? Always be well aware of the conditions you're putting yourself into. Ask questions of the lifeguards and the other surfers – don't just jump out of your car and head for the waves.'

BEACH AND SEA SAFETY

The main water hazards you're likely to encounter on a tropical beach are rip currents, along-shore currents, undertow, backwash and shorebreaks.

Rip currents, which flow directly from the beach straight out to sea, are potentially the greatest hazard simply because people don't understand how they work or how to deal with them. Rips are caused by a volume of water being temporarily dammed up in-shore and unable to escape because of continuous waves coming in behind. This build-up of water attempts to flow back out to sea along the line of least resistance, such as a trough between sandbars or a channel in the reef, and the result is a strong, steady current flowing seawards. Rips can be recognized by sand, seaweed or debris swirling around and being carried swiftly away from shore and by areas of turbulence in a calm sea.

There is no need to panic if you get caught in a rip since it will invariably lose its strength a short distance out to sea. The worst possible mistake you can make is to try and swim back against the rip, since this will lead to exhaustion and possibly drowning. A strong current can run at 10-12 mph/16-19kph and even a good swimmer only manages 3-5/5-8kph. Allow the current to carry you out until it has weakened, and then swim parallel to the shore and back in again. Whatever you do, don't fight the current.

Along-shore currents flow parallel to the land and if they're powerful enough can carry you for several miles or more. Again, the important thing to remember is not to fight it but to swim at an angle to the current in the direction of the shore.

Undertow is caused by one wave going back out to sea underneath an incoming wave and although it can be quite powerful, it is always short-lived. Undertows are not like underwater currents – they cannot pull you down into the depths or out to sea. If you're knocked over by undertow it might be frightening but just go with it and in a few seconds it will return you to the surface behind the incoming wave.

Backwash is a strong out-going wave which usually occurs on steep beaches. If you're on the shore's edge or in shallow water it can knock you off your feet and carry you out into the surf – this can be dangerous for children or weak swimmers. Always be conscious of ocean conditions on beaches with steep slopes.

A shorebreak is a powerful wave breaking close to shore or directly on it, often the cause of neck injuries and fractures because of its downward force and the strength with which it tosses people around. Big waves like this are fun to play in and often terrific for body-surfing but it's important to remember never to stand around with your back to the waves or try to go through them backwards (as you might normally do with small waves). Hold your breath and dive under each wave to reach calmer seas behind it.

SEA SURVIVAL

Should you have the misfortune to be swept out to sea or to be in a shipwreck, there are several swimming techniques which can be learned to increase your chances of survival. Most of them involve trying to stay afloat with the least expenditure of energy and to relax in the water. The basic survival swimming position is with the body bent at the waist, arms floating on the surface, and head *under* the water. In order to breathe you raise your head long enough to exhale rapidly through the mouth and nose, followed by an intake of breath through the mouth only. The reason for this is that floating on the back allows water to enter the mouth and nose. Another drown-proofing technique is to float vertically just beneath the surface of the water, raising your head above it to breathe when necessary.

Once you've practised enough you're considered to be drown-proof. The classic reference work is Fred Lanoue's *Drownproofing* (now out of print). It's also worth remembering that with a mask and snorkel you're automatically drown-proof and can float for an unlimited amount of time if the water is warm enough.

Shipwrecks may seem a rather remote consideration as you laze underneath a palm tree on the warm sand, but for travellers in Asia capsizing boats are a real hazard. During the time I spent writing this book at least three inter-island ferries in the Philippines and one small ferry in Thailand capsized, all of them on regular routes on the beaten track.

You cannot assume that small boats like these have life-belts or any other equipment and with a mask and snorkel your chances of survival are considerably increased. You can float face down, breathe easily and see what's going on underneath you. This is the best possible way to survive in the sea for long periods of time. In this situation, a snorkel can even be used on its own without a mask.

POTENTIAL MARINE HAZARDS

BARRACUDA

Barracuda virtually never attack humans and have a totally unjustified reputation for viciousness. Although they will sometimes circle snorkellers or divers or follow them at close quarters, attracted by their bright metallic equipment, this is unlikely to result in an attack. Barracuda normally only eat fish much smaller than themselves and in the few recorded instances where they have attacked humans it has been in turbid and murky shallow water where they have mistaken a flash of jewellery or a splashing foot for prey. Don't wear shiny jewellery, especially ankle bracelets, whilst snorkelling.

BRISTLE WORMS

Bristle worms can grow up to eight inches long and are green or orange-coloured with short, white-tipped bristles running down their sides. If touched, the bristles will break off under the skin and can cause severe pain for several hours. Take the bristles out with tweezers and apply ammonia or alcohol.

CONE SHELLS

Several cone shells are venomous and possibly lethal. The Geographer cone, *Conus geographus*, and the textile cone, *Conus textile*, are both prevalent throughout the Indo-Pacific region, the Red Sea and tropical Australia. Cone shells have a tooth-like tongue which acts as a hypodermic needle to inject venom into worms, molluscs and other small prey. If live shells are handled by humans they can cause severe pain, paralysis and death. First aid is as for venomous fish stings and medical help should be sought. Cone shells should not be picked up or handled.

CORAL CUTS

The most likely injury you'll be subject to in the Tropics is a coral cut. Because corals are so sharp even just lightly brushing against them can cause grazes or cuts which in some cases can be quite severe. Coral wounds heal very slowly and can lead to serious infections. Cleanse the wound with water, remove all particles of coral and apply an antiseptic and/or antibiotic powder. Many snorkellers and divers have stories of coral wounds which refused to heal for weeks or even months, and this is especially true if you remain in the Tropics where wounds heal more slowly anyway. I had a particularly painful experience on the Barrier Reef several years ago when just one small coral cut landed me in hospital for four days – even the lightest scratch should be taken seriously. Wear gloves and try and avoid touching corals.

FIRE CORALS

Also known as stinging corals, fire corals are in fact more closely related to hydroids than corals. The two different species of fire coral, *Millepora platyphylla* and *Millepora dichotoma*, are both normally coloured dull brown and are very common. *Millepora platyphylla* is a solid-looking coral with a smooth surface which grows in clumps and looks somewhat like a set of mis-shaped plates stacked up in a drying rack. In the Caribbean, the equivalent is the leafy stinging coral *Millepora complanata*. *Millepora dichotoma* has a much more delicate structure and grows in branching colonies to form a large lattice of bifurcating fingers.

Both these corals can cause mild pain in the areas they touch and the longer you're in contact with fire corals the more painful they're likely to be. Otherwise there are no harmful effects. Alcohol or an anaesthetic ointment should be applied to the sting.

FIRE SPONGES

Most sponges are as harmless as they seem apart from two particular – and appropriately named – species, the red fire sponge, *Tedania ignis*, and the 'touch-me-not' sponge, *Neofibularia nolitangere*. The red fire sponge is bright orange or red whilst the 'touch-me-not' sponge is usually a duller brown-red colour and found in deeper water. When touched, either of these will cause a stinging sensation, irritation and swelling. The stinging usually disappears within half-an-hour although it can sometimes persist much longer. Affected areas can be treated with a mild vinegar solution.

JELLYFISH

Jellyfish tentacles are equipped with stinging cells (nematocysts) which discharge toxins into the skin on contact. Jellyfish stings normally only result in mildly painful and itchy skin rashes but all jellyfish should be treated with caution and avoided unless you know they're harmless. If there are a number of jellyfish in the sea, ask the local dive shop whether it's safe to swim.

If you get stung the bits of tentacle still stuck to the skin must be removed with extreme care, since otherwise they will discharge more nematocysts.

Put dry sand on the skin and brush off the fragments of tentacle with a towel. Don't use water or wet sand, since this will activate the nematocysts. Tentacles can possibly also be removed with a safety razor and shaving cream. Alcohol (gin will do), commercial vinegar or even sun-tan oil will stop any further release of stinging cells. If you're travelling and diving or snorkelling a lot I suggest keeping a small bottle of a commercial preparation such as Dacor's Sea-Sting solution (an alkaline pH neutralizer) in your dive bag – it'll win you a lot of friends on dive boats!

The two most dangerous jellyfish are the Portuguese Man-o'-War, *Physalia physalis*, and the box jellyfish, *Chironex fleckeri*. The Portuguese Man-o'-War (also known as a blue-bottle) is easily recognized by its balloon-like float with long, blue stinging tentacles trailing beneath. Contact may lead to severe pain, shock and possibly respiratory failure in allergic individuals. This also applies even when the jellyfish is high and dry on the beach. Normally stings from these jellyfish aren't fatal and the red weals left by their tentacles will heal without scarring.

Box jellyfish stings can kill a human within 30 seconds to three minutes. Also known as Sea Wasps, box jellyfish occur mostly in the Western Pacific and are especially prevalent along the tropical coast of Australia between November and March/April. More than 50 people in Australia have died from box jellyfish stings, which makes them more dangerous than sharks, crocs and everything else rolled together. During the stinger season, only swim in netted areas or from off-shore islands or else make sure that your trunk, arms and legs are completely covered before entering the water. Box jellyfish aren't found in the Indian Ocean or the Red Sea and although there is a Caribbean variety, its sting isn't lethal.

Box jellyfish are semi-transparent and box-shaped with a fleshy protruberance on each corner trailing tentacles which can be up to 10-16ft/3-5m long. The venom in the tentacles is likely to produce shivering, vomiting, diarrhoea, severe pain, shock and respiratory arrest. Vinegar is kept on many Queensland beaches and this should be applied to prevent the further release of stinging cells, taking care not to touch the tentacle. First aid involves the application of a tourniquet to prevent the venom being absorbed into the general circulation. Cardiac massage and artifical respiration may be necessary before the victim is taken to hospital for the administration of the anti-venom. If mouth-to-mouth resuscitation can be maintained for at least 30 minutes, the victim will probably live. Recovery may take months and permanent scarring is likely.

MORAY EELS
Morays, like barracuda, have suffered the calumny of humans projecting our fears onto them, but unless provoked they are normally harmless. Morays just happen to look fierce because they have to open and close their mouths continually in order to breathe. However, they are quite likely to deliver an extremely painful bite if you put your hand into a hole or crevice where they live. Because their fangs are often covered in detritus and slime, serious secondary infections can result from moray wounds. Clean the wound and seek medical attention as soon as possible. It's quite normal in many countries for dive guides to tame morays so that they can be petted and photographed and there is no need to be afraid of them as long as you respect their territory. There are numerous varieties of morays, many of them with very beautiful markings, and most are poisonous to eat.

OCTOPUS
Octopus are shy and incapable of causing harm, except for one species, the Australian blue-ringed octopus. This small octopus is a yellow to brown or grey colour with dark brown bands on its arms. It is harmless unless provoked, in which case it turns a darker colour and its blue circles start to expand. A bite is likely to result in death from respiratory failure. Artificial resuscitation and the appliction of a tourniquet are the only effective treatments until the victim reaches hospital.

RAYS
Rays are amongst the most graceful of creatures when seen gliding through the water and under normal circumstances do not pose a threat to humans. However, rays spend a proportion of their time resting partially buried in the sand and if you step on one accidentally it will lash out with the venomous spine at the base of its tail. Should this occur wash the wound with salt water, carefully remove the barbed spine and soak the infected area in hot water until the pain stops. Seek medical help as soon as possible since more severe symptoms may follow.

The ones to watch out for in the Indian Ocean are reef sting rays, *Taeniura lymma*, smallish with blue spots, and in the Caribbean yellow stingrays, *Urolophus jamaicensis*, about the size of a frisbee with mottled spots, and southern stingrays, *Dasyatis americana*, diamond-shaped and up to five-feet wide. In the Red Sea there are also electric rays, *Torpedo fuscomaculata*, which are capable of generating a 200 volt shock if you step on them but which will not otherwise cause any damage. Perhaps the most awesome member of the ray family is the majestic manta, which can have a wingspan of 20ft/16m or more. Mantas are filter feeders and do not constitute any sort of risk.

SCORPIONFISH

Two members of the scorpionfish family, the lionfish and the stonefish, must on no account be touched. Any fish which allows you to approach too closely has to be regarded with suspicion – it must have a powerful defence mechanism to feel that confident – and these two fish are prime examples of that rule.

Lionfish (also known as turkeyfish, zebrafish, scorpionfish, butterfly cod, firefish and sea dragons) look elegant and harmless as they hover effortlessly a few feet away from the reef in their delicate plumage but should you happen to touch one, the toxins in their feathery fins are capable of inflicting considerable pain for several hours (normally between three to eight hours). Clean the wound with salt water, immerse it in hot water to reduce the pain and seek medical help as soon as possible. Lionfish stings are not as dangerous as stonefish stings.

Stonefish are amongst the most bizarre, even grotesque fish you're likely to come across. Their camouflage is almost perfect and they lie on the seabed or amongst coral debris looking like a small lump of algae-covered rock, preying on small fish who thought they were just that. Their dorsal spines are venomous and potentially lethal if you tread on them. Severe reactions including paralysis, shock and cardiac arrest are likely. To relieve the pain, the affected limb should be immersed in hot water for an hour or more and medical help should be sought. Dr Peter Vine reports in *Red Sea Safety* (Immel Publishing 1986) that the Australian aborigines use mangrove sap as a natural cure for stonefish stings.

SEA URCHINS

Sea urchins are present throughout the tropics and probably cause more problems for swimmers, snorkellers, divers and anyone who spends time in the water than any other marine creature. The reason for this is that not only are they often abundant on the seabed but their spines are easily capable of penetrating wetsuits or diving gloves. However, they are at worst only a minor hazard.

Sea urchins have brittle domed shells and their spines are often over a foot long, also brittle, and very sharp. If touched or stepped on, the spines break off in the skin and can cause excruciating pain for several hours. There may be swelling in the affected area and a purple discoloration of the flesh; the latter is due to dye in the spines and is harmless.

Because they're so brittle and also have barbs on them, the spines are almost impossible to remove by normal methods. They will eventually dissolve and the wound will heal naturally but one way of speeding up the process is by applying ammonia to break down the calcific material in the spines and neutralize the toxins. The most handy source of ammonia is in urine – applying urine to sea urchin wounds is a time-honoured remedy in many parts of the world. In the South Pacific they also pound the flesh with a hard object to assist the process beforehand. Soothing creams or a compress of magnesium sulphate will also help reduce the pain, as will the application of pawpaw (papaya) flesh.

Crown of thorns starfish have short, thick spines which are venomous. When touched, they can cause pain, nausea and vomiting.

SHARKS

Contrary to popular opinion and phobias fuelled by the book and three *Jaws* films, shark attacks on humans are rare: there are less than 100 attacks reported worldwide every year, and of these less than 50 per cent are fatal. Considering the number of sharks in the sea and the number of people who go swimming, snorkelling or diving all the time your chances of being attacked while doing any of these activities are minimal.

The greatest attraction for sharks is the smell of blood, which they are capable of detecting in minute quantities at great distances. Seventy per cent of a shark's brain is concerned with olefactory sensations. Over a third of shark attacks are associated with the presence of dying fish where people are spear, net or line fishing, so avoid snorkelling or swimming if anyone is fishing nearby. If you suspect sharks are present don't swim in deep channels, at dusk or after dark, when their feeding activity is greatest. Sharks are less likely to attack groups of swimmers than lone individuals, and are also less likely to attack in areas where they are used to humans – the greatest danger is from sharks which have never seen a human before. A shark's visual definition is poor, and it's possible that they only find out if something is prey or not by having a bite at it. In areas with a lot of divers, sharks are amongst the first to leave for less disturbed habitats.

If you see a shark, keep calm and keep your eyes on it all the time. Whatever you do, don't panic and splash around. The greater your excitement the more the shark will be interested. Sharks have extremely acute sensory perception and can detect fear in humans, as many animals can. Act confidently, watch the shark, and back off slowly if you think it's necessary. If the shark starts closing in, shouting into your snorkel and throwing your arms out can act as a deterrent. Whatever you do, *freeze* rather than flee: fleeing is a universal trigger for a predator to attack. If it does close in, make an effort to defend yourself. Poke it with anything that's available, aiming for the eyes, gill or nose. Use any heavy object to hit it on the nose and as a last resort stick your fingers in its eyes or nose. In all the shark books I've read, no one has ever suggested taking off a fin and trying to shove it down the shark's throat, and although I haven't yet had occasion (happily) to test this theory, I'm sure it wouldn't come back if its first mouthful was a lump of indigestible plastic. Several books suggest using a stick to fend it off, but apart from those carried by divers for just this purpose, I can't say I've ever seen sticks handily floating around coral reefs.

Attacks are often preceded by an easily recognized and distinctive behaviour pattern known as exaggerated swimming display. The shark starts moving faster, bending and twisting its body from side to side, arching its back and lifting its snout, with the pectoral fins in an almost vertical downward position. If you see a shark doing this it would be foolish to ignore the message. Back off as calmly as you can and get out of the water or put some solid reef between you and the shark. It's not necessary to leave the water if you're snorkelling or diving unless the shark starts behaving in this way or it just gets too close for your comfort.

Even small sharks shouldn't be provoked. Nurse sharks are normally considered docile but they have been known to bite divers if harassed or had their tails pulled. Most shark deaths amongst divers are due to divers provoking sharks or are associated with spearfishing.

In case of attack, get the victim out of the water and put them sloping head-down on the beach, so that blood flow to the head is increased. Don't remove wetsuits. Control bleeding with direct pressure, but don't administer any other first aid. Reassure the victim constantly. Call a doctor or paramedic. Protect the victim from cold and only give water to drink. Don't move them, since this can increase shock. Most people die from blood loss and shock rather than the bite.

MARINE TOURISM AND CORAL REEFS

Coral reefs cover a vast area of the tropics: the official estimate is 230,000 square miles/600,000 square kms, but this is probably an underestimate. Reefs are the aquatic equivalent of the tropical rainforest, an ancient and diverse ecosystem with enormous economic and scientific potential.

With the exception of the Red Sea coral reefs only grow in the tropics, and most of the countries where they're found are in the Third World. The economic imperative to reap profits (through exporting coral or aquarium fish) or simply to harvest fish to feed mouths has had to take priority over conservation issues. Pollution, either directly or indirectly, has taken its toll and natural phenomena such as cyclones, El Niño and crown of thorns starfish have also caused havoc.

Marine environments all over the world are under threat from human activities, but it's just possible that the tide has turned in many tropical countries. There has been an enormous growth in marine tourism and numerous marine parks have sprung up all over the tropics, proving themselves to be both profitable and ecologically beneficial.

A recent survey by *Skin Diver* magazine showed a direct correlation between marine parks and dive tourism. Most of the world's popular and profitable dive travel destinations have established marine parks, amongst them Australia, the Bahamas, Bonaire, the British Virgin Islands, the Caymans, Cozumel, Hawaii, and others.

This is the aquatic equivalent of green capitalism, an awareness that on a long-term basis caring for the underwater world is more profitable than stripping it of its assets. Colourful, thriving reef communities are one of the chief attractions of the tropics for divers. Every dive centre knows this, and with few exceptions they're diligent in protecting the future of their business by protecting their reefs. However, there are now so many divers travelling to the tropics on a regular basis that even governments are sitting up and taking notice of this potential goldmine.

A graphic example of the new-found power of the sport diving business was given to me by a dive operator in the Sinai, where the Egyptian government recently relaxed regulations to allow foreign investment. This liberalization came about, my informant told me, as an indirect consequence of the shooting of an American toursist on the *Achillo Lauro* in 1986. This had the immediate effect of causing all normal tourism (and with it the vital flow of foreign exchange) to dry up completely but, much to everyone's surprise, the divers just kept on coming. No one is sure whether this was due to political ignorance, insensitivity, or just plain pig-headedness, but the net effect was that the Egyptian government woke up to the potential importance of this segment of the tourist market and decided to develop it further. The result has been a boom in sophisticated facilities for divers (including a brand new Hilton hotel) and the initiation of direct charters from northern Europe.

There is no longer any doubt that marine tourism (which includes sport diving) has become an important worldwide business. In Australia, 1.2 million people visited the Great Barrier Reef in 1987, generating an estimated US$190 million in revenue. In the Caymans, one of the Caribbean's prime diving destinations, income from dive tourism is estimated at around US$53 million annually. In Hawaii, marine parks generate enormous sums of money: at the Molokini crater off-shore from Maui, as many as 35 boats every day dump something in the region of 1,000 snorkellers in the water. A leading operator at Molokini, with four boats to look after and 80 people on his payroll, estimates that the revenues generated by Molokini average between US$10-20 million per annum.

The message is simple: the marine world is a source of fascination to us all and a thriving, healthy marine environment is a profitable business. Although there are problems (increased marine tourism means increased damage to corals; for instance) the signs are promising, and most marine life recovers remarkably quickly once protected. Just as important, marine reserves provide a nursery for fish and generate increased catches for local fishermen in adjacent areas.

DOLPHINS

Contact with dolphins can be an intense, life-changing experience. The world's most famous location for guaranteed human-dolphin contact is Monkey Mia, a campsite in Shark Bay, Western Australia, 520 miles/840 km north of Perth. Dolphins started coming to Monkey Mia in 1964 and now at least eight visit regularly, arriving in the shallow bay to be fed and petted by visitors. Monkey Mia has a new, purpose-built dolphin information centre, and buckets of fish for feeding them are dispensed from a counter overlooking the beach. Wilf and Haze Mason, who run the campsite and look after the dolphins, have discouraged people from snorkelling with them on the grounds that they might then be led away from the beach and non-swimmers would be denied contact: at present, anyone can hand-feed them. Monkey Mia is two days' driving from Perth or you can fly to Denham, 16 miles/25 km from the campsite.

On Grand Bahama island a group of four Atlantic bottlenose dolphins are being trained at the Underwater Explorers Society (UNEXSO) to leave their enclosure and follow scuba divers and snorkellers out to the open ocean to swim and play on the coral reefs. 'Releasing dolphins and expecting them to come home again has never been tried before in a non-military context,' says UNEXSO. 'There's a possibility we could lose one, two or possibly all of the dolphins .

UNEXSO runs an assistant trainer programme and the day's activities include feeding them their fish and vitamins, taking part in an 'acoustic workshop', helping with training, swimming with them in their enclosure, and also working with the dolphins in the harbour on board UNEXSO's boat.

The one-day assistant trainer programme costs US$159, two days US$289, five days US$629. Advance reservations (allow two or three months) are necessary.

From early May to early September you can take a seven- or ten-day boat trip to observe and swim with a school of wild dolphins on the Little Bahamas Bank, 12-15 miles/19.2-24 km north of Grand Bahama. Run by an organization called Wild Dolphin Project, these trips (which have proved enormously successful in previous years) are part of a long-term study of dolphin communications. The catamaran takes a maximum of six guests and the dolphins are now quite comfortable and confident of making contact in the water: sometimes you'll get up to a hour at a time of acrobatic swimming with as many as 20 or 30 dolphins. 'The dolphins show off and play underwater and if you're a good swimmer and you're willing to extend what you can do they get much more interested' says Tom French of Wild Dolphin Project. 'You feel that they're interacting with you and making you feel welcome – it's an amazing experience.' You can also help with research on board. Pick-up for the trips alternate between West Palm Beach, Florida, and Grand Bahama.

In Hawaii you can swim with dolphins at the new Hyatt Regency Waikoloa on the Big Island. Eight Atlantic bottlenose dolphins live in a huge lagoon at the centre of the resort, the largest and most 'natural' man-made dolphin habitat in the world. The dolphin lagoon also serves as a research facility for marine scientists. A 30-minute swim with the dolphins costs US$55, and they recommend making a reservation up to three months in advance. These are, of course, captive dolphins.

In Europe, wild dolphins regularly associate with humans at several specific locations in Ireland, France, Spain and Yugoslavia. Information on where to go is published in *Dolphin*, a newsletter for members of the non-profit organisation International Dolphin Watch.

● *UNEXSO*, Box F2433, Freeport, Bahamas, tel: (809) 373 1244. Reservations: USA, tel: (800) 992 DIVE.
● *Wild Dolphin Project*, 1795 8th Avenue, San Francisco, CA 9412, tel: (415) 731 3264.
● *Hyatt Regency Waikoloa*, 1 Waikoloa Beach Resort, Kohala Coast, HI 98743, USA, tel: (808) 885 1234.

Reservations: USA, tel: (800) 228 9000; UK, tel: (01) 580 8197.
● *International Dolphin Watch*, Parklands, North Ferriby, Humberside HU14 3EY, tel: (0482) 634895.

MARINE ENVIRONMENTAL ORGANIZATIONS

UK

• *The Marine Conservation Society:* Campaigns related to marine life in British waters include the plight of basking sharks, bottlenose dolphins and harbour porpoises. They sometimes use volunteer divers to explore coastal sites. Annual membership £8 (overseas £11), life membership £100, includes the quarterly magazine *Marine Conservation*. **A** 4 Gloucester Rd, Ross-on-Wye HR9 5BU, tel: (0989) 66017.

• *Whale Conservation Society*: Campaigns on dolphins and whales. **A** 22 Hughender Road, Weston-super-Mare, Avon BS23 2VR, tel: (0934) 21089.

USA

• *Earthwatch:* Earthwatch sponsors scientific field expeditions in which volunteers can participate in over 35 countries worldwide. It is the largest organization of its kind in the world and because it has a non-profit status, the cost of your diving trip is tax deductible.

Previous projects involving diving have taken place in the Gulf of Aqaba, Africa (lake diving), Bonaire and Australia (Lizard Island and Adelaide). Projects last from two to three weeks and you pay on a cost-sharing basis which ranges from US$400-2,800. Membership of Earthwatch costs US$25 and includes a quarterly magazine, a newspaper, regular bulletins and an expedition planner. A list of forthcoming expeditions can be obtained free of charge. **A** 680 Mt. Auburn Street, PO Box 403, Watertown, Massachusetts 02172, tel: (617) 926 8200.

• *The Center for Environmental Education* (CEE): Established in 1972, the CEE campaigns for the protection of marine wildlife and the conservation of ocean and coastal resources. Much of their work is carried out through their Whale Protection Fund, Seal Rescue Fund and Sea Turtle Rescue Fund, as well as the Marine Habitat Programme which helps establish protected marine areas in the US and abroad. **A** 1725 DeSales Street, N.W. Washington, D.C. 20036, tel: (202) 737 3600.

• *The Cousteau Society:* Lobbies on marine issues and helps support Cousteau's *Calypso* projects. Annual membership of US$15 includes quarterly issues of the *Calypso Log* and seven issues of the *Calypso Log Dispatch* with up-to-date developments (overseas airmail charge US$7 extra). **A** 930 West 21st Street, Norfolk, Virginia 23517, tel: (804) 627 1144.

• *Pacific Whale Foundation:* Based in Maui, the PWF is a non-profit organization for studying whales. Members of the public are invited to participate through joining whale-watching trips (see under Maui, p 213), adopting a whale or taking part in an internship programme to work with marine scientists studying whales.

The Adopt-A-Whale programme involves either Hawaiian or Australian humpback whales and costs US$75, for which you get an adoption certificate with a photograph of 'your' whale, an informative letter about that particular individual, and a map showing its last recorded location. A newsletter will keep you informed of any subsequent sighting of your whale and what it's been up to.

Internship programmes are open to anyone with an interest in marine mammals between the ages of 16 and 70, no background in science or diving required. Research projects take place in Hawaii, Australia and New Zealand and cost from US$2,000 for two to four weeks of intensive research with whales. **A** Kealia Beach Plaza, 101 North Kihei Rd, Kihei, Maui, Hawaii 96753, tel: (808) 879 8811.

AUSTRALIA

• *Sea-Studies Services:* Marine study courses leading to PADI Research Diver, FAUI Underwater Naturalist or NAUI Environment Diver awards. Courses take place in several locations in Australia and involve lectures, discussions, practical work and diving. Costs vary from around A$200-250 (US$153-192) for those held near Melbourne up to around A$700 (US$538)

for those held on the Great Barrier Reef. **A** 70 Railway Parade South, Chadstone, Victoria 3148, tel: (03) 2770773.

WORLDWIDE

• *The TRAFFIC network:* TRAFFIC (Trade Records Analysis of Flora and Fauna in Commerce) is an international network of offices which monitors and reports on global trade in wild animals and plants, including sea turtles, corals and ornamental fish.

A *Wildlife Trade Monitoring Unit,* World Conservation Monitoring Centre, 219c Huntington Rd, Cambridge CB3 ODL, tel: (0223) 277427.

• *Greenpeace:* Marine campaigns include whaling, sealing, turtle ranching and water pollution. UK subscriptions £10 for individuals, £15 for families, includes quarterly newsletter, *Greenpeace News.* Offices in eighteen countries worldwide.

BEACH AND MARINE BOOKS

• See the end of this section for mail-order addresses.

• *Classic Dives of the World.* Horace Dobbs (The Oxford Illustrated Press, 1987). Hardback, 152 pp, colour and B&W photos. Covers 17 diving locations around the world, including nine in the tropics. Very biased selection (a third of the world's best dive sites are around Great Britain, apparently!). £14.95 + £1 p&p from Underwater World Publications.

• *The Complete Scuba Diving Guide,* Dave Saunders (A & C Black, 1987). Hardback, 144pp, £12.50. Covers the theory and practice of diving, illustrated with diagrams and photos. More read-

able than the BSAC manual, and with fewer technical errors.

• *Easy Diving,* Lou Fead and Alan Watkinson (Underwater World Publications, 1985). Hardback, 190pp. Full of down-to-earth common sense, well worth reading if technical diving manuals turn you off but you still want to know more about diving once you're qualified. 'Dive with your brains, not your back', is the book's motto, and it's full of ideas designed to make your diving easier, lazier, and more fun – and they work. £5.95 + 50p p&p from Underwater World Publications.

• *Guide to Corals and Fishes,* Idaz and Jerry Greenberg (Seahawk Press,

313

1977). Waterproof, 64pp. Well-laid out, handy underwater guide with 260 species of corals and fish illustrated in colour. And yes, fish do sometimes swim up to look at the images on the pages! These waterproof guides are fairly tough and last quite a long time before they start falling apart but the main problem is that if you're not careful they're likely to float out of your BC pocket and become lost. It would be useful to have a hole through the corner of the book so that you could tie it on, as they do with the submersible fish cards. US$6 including postage from Seahawk Press or £8.95 + £1.50 p&p from Ocean Optics.

• *How to Survive on Land and Sea,* Frank and John Craighead (Airlife Publishing, Shrewsbury, 1986). Hardback, 415pp, £10.95. The classic guide to survival outdoors in 'life-threatening situations', with advice on everything from wild foods to seashore survival to how to make rafts.

• *Landfalls of Paradise: The Guide to Pacific Islands,* Earl R. Hinz (Western Marine Enterprises Inc, 2nd edition 1986). Hardback, 385pp, 150 photos and 90 charts. Based on the author's seven years of research, covers 33 island groups including Polynesia, Melanesia, Micronesia and other islands of Oceania. If you've ever longed to escape to the South Seas on a yacht, this is the book to fuel your dreams. US$39.95 from Helix or £32.95 + £2.20 p&p from Warsash Nautical Bookshop, tel: (04895) 2384.

• *The Living Reef,* Jerry and Idaz Greenberg (Seahawk Press, 1979). Softback, 127pp. Introduction to fishes and corals of the Caribbean, Florida, Bermuda and the Bahamas. US$8.95 + US$1.05 p&p from Seahawk Press or £7.95 + £2.00 p&p from Ocean Optics.

• *Pocket Guide to Underwater Diving,* Reg Vallintine (Bell & Hyman, London 1985). Hardback, 94pp, £4.95. A pocket guide which could be carried in a dive bag and used to refresh your memory prior to diving would be extremely useful, but unfortunately this book doesn't fulfil that function, and nor is it comprehensive enough to replace existing diving manuals.

• *Sport Diving – the British Sub-Aqua Club Diving Manual* (Stanley Paul/Century Hutchinson, revised editon 1985). Softback, 256pp, £11.95. Covers training, use and maintenance of equipment, dive planning, safety precautions and special interests such as wreck diving and cold water diving.

• *Shark –A Photographer's Story,* Jeremy Stafford-Deitsch (Headline Publishing, London, 1987). Hardback, 200pp. A personal narrative of a three-year quest across tropical oceans diving with and photographing sharks. Absorbing and informative, fully illustrated. £14.95 + 50p p&p from Underwater World Publications.

• *Sharks – Silent Hunters of the Deep,* Ron and Valerie Taylor (Reader's Digest, 1986). Hardback, 208pp, £13.95. Popular, authoritative guide with contributions by some of the world's leading shark experts.

• *Sharks and other Dangerous Sea Creatures,* Idaz and Jerry Greenberg (Seahawk Press, 1981). Softback, 65pp. Brief but well-illustrated résumé of common marine dangers. £4.95 + £1.50 p&p from Ocean Optics.

• *Submersible Field Guides:* These excellent waterproof plastic cards are designed to help snorkellers and divers identify fish and corals on the spot and are printed on both sides with full colour drawings. They measure 6''x 9'' and have holes at either end for securing them with a thin line. The Tropical Atlantic series (valid for Florida, Bermuda, the Bahamas and the Caribbean) includes *Marine Invertebrates* (61 corals, sponges and crustaceans), *Shells* (74 species), *Reefcomber's Field Guide* (47 fish and 23 invertebrates) and *Fishwatcher's Field Guide* (75 fishes). The Tropical Pacific and Indo-Pacific series includes the *Great Barrier Reef* (56 fishes of Australia, New Guinea and the tropical Pacific), *Hawaii* (58 fishes) and the *Red Sea* (65 fishes of the Red Sea and Indo-Pacific). The cards cost US$5 each plus US$1 airmail per card from Seahawk Press or £2.95 each + 75p p&p from Ocean Optics.

• *The Tropical Traveller,* John Hatt (Penguin, 2nd edition 1985). Softback, 270pp, £2.95. Enlarged and updated edition of John Hatt's witty, eccentric and highly-readable guide. Particularly recommended for first-time travellers in the tropics.

• *Travellers' Health,* Dr Richard Dawood (Oxford University Press, 1986). Softback, 500pp, £6.95. Useful compendium, covers most tropical problems.

• *Undersea Predators,* Carl Roessler (Facts on File, New York, 1984). Hardback, 192pp. Carl Roessler is one of the world's top diving photographers and this book covers a wide range of marine life, accompanied by personal observations and insights into the mechanisms of predation. US$24.95 + US$3.50 p&p from Pisces Books or £14.95 + £2.50 p&p from Ocean Optics.

• *Uninhabited and Deserted Islands,* Jon Fisher (Loompanics, Australia, 1983). Softback, 111pp, 41 maps. A gazetteer of potential hideaways for aspiring Crusoes, covering the Pacific Ocean, the South Atlantic and the Indian Ocean. Unfortunately, as the author points out, most desert islands are uninhabited for a good reason – they're uninhabitable. US$7.95 from Moon Publications.

• *Whale Nation,* Heathcote Williams (Jonathan Cape, London, 1988). Softback, 190pp, £8.95. Part poem and part photographic essay, this paean to the virtues of whales also catalogues the senseless destruction which has driven them close to extinction. A brilliant and vital book.

Mail Order Addresses

USA

• *Helix Books*: The world's largest mail order business for books on diving, snorkelling and the underwater world, also stockists of a huge range of underwater photography equipment. **A** 310 South Racine Avenue, Chicago, Illinois 60607, tel: (312) 421 6000 or (800) 33-HELI.

• *Moon Publications*: Huge range of travel guides available by mail order. Catalogue US$2.95 not including postage. For US domestic book orders, add US$1.25 for each item and US$.50 per additional item for book rate delivery. For overseas orders, add US$2 per item and US$1 per additional item for surface rate delivery. For airmail rates, call or write for a quote. **A** 722 Wall Street, Chico, CA 95928, tel: (916) 345 5413. Credit card orders: (916) 345 5473.

• *Pisces Books*: For diving and snorkelling guides listed under individual countries; add US$5 for domestic orders and US$7.50 for overseas orders. **A** One School St, Glen Cove, NY 11542, tel: (516) 676 2727.

315

• *Seahawk Press*: For overseas air-mail orders, add US$2 per book, US$1 per card **A** 6840 S.W. 92nd St, Miami, Florida 33156.

• *Ocean Optics*, 4 Greyhound Rd, London W6 8NX, tel: (01) 381 6108.
• *Underwater World Publications*, 40 Gray's Inn Rd, London, WC1X 8LR, tel: (01) 405 0224.

DIVING MAGAZINES

USA
• *Sea Fans:* Quarterly video magazine, each issue is 90 minutes' long and covers diving holiday destinations, interviews with top photographers, practical diving tips and marine life studies. Single issues US$19.95 plus US$2 handling, overseas orders add US$4 (surface), US$13 (air); four quarterly issues US$59.95, overseas orders add US$14 (surface), US$39(air). Specify VHS or Beta (PALM/SECAM available at extra cost). **A** 7800 East Iliff, Suite E, Denver, Colorado 80231, tel: (800) 622 8767.
• *Skin Diver:* Glossy monthly, features extensive dive destination guides, technical equipment reviews and underwater photography and video tips. Subscriptions US$19.94, overseas add US$10 (surface). **A** 8490 Sunset Blvd, PO Box 3295, Los Angeles, CA 90078, tel: (213) 854 2470.
• *Undercurrent:* Monthly newsletter, (no photos or adverts), features extensive and detailed independent critiques of dive destinations. An invaluable source of objective advice for serious divers. Subscriptions US$55, overseas US$80 (surface), US$90 (air). **A** Atcom Publishing, 2315 Broadway, New York, N Y 10024-4397, tel: (212) 873 5900. Credit card orders: tel: (800) 521 7004.

UK
• *Diver:* Monthly, the official publication of BSAC. Subscriptions £18.50 (UK), US$40 (USA and Canada). **A** 40 Gray's Inn Rd, London, WC1X 8LR, tel: (01) 405 0224.
• *Subaqua Scene:* Monthly. Subscriptions £18 (UK), £26 (overseas). **A** Sunseeker House, West Quay Road, Poole, Dorset BH15 1JF, tel: (0202) 665616.
• *Sport Diver:* New independent bi-monthly magazine, incorporating Peter Rowlands' Underwater Photography. Subscriptions £15 (UK), £25 (overseas). **A** Ocean Optics, 4 Greyhound Rd, Hammersmith W6 8NX, tel: 385 3218.

AUSTRALIA
• *Scuba Diver:* Bi-monthly. Subscriptions A$19.80 (Australia), A$39 (overseas). **A** PO Box 606, Sydney, NSW 2001, tel: (02) 281 2333.
• *Sportdiving in Australia and the South Pacific:* Bi-monthly. Subscriptions A$24 (Australia), A$30 (Asia and Pacific), A$36 (elsewhere). **A** PO Box 167, Narre Warren, Vic 3805, tel: (03) 794 0793.
• *Underwater Geographic:* Quarterly magazine, edited by Australian diving guru Neville Colman. Subscriptions A$20, overseas A$30 (surface). **A** PO Box 702, Springwood, Qld 4127, tel: (07) 341 8931.

INDEX

This is chiefly an index of beaches and islands. Bold type indicates a featured beach entry. Maldive islands are listed alphabetically between pages 55-63.

Aguada, *Goa* 78, **82**
Ahihi Bay, *Maui* 223
Ahungalla, *Sri Lanka* 64, **71**
Aitutaki, *Cook Islands* 185, **190-1**
Aldabras, *Seychelles* 37
Alona Beach, *Panglao* 114, **124**
Amirantes, *Seychelles* 37
Anjuna, *Goa* 78, **85-6**
Anse Banane, *La Digue* 43
Anse Chastanet, *St Lucia* 240, **243-5**
Anse Cocos, *La Digue* 43
Anse Gaulettes, *La Digue* 43
Anse Grosse Roche, *La Digue* 43
Anse Intendance, *Mahé* 31
Anse La Réunion, *La Digue* 33, 43
Anse Lazio, *Praslin* 33, 41
Anse Parc, *Frégate* 47
Anse Patate, *La Digue* 43
Anse Victorin, *Frégate* 47
Anse Volbert, *Praslin* 33, 41, 42
Aride, *Seychelles* 34, 42
Arugam Bay, *Sri Lanka* 68
Australs, *French Polynesia* 193

Badian Island, *Cebu* 114, **122**
Baga, *Goa* 78, **82-3**
Bali, *Indonesia* 133, 137-41
Balingay Beach, *Boracay* 120
Barbados 246-61
Bathsheba, *Barbados* 247, 258
Batu Ferringhi, *Penang* 125, 128
Beachcomber Island, *Fiji* 170, 171, **177-8**
Beau Vallon, *Mahé* 31, **39-41**
Bedarra Island, *Australia* 148
Belize 230
Benualim, *Goa* 83
Benston Beach, *Barbados* 247, **254-5**
Bentota, *Sri Lanka* 64, **70-1**
Beruwala, *Sri Lanka* 64
Beqa Island, *Fiji* 171
Big Buddha, *Koh Samui* 92, **110**
Bird Island, *Seychelles* 33, 37, **45-6**
Bloody Bay, *Jamaica* 232
Blue Lagoon, *Jamaica* 228, 236, **237**
Bo Phut, *Koh Samui* 92, **110**
Bogmalo Beach, *Goa* 80
Bohol Beach Club, *Panglao* 114, **123**
Bora Bora, *French Polynesia* 195, 198, 201-5

Boracay, *Philippines* 114, **119-122**
Boston Beach, *Jamaica* 228
Buitan Beach, *Bali* 140
Bulabog Beach, *Boracay* 120

Cagban Beach, *Boracay* 120
Calangute, *Goa* 78, **82-3**
Candi Dasa, *Bali* 133, **140**
Candolim, *Goa* 82
Cape Tribulation, *Australia* 151, **164**
Cariblue Beach, *St Lucia* 238
Carlisle Bay, *Barbados* 246, 260
Castaway Island, *Fiji* 171
Cayman Islands 230, 261, 309
Cebu, *Philippines* 114, **122**
Cha-am, *Thailand* 90
Chankanaab, *Cozumel* 263, **269**
Chaweng, *Koh Samui* 92, **108**
Cheong Mon, *Koh Samui* 92, **111**
Cherating, *Malaysia* 125, 126
Club Caribbean, *Jamaica* 226
Club Med, *Bali* 127, 138
Club Med, *Bora Bora* 204
Club Med, *Cherating* 125, 127
Club Med, *Moorea* 195, 199
Club Med, *Phuket* 100, 102, 127
Club Med, *St Lucia* 241
Club Naitasi, *Fiji* 171
Club St Lucia, *St Lucia* 238
Cobbler's Cove, *Barbados* 250, 253, 254
Coconut Beach, *Queensland* 164
Cocos Islands, *Seychelles* 34
Cod Hole, *Australia* 151, 162, 163, 167, 168
Colva, *Goa* 78, **83-5**
Cook Islands, 184-91
Cook's Bay, *Moorea* 195, 200
Coral Coast, *Fiji* 169
Coral Sea, *Australia* 167, 168
Côte D'Or, *Praslin* 41, 42
Cozumel, *Mexico* 230, 262-72
Cousin, *Seychelles* 34
Crane Beach, *Barbados* 247, **257-8**
Curieuse, *Seychelles* 34
Cuyo Islands, *Philippines* 116

Dahab, *Egypt* 276, **285-6**
Daydream Island, *Australia* 147
Denarau Beach, *Viti Levu* 170
Denis Island, *Seychelles* 33
Diani, *Kenya* 17, **26-9**
La Digue, *Seychelles* 33, 34, 36, 37, 42, **43-4**
Diamond Head, *Waikiki* 217
Dikwella, *Sri Lanka* 65, **76-7**
Discovery Bay, *Barbados* 250, 252, 254
Discovery Bay, *Jamaica* 229
Dunk Island, *Australia* 148, **159-60**

Egypt 274-86
El Nido, *Philippines* 115
El Presidente, *Cozumel* 263, **268-9**
Ekuhai Beach, *Oahu* 210, **219-20**, 301

Félicité Island, *Sychelles* 34
Fiji 169-183
Fijian Resort, *Viti Levu* 170, **175-6**
Fisherman's Beach, *Gt Keppel Island* 156
Fitzroy Island, *Australia* 151, **160-1**
Flores, *Indonesia* 134, **144**
Fort de Russy, *Waikiki* 216
Frégate, *Seychelles* 33, 37, 42, **46-7**
Frenchman's Cove, *Jamaica* 228, **236**

Galu, *Kenya* 26, 28
Gambiers, *French Polynesia* 193, 197
Gili Air, *Indonesia* 134, **142-3**
Gili Meno, *Indonesia* 134, **142-3**
Gili Trawangan, *Indonesia* 134, **142-3**
Ginger Bay Beach, *Barbados* 247, **257-8**
Grand Anse, *La Digue* 43
Grand Anse, *Frégate* 47
Grand Anse, *Mahé* 31
Grand Anse, *Praslin* 33, 41
Great Barrier Reef, *Australia* 48, 149, **166-8**
Great Keppel Island, *Australia* 146, **156-8**
Green Island, *Australia* 149, 151
Grenadines 241
Goa, *India* 78-88

Haat Rin, *Koh Phangan* 93, **113**
Halcyon Beach Club, *St Lucia* 238
Hamilton Island, *Australia* 147
Hanuama Bay, *Oahu* 209, 216, **218**, 220
Hapuna, *Hawaii* 214
Harambol, *Goa* 80, **86-7**
Hawaii 208-224
Hawaii, *Hawaii* 214, 261
Hayman Island, *Australia* 146
Heron Island, *Australia* 146, **154-5**
Hideaway Resort, *Viti Levu* 170, **176**
Hikkaduwa, *Sri Lanka* 64, **71-4**
Hinchinbrook Island, *Australia* 148, **158-9**
Honulua Bay, *Maui* 223
Ho'okipa, *Maui* 223, 224
Hua Hin, *Thailand* 90
Hurghada, *Egypt* 276, 277, 284

Isla Mujeres, *Mexico* 264, 265
Isla Chauve Souris, *Praslin* 42
Isle St Pierre, *Praslin* 42
L'Islette, *Mahé* 31

Jamaica 226-37
Jamaica Jamaica, *Jamaica* 228, **235-6**

Kaanapali, *Maui*   210, **220-1**, 223
Kahoolawe, *Hawaii*   212, 222
Kahului, *Maui*   212
Kailua Bay, *Oahu*   209
Kalkudah-Passekudah, *Sri Lanka*   68
Kanaha, *Maui*   224
Kandavu, *Fiji*   170
Karon, *Phuket*   91, **99-100**
Kata, *Phuket*   91, **100-1**
Kata Noi, *Phuket*   91, **102**
Kaui, *Hawaii*   213
Kenya   16-30
Kihei, *Maui*   212, 213, 223
Kisite Marine Park, *Kenya*   19, **30**
Kiunga Marine Park, *Kenya*   19
Krabi, *Thailand*   92, **107-8**
Koggala, *Sri Lanka*   64, **76**
Koh Samet, *Thailand*   90, **96-7**
Koh Samui, *Thailand*   92, **108-11**
Koh Phangan, *Thailand*   93, **112-13**
Koh Phi Phi, *Thailand*   92, **106**
Koh Tae Nok, *Thailand*   95
Koh Tao, *Thailand*   95
Kovalam, *India*   81, **87-8**
Kuanaoa, *Hawaii*   214
Kuhio Beach Park, *Waikiki*   216
Kuta, *Bali*   133, **139-40**
Kuta, *Lombok*   134

Lady Elliott Island, *Australia*   146, **152-3**
Laem Set, *Koh Samui*   92
La Laguna, *Puerta Galera*   115
Lamai, *Koh Samui*   92, **109-10**
Lamu, *Kenya*   17, **23-6**
Lanai, *Hawaii*   212, 222
Legian, *Bali*   133, 139
Lighthouse Beach, *Kovalam*   87
Little Makena, *Maui*   212
Lizard Island, *Australia*   151, **162-3**, 168
Lombok, *Indonesia*   134, 142, 143
Long Bay, *Barbados*   247, **257-8**
Lovina, *Bali*   134

Mae Haat, *Koh Phangan*   93, **112-13**
Mae Nam, *Koh Samui*   92, **110**
Magnetic Island, *Australia*   147
Mahé, *Seychelles*   31, 33, 34, 36, 37, 39-41
Majorda, *Goa*   83
Makaha, *Oahu*   210
Makapu'u, *Oahu*   209, 218-19
Makena, *Maui*   212, 223
Malaysia   125-132
Maldives   48-63
Malololailai, *Fiji*   171, **179-80**
Malindi, *Kenya*   17, 19, 21
Mamanuthas, *Fiji*   170, 171, 177-80

Mana Island, *Fiji*   171, **178-9**
Manihi, *French Polynesia*   197
Marigot Bay, *St Lucia*   240
Marquesas, *French Polynesia*   193, 197
Martinique   241
Matamamanoa, *Fiji*   171
Mataqi, *Fiji*   172, **183**
Matira Point, *Bora Bora*   202, 203
Maui, *Hawaii*   210, 212, 213, 220-4
Middle Keppel, *Australia*   156
Moalboal, *Cebu*   114, **122-3**
Mokuleia Bay, *Maui*   223
Molokai, *Hawaii*   212, 222
Molokini, *Hawaii*   222, 223
Mombasa, *Kenya*   16, 19, 25, 26, 29
Monkey Mia, *Australia*   310
Montego Bay, *Jamaica*   226, 230
Moorea, *French Polynesia*   195, 199-201
Morgan Lewis Beach, *Barbados*   248
Mount Lavinia, *Sri Lanka*   65
Mrs Watson's Beach, *Lizard Island* 162
Muri Beach, *Cook Islands*   184, **186-8**
Myall Beach, *Cape Tribulation*   164
Muroroa, *Tuamotus*   192, 197

Na'ama Bay, *Egypt*   274, 276, **280-4**
Na Koro Resort, *Vanua Levu*   171
Nai Harn, *Phuket*   91, **103-4**
Namale Plantation, *Vanua Levu*   171
Namena, *Fiji*   172, **180-1**
Nananu-I-Ra, *Viti Levu*   170, **176-7**
Narigama, *Sri Lanka*   72
Natandola, *Viti Levu*   170
Negombo, *Sri Lanka*   65
Negril, *Jamaica*   226, **231-4**
Nilaveli, *Sri Lanka*   68
North Coast, *Koh Samui*   92, **110-1**
North Shore, *Oahu*   209, 210, **219-220**
North West Coast, *Moorea*   195, **199-200**
Nusa Dua, *Bali*   133, **138-9**
Nusa Lembongan, *Indonesia*   134
Nusa Penida, *Indonesia*   140
Oahu, *Hawaii*   208, 209, 210, **216-220**
Ocho Rios, *Jamaica*   226, 228, 230
Orpheus Island, *Australia*   148

Pacific Harbour Resort, *Viti Levu* 171
Paia, *Maui*   212, 224
Palawan, *Philippines*   115, 116
Pangkor Island, *Malaysia*   125, **128**
Panglao Island, *Philippines* 114, **123-4**
Paradise Beach, *Barbados*   250, 261
Patong, *Phuket*   91, **98**
Pattaya, *Thailand*   90
Payne's Bay, *Barbados*   250
Petite Anse, *La Digue*   43

Penang, *Malaysia*   125
Philippines   114-124
Phuket, *Thailand*   91, 92, 96-106
Pier Beach, *Cozumel*   263, **267-8**
Playa Chen Rio, *Cozumel*   263
Playa Los Cocos, *Isla Mujeres*   265
Playa Maya, *Cozumel*   263, **269-70**
Playa San Francisco, *Cozumel* 263, **269-70**
Playa San Juan, *Cozumel*   263
Point Raititi, *Bora Bora*   201
Praslin, *Seychelles*   33, 34, 36, **41-3**
Puerta Galera, *Philippines*   115
Puka Beach, *Boracay*   120
Punta Morena, *Cozumel*   263
Putney Beach, *Gt Keppel Island*   156

Qamea, *Fiji*   172, **182-3**
Queensland, *Australia*   148-168
Queen's Surf, *Waikiki*   216

Rantau Abang, *Malaysia*   125, **129**
Rangiroa, *French Polynesia* 196, 197, **205-7**
Rarotonga, *Cook Islands*   184, 186-90
Rarotongan Resort, *Rarotonga* 184, **188-9**
Ras Muhammed, *Egypt*
                274, 278, 279, 282, 283
Rawa Island, *Malaysia*   127
Rawai, *Phuket*   91
Reduit Beach, *St Lucia*   238, **242-3**
Relax Bay Meridien, *Phuket* 91, **103**
Round Rock Beach, *Barbados*   256
Runaway Bay, *Jamaica*   228, **235-6**

St Anne Marine Park, *Mahé*   37, 39
St Lucia   238-45
Sabang, *Puerto Galera*   115
Sandy Beach, *Oahu*   209, **218-9**
Sandy Lane, *Barbados*   250, 253
San San Beach, *Jamaica*   228, **237**
Sans Souci, *Waikiki*   216
Sanur, *Bali*   133, **137-8**
Sao Wisata, *Flores*   134, **144**
Senggigi, *Lombok*   134, **142**
Seychelles   31-47
Sharm el Sheikh, *Egypt*   274, 277, 279,
                           280, 285, 286
Shela, *Kenya*   17, **23-6**
Sicogon, *Philippines*   115
Silhouette Island, *Seychelles*   36
Silver Sands, *Barbados*   247, **255-6**
Silver Sands, *Jamaica*   228, **235**
Similan Islands, *Thailand*   92, 105, 106
Small La Laguna, *Puerta Galera*   115
Small Vagator, *Goa*   78, **86**
Sombrero Island, *Philippines*   116
South Coast, *Bora Bora*   198, **201-5**

South East Coast, *Barbados* 247, **257-8**
Spreckelsville, *Maui* 223, 224
Sri Lanka 64-77
Sulu Sea, *Philippines* 116
Sumilon Island, *Philippines* 116
Sunrise Beach, *Koh Phangan* 113
Sunset Beach, *Koh Phangan* 113
Sunset Beach, *Oahu* 210, **219-20**
Surin, *Phuket* 91, **98**

Tahiti, *French Polynesia* 38, 192, 193, 195
Talipanan, *Puerto Galera* 115
Tangalle, *Sri Lanka* 65, **77**
Taveuni, *Fiji* 172, **181-2**
Telok Chempedak, *Malaysia* 127, **129-30**
Temae Beach, *Moorea* 195, **200-1**
Tenggol Island, *Malaysia* 130
Thailand 90-113
Three Quarter Mile Beach, *Nananu-I-Ra* 177
Tioman Island, *Malaysia* 127, 128, **130-2**
Tiwi, *Kenya* 17, **29**
La Toc, *St Lucia* 240
Treasure Island, *Fiji* 170, **177-8**
Tuamotus, *French Polynesia* 192
Turtle Island, *Fiji* 171

Unawatuna, *Sri Lanka* 64, **74-5**

Vagator, *Goa* 78, **86**
Vanua Levu, *Fiji* 171, 172
Vigie Beach, *St Lucia* 240
Viti Levu, *Fiji* 169, 170, 171

Waikiki, *Oahu* 208, 210, **216-18**
Wailea, *Maui* 211, 212, 223
Waimanalo, *Oahu* 209
Waimea Bay, *Oahu* 210, **219-20**
Watamu, *Kenya* 17, **21-3**
West Coast, *Barbados* 246, **250-4**
White Beach, *Boracay* 119
Whitsunday Islands, *Queensland* 146

Yanuca Island, *Viti Levu* 175

Photo Credits
Mandy Williams-Ellis 13, 141; Lorenz Riedl 16, 17, 20, 21 b; Seychelles National Tourist Office 33, 36, 37; Ueli Weibel 52, 56; Feature-Pix 81, 84, 85; Malaysia National Tourist Office 128; Martin Coleman/ Planet Earth Pictures 153; Valerie Desheulles/ Colorsport 208, 209 t, 217 t, 224; Al Giddings/Ocean Images /Planet Earth Pictures 213; Chris Huxley 241.